Readings in
U.S. IMPERIALISM

Readings in
U.S. IMPERIALISM

K. T. Fann & Donald C. Hodges, editors

AN EXTENDING HORIZONS BOOK

Porter Sargent Publisher   Boston   Massachusetts 02108

Library of Congress catalog number 78-133507
International Standard Book Number: 0-87558-053-X (hardbound)
International Standard Book Number: 0-87558-054-8 (paper)

PREFACE

The war in Vietnam (now the war in Indochina) has brought an increasing number of Americans to the realization that the series of so-called foreign policy "mistakes" underlying our involvement may very well be no mistakes at all, but rather part of a consistent policy to defend an empire. That the U.S. is an imperialist power, second to none in the world today, can no longer be dismissed as empty rhetoric or a mere piece of communist propaganda. The nature or unique character of this imperialism, however, is still a much debated issue. There is an urgent need for the antiwar movement to gain a clear understanding of the operation of U.S. imperialism, in order to resist it more effectively. We hope that this anthology will serve as an aid toward the first of these objectives.

Collected here are essays written by those who have become

concerned over the increasing role of U.S. involvement abroad. They deal with matters which the editors believe to be the most significant aspects of this involvement. Although primary importance has been assigned to the economic aspect, the readings also include selections covering instances of U.S. political, military and cultural imperialism. Though recent events have already dated some of the particulars, we included these articles for their overall relevance, their historical perspective, and their varying responses to U.S. imperialism during the sixties.

Of all the spheres of U.S. involvement, and especially economic penetration, the most important in the editors' judgment is our own backyard in Latin America. This explains the concentration on Latin America rather than Asia or Africa as still the most promising foreign preserve of U.S. imperialism. Geographical continuity with the North American continent and the historical continuity of the Monroe Doctrine, which in effect makes Latin America our special sphere of influence, account only in part for the emphasis on this area. More important is the fact that U.S. economic domination of most of the countries south of the Rio Grande represents the first historic instance of what is currently called neo-colonialism, i.e., economic domination under conditions of at least *de jure*, if not always *de facto*, political and military sovereignty. Prior to World War II, the major European powers were typically annexationist, which is to say that military and political domination were inseparable from economic and cultural imperialism. Increasingly, however, this old model of imperialism is being replaced by a new one made in the U.S.A. The U.S. showed the European powers that political annexation is now an obsolete form of domination, the most expensive in view of the costs of military occupation and direct legal administration, and the most unstable because of the aspirations of subject peoples to self-government and national independence. To a much greater extent than the new imperialism, the old annexationist form was morally and politically responsible for the economic well-being of its subjects. Hence the advantage of U.S. imperialism over its several rivals: it permits economic domination within the scope of international laws, yet without strict legal accountability or instruments of redress.

We are already familiar with the effect of U.S. imperialism in Vietnam on the quality of life at home, notably increased domestic disorders, spreading cynicism, a government credibility gap, resistance to the draft, student rebellions, and racial violence. The cost of U.S. foreign involvement in domestic oppression is somewhat less evident, though hardly less important. In a manner indicative of the way in which U.S. economic domination rides roughshod over the interests of subject peoples, the great majority of citizens in this country are also increasingly exploited, whether directly in producing military hardware of little or no benefit to them, or indirectly in paying for our venture in Vietnam through increased taxation and economic inflation. Add to this the recession of 1969-70, with its own toll in decreased industrial output and increased unemployment, not to mention the blood tax or military casualties from the war itself, and our picture of the quality of life in the U.S. at the beginning of the 70's is a dismal one indeed.

The concluding selections cover the revolutionary response to U.S. imperialism not only from inside the U.S., but also, and especially, from without. Currently, Southeast Asia and Latin America are the two main areas in which the U.S. has intervened militarily in support of the vested economic and global interests of U.S. corporations operating abroad. Here we need to be reminded that China, as well as Cuba, is today suffering the effects of a U.S. blockade, and that our Pacific fleet continues to patrol the Formosa straits, in effect detaching the Chinese province of Formosa (Taiwan) from the Mainland. In other words, the struggle against U.S. imperialism is not likely to meet with much success if it is narrowly focused on our involvement in Vietnam or even the expansion of that war into Laos and Cambodia. The hardships we face because of our present Vietnamese policy may not be the last of their kind. But they are more likely to be the last if realistic and effective measures are devised for countering such policy "mistakes."

K. T. Fann and Donald C. Hodges
The Florida Center for Social Philosophy
Tallahassee, Florida
June 21, 1970

CONTENTS

BERTRAND RUSSELL

Peace through Resistance
to U.S. Imperialism

Throughout the world today increasing numbers of people concerned with peace and with social justice are describing U.S. imperialism as the common destroyer of peace and justice. To some, the expression "U.S. imperialism" appears as a cliché because it is not part of their own experience. We in the West are the beneficiaries of imperialism. The spoils of exploitation are the means of our corruption. Because imperialism is not part of our experience we do not recognize the aptness of the description for the economic and political policies of what President Eisenhower termed "the military industrial complex." Let us consider briefly the nature of U.S. power.

Three thousand three hundred military bases and vast mobile fleets, bearing missiles and nuclear bombers, are spread over our planet to protect the ownership and control by U.S. capitalism of sixty per cent of the world's resources. Sixty per cent of the world's resources are owned by the rulers of six per cent of the world's population. The aggressiveness of this empire imposes on mankind an expenditure of 140,000 million dollars annually or 16 million dollars each hour. The current arms expenditure exceeds the entire national income of all developing countries. It exceeds the world's annual exports of all commodities. It exceeds the national income of Africa, Asia and Latin America. The U.S. Military budget is nearly 60,000 million dollars per year. One Atlas missile costs thirty million dollars, or the equivalent of the total investment for a nitrogen fertilizer plant with capacity of 70,000 tons per annum.

Consider this in terms of the United Kingdom only, to take the example of a prosperous country: one obsolete missile equals four universities, one T.S.R. 2 equals five modern hospitals, one ground-to-air missile equals 100,000 tractors.

During the past fourteen years the U.S. spent 4,000 million dollars to purchase farm surpluses. Millions of tons of wheat, oats, barley, maize, butter and cheese have been stored and poisoned to keep prices up in the world markets. Blue dye is poured into great mountains of butter and cheese to render them unusable. By 1960, 125 million tons of bread grain had been stored in the United States to rot—enough food for every citizen of India for one year. Unimaginably vast quantities of foodstuffs are calculatedly destroyed by the rulers of U.S. capitalism, for no other purpose than the continuation of their profits and the retention of their power. Like vultures the handful of the rich batten on the poor, the exploited, the oppressed. A drop of five per cent in the world price of staple exports of any country would, according to Dag Hammarskjold, wipe out all investments of the World Bank, of the United Nations and all bilateral and other investments.

These were the fears of Hammarskjold. What are the facts? In recent years prices have operated against poor countries not merely at five per cent but at forty per cent. The industrial production of Western capitalism is consciously employed not only to perpetuate the hunger which exists in the world, but to increase it vastly for profit.

In South Africa, 10,000 children die annually from gastroenteritis. The smallpox which haunts many countries could be eliminated at a cost of 500,000 dollars. Hundreds of millions who suffer from yaws could be cured by a fivepenny shot of penicillin. Five hundred million people have trachoma. Sixty per cent of the children of Africa suffer from protein deficiency diseases such as kwashiokor, beri-beri or pellagra. When U.S. capitalists hoard food and poison it they not only deprive the starving, but force the developing countries to buy food at high costs. The riches of the earth are destroyed, wasted, stolen by the few and used to murder the millions. 3,300 military bases are spread across the planet to prevent the peoples from destroying this evil system.

Let us examine the role of the war industry in the United States. The United States Defense Department owns property valued in 1954 at 160 billion dollars.

This value has almost doubled. The U.S. Defense Department is the world's largest organization. The Pentagon owns millions of acres of land, including thirty-two million in the United States and over three million acres of land outright in foreign countries. The Pentagon building is so large that the Capitol, which contains the United States Government, could be swallowed in any one of the five main segments of the Pentagon. The 1962 budget involved $53 billion for arms, exclusive of the military space program.

Thus, by 1962, sixty-three cents out of every dollar were spent on appropriations for arms and space. A further six cents were for army services, and more than eighty per cent of interest payments were for military debts. Seventy-seven cents out of every hundred are spent on past wars, the Cold War and preparations for future war. The billions of dollars placed in the pockets of the U.S. military give the Pentagon economic power affecting every aspect of American life, and of the lives of mankind.

Military assets in the U.S. are three times as great as the combined assets of the great monopolies, greater than the assets of U.S. Steel, Metropolitan Life Insurance, American Telephone and Telegraph, General Motors and Standard Oil. The Defense Department employs three times the number of all these great world corporations.

This immense world concentration of power and wealth is directly linked to large scale capitalism in America. The billions of dollars in contracts are awarded by the Pentagon and filled by large industry.

In 1960, 21 billion dollars were spent on military goods. Ten capitalist corporations received 7½ billion dollars, three received one billion each and two others 900 million dollars. In these corporations there are more than 1,400 retired officers of the army above the rank of major. This includes 261 Generals and flag rank officers.[1]

The largest company, General Dynamics, has 187 retired officers, 27 generals and admirals and the former Secretary of the Army on its payroll. American policy and the military bases serve a vast power complex interconnected and interested in the perpetuation of the arms race for its own sake. This concentration of power spreads throughout the economy of the United States. Sub-contracts awarded by war contractors involve every city of any size. The jobs at stake involve millions of people.

Four million people work for the U.S. Defense Department alone. The payroll of twelve billion dollars is twice that of the U.S. automobile industry. A further four million people are employed directly in arms industries. Thus eight million people depend for their jobs on the military adventures of the U.S. rulers. Eight million jobs mean twenty-five million people in total.

Missile production accounts for eighty-two per cent of all manufacturing jobs in San Diego, California, seventy-two per cent in Wichita, Kansas. Military contracts alone account for thirty per cent of all manufacturing jobs in six States, including California. In Los Angeles nearly sixty per cent of jobs are directly or indirectly dependent on the arms race. Thus the United States as a whole devotes over fifty per cent of all its public expenditure to military spending.

This colossal investment is in exploiting and domination. Every food store and every gas station in America requires, under capitalism, the perpetuation of war production.

This is the world system of imperialism. And the system also has a silent army: the Central Intelligence Agency. The CIA has a budget fifteen times the size of all diplomatic activity of the U.S. This vast agency purchases members of the army and police in countries all over the world. It draws up lists of popular leaders to be assassinated. It plots to start wars. It invades countries.

In Latin America, a band of reactionary generals, at the instigation of the Central Intelligence Agency and the U.S. Ambassador in Brazil, Mr. Lincoln Gordon, crushed the democratic government of João Goulart. In Argentina, American tanks smashed the civilian government of Arturo Frondizi, solely because this conservative spokesman for middle-class interests was insufficiently subservient to U.S. capitalism. Brutal military putsches have been imposed upon Ecuador, Bolivia, Guatemala and Honduras. For decades, the United States armed and supported one of the most barbaric and savage rulers in modern times, namely, Trujillo. When Trujillo no longer served their interests, they allowed him to suffer the fate of Ngo Dinh Diem, but the United States remained the enemy of the people of the Dominican Republic, as can be seen by the arrogant military intervention to crush the brave revolution of April, 1965.

The fact that this naked aggression is condoned by the United Nations, and the ability of the United States to escape expulsion from the United Nations for its gross violation of the Charter, demonstrates that the United Nations has become a tool of American aggression of the kind displayed in the Dominican Republic. All my sympathy lies with the struggle of the people of the Dominican Republic, which continues at this very moment.

In the Congo, mercenary troops, acting for Belgian and American interests and shamelessly supported by the British Government, have killed indiscriminately every living villager in the path of the advancing mercenary armies. The dregs of American militarism have been used for this purpose: the mercenary soldiery of South Africa and of the Cuban counter-revolution.

In the Middle East, United States' and European oil interests force poverty and tyranny on the people. British imperialism, relying on the military and financial power of the United States, is showering the people of Aden with napalm and high explosives in an attempt to suppress the popular movement.

In Southern Africa, incalculable riches are taken out of the Copper Belt of Rhodesia and of South Africa and the fascist states of Salazar and Verwoerd survive through NATO arms. In South-East Asia, 50,000 troops prop up the puppet state of Malaysia, and right-wing generals, with United States' money, have taken control of Indonesia. Throughout the South China seas, every patriotic and radical force is jailed and persecuted by the imperialist powers. The United States boasts of its intrigues in the Maghreb. It brazenly publishes its plans to subvert all nationalist governments.

This is a predatory imperialism and nowhere has it been more cruel and reckless than in Vietnam. Chemicals and gas, bacteriological weapons and phosphorus, napalm and razor bombs, disembowelment, dismemberment, forced labor, concentration camps, beheadings, elaborate torture—every species of cruelty— have been employed by American imperialism in Vietnam. Clinics, sanatoria, hospitals, schools, villages have been relentlessly saturated with fire bombs; and still the people of Vietnam resist, after twenty-five years of struggle against three great industrial powers.

The people of Vietnam are heroic, and their struggle is epic: a stirring and permanent reminder of the incredible spirit of which men are capable when they are dedicated to a noble ideal. Let us salute the people of Vietnam.

In the course of history there have been many cruel and rapacious empires and systems of imperialist exploitation, but none before have had the power at the disposal of United States' imperialists. This constitutes a world system of oppression, and represents the true threat to peace and the true source of the danger of world nuclear war.

I have supported peaceful coexistence, out of the conviction that conflict in a nuclear age can only be disastrous. This conviction was based on the hope that the United States could be persuaded to come to an agreement with the socialist and communist countries. It is now painfully clear that U.S. imperialism cannot be persuaded to end its aggression, its exploitation and its cruelty. In every part of the world the source of war and of suffering lies at the door of U.S. imperialism. Wherever there is hunger, wherever there is exploitative tyranny, wherever people are tortured and the masses left to rot under the weight of disease and starvation, the force which holds down the people stems from Washington.

Peaceful coexistence, therefore, cannot be achieved by requesting U.S. imperialism to behave better. Peace cannot be realized by placing hopes on the goodwill of those whose power depends on the continuation of such exploitation and on the ever-increasing scale of military production. The system which oppresses the people of the world is international, co-ordinated and powerful; but it is hateful and oppressive and in various ways resisted by the people of the world.

A united and co-ordinated resistance to this exploitation and domination must be forged. The popular struggle of oppressed people will remove the resources from the control of U.S. imperialism and, in so doing, strengthen the people of the United States itself, who are striving first to understand and second to overcome the cruel rulers who have usurped their revolution and their government. This, in my view, is the way to create a secure peace, rather than a tenuous and immoral acquiescence in U.S. domination, which can neither work nor be tolerated by humane men.

If the Soviet Union, in its desire for peace, which is commendable, seeks to gain favor with the United States by minimizing, or even opposing, the struggle for national liberation and socialism, neither peace nor justice will be achieved. U.S. imperialism has provided us with all the evidence to which we are entitled as to its nature and its practice. The peoples of the world bear witness to it.

War and oppression have a long history in human affairs. They cannot be overcome except through struggle. A world free of exploitation and foreign domination, a world of wellbeing for the masses of people of all continents, a world of peace and of fraternity, has to be fought for. This is the lesson U.S. imperialism teaches us. It is not a palatable lesson, but nothing will be accomplished by ignoring it.

The danger of nuclear war will not be averted through fear of United States' power. On the contrary, the more isolated the wielders of power in the United States become, in the face of world rejection of their values and resistance to their acts, the more likely we are to succeed in avoiding a nuclear holocaust. It is the illusion on the part of U.S. imperialism that it can accomplish an aim and defeat people by the use of such weapons that constitutes today the main source of nuclear danger. But when the people of Peru, Guatemala, Venezuela, Colombia, Vietnam, Thailand, the Congo, the Cameroons, the United States, Britain— all the people—demonstrate and struggle and resist, nuclear power is of no avail. Its possession will destroy its user. Let us join together to resist U.S. imperialism.

Notes

[1] See the report of the Hebert Investigating Committee of the House of Representatives in the U.S. *Congressional Quarterly.*

1

CONOR CRUISE O'BRIEN

Contemporary Forms of Imperialism

We know that when J. A. Hobson found the economic tap-root of imperialism in the workings of the capitalist system at a given stage, several conditions applied which no longer apply today. Apart from the question of the validity of his economic analysis as applying to the conditions of his own day—one of the many questions on which I look forward to hearing the views of other members of the panel—and apart from the great technological and economic changes which the past sixty years have brought, there have also been *political* changes of such a character and on such a scale as to transform the whole discussion. In Hobson's day—and Lenin's—there could be no doubt, on any side, about the relevance and usefulness of the term "imperialism." There were then British and French and Russian empires, openly labelled as such, and there were many men, and important men, who not merely defended but gloried in the existence of these empires. There were

1

also influential men who openly preached the doctrine of America's imperial destiny. These men could properly be called "imperialists" and their doctrine "imperialism"; they and their increasingly vocal critics had at least these basic words and concepts in common. There was also something else in common: since all the powerful states of the early twentieth century—with the partial exception of a Russia in transition—were capitalist states, it was natural, and indeed inevitable, that contemporary imperialism should be discussed as a function or outgrowth of capitalism.

Two world wars and two major revolutions have changed that landscape out of recognition. The old empires seem to have disappeared; if they have not entirely disappeared, they have at least lost the name of empire. A new vocabulary has arisen—Commonwealth, *Communauté*, Union—"imperialist" is in popular present use solely as a term of abuse. Of the five great powers, recognized as such in the Charter of the United Nations by permanent seating on the Security Council, two now have Communist governments—a situation only flimsily disguised by the insertion of an American satellite delegation in China's place. None of the five great powers would admit to having today anything resembling an empire; all officially are against imperialism or deny its existence, although France's conversion from open imperial practice is so recent that the vocabulary of her spokesmen is still under repair. Imperialism, in the Hobsonian sense, can have no economic tap-root in those powers which have ceased to be capitalist; as for the capitalist countries, these claim to have overcome the supposedly inbuilt Hobsonian compulsion and to have divested themselves of their empires and of any thought of acquiring empires.

Yet the term imperialism has not only survived the overt phenomena which it was used to designate in Hobson's day; it has acquired new life and is in far more frequent international use today than it was in the heyday of the empires. Why should this be? Is it, as some maintain, that the term has become purely emotive, of propaganda value only? Or has it still rational relevance, as a general descriptive term grouping sets of relations still existing, though officially unacknowledged, and continuing certain crucial patterns of the old imperial systems and ambitions? It is obvious that the most frequent uses of the term are operational, that is to say propagandist, and that it is thus used by both sides in the cold war. The Communist side, or rather the Communist sides, have used it most persistently and aggressively, concentrating in recent years on "American imperialism" especially in Latin America, the Near East, Southeast Asia and the Congo. Western spokesmen have retorted by attacks on "Soviet imperialism" in Eastern Europe and "Chinese imperialism" in Tibet, Southeast Asia and the Indian border, and Chinese imperial ambitions towards Indonesia, Africa, etc. The peoples of the newly independent countries are warned from time to time, mainly by American writers and speakers, to be careful not to fall under the sway of a far more cruel form of imperialism than that which they have just shaken off. There has, however, been something half-hearted and ineffective about Western propaganda on these lines; it remains a *tu quoque* and an intellectual gimmick rather than a driving force as Communist anti-imperialism is. The peoples addressed—Africans, Asians, Latin Americans—find it impossible, on the basis of their historical experience, to believe in the sincerity of Western anti-imperialism, and many non-Communist Westerners also find such propaganda distasteful. Many Englishmen and Frenchmen dislike hearing Americans tell the peoples of Ghana or Guinea that Russian rule will be "even more oppressive" than English or French rule was. And many feel—though they do not say—that the rule of more advanced over less advanced people is part of the law of nature and that if the Russians and Chinese were genuinely imperialists, and only imperialists, it would be possible to reach agreement with them. At bottom the West objects to Communists not in so far as they may be imperialists, but in so far as they are revolutionaries.

Western propaganda on "Communist imperialism" lines also errs when it assumes that African and Asian governments necessarily shrink in horror from the thought of the domination of one people over another. Most of these governments are themselves the instruments of such rule over "minority" peoples—and most of them feel that unless they are ready when necessary to take repressive action against minorities, or against refractory elements among the minorities, their states will break up and collapse. Thus many of these states were sympathetic to the Chinese action in Tibet, when this action was presented to them in the light of bringing a dissident peripheral minority to heel—which is of course how the Chinese government envisaged the action. Again Asian and African governments are impressed when an Asian nation like China—or formerly Japan—shows the capacity to act as a great power acts, even in ways which would be stigmatized as imperialist if used by a Western power against Africans or Asians. In such contexts even left-wing African spokesmen are themselves liable to use the classic language of imperialism. Thus I have heard an African delegate, speaking against the inclusion of the question of Tibet on the agenda of the U.N. General Assembly in 1958, argue that the Chinese action was justifiable because Tibetan society was archaic, stagnant and monk-ridden, and the Chinese would bring roads, medicine and education. There was truth in much of what he said, but every argument he used could have been—and was—used to justify, say, Mussolini's conquest of Ethiopia. The man who spoke thus at the U.N. was the delegate of Ethiopia.

Not unnaturally such contradictions have enabled some Western and other spokesmen to pour scorn on the moral position of African and Asian governments, and to deny to these governments any moral right to challenge Western imperialism, or colonialism or the actions of white settler governments. It was the practice of Mr. Eric Louw, representing South Africa when that country still defended its practices in the U.N. General Assembly, to rattle the bones of all the minority skeletons in the U.N. cupboard—caste discrimination in India, oppression by Ethiopia of its Moslem subjects, by Sudan of its non-Muslim subjects and so on. Again there was truth in much of what he said, but he left his audience at best indifferent. Outside a few Western delegations, no one felt that the treatment of minorities in some independent African and Asian countries was seriously comparable to *apartheid*.

White domination over non-white has been after all an almost universally experienced reality. South Africa is a symbol of the continuance of this reality. It is not surprising that the non-white peoples, guilty though some of them are of particular and local acts of aggression, should resent the symbol of their universal bondage. In their reaction to pictures from South Africa or Dixie, the Moslem from Khartoum and his rebellious subject, the pagan from Southern Sudan, would be at one. It is quite true that the moral altitude from which African and Asian governments criticize the West is often less elevated than those governments assume; such governments are not wiser or nicer than other governments, only weaker, and therefore more limited in the scale of their depredations. But the consensus of non-white opinion which they reflect is important and it is this consensus, and not the morals of those through whom it finds expression, that Western policy-makers should take into account. Western policy should—and hopefully must—ultimately be based on the values professed in the West, including that of consent of the governed, and not on, say, the example of Baghdad's treatment of the Kurds. Yet some Western commentators write as if the policies of Baghdad, Khartoum, etc. constitute a vindication of Western imperialism.

In the propaganda battle over "imperialism" the West has been the losing side; the Western nations, and in particular the United States, are still widely regarded as the imperialists and have generally failed in their efforts to pin this label on to the Communist countries. Is this due to resentments arising from past history, including the deep resentments generated by white color-consciousness? Or has the fear of Western imperialism an objective referent in the present? When we are discussing the reactions of many thousands of people, representing in some fashion hundreds of millions of others, the answer to the first question has necessarily to be a qualified one. On personal observation, however, I would say that the role of resentment of *past* wrongs is less than it is often represented to be, and in many of the countries concerned is no more than a latent factor, which in normal circumstances does not become manifest at all. No country is more militantly anti-imperialist in its language than Ghana, yet it is almost impossible to find a Ghanaian who has any really bitter memories of British rule; villagers everywhere respond with spontaneous friendliness to the sight of a white face; the products of the secondary schools and University who man the civil service, the embassies and the U.N. delegation are pro-British to a degree which seems to an Irishman even a little mawkish. It is true that the class in between villager and elite, the class of those whose education stopped at primary level, is a somewhat embittered body, as well as an important one, and not disposed to be sentimental about the benefits of British rule. The real bitterness however is directed against the Ghanaian elite, who have enjoyed secondary and higher education; the anti-Western attitudes of the "Standard VII" boys are principally directed not so much against the West as such as against a native elite which happens to be, on the whole, pro-Western. A similar problem, though at present with greater dominance of pro-Western elites, prevails in Nigeria. Combinations of this kind, whether with a "Nigerian" or "Ghanaian" balance, are to be found throughout all those territories of the former British—and with some qualification French—empires which were not burdened with settlers from the metropolis. (The Belgian Congo, exposed within living memory to the most ferocious and unbridled form of colonial rapacity, is of course quite a different matter.) I find it hard to believe, therefore, that among most of the newly independent countries, resentment of *past* wrongs is a really live factor, actively and independently inspiring present choices. But past experience illuminates contemporary events. Most Algerians, for example, are far too pre-occupied with the pressing problems of the present to waste much time in brooding over the wrongs inflicted on them by the French. But when Algerians hear on the radio, from a Western source, that peasants in certain parts of Vietnam are being brought together in special villages for their protection against terrorists, it is inevitable that these Algerians should think of the French regroupment camps and of the realities which underlay the French army's claim that it was protecting villagers from terror. From this it is a short step to concluding that America's war in Vietnam, like France's in Algeria, is in reality an imperialist war accompanied by mendacious slogans. As this is just what the Communist press and radio say it is, the net effect for so many people, will be to strengthen confidence in the Communist picture of world events, while deepening scepticism about the picture presented by the Western media; this scepticism extends of course to stories of Soviet and Chinese imperialism. (Similarly, those who have lived under people like Trujillo or Batista are not likely to be roused to free world enthusiasm by news of the emergence of another anti-Communist strong man in, say, the Congo.) Algeria is, of course, an extreme example, but even those—like, say, the English-speaking West Africans—whose recent experience of colonial rule has been on the whole a benign one, are sensitized by their past history in such a way as to be repelled by much in the present conduct of the Western powers. Even the benevolent generations of British rulers carried with them their racial exclusiveness and assumptions of superiority, and even the most pro-Western Ghanaian or Nigerian is necessarily affected by corresponding doubts and suspicions—which normally he will seek to repress—about white attitudes towards non-white peoples. These doubts and suspicions can be fanned into hostility by certain news and above all news pictures. An African who has just seen pictures of white Americans using dogs and cattle prods against black men is not psychologically prepared to believe that the white Americans who land in Vietnam have come to help the yellow man. And the more closely he follows the news from Vietnam the less he will be disposed to accept the American official version.

One may note here, to the credit of the American system, how ill-adapted that system is, in certain respects, to the successful waging of a colonial-type war. The French in Algeria did not distribute to the world pictures of their harkis torturing prisoners; British reporters covering Mau Mau had plenty to say about Mau Mau atrocities but little or nothing about atrocities committed by the suppressors of Mau Mau. But American wire services do distribute to the world pictures of "Viet Cong suspects" being tortured by America's Vietnamese allies; American reporters tell of indiscriminate shooting, including the shooting of children, by American marines. Critics of American imperialism can buttress their case with abundant and horrifying detail supplied by impeccable American sources. No corresponding facilities are available to critics of Soviet or Chinese policies and activities.

It seems fair, then, to conclude that the hostility of the newly independent countries to Western imperialism derives not so much from past resentments as from the actual flow of world news, interpreted, as we all must interpret news—in the light of personal and community experience. That news, so interpreted, makes up a pattern in which the Western whites, who control almost all the physical resources of the non-Communist world, seek also with a high degree of success to control its non-white peoples, indirectly and by guile where possible, directly and by force where necessary. This is what is meant by "Western imperialism" today.

How far is this picture valid? Personally I believe that it is substantially accurate, and it is meaningful to speak of Western imperialism, in this sense, as one of the greatest and most dangerous forces in the world today. Those who would deny or minimize its existence assert, with some degree of truth, that the Hobsonian version of imperialism no longer applies if ever it did apply, and that there is no adequate economic motive for imperialist activities. Thus, if France, for example, has a powerful say in the political life of Upper Volta, this is not because she needs the resources or the market—both of them almost non-existent—of that desolate and destitute country, but on the contrary, because France annually makes up the deficit in the Upper Volta budget. This might be defined as *un*economic imperialism. Such examples can easily be multiplied, by writers like Mr. Brian Crozier, to bring into ridicule the idea of economic imperialism and, implicitly, of *all* forms of Western imperialism. I have heard Barbara Ward explain to a Ghanaian audience that the advanced countries of the West have no longer any serious need either for the markets or the resources of the underdeveloped countries generally, and consequently have no economic need either to control or to develop these countries; without the underdeveloped countries, according to this thesis, the advanced countries will continue to progress while, without the advanced countries, the underdeveloped are doomed to continue to stagnate. (It is a measure of Barbara Ward's charm and powers of presentation that this bleak doctrine was received with loud applause by her Ghanaian audience—admittedly an "elite" one of

University students.) The Ward thesis, at least as understood and here summarized by me, itself seems open to some question. I find it hard to believe that Britain is so indifferent to the resources of Kuwait, the United States to those of Venezuela, or Belgium to those of Katanga, as this thesis seems to suggest. Nor does the thesis seem to take sufficient account of the overseas interests of particular groups in the advanced countries. It is uneconomic for France to pay prices higher than world market prices for Ivory Coast *robusta* coffee, but this practice is highly economic for those Frenchmen who own Ivory Coast coffee plantations. Political leverage of interested groups (Standard Oil, United Fruit, etc.) has done much to create, through the mass media, the pattern of anti-Communist public opinion and, by now, anti-Communist *reflexes.* One may, however, agree with the Ward thesis to the extent that economic motives are not in *themselves* sufficient to account for a world-wide effort by the Western countries and especially by the United States to control the politics of the underdeveloped countries generally.

That such an effort exists, is, I think, undeniable. It is a declared goal of the United States, not merely to prevent Soviet and Chinese territorial expansion, but to check the spread of a political doctrine: Communism. This cannot be done without close surveillance of the internal politics of all countries deemed vulnerable to Communism—including all underdeveloped countries—without discreet guidance of these politics when necessary, without economic pressure and without in the penultimate resort intervention by all the methods practiced by all secret services including bribery, blackmail and political assassination. The Congo is an obvious case in point. I have myself heard a senior and responsible American official state that it was not America's responsibility to prevent the Congolese from massacring each other, but it *was* America's responsibility to keep Communism out of the Congo. In practice, American officials, some employed by the C.I.A. and at least one by the United Nations, actively intervened in Congolese politics in order to bring about the downfall of Lumumba and the triumph of his enemies; his subsequent murder and the murder of his principal associates at the hands of these enemies were then regarded as an internal Congolese affair. Professor Paul W. Blackstock in *The Strategy of Subversion: Manipulating the Politics of Other Nations* writes approvingly of the effectiveness of U.S. intervention in this period. C.I.A. intervention in the troubled Congo in support of Colonel Joseph Mobutu contributed materially to the stabilization of the fledgling native regime during the first year (1960-61) of independence. "Stabilization" here appears to be a technical term meaning American control. It should be noted, as demonstrating the formidable and unexpected political weapons which the United States can deploy in an anti-communist effort, that although Mobutu was, as Andrew Tully states, "discovered" and backed by the C.I.A., it was actually from the United Nations—as has recently been shown by Catherine Hoskyns in *The Congo Since Independence*—that he got the money to pay his troops. The United Nations, on the authority of Andrew Cordier, also saw to it that the credit for raising this money went to Mobutu, and that Mobutu's superior, General Lundula, suspected of being loyal to Lumumba, was prevented, through U.N. control of the Congo's airports, from returning to the capital at the critical time.

The Congo in some ways is an extreme case, a *cas limité*, and the limit it stands for, in the eyes of many Africans and Asians, is the limit to their own freedom. From this example they see that if their government shows what are, in the eyes of U.S. officials, Communist tendencies, the diplomatic, political, secret service, and financial resources of the greatest of world powers may be turned against them and that a political receiver nominated by Western interests—a Tshombe—may be put in charge of their affairs. They know further that if they withstand the political shock—which few of them indeed feel strong enough to do—they may have to face actual military intervention, as those other *cas limités*, Santo Domingo and Vietnam, have demonstrated. If there are sizeable Western business interests in their territory they will know that their position in relation to these interests is less than that of a fully sovereign state, for their dealings with these interests will be among the criteria of their non-Communism, that is to say of their continued existence. But even if they have little or nothing, like many of the so-called French-speaking African territories, this does not exempt them from Western surveillance, for even these wastelands form part of that "reservoir of strategic space" which is Africa in the eyes of such competent Western observers as Professor Hans Morgenthau. The position of these countries, with backward economies, often dependent on the export of a single raw material, would be weak in any case in relation to the advanced countries, agreement of whose nationals sets the price of the commodities. When to these structural conditions of dependence is added the latent, and sometimes overt, tutelage implied in the doctrine of "containing Communism" it is not surprising that many people in the poor countries should feel their present independence is little more than a facade, and that in reality they still form part of a sort of Western empire, which is not the less real, economically and politically, for having no legal existence. If the Communist parties have taken up the slogan of "the struggle against neo-colonialism"—a word not of their coinage according to Professor I. I. Potekhin—it is that they see in this situation, and in the resentments generated by it, the point of departure for revolutionary change. In other words the application of the American policy of "containing Communism" is regarded by Communists themselves as a principal generator of Communism. This is of course especially so in those "end-games" where, as in Indo-China, the Congo and much of Latin America, the "containment" process, working by elimination, has thrown up, as "friends of the West" and holders of power, discredited and parasitic groups with little or no unpaid support within their own countries.

The policy of "containing Communism," which is both the mainspring and the justification of contemporary Western forms of imperialism, has a number of points in common with Stalin's policies in post-war Europe. The anti-Communists, like Stalin, seem to envisage their policies as essentially defensive; like Stalin they prefer to work through stooges, reserving military action for the last resort; like Stalin they describe the state of affairs which results from their maneuvers as "freedom," and like Stalin they are in fact adept at the manufacture of satellite states. More adept than he, indeed, for every member of the United Nations which, in a critical vote, accepts the "whip" of the Soviet Union, there are at least five members which will follow the "whip" of the United States. In part as a result of this, and in part because of other pressures, the United Nations on most important matters and at every level—Security Council, Assembly and Secretariat—is preponderantly influenced by United States policy. The delegation seated as representing China is symbolic of this preponderant influence.

If indeed it is to remain the settled and official policy of the United States to prevent the spread of Communism, the quasi-imperial involvement of the United States in the domestic affairs of every country in the "free world" becomes inevitable. There is no way of being sure of "stopping Communism" without interfering, by force if necessary, in the internal affairs of every country in which Communism may appear. What such interference means in the penultimate resort we have seen in the Congo. What it means in the last resort we are seeing in Vietnam. There seems to be no doubt that, left to itself, Vietnam would go Communist; in the effort to prevent this, the United States has taken France's place as imperial power in Southeast Asia; the shadowy governments in Saigon disguise this fact, by now, even less effectively than France's role was disguised by the Emperor Bao Dai. It seems clear that the policy of "containing Communism" is likely to lead to other accretions of direct imperial responsibility—as distinct from indirect rule, as in the Congo—in other parts of the globe. And in an age of awakened nationalism, and of the existence of great powers outside the western system, imperial responsibilities are likely to involve wider resentments and greater bloodshed and infinitely greater risks than they did in the nineteenth century.

On a recent television program we saw the President and the Secretary of State defending their Vietnam policy. They gave three reasons for continuing the war: prestige, honor—meaning the necessity to abide by pledges—and the defense of the freedom of South Vietnam. The first two are contingent, that is to say that they are reasons which can be invoked for persisting in *any* policy, however bad; both were invoked in defense of France's Algerian war policy, until the time came when they had to be dropped. The only *substantive* reason invoked—and that briefly and skimpily— was the so-called defense of freedom. But what meaning can be assigned to the defense of freedom in South Vietnam? It is obvious that the people of South Vietnam do not enjoy freedom in any of the senses in which we so commonly understand the word; they are subject to the arbitrary will of juntas dependent on foreign military and economic support. "Freedom" here is a purely technical term, meaning the exclusion of Communists from power by force if necessary. Mr. James Reston, in a recent article in *The New York Times,* seemed puzzled by the failure of Asians to understand the fact that the U.S. championed their independence and nationalism. He himself failed to understand that the concepts of independence and nationalism are wholly vitiated by the qualifications which current U.S. policy attaches to them. In terms of that policy, independence must be non-Communist or it is not independence; nationalism must be non-Communist, or it is not nationalism. But what happens in a country where nationalists are Communists or pro-Communists, and where independence is thought of as being able to have one's own form of government, even if it should be a Communist form? What happens then is that an outside power, the United States, intervenes to impose its own doctrine of what independence and nationalism should constitute in the country concerned. This, it seems to me, constitutes the ideological mainspring of the most widespread form of contemporary "imperialism." The doctrine of the containment of Communism is necessarily an imperialist doctrine.

Here are certain questions which I would like to have considered by the members of the panel:

Is it really in the national interests of the United States to fight Communism wherever it appears? If so, why?

Why should it be assumed that a state which becomes Communist as Yugoslavia did—i.e. without either Russian or Chinese intervention or active American opposition—should be any more hostile to the United States than Yugoslavia is?

Should not the emergence of a plurality of centers and forms of Communist doctrine and power lead to a radical re-examination of policies formed in the days when it was assumed that any new Communist territory represented an automatic extension of the monolithic power of the Kremlin?

Has anti-Communism become so rooted in the American way of life that no American government can at present afford to allow any country which is at present non-Communist to become Communist?

If so, how is such an attitude likely to be affected by the deepening of the American involvement in the Vietnamese war? Is the doctrine of the necessity to fight Communism likely to be hardened by this involvement—leading perhaps to other similar involvements elsewhere—or will the doctrine be brought into question, once the cost becomes more clear?

Granted that the foreign policies of the United States are increasingly challenged in academic or other intellectual circles, has this challenge now any effect, or is it likely to have any effect, on U.S. public opinion generally?

An outsider like myself sees something of the impact of present U.S. policies on the outside world. Only insiders like yourselves however can come near to gauging the likelihood of a revision of these policies. That is why I should like to know how you would answer such questions as these. A great deal surely depends on the answers, for all of us.

2

TIMOTHY F. HARDING

The New Imperialism in Latin America: A Critique of Conor Cruise O'Brien

In trying to frame in my own mind an adequate description of modern imperialism I found many of Mr. Conor Cruise O'Brien's ideas useful, but I feel that they must be complemented and supplemented if we are to understand imperialism today in any meaningful way. I wish that instead of hearing me comment on his paper you could hear James O'Connor, André Gunder Frank, and others I can name who are currently trying to describe in economic terms the new essence of imperialism in Latin America.

Mr. O'Brien suggests (does he really believe?) that economic imperialism no longer exists, at least as described by Lenin and Hobson. He seems to reduce imperialism to a desire on the part of powerful nations to dominate other nations. But why do they want to dominate them? I'm not sure if he thinks Barbara Ward and Brian Crozier explain away the "economic tap-root" of imperialism in capitalist countries or not. Should I quote Nelson

Rockefeller to demolish Ward? He said of raw materials, "With critical shortages developing rapidly, a quickened and enlarged production of materials in the underdeveloped countries is of major importance." Adolph Berle, like Ward, argued to Latin Americans that their resources were not indispensable to the U.S., but what he meant was the U.S. did not need Bolivian tin, it could buy Nigerian or Malayan tin; it did not need Chilean copper, it could get Rhodesian; Brazilian coffee was being undersold in Africa, and so on. The point of his argument was that Latin Americans had better behave themselves and provide a good atmosphere for U.S. investment, but the argument as a whole shows how dependent the U.S. economy is on the underdeveloped world.

Unless Mr. O'Brien wishes to specify which aspects of economic imperialism are no longer valid, I hesitate to review them all. The arguments of Ward and Crozier are adequately demolished in Paul Baran's *The Political Economy of Growth*[1] and Michael Barratt Brown's *After Imperialism*[2] from two different points of view.

Just as there is no apparent economic justification for France's domination of the Upper Volta, so one might question the economics of the U.S. underwriting one-fourth to one-third of the Bolivian budget for the last decade, and one could ask if the small U.S. economic interests in the Dominican Republic justified the military expenditure in our invasion and occupation of the island. The point is that it is in the economic interests *in general* of the United States to maintain control of Latin America, and that involves subsidizing the weakest links in the chain out of all proportion to the specific profits to be made from these links.

The U.S. financed the Bolivian revolution of 1952 to keep it from moving toward Socialism and becoming a revolutionary spark for Latin America, and much of the "aid" was spent in the U.S. (which means it was aid to U.S. business).

In the Dominican Republic it was to "stop another Cuba" from happening that we intervened, because if Cubas can happen in two islands, "we might lose the hemisphere."

Mr. O'Brien suggests no other adequate explanations for imperialism to replace the economic one. To maintain power a government or ruling group needs prosperity, and to maintain prosperity a capitalist nation must eventually expand its economic control abroad. The spokesmen of U.S. leadership have been very clear on that issue, whether you read the statements of Woodrow Wilson, Dean Acheson or President Eisenhower. The U.S. search for power, prestige and security is inseparable from the U.S. interest in free trade throughout the world. As the most powerful and advanced capitalist nation, the United States stands to benefit from free trade, just as Britain did when it was the leading world capitalist power.

Even in the economic sense, if the economic advantages of imperialism are viewed in their entirety, they include not just trade advantages, but the expenditures on the military establishment to protect areas and enforce policies abroad, the loans and grants (spent in the home country) used to control underdeveloped nations, the expenditures on propaganda, subversion, etc. All these Baran calculates at twenty per cent of the U.S. GNP in the last decade.[3]

Have these means of imperialism become more important to the functioning of the economy than the original ones?

But, given the real economic basis for imperialism, the ideology (anti-Communism), the institutions (the military and CIA) and the policies (containment) take on a life of their own which become self-justifying. Thus, "The cold war is also more than just the defense of capitalist and imperialist positions . . . it is concerned with the overall capitalist position, the whole way of life of what is called 'the free world.' "[4]

The existence of economic imperialism is most obvious to a person living in a "poor" nation. I do not agree that it is perceived primarily, in Latin America, in terms of light dominating dark peoples. The central concern of Latin Americans is to achieve *economic development,* and yet the gap between rich and poor nations continues to grow. Economic imperialism to Latin Americans means the very nature of the relations between industrial and underdeveloped nations that work to widen the gap between them and frustrate the development of their nations. Imperialism is the set of relationships resulting in the nonutilization of available resources for development, in spite of the fact that the techniques for utilizing the potential (but unused) investment capital are known.

To prove that the nature of these economic relations inherently exploits the underdeveloped country, the Latin Americans point to the terms of trade: greater and greater quantities of raw materials are exchanged for less and less finished goods, as prices on raw material exports decline. On a world scale, the industrial worker earns more and more, the raw material producer earns less. The resources of Latin America continue to be controlled from abroad.

The export of profits on foreign investment leads to a net capital drain on Latin American countries. Other concealed payments on royalties and manipulation of prices by huge international corporations increase the net outflow of capital. Local capital is sucked into foreign enterprises and much of the return on it is sent abroad. All this results in a net de-capitalization.

Foreign investment distorts Latin American economies inter-nally by making them economic appendages of the United States. Service and transportation payments go to foreign shipping companies putting an extra drain on their economies. Control of the financial policies of Latin American governments by inter-national banks and the U.S. government through political pressure, threats, loans and bribery operates to keep these policies favorable to U.S. business. Austerity plans and other policies disastrous to economic growth have been imposed from outside.

If insurgent forces in Latin America or elsewhere rise up and put into power a government designed to end acquiescence to economic imperialism, then that country is subjected to political and military pressures which are the most obvious manifestations of imperialist control. This may take the form of subversion, as in Guatemala in 1954, counter-insurgency, or invasion, as in Cuba and the Dominican Republic.

Local ruling oligarchies in Latin America, fearing genuine reform movements, are only too willing to become the tools of the U.S. in return for financing that keeps them in power. Nationalist movements in Latin America have not resulted in national liberation. They have acted as escape valves for radical pressure and in the end helped keep local ruling groups subservient to the United States. The Communist parties have supported the nation-alist movements. Fidelista groups are something qualitatively different from earlier nationalist movements. They concentrate on taking power.

Leaving aside Mr. O'Brien's comparisons of Stalin's control of Eastern Europe with Western imperialism, it is worth noting that Rumania and Cuba complain of economic exploitation by the more developed countries in the Soviet Bloc. Speaking at the Afro-Asian Unity Congress in Algiers, Cuba's Ernesto "Che" Guevara explained how the low prices for raw materials and the high prices for manufactured goods in capitalist world trade worked to exploit the underdeveloped nations. He then said that the developed Socialist countries acted as "accomplices of imperialist exploitation" by using the world market prices as the basis of trade with underdeveloped countries. He accused the Soviet Union and Czechoslovakia in effect of "immorality" in this regard.[5]

What are the new aspects and trends of economic imperialism in Latin America? It used to be that imperialist nations used poor countries almost exclusively as markets and sources of raw materials. In the second stage, in Latin America, until World War II, foreign public utility investment (electricity, railroads, street cars) became nearly as important as the development of agricultural and mineral exports. Since World War II there has been an important swing toward foreign investment in industry for production and sale in the Latin American countries, particularly in those with the largest internal markets: Brazil, Mexico, Argentina and Colombia. The Latin American Common Market will increase this trend. Under the threat of expropriation and government price controls, foreign capital is actually shifting away from utilities and minerals (with the exception of oil, the most important one) into steel, automobiles, refrigerators, Sears Roebuck, supermarkets, and services such as management consulting.

The economic implications of this new form imperialism is taking are still to be studied, but as long as these new industries are controlled from abroad and export their earnings, they do not really contribute to sound economic development of the nation as a whole.

Lenin described the changeover from manufacturing-interest imperialism to bank-financial imperialism. Since then the big banks, it seems to me, have fallen under the control of the large corporations which now direct the economic imperialism of the developed countries. The giant corporations seem to finance their operations abroad by themselves, without coming under bank control, and they are able to use the local banking system and the international banks (Export-Import Bank, World Bank, Inter-American Development Bank) to help finance their activities abroad without being controlled by them.

Massive U.S. economic aid is a new facet of imperialism since World War II. U.S. aid abroad, much of it military, has been an important element in sustaining the U.S. economy by paying for goods and services exported. While most of this aid went to Western Europe and "crucial" countries like Korea, Taiwan and Vietnam, since the "Alliance for Progress" was announced more has gone to Latin America. It has been a decisive element in keeping governments in power who respected U.S. economic interests.

In 1962, Alliance for Progress money went to Honduras partly because, following the spirit of the Alliance for Progress, the government of Villeda Morales passed a land reform program.

However, when the implementation of the program involved the expropriation of United Fruit Company land, the Hickenlooper amendment was called into play, and aid was cancelled. Shortly after, presumably with support of the U.S. military mission, the civilian government was overthrown by the military and the officers still rule in Honduras. U.S. aid was resumed. Such are the contradictions of U.S. aid.

Another new aspect of U.S. imperialism is the extent to which the interests of specific corporations have been sacrificed to the interests of the U.S. corporation in general, as interpreted by those super-managers, McNamara, McGeorge Bundy, Dean Rusk and Thomas Mann. McNamara seems truly to have graduated from the Ford Motor Company in a way that Charles Wilson never did from GM.

It is true that during the "Good Neighbor Policy" Franklin Roosevelt was able to sacrifice particular interests of the U.S. oil companies expropriated in Mexico in the interests of the larger question of U.S. control of the hemisphere as World War II drifted near (he then made Nelson Rockefeller coordinator of Inter-American Affairs). But after the war, the aggregate interest of the U.S. in the hemisphere was abandoned to the specific interest of each small pressure group and large corporation. Hemisphere affairs were ruled by the Trujillo lobby, etc., symbolized by Earl T. Smith's ambassadorship in Cuba.

Eisenhower gave the Bolivian revolution the right to expropriate the tin mines in 1952 (they were not predominantly U.S.-owned) and successfully bought out the middle class revolutionary leadership there to keep it from going further left. In return, the Bolivians allowed U.S. oil concessions east of the Andes, concessions that proved to be of little value, although they seemed important to U.S. economic security during the Korean war. While weaning the Bolivian leadership away from worker and peasant support, the U.S. convinced the Paz Estenssoro leadership to revive the professional army that had been destroyed during the revolution. In 1964 the army threw out Paz.

The CIA's overthrow of the Arbenz regime in Guatemala in 1954 took place amid a sea of decorations for dictators.

However, the Cuban revolution and its movement toward the Soviet bloc changed the nature of the situation in Latin America. Convinced that Cuba was bluffing, in 1959 and 1960 pressure by the U.S. was designed to bring Cuba to heel so that it would accept aid on U.S. terms (austerity programs and guarantees for U.S. property). But Fidel could not be bought out or pressured to the right like the Bolivians, or thrown out by invasion like the Guatemalans.

To keep the Cuban Revolution from spreading, the Alliance for Progress was constructed. Justifiably called the Castro plan, it provided for two-thirds of the U.S. investment Fidel had called for in his speech in Buenos Aires in May of 1959 over a ten-year period. The hope was that the oligarchies could be bribed into reform while the U.S. paid to clean up the slums.

But Cuba so polarized the situation, and the timid encouragements to reform so shook the stability of the oligarchies and U.S. property, that the military intervened in nation after nation to stabilize the old order. Military officers took over Argentina, El Salvador, Peru, Honduras, Ecuador, the Dominican Republic and Brazil.

The U.S. State Department at first slapped these generals on the wrist: "This is not what we had in mind at all!" To which the generals replied, "Who makes policy in Washington? Our friends in the Pentagon or you civilians?" To quiet the Kennedy liberals, the generals had only to wave the red shirt of the Communist threat, or ask the CIA to plant some arms on their beaches.

A new turn in the short-lived U.S. policy came after Kennedy's death when Thomas Mann, the new Under Secretary of State for Latin America, declared that henceforth the U.S. would put no obstacles in the way of military regimes taking over since they were more likely than civilian governments to provide the progressive stability cherished by the U.S. Two weeks later the Brazilian military overthrew Joao Goulart. President Belaunde Terry of Peru, in combat with the conservative forces who controlled the Congress in Peru, had been threatening to by-pass the Congress with a "progressive dictatorship." After Goulart fell he abandoned that idea and acquiesced to filling out his term as a do-nothing president.

An important new trend in U.S. control over Latin America is the control exercised over Latin American nations by the Pentagon through the local Latin American military, completely by-passing the State Department. This was apparently the case in the Dominican Republic, where the U.S. military mission encouraged the overthrow of Bosch while the State Department supported him. U.S. counter-insurgency forces have directed anti-guerrilla operations in Venezuela and Colombia and have prepared "contingency plans" to deal with instability in nearly every country in Latin America. However, with all the military aid, the U.S. cannot count on the Latin American military one hundred per cent, as shown in military revolts at Carupano and Puerto Cabello in Venezuela, the military "Constitutional" leadership in the Dominican Republic, and the participation of young Guatemalan officers in the guerrilla movements in Guatemala. The Guatemalan guerrilla leader Yon Sosa was trained by the U.S. in counter-insurgency and Francisco Camaño Deño was also trained by U.S. military forces.

Intervention in the Dominican Republic was further confirmation of the rightist trend of U.S. policy in Latin America. Since that intervention the U.S. has been trying to get the Brazilian military to take the lead in the construction of a multilateral "peace-keeping force" that would try to snuff out the flames of revolution in Latin America wherever they threaten to consume the old order.

The Mann policy is a return in *form* to marine diplomacy, and to support of dictators, but it is essentially different in that it is dictated by the collective anti-Communist interest of U.S. corporations and not the individual desires of small economic pressure groups.

I do not agree that containing Communism is the "mainspring" of Western imperialism, because I think the mainspring is economic. Anti-Communism is an ideology and a justification, and it must be very loosely defined. If it was essentially the distribution of arms to the people in the Dominican Republic by the rebels, and not the presence of a few Communists that led to the U.S. invasion, then the real reason for U.S. imperialism is only indirectly related to anti-Communism.

Why is Communism in underdeveloped countries a danger to the United States, as Mr. O'Brien says? Because Communism puts an end to economic imperialism. In China, the Open Door is now closed! But non-Communist guerrillas in Guatemala are perceived as more of a threat than Communists in the Kremlin with whom one can make a deal.

If capitalism is going to survive, then "Communism" must be contained. Revolutions must be stopped in Vietnam or the Dominican Republic.

The fact that the U.S. recognizes no limits to its power to intervene terrifies even Arnold Toynbee.[6] But it seems to me misleading to argue that whether or not Vietnam and the Dominican Republic become "Communist" should not concern the United States. The difference today between English and French imperialism and U.S. imperialism is that the British and French are willing to accommodate themselves to a revolution if it becomes too expensive to stop, as in Algeria or Vietnam. They cannot afford an all-out commitment to reaction. But ever since Churchill gave the leadership of the capitalist world to the United States in his speech in Fulton, Missouri, in March, 1946, and Truman accepted that responsibility by proclaiming the Truman Doctrine a year later, the United States has recognized no economic limitations to the defense of capitalism. Each encounter is a precedent, and each is more desperate. Because the survival of the Cuban revolution may well be bound up in what happens in Vietnam, Fidel has pleaded with the Soviet Union and China to patch their differences and give effective aid to North Vietnam. Cuba gave North Vietnam 10,000 tons of sugar, the only thing Cuba had to give.

Mr. O'Brien asks me if it is really in the U.S. interest to fight Communism anywhere. Certainly such a fight is diametrically opposed to the interests of most Americans in the long run and it is morally indefensible. Socialists have the job of explaining this to Americans in spite of the short-term advantages to the U.S. economy of war. For the giant corporations whose survival is linked to the survival of capitalism, it *is* in their interest to fight "Communism" everywhere, and the revolutions they call "Communism" can only be checked with unspeakable brutality.

The United States is not likely to accept Cuba as another "Yugoslavia," although a Yugoslavia could be tolerated in Africa. The U.S. attitude toward Yugoslavia was based on three considerations: Yugoslavia broke away from the Soviet Union, it was situated in the Soviet sphere of influence, and Tito renounced attempts to encourage revolution in the rest of the world. But compare the U.S. attitude toward Yugoslavia with the U.S. attitude toward the possibility of revolution in Greece. Countries like Cuba and North Vietnam which are perceived to be supporting the spread of revolution are considered much more dangerous than Poland or the Soviet Union.

Cuba considers the very survival of its revolution to be bound up with the spread of revolution in Latin America, and the supporting evidence is convincing. A Communist-unified Vietnam might not be hostile to the U.S., but it would be an admission that Communism cannot be "contained," and I believe this would and should encourage revolution elsewhere, because, as Mr. O'Brien pointed out, revolutionary forces in most countries do not have the courage to move when confronted by the threat of massive retaliation.

On the other hand, where there is a minimum of stability, as in most Latin American countries, revolution will be postponed for years. Socialist revolutions will occur only when there is no more possibility for capitalist development (given the social structure, available leadership and the economic conditions). In understanding why there might be room for capitalist development in Chile, Brazil and Mexico, socialist scholars have not made significant contributions. Guerrillas in Venezuela themselves admit they are at least a decade from taking power.

I see some hope in Mr. O'Brien's statement that the way in which Communism is contained has become the principal generator of Communism. U.S. actions in Bolivia and Guatemala contributed to the Cuban revolution. U.S. intervention in the Dominican Republic destroyed any remaining illusions about the Alliance for Progress.

Mr. O'Brien describes imperialism as the control of the resources and people of the non-white world by Western whites. This description has severe limitations when applied to Latin America. Racial discrimination was abolished in Cuba by a white revolutionary leadership. Chile and Uruguay are no less subject to U.S. imperialism because they happen to be mostly white. Even in Africa, it was the white revolutionary leadership in Algeria that convinced Malcolm X of the limitations of making a fetish of black nationalism. To the extent that Indians in Peru do identify their exploiters as light-skinned, it provides an almost unbridgeable chasm between them and the middle class radicals which is only now being broken down.

Notes

[1] Baran, Paul, *The Political Economy of Growth* (Monthly Review Press, New York, 1957).

[2] Brown, Michael Barratt, *After Imperialism* (Heineman, London, 1963).

[3] Baran, *op. cit.*, p. 118.

[4] Brown, *op. cit.*, p. 204.

[5] Ernesto Guevara, "Discurso del Comandante Ernesto Guevara, Ministro de Industrias de Cuba, Pronunciado en Argel (Argelia) el 24 de Febrero de 1964," *Politica*, Mexico City (March 1, 1965), pp. I-VI.

[6] Arnold J. Toynbee, "The Failure of American Foreign Policy," *Fact* (September-October, 1965), pp. 4-5.

3

JAMES O'CONNOR

The Meaning of Economic Imperialism

THEORIES OF IMPERIALISM

There is still much controversy, and more confusion, about the meaning of economic imperialism. Monopolistic privileges and preferences, plunder of raw materials, seizure of territory, enslavement of local peoples, nationalism, racism, militarism—all of these phenomena have been closely identified with imperialism. Only on the association of imperialism with expansion—economic, political, cultural and territorial expansion—has there been any general agreement. But if imperialism means "the extension of political power by one state over another, (then) all through the sixty centuries of more or less recorded history" it has been a principle feature in human relations.[1] Beneath the undergrowth of over half a century of historical, theoretical, and polemical writings, however, three general doctrines can be distinguished. Two of

23

these reflect the period of European expansion which began during the 1880's and ended in 1914. The third is an interpretation of contemporary world capitalism, and, in particular, United States expansionism.

Imperialism: A Political Phenomenon

The first doctrine dissociates capitalism from imperialism. For Joseph Schumpeter, the leading exponent of this view, imperialism is "a heritage of the autocratic state . . . the outcome of precapitalist forces which the autocratic state has reorganized . . . (and) would never have been evolved by the inner logic of capitalism itself."[2] The "inner logic" of capitalism consists of nothing more or less than free trade and "where free trade prevails *no* class has an interest in forcible expansion as such . . . citizens and goods of every nation can move in foreign countries as freely as though those countries were politically their own." Only the "export monopolist interests"—in particular, monopolies in the metropolitan countries which dump surplus commodities abroad behind high tariff walls—profit from imperialism. Schumpeter was confident that these interests would not survive capitalism's "inner logic." His confidence was, of course, misplaced; as we will see, the national and regional economic policies of the advanced capitalist countries today rightly merit Mrs. Joan Robinson's label—the New Mercantilism. The reason is not hard to find: Schumpeter selected one characteristic of capitalism, "rationality," which he considered central, to the exclusion of other features.

The vast majority of bourgeois economists in the past and present adopt a position similar to Schumpeter's, even though few today would share his optimism in connection with the revival of free trade. The generally accepted "comparative advantage" theory of Ricardo and Mill holds that all parties in international commodity trade under competitive conditions benefit in accordance with the strength of the demand for their respective commodities. Nationalist economic policy and monopoly restricted free trade and inhibited the growth of income and economic well-being, but these barriers have been lowered by the breakup of the European empires. The trademark of this doctrine is that exploitive economic relations between the advanced and backward capitalist countries cannot survive in a world of politically independent countries. According to this line of thinking, the real problems of world capitalism today spring from the misplaced faith of the ex-colonies that nationalist economic policies which have created new and higher barriers to international investment and trade can put the backward countries on the path of self-sustained economic growth.

Schumpeter and other bourgeois writers uncritically dissociate capitalism from imperialism for three reasons: first, because their criteria for distinguishing and identifying imperial and colonial relationships are ordinarily political and not economic (for example, Hans Kohn has developed the most sophisticated typology of imperialism, which he understands in terms of the distribution of political power);[3] second, because they do not consider capitalism as such to be an exploitive system; third, because imperialism historically has contained certain features identified with the theme of expansionism which have not been uniquely associated with any given economic and social system. Thus bourgeois writers have concluded not only that imperialism pre-dates capitalism but also that imperialism is essentially an anachronistic system. For this reason, there have been few investigations of the specific features of capitalist imperialism.

In connection with economic expansionism, pre-capitalist and capitalist societies differ in five general ways. First, in pre-capitalist societies, economic expansion was irregular, unsystematic, not integral to normal economic activity. In capitalist societies, foreign trade and investment are rightly considered to be the "engines of growth." Expansion is necessary to maintain the rhythm of economic activity in the home, or metropolitan economy, and has an orderly, methodical, permanent character. Second, in pre-capitalist societies, the economic gains from expansion were windfall gains, frequently taking the form of sporadic plunder. In capitalist societies, profits from overseas trade and investment are an integral part of national income, and considered in a matter-of-fact manner.

Third, in pre-capitalist societies, plunder acquired in the course of expansion was often consumed in the field by the conquering armies, leaving the home economy relatively unaffected. In capitalist societies, exploited territories are fragmented and integrated into the structure of the metropolitan economy. Imperialism in effect potentially emancipated space-bound and time-bound man. Fourth, in pre-capitalist societies, debates within the ruling class ordinarily revolved around the issue whether or not to expand. In capitalist societies, ruling-class debates normally turn on the question of what is the best way to expand.

Last, in relation to colonialism, pre-capitalist and capitalist societies also differ in a fundamental way. In the former, colonialism (land seizure, colonist settlement, or both) was the only mode of control which the metropolitan power could effectively exercise over the satellite region. As we will see later in detail, capitalist societies have developed alternative, indirect, and more complex forms of control.

Mercantile vs. Industrial Capitalism.   Not only do pre-capitalist and capitalist expansion depart from each other in significant ways, but also the character of expansion (especially the nature of trade and colonialism) in mercantile capitalist societies differs from that in industrial capitalist societies. To be sure, the definition of colonialism adopted by some writers— monopolistically regulated trade and investment at higher rates of profit than those obtaining in the home economy—applies with equal force to both the mercantilist and the industrial capitalist eras. In fact, the term "neo-mercantilism" has frequently been used to describe nineteenth century imperialism, and, as we have mentioned, mid-twentieth century nationalist economic policy has been labeled the "new mercantilism." In addition, throughout the history of capitalism, businessmen and traders have followed the same rule—extract capital from areas where the cost is lowest, invest where anticipated returns are highest.

The differences between mercantilism and nineteenth century imperialism, however, outweigh the similarities.[4] First, the resemblance between monopolistic commerical organization in the two political-economic systems is only superficial. Mercantilist monopoly trading companies did not spring from the prevailing modes of production. They were formed to minimize physical and commercial risks along uncertain and distant trade routes. As "normal" patterns of trade were established, risk and uncertainty were reduced, and the great monopoly companies met increasing competition from other nationals and foreign companies. The East India Company, the last of the great monopolies, was dissolved early in the nineteenth century. From then until the last quarter of the nineteenth century, British manufacturers and merchants adopted free trade on principle because their control over advanced methods of production gave them a decisive competitive advantage. But Britain's foreign investments in Europe and the United States and the diffusion of industrial technology eliminated this advantage. And further advances in technology which were not consistent with small-scale enterprise led to the cartelization and monopolization of industry. Latter-day monopolies, unlike their forerunners, have proven not to be transitory.

A second important difference between mercantilism and imperialism is related to the character of trade. Early mercantilism was commercial capitalism in its purest essence, middlemen exchanged goods for goods in a lively *entrepôt* trade, and mercantilist wars were mainly trade wars—the Anglo-Dutch wars of the seventeenth century were the purest commerical wars in history.[5] It is true that as early as the first decades of the seventeenth century the East India Company purchased raw materials in exchange for British manufactured goods. But this was not typical. It was only in the late mercantile and early industrial capitalist periods that Britain increasingly exported manufactured commodities for agricultural raw materials and minerals.[6] As late as 1800, for example, British ships took woolens and hardware to India and returned with cotton and silk products. Then, as the nineteenth century wore on, a new dimension was added to trade: capital goods financed by foreign loans and investments, as well as consumer manufacturers, were exchanged for foodstuffs and industrial raw materials.

Finally, there are superficial similarities between mercantilism and imperialism in the sphere of state economic policy. Both systems of political economy relied on active state participation in the direction, organization, and character of trade or investment. But the nature of state policy was fundamentally different. In England, after the prohibition on the export of bullion was abolished in 1663, the State employed commodity import and export controls with the aim of maintaining a favorable balance of trade, or export surplus, with *each* of Britain's trading partners, colonies and non-colonies alike. Gradually, a system of multilateral trade replaced the more primitive bilateral trade patterns. It was this system of multilateral trade which the imperialist states of the late nineteenth century inherited. Imperialist state policy revived the older technique of export promotion and import restriction (and invented new techniques, as well) with the aim of maintaining a favorable balance of trade *with the world as a whole,* not with any specific trading partner.

These contrasts between mercantilism and imperialism give rise to important differences with respect to colonization. In the first place, it is certainly true that the leading late mercantilist and imperialist powers discouraged both subsistence production and the manufacture of commodities in the colonies. But mercantilist industry was technologically primitive, small-scale, and, most important, not vertically integrated. Thus the exploitation of raw materials under mercantile impulses, and colonization itself, were of necessity *national* policies, and generated fierce national rivalries. From the late nineteenth century down to the present, however, national rivalries have increasingly given way to struggles between fully-integrated corporations based in the metropolitan countries. These struggles have typically been resolved in compromise. The sharing out of oil resources between the great oil monopolies in the Middle East is an excellent example of cooperation between integrated corporations (and, by extension, imperialist nations). To make the point slightly differently, in the mercantilist era it was impossible to conceive of an international ruling class; in the contemporary imperialist period, an international ruling class is an accomplished fact.[7]

Secondly, colonial conquest in the sixteenth and seventeenth centuries had as its chief purpose the mitigation of the hazards of trade and the preservation of monopoly control. The mercantilist powers established factories, trading bases, and forts where regional trade was already established.[8] By contrast, the seizure of territories in the late nineteenth century was motivated less to preserve commercial positions which had already been won by peaceful methods than to open up possibilities for trade and investment where none had existed before. Colonialism under mercantilism was therefore defensive in nature and required a passive state presence, while latter-day imperialism, by contrast, exhibited an aggressive character which stood in need of active state participation.

Mercantilism and imperialism departed from each other in still another important respect. The doctrine used to support rigid trade restrictions, and an important element of the theory which the mercantile colonial system was based on, was that the maximum inflow of bullion required a favorable balance of trade with each colony. This doctrine limited the scope of territorial conquest and seizure, as well as the development of commerical relations with other colonial powers. In the late mercantile era, however, the state gradually realized that an expansion of output was the key to maximum trade and therefore the nursing of home industry and creation of employment became central goals of state policy. Thus were created the pre-conditions for the growth of complex, multilateral trade patterns, which in turn awakened the interests of the imperial powers in any and all under-exploited regions.

In sum, industrial capitalist expansionism distinguished itself in the following important respects: it exhibited a more aggressive attitude toward the under-exploited lands; it was less particular and more universal in character; it more fully integrated under-exploited economic regions into the structure of the metropolitan country; it required the active participation of the state; and, finally, internecine warfare between the economic monopolies tended to be less acute. Imperialism thus contained the important contradiction which has afflicted the advanced capitalist countries down to the present day. On the one hand, the *national* power elites seek to advance the economic interests of their respective countries; on the other hand, the integrated, multinational corporations, or the *international* ruling class, extend their sway irrespective of the interests of the countries in which they are based. This contradiction is heightened by the aggressive, universal character of modern imperialist expansion.

(In our comparison of mercantilism and imperialism we have neither surveyed the differences between the early, middle, and late mercantilist era, nor reviewed satisfactorily the relation of the free trade period to either mercantilism or imperialism. One school of thought sees a great deal of continuity between mercantilism and early industrial capitalism. M. Barratt-Brown, for example, argues that the decades after 1815 saw the expansion and consolidation of the British Empire based on the need to conquer and secure markets and keep trade routes open in the face of rivalries from developing European and United States capitalism and the first outbreaks of nationalism and anti-imperialism in the colonies. D. Fieldhouse, on the other hand, asserts that Britain's industrial supremacy after 1815 meant that the colonies and monopolistic privileges involved few benefits and large costs. He claims that the acquisition and defense of colonies were motivated chiefly for reasons of military security and administrative efficiency.)

Imperialism: An Aspect of Monopoly Capitalism

Against the view that dissociates capitalism and imperialism, Marxist economists have put forward many variations on fundamentally the same argument. The second doctrine of imperialism, also inspired by European expansionism in the late nineteenth and early twentieth centuries, holds that monopoly capitalism, imperialism, and colonialism are basically the same phenomena. Perhaps it is more accurate to call this view "neo-Marxist" because those who hold it have inherited few clear theoretical guidelines from Marx himself. In the three volumes of *Capital,* apart from the brief concluding chapter in Volume 1, there are only two or three references to the economics of colonialism, the gist of which is that commmodities produced under conditions of high labor productivity and sold in countries where labor productivity is low will command an abnormally high rate of profit.[9] Marx's relative silence on the economics of imperialism may have handicapped the development of Marxist theory, or it may have been a blessing in disguise. The absence of any theoretical precedent has forced (and continues to force) Marxists back on their own experiences and intellectual resources. Thus older interpretations of imperialism as far apart as those of Lenin and Rosa Luxemburg, and modern theories as disparate as those of Paul Baran and Joseph Gillman have arisen from basically the same critical tradition.

Nothing succeeds like success, however, and Lenin's ideas have dominated the field. Yet Lenin owed much to John A. Hobson's *Imperialism,* published in 1902, a book which is frequently (and legitimately) read as the precursor of Lenin's study. Thus we will begin by sketching out the main ideas of Hobson and Lenin, later subjecting them to analysis on the basis of theoretical and historical studies published in recent years.

Hobson and Lenin wrote about imperialism during the heyday of colonialism (1885-1914), which naturally enough appeared to be *the* most significant economic-political phenomenon of the time. By making colonialism their focal point, however, both men equated imperialism and colonialism and thus failed to understand the significance of the "imperialism of free trade"—an expression coined to describe British economic expansion from the 1840's to the 1880's. Moreover, they barely acknowledged United States expansion and could not anticipate future modes of imperialist controls which have proved to be even more effective than formal colonial rule.

The distinctive feature of Hobson's theory is his conception of colonialism as the reflection of the unfulfilled promise of liberal democracy. As Hobson saw it, inequalities in the distribution of wealth and income in Britain dampened the consumption power of the British working classes, which in turn made it unprofitable for capitalists to utilize fully their industrial capacity. Unable to find profitable investment outlets at home, British capitalists subsequently sought them abroad in the economically under-exploited continents. Britain therefore acquired colonies as a dumping ground for surplus capital. The end of imperialist conquest and de-colonization would come about only when the British working classes acquired more economic and political power through trade unionism and parliamentary representation, which would set the stage for a thoroughgoing redistribution of income and hence the development of a home economy in which the volume of consumption corresponded more closely to the volume of production.

Hobson supported his thesis not only by his faith in the promise of liberal democracy, but also by reference to changes in Britain's trade and investments. He tried to show that the expansion of empire during the last two decades of the nineteenth century, when most of the world not already independent or under European rule was carved up among the European powers, resulted in a *decline* in British trade with her colonies in relation to trade with non-colonies.[10] He also underlined the obvious fact that the new colonies in Africa and Asia failed to attract British settlers in significant numbers. Through a process of elimination Hobson thus hit on what he considered to be the crucial element in British imperialism—foreign investments. He linked the vast outflow of capital from Britain during this period—British overseas investments rose from £785 million in 1871 to £3,500 million in 1911 and annual net foreign investments were frequently greater than gross domestic fixed investments—with the frantic struggle by the European powers for colonies, and inferred that the former caused the latter. The political struggles between the major European powers were thus dissolved into struggles for profitable investment outlets, and the explorers, missionaries, traders, and soldiers of the period were seen as the puppets of London's financial magnates.

Lenin's views. Lenin agreed with Hobson that the prime cause of capital exports was the vast increase in the supply of capital in the metropolitan countries, especially Britain, and played down the role of the demand for capital in the underdeveloped regions. He also, like Hobson, causally linked foreign investments with the acquisition of colonies. The distinctive element in Lenin's theory related to the *cause* of the surplus of capital.

Lenin understood that imperialism is a *stage* of capitalist development, and not merely one possible set of foreign policy options among many. In particular, imperialism is the monopoly capitalist stage, and exhibits five basic features:

1. The concentration of production and capital, developed so highly that it creates monopolies which play a decisive role in economic life.
2. The fusion of banking capital with industrial capital and the creation, on the basis of this financial capital, of a financial oligarchy.
3. The export of capital, which has become extremely important, as distinguished from the export of commodities.
4. The formation of the international capitalist monopolies which share out the world among themselves.
5. The territorial division of the whole earth completed by the great capitalist powers.[11]

The key element is the formation of local and international monopolies behind high tariff barriers in the metropolitan countries. Monopolistic organization develops "precisely out of free competition" in essentially four ways. First, the concentration (growth in absolute size) of capital leads to the centralization (growth in relative size) of capital. Second, monopoly capital extends and strengthens itself by the seizure of key raw materials. Third, financial capital, or the investment banks, "impose an infinite number of financial ties of dependence upon all the economic and political institutions of contemporary capitalist society," including non-financial capital. Fourth, "monopoly has grown out of colonial policy. To the numerous 'old' motives of colonial policy the capitalist financier has added the struggle for the sources of raw materials, for the exportation of capital, for 'spheres of influence,' i.e., for spheres of good business, concessions, monopolist profits, and so on; in fine, for economic territory in general." In short, the new colonialism opposes itself to the older colonial policy of the "free grabbing" of territories.

The cause of the surplus of capital and capital exportation, and monopolistic industry, is the tendency of the rate of profit to fall.[12] Two underlying forces drive down the rate of profit in the metropolitan country: first, the rise of trade unions and social democracy, together with the exhaustion of opportunities to recruit labor from the countryside at the going real wage, rule out possibilities for increasing significantly the rate of exploitation; second, labor saving innovations increase the organic composition of capital. Monopoly is thus in part formed in order to protect profit margins. At the same time, economies of large-scale production (internal expansion) and mergers during periods of economic crises (external expansion) strengthen pre-existing tendencies toward monopolistic organization.

Meanwhile, in the economically under-exploited regions of the world, capital yields a substantially higher rate of return. For one thing, the composition of capital is lower; for another, labor is plentiful in supply and cheap; and, finally, colonial rule establishes the pre-conditions for monopolistic privileges. Rich in minerals and raw materials required by the development of the metals, the automotive, and other heavy industries in the metropolitan powers, the under-exploited regions naturally attract large amounts of capital. Consequently, foreign investment counteracts the tendency for the rate of profit to fall in the metropolitan economy. On the one hand, high profit margins in the colonies pull up the average return on capital; on the other hand, the retardation of capital accumulation in the home economy recreates the reserve army of the unemployed, raises the rate of exploitation, and, finally, increases the rate of profit.

Pushing this thesis one step forward, the precondition for a truly "favorable" investment climate is indirect or direct control of internal politics in the backward regions. Economic penetration therefore leads to the establishment of spheres of influence, protectorates, and annexation. Strachey suggests that the backward regions assumed a dependency status (the last step before outright control) in relation to the metropolitan powers chiefly because the former were in debt to the latter. What was significant about the shift from consumer goods to capital goods in world trade was that the colony-to-be needed long-term credits or loans to pay for the capital goods, and that, finally, the relationship between the backward country and the metropolitan country became one of debtor and creditor. And from this it was but a small step to dependence and domination.

Whatever the exact sequence of events which led to colonialism, Lenin's economic definition of colonialism (and imperialism) is monopolistically regulated trade and/or investment abroad at higher rates of profit than those obtaining in the metropolitan country. "As soon as political control arrives as handmaid to investment," Dobb writes, "the opportunity for monopolistic and preferential practices exists." The essential ingredient of colonialism therefore is "privileged investment: namely, invest-ment in projects which carry with them some differential advantage, preference, or actual monopoly, in the form of concession-rights or some grant of privileged status."[13]

Criticisms of Hobson and Lenin. The criticisms of Hobson and Lenin's theories, and the alternative views which have been put forward, do not constitute a new theory so much as a catalogue of historical facts which are not fully consistent with the older theories. These criticisms bear on three key aspects of Lenin's theory, two of which also figured importantly in Hobson's thought.

One line of criticism is that Lenin ignored the theme of continuity in European expansionism and was too eager to interpret the partition of Africa and the Pacific as a qualitatively different phenomenon. Alexander Kemp has shown that throughout the *entire* nineteenth century British net capital exports in relation to national income amounted to just over one per cent during recession periods and about six to seven per cent during boom years.[14] Pointing to a similar conclusion is Richard Koebner's judgment that British "imperial responsibilities were enlarged step by step by a hesitant government."[15] Gallagher and Robinson also reject the idea that there were important qualitative differences between British expansionism in the first and in the second parts of the nineteenth century. In both periods the formula was "trade with informal control if possible; trade with the rule if necessary."[16] In Egypt and South Africa, for example, they maintain that Britain was only responding to internal upheaval and that traditional controls could no longer be relied upon.

Lenin was aware of the continuity in European expansionism but maintained that the development of monopoly capitalism led to a break in this continuity. In principle Lenin had solid earth under his feet because the generation of business savings and their absorption by new investments are governed by different laws in a competitive capitalist society than under monopoly capitalism. But in practice it is by no means certain that Lenin was right when he asserted that "at the beginning of the twentieth century, monopolies have acquired complete supremacy in the advanced countries."

In the most powerful imperialist country, Great Britain, there were few trusts or cartels of any consequence in 1900.[17] One highly qualified economic historian maintains that the British economy failed to enter the monopoly state until the early 1930's.[18] Lenin was aware that British capitalism was far from a model of monopoly domination, but slurred over the problem by referring to a "monopoly" of a few dozen companies and by interpreting Chamberlain's Imperial Preference System as Britain's reply to the European cartels. The German economy was not thoroughly trustified until after 1900, even though bank control of industry was established at a much earlier date. As for the

United States economy, recent research has thrown doubt on the received idea that the great merger movement around the turn of the century resulted in the cartelization and trustification of heavy industry, and has substituted the thesis that the economy was more competitive in the first decade of the twentieth century than in the last decade of the nineteenth.[19]

The same line of criticism developed from a different perspective also casts doubt on Lenin's major thesis. The truth is that British capital exports to Africa were mobilized by small-scale speculators, not mainly by the big London banking houses. For the former, although not the latter, foreign lending was a precarious undertaking. One of the first of the African companies, The Royal Niger Company, "had to . . . enlist subscribers in order to make certain that the Company would be equal to its administrative undertaking."[20] Similarly, subscribers to the Imperial British East Africa Company and Cecil Rhodes' South African Company were mainly small-scale savers, such as pensioners and retired military officers. If monopoly capitalism is essentially a post-Lenin phenomenon, it is readily understandable why the African companies were financed by small capital. The interesting point in this connection is that capital exports to the underdeveloped regions today conform closely to the Leninist vision. It is not the small investor attracted to an empire builder like Rhodes who provides the savings for foreign investment, but the giant multinational corporations such as Standard Oil, General Motors, and General Electric.

The second line of criticism challenges directly the thesis of Hobson and Lenin that the vast amounts of capital from Britain flowed into the new colonies. As Cairncross has shown in his definitive study, the great mass of British foreign investments penetrated India and what Ragnar Nurkse has termed the regions of recent settlement—the United States, Canada, Australia, Argentina, and South Africa.[21] These areas contained primary commodities, chiefly agricultural goods, which Britain required and which in turn needed a steady flow of foreign capital, mainly to finance railroad construction, to exploit. This analysis lays great stress on the increase in the demand for capital (and is sometimes called the capital-pull thesis) and plays down the significance of the capital surplus which Hobson and Lenin saw piling up in the metropolitan countries.

Maurice Dobb has countered this reasoning with the observation that Britain's need for foodstuffs and raw materials was specific to Britain and in no sense characteristic of the other imperial powers. Thus while the demand for British capital may have increased more rapidly than the supply, the same conclusions cannot be applied to France or Germany. What is more, repatriated interest and dividend payments on investments "pulled" from Britain in the early years of the colonial epoch may have been during later decades "pushed" out into both the old and new colonies. Fieldhouse has pointed out that there were not important differentials between home and foreign interest rates during the pre-World War I colonial era, concluding that capital could hardly have been attracted by colonial super-profits.[22] Taken at face value, this conclusion supports the Nurkse-Cairncross "capital pull" thesis. But the conclusion is fallacious because it was precisely the vast outflow of capital which depressed interest rates abroad and kept them firm at home.

The new colonies did fail to attract many investments during the period directly before and after their conquest. Egypt's indebtedness to Britain was a factor, to be sure, but it was the collapse of the Egyptian government which led Britain to occupy that country in 1882 in order to protect Suez and the routes to the East.[23] As for the rest of Africa, British enterprise in the nineteenth century was restricted mainly to the palm oil trade on the West Coast, and moderate investment activity in the Transvaal and Rhodesia. As Robinson and Gallagher have shown, Africa provided little trade, less revenue, and few local collaborators, and Britain supplied little capital and few settlers. Certainly, until the twentieth century, British ruling class opinion held widely that there was no real economic reason for the partition of Africa.[24] In the Pacific, large-scale investments in Malayan tin and rubber were made considerably after the annexation of that country, and other late nineteenth century conquests in Asia and the Pacific failed to attract new investments in any significant quantity. This of course does not prove that these acquisitions were not economically motivated, but only that investors may have had overoptimistic expectations.

Lenin's description of the chief characteristics of the new colonial era—foreign investments, seizure of territories, monopolistic preferences—was therefore largely accurate. A single, or simple, theoretical pattern, however, cannot be imposed on the complex sequence of events which revolutionized the world capitalist system between the 1880's and World War I. More often than not, in Robinson and Gallagher's words, the "extension of territorial claims . . . required commercial expansion." Certainly the attitudes expressed by the German Colonial Congress in 1902 suggests that in point of time investment and trade followed the flag, rather than vice versa: "The Congress thinks that, in the interests of the fatherland, it is necessary to render it independent of the foreigner for the importation of raw materials and to create markets as safe as possible for manufactured German goods. The German colonies of the future must play this double role, even if the natives are forced to labor on public works and agricultural pursuits." Similar sentiments were expressed in one form or another by Joseph Chamberlain, Theodore Roosevelt, and a host of lesser leaders and ideologists of imperialism.

We have finally to discuss a criticism of Lenin's thesis which arises from the experiences of Britain in the period directly after World War II. Although domestic investment has been considerably in excess of foreign investment (thus reversing the pre-1914 ratio of home to foreign investment),[25] capital exports did not come to a complete halt with the political independence of Britain's colonies. It has been inferred from this that formal colonial rule was really not necessary to provide profitable investment outlets. In defense of Lenin, the argument has been raised that British economic stagnation in the immediate post-war era can be attributed to the decline in repatriated earnings from foreign investments, and therefore a decrease in the rate of profit, in turn due to the removal of British economic interests from their monopoly over trade, banking, agriculture, and other branches of politically independent ex-colonies.[26] The empirical work published by Michael Barratt-Brown tends to confirm this line of reasoning: Brown estimates that after deducting payments to foreign owners of property, net earnings from overseas investments in the post-war period amounted to only one per cent of Britain's national income.[27]

These estimates, and the conclusion implicit in them, have been questioned by Hamza Alavi, who argues that informal economic control exercised by the advanced capitalist countries can be as effective, and as profitable, as formal political rule.[28] In our subsequent interpretation of contemporary imperialism we lay great stress on this idea and develop it in detail. Alavi challenges the estimates on three grounds. First, he maintains that the gross return, not the net return, on capital invested abroad is the relevant figure on the grounds that Britain incurred her liabilities independently. Second, he rightly stresses that profit remittances represent but a portion of the return flow on foreign investments. Although it proved impossible to arrive at any accurate estimates, income remitted in the form of monopolistic prices, "services" such as commission royalties, and head office charges, should be included in the return flow. Lastly, Alavi states that income remissions in relation to the domestic economic surplus (and not relative to national income) is the relevant comparison for measuring the impact of foreign investments on the metropolitan economy. Alavi calculates that gross income from overseas investments in the postwar period (excluding the disguised income remissions listed above) amounted to 3.3-4.0 per cent of the national income and 40-55 per cent of domestic net investment. Clearly, if Britain financed perhaps one-half of her home investments from overseas profits, foreign asset holdings must have been a decisive element in the maintenance of the rate of profit at home.

Neo-Imperialism: Control without Colonialism

A brief sketch cannot even begin to resolve the many theoretical and historical questions which run through the two major contending doctrines of nineteenth century imperialism. It is clear, however, that two features of imperialism are not in dispute. The first concerns the general description of economic organization and economic policy. As we have seen, Dobb considers the essential ingredient of imperialism to be "privileged investment . . . investment in projects which carry with them some differential advantage." This feature must be placed in a wider frame of reference, as in Paul Sweezy's description of imperialism as "severe rivalry (between advanced capitalist countries) in the world market leading alternatively to cutthroat competition and international monopoly combines."[29] Schumpeter's view of imperialism is very similar. Cutthroat competition and international monopoly combines are seen as "protective tariffs, cartels, monopoly prices, forced exports (dumping), an aggressive economic policy, and aggressive foreign policy generally. . . ."[30] A second general area of agreement (generally implicit in the writings of both Marxists and non-Marxists) is that modern imperialism, whatever its causes, depends on colonial rule as the main form of economic and political control of the economically backward regions and that political independence would significantly reduce, or eliminate entirely, exploitive imperialist relations.

Opposed to these doctrines is what may be called the neo-Leninist, or modern Marxist theory of imperialism. The increasing economic domination exercised by the United States in the world capitalist economy and the failure of the ex-colonies to embark on sustained economic and social development have caused older Marxist economists to re-work original doctrines and have given rise to a new theory of neo-colonialism. Many of its outlines are still indistinct, but there is broad agreement that a sharp distinction should be made between colonialism and imperialism, while the original Leninist identity between monopoly capitalism and imperialism should be retained. In this view, which we adopt throughout this study, monopoly capitalism remains an aggressively expansionist political-economic system, but colonialism is seen as merely one *form* of imperialist domination, and frequently an ineffective one at that.

The phrase "neo-colonialism" was first used in the early 1950's. Anti-colonial leaders in Asia and Africa focus on the element of control—in the words of Sukarno, "economic control, intellectual control, and actual physical control by a small but alien community, within a nation."[31] To cite a specific illustration of economic neo-colonialism, Nkrumah denounced as "neo-colonialism" the economic association of France's African colonies with the European Common Market. An example in which the political element was in the fore was France's claim to the right to suppress the revolt against the puppet ruler of Gabon in February 1964 in order to defend French economic interests in that country. A comprehensive summary of the chief manifestations of neo-colonialism was made at the Third All-African People's Conference held in Cairo in 1961:

> This Conference considers that Neo-Colonialism, which is the survival of the colonial system in spite of formal recognition of political independence in emerging countries, which become the victims of an indirect and subtle form of domination by political, economic, social, military or technical (forces), is the greatest threat to African countries that have newly won their independence or those approaching this status . . .

> This Conference denounces the following manifestations of Neo-Colonialism in Africa:

> (a) Puppet governments represented by stooges, and based on some chiefs, reactionary elements, anti-popular politicians, big bourgeois *compradors* or corrupted civil or military functionaries.

> (b) Regrouping of states, before or after independence, by an imperial power in federation or communities linked to that imperial power.

(c) Balkanization as a deliberate political fragmentation of states by creation of artificial entities, such as, for example, the case of Katanga, Mauritania, Buganda, etc.

(d) The economic entrenchment of the colonial power before independence and the continuity of economic dependence after formal recognition of national sovereignty.

(e) Integration into colonial economic blocs which maintain the underdeveloped character of African economy.

(f) Economic infiltration by a foreign power after independence, through capital investments, loans and monetary aids or technical experts, of unequal concessions, particularly those extending for long periods.

(g) Direct monetary dependence, as in those emergent independent states whose finances remain in the hands of and directly controlled by colonial powers.

(h) Military bases sometimes introduced as scientific research stations or training schools, introduced either before independence or as a condition for independence.[32]

This description supports two broad generalizations. First, modern imperialism requires the active participation of the state in international economic relationships; imperialist nations can not singly or collectively implement a neo-colonialist policy—via agencies such as the European Common Market, for example— without state capitalism. Secondly, neo-colonialist policy is first and foremost designed to prevent the newly independent countries from consolidating their political independence and thus to keep them economically dependent and securely in the world capitalist system. In the pure case of neo-colonialism, the allocation of economic resources, investment effort, legal and ideological structures, and other features of the old society remain unchanged—with the single exception of the substitution of "internal colonialism" for formal colonialism, that is, the transfer of power to the domestic ruling classes by their former colonial masters.[33] Independence has thus been achieved on conditions which are irrelevant to the basic needs of the society, and represents a part-denial of real sovereignty, and a part-continuation of disunity within the society. The most important branch of the theory of neo-colonialism is therefore the theory of economic imperialism.

The definition of economic imperialism which we employ is the economic domination of one region or country over another— specifically, the formal or informal control over local economic resources in a manner advantageous to the metropolitan power, and at the expense of the local economy. Economic control assumes different forms and is exercised in a number of ways. The main form of economic domination has always been control by the advanced capitalist countries over the liquid and real economic resources of economically backward areas. The main liquid resources are foreign exchange and public and private savings, and real resources consist of agricultural, mineral, transportation, communication, manufacturing, and commercial facilities and other assets. The most characteristic modes of domination today can be illuminated by way of contrast with examples drawn from the colonial period.

Control over Money. Examples of control over foreign exchange assets are numerous. In the colonial era the metropolitan powers established currency boards to issue and redeem the local circulating medium against sterling and other metropolitan currencies. In its purest form, the currency board system required 100 per cent backing of sterling for local currency. The East African Currency Board, for example, was established in 1919, staffed by British civil servants appointed by the Colonial Office, and at one time exercised financial domination over Ethiopia, British and Italian Somaliland, and Aden, as well as the East African countries.[34] The Board did not have the authority to expand or contract local credit, and therefore expenditures on local projects which required imported materials or machinery were limited to current export earnings, less outlays for essential consumer goods, debt service and other fixed expenses. Measures to expand exports were thus necessary pre-conditions of local initiatives toward economic progress. In this way, British imperialism indirectly controlled the allocation of real resources.

This mode of control still survives in modified form in the Commonwealth Caribbean economies and elsewhere.[35] The Jamaican central bank, for example, has limited power to influence the domestic money supply, but sterling and local currency are automatically convertible in unlimited amounts at fixed rates of exchange. The local government is thus prohibited from financing investment projects by inflation, or forced savings, nor are exchange controls and related financial instruments of national economic policy permitted. The structure and organization of the commercial banking system aggravates the situation. Local banks are branches of foreign-owned banks whose headquarters are located in the overseas financial centers and are more responsive to economic and monetary changes abroad than in the local economy; specifically, local banks have contracted credit at times when foreign exchange assets have been accumulating. This combination of monetary and financial dependence has caused artificial shortages of funds and prevented the Jamaican government from allocating local financial resources in a rational manner.

A more characteristic form of control over foreign exchange today is private direct investment. In the nineteenth and early twentieth centuries, backward countries were often able to attract portfolio investments, and local governments and capitalists were thus able to exercise some control over the use of foreign exchange made available by long-term foreign investment. Today direct investment constitutes the great mass of long-term capital exported on private account by the metropolitan countries. Foreign exchange receipts typically take the form of branch plants and other facilities of the multinational corporations—facilities which are difficult or impossible to integrate into the structure of the local economy. What is more, satellite countries which depend on direct investment ordinarily provide free currency convertibility and hence foreign-owned enterprises which produce for local markets have privileged access to foreign exchange earned in other sectors of the economy.

Another feature of economic domination is the control of local savings, which assumes two forms. First, economic rule means that local government revenues, or *public* savings, are mortgaged to loans received from the metropolitan powers. An extreme example is Liberia—a country with an open door policy with regard to foreign capital—which in 1963 expended 94 per cent of its annual revenues to repay foreign loans.[36] In the nineteenth century, persuasion, coercion, and outright conquest often insured that tariffs and other taxes were turned over to foreign bondholders. In the absence of direct colonial rule, however, foreign lending was frequently a precarious undertaking. Latin American countries, for example, had an uneven history of bond payments.[37] Foreign loans today are secured in more peaceful and more effective ways. The international capital market is highly centralized and dominated by the agencies of the main imperialist powers—the International Bank for Reconstruction and Development, the International Monetary Fund, and other financial institutions. No longer is it possible for borrowing countries to play one lending country off against another, or to default on their obligations or unilaterally scale down their debt without shutting the door on future loans. That no country has ever defaulted on a World Bank loan, or failed to amortize a loan on schedule, is eloquent testimony to the ability of the advanced capitalist countries to mortgage local tax receipts to foreign loans.

Secondly, *private* savings are mobilized by foreign corporations and governments in order to advance the interests of foreign capital. Foreign companies float local bond issues, raise equity capital, and generally attempt to monopolize available liquid resources in order to extend their field of operations and maximize profits. World Bank affiliates finance local Development Banks which scour the country for small and medium size savings to funnel into local and foreign enterprise. The United States government acquires a significant portion of the money supply of India and other countries through its policy of selling surplus foodstuffs for local currencies which it makes available to United States corporations. In these and other ways foreign interests today exercise control of local private savings.

A final feature of economic domination is the control of mineral, agricultural, manufacturing, and other real assets, and the organization and management of trade by foreign corporations. In Africa, for example, French bulk-buying companies in the ex-colonies monopolize the purchase and sale of coffee, peanuts, palm-oil products, and other commodities produced by small and medium-sized growers. In Mexico, one foreign corporation organizes the great part of cotton production and exportation. Frequently control of commerce necessitates financial domination. The United States, for example, has penetrated Mexico's financial structure with the aim of restricting Mexican-Latin American trade in order to insure control of Latin American markets for itself.[38] Control of iron, copper, tin, oil, bauxite, and other mineral resources is in the hands of a handful of giant corporations. In some countries, foreign interests dominate the commanding heights of the economy—transportation, power, communication, and the leading manufacturing industries. These examples should suffice to show that foreign control of real, as well as of liquid, assets extends into all branches of local economies and penetrates every economically backward region in the world capitalist system.

The Main Features of Contemporary Imperialism. The examples of specific kinds of economic domination illustrate most of the main features of contemporary imperialism which can be summarized as follows:

First, the further concentration and centralization of capital, and the integration of the world capitalist economy into the

structures of the giant United States-based multinational corporations, or integrated conglomerate monopolistic enterprises; and
the acceleration of technological change under the auspices of
these corporations.

Second, the abandonment of the "free" international market,
and the substitution of administered prices in commodity trade
and investment; and the determination of profit margins through
adjustments in the internal accounting schemes of the multinational corporations.

Third, the active participation of state capital in international
investment; subsidies and guarantees to private investment; and a
global foreign policy which corresponds to the global interests and
perspective of the multinational corporation.

Fourth, the consolidation of an international ruling class
constituted on the basis of ownership and control of the
multinational corporations, and the concomitant decline of national rivalries initiated by the national power elites in the
advanced capitalist countries; and the internationalization of the
world capital market by the World Bank and other agencies of the
international ruling class.

Fifth, the intensification of all of these tendencies arising from
the threat of world socialism to the world capitalist system.

WHY IMPERIALISM?

The general features of contemporary imperialism are much
better understood than the sources of economic expansion, the
specific contradictions in the metropolitan economies which drive
the multinational corporations to extend their scale of operations
over the entire globe. As we have seen, Hobson explained
nineteenth century British imperialism by way of reference to
inequalities in the distribution of income, while Lenin rested his
case on the declining rate of profit in the home economy. Neither
of these explanations is very useful today, at least in the form
which they have come down to us. In the first place, the advanced
capitalist economies have become mass consumption societies;
secondly, savings have become concentrated in the hands of the
government, financial intermediaries, and trust funds, as well as a
relatively few giant corporations; thirdly, the concept of "the"
rate of profit is out-of-date. In the overcrowded competitive sector
of the advanced capitalist economies the profit rate remains a
datum, a given, but in the oligopolistic sector profit margins are

themselves determined by corporate price, output, and investment policies.

Economic Surplus

Some contemporary Marxist economists have proposed an alternative approach to the problem of identifying the important economic contradictions in advanced capitalist societies. These approaches are based on the elementary concept of economic surplus, which Baran and Sweezy define as the difference between total national product and socially necessary costs of production.[39] Total product is the aggregate value of all commodities and services produced in a given period of time, or, alternatively, total business, worker, and government expenditures. Nowhere in the literature is there a satisfactory discussion of the meaning of socially necessary costs. A working definition is the outlays which are required to maintain the labor force and society's productive capacity in their present state of productivity or efficiency.

Economic surplus consists of outlays which either augment productive capacity and increase labor skills and efficiency, or are used for economically wasteful or destructive ends. Any specific expenditure item which can be reallocated from one use to another without affecting total production (e.g. military expenditures to foreign gifts) falls into the general category of economic surplus. An expenditure item which can not be reallocated from one employment to another (e.g. wages of workers in basic food industries to military expenditures) without reducing total production can be defined as a necessary cost. Unlike total output, neither necessary costs nor surplus is easily quantifiable, particularly since many outlays, highway expenditures for example, comprise both costs and surplus. Hence it is not possible to calculate with any great precision the proportion of total product which is constituted by surplus, nor can the relation between total product and surplus over a span of time be known with absolute certainty. Nevertheless, there is powerful indirect evidence that the surplus in relation to total product in the advanced capitalist countries tends to increase historically.

Provisionally identifying surplus with corporate profits, sales expenditures, and taxes, Baran and Sweezy demonstrate easily that corporate price and cost policies result in an absolute and relative increase in the surplus. In a nutshell, the corporations stabilize prices around an upward secular trend, while constantly seeking to increase efficiency by reducing production costs. Cost reductions are not transmitted to consumers in the form of lower prices, but rather are channeled into new investment, sales expenditures, and taxes.

The questions thus arise: what are the various ways available to advanced capitalist countries of absorbing the increasing economic surplus, or raising the level of demand? and, what are the limits on their absorptive capacity? These are obviously large and complex questions the answers to which we can do no more than suggest here.

Within the metropolitan economy the economic surplus is absorbed in three distinctive ways.[40] Expenditures on productive investment in both physical and human capital are the first, and historically most important, mode of surplus utilization. Investment outlays are made on both private and government account. In the private sector of the economy, investment opportunities are available in two distinct spheres, oligopolistic industries, dominated by the giant conglomerate corporation, and competitive industries, characterized by relatively inefficient, small-scale enterprise. In the former, technological change, which was at one time the most important outlet for investment-seeking funds, no longer can be relied upon to absorb more than a tiny fraction of the surplus. In the first place, in the few older, stabilized industries where competition between firms for larger shares of the market is at a minimum, there is a tendency to suppress new technologies in order to preserve the value of the existing productive capacity. There is, in Dobb's words, "an increasing danger of the ossification of an existing industrial structure owing to the reluctance or inability of entrepreneurs to face the cost and the risks attendant upon such large-scale change."[41]

Secondly, Baran and Sweezy have shown that in industries in which firms struggle to increase their share of the market, and hence are under considerable pressure to lower costs, the rate of introduction of new technology is reduced, thus limiting the amount of investment-seeking funds which can be profitably absorbed during any given period. Lastly, as Gillman and others have demonstrated, there has been a historic rise in fixed capital stock per employed worker, and a decline in business fixed investment and producer durable equipment expenditures in relation to total national product. Thus technological change— independent of the rate at which it is introduced into the production processes—tends increasingly to be capital-saving.[42] To put it another way, oligopolistic enterprises favor input-saving, rather than output-increasing innovations when (and if) the industrial structure becomes relatively stabilized and a provisional market-sharing plan has been agreed upon. For their part, competitive industries are overcrowded, the turnover rate is high, profit margins are minimal, and they offer few incentives to corporations with investment-seeking funds.

Productive investment outlays are also made on government, or state account, but most of these are merely special forms of private investment and hence are determined by the rhythm of capital accumulation in the private sector. The costs of these complementary investments—water investments in agricultural districts, for example—are borne by the taxpayer, while the benefits are appropriated by private capitalists. The state also finances investments which aim to create future profitable opportunities for private capital—examples are industrial development parks—but these discretionary investments are limited by the need on the part of the state bureaucracy to justify the extra tax burden (due to the absence of long-term investment horizons generally shared by capitalist class and state officials), as well as by the lack of new markets for final commodities.

Consumption-related Use of Surplus.   Expenditures on private and social consumption over and above economic needs, or in excess of outlays on necessary costs, constitute the second mode of surplus utilization. These expenditures, like all economically wasteful outlays, are limited to the degree that they can be rationalized within the logic of capitalist economy—that is to say, insofar as they lead to greater profits. The proportion of current earnings which the corporation can channel into advertising expenditures, product differentiation, forced obsolescence, and other selling expenses, as well as other socially wasteful uses of the surplus, is limited to the extent to which these outlays increase commodity demand, sales, and profits. There are also limits on the absorption of the surplus via borrowing private consumption demand from the future—that is, by the expansion of consumer credit—which are determined by the relation of current consumer income to loan repayments. (In general, a consumer will not be able to borrow in order to finance new consumption when economically necessary outlays [or costs], together with loan repayments, equal current income.)

Consumption outlays are also made by local, state, and Federal government bodies. A greater or lesser portion of education, transportation, recreational, and cultural expenditures—in general, spending on social amenities—constitutes social consumption, a special form of private consumption. Socially necessary costs make up a large part of social consumption, while much of the remainder comprises economic waste. Again, government expenditures are limited by the ability of the political authority to rationalize waste within the framework of private profit-making. In addition, there are political limits on the expansion of spending destined for public housing, health, and other socio-economic activities which are inconsistent with the hierarchy of rank and privileges in a capitalist society, or which compete with private capital. The same conclusion can be drawn in connection with the possibilities of redistributing income with the aim of raising the wage and salary share of total product—and hence private consumption expenditures—at the expense of private profits. The only major type of discretionary state expenditure consistent with private ownership of the means of production, social and economic inequality, and other central features of a capitalist society is military spending.

Imperialism as a Use of Surplus

The preceding sketch in no sense substitutes for a full-dress analysis of the surplus absorption capacity of the advanced capitalist countries, in particular the United States, but rather provides a general background for the detailed exploration of the possibilities of utilizing the economic surplus in the backward capitalist countries and the other advanced capitalist societies. Our general conclusions are two-fold: first, the multinational corporations are under unceasing pressure to extend their field of operations outside the United States. Economic prosperity in the United States during the two decades since World War II has increasingly depended on military expenditures and overseas expansion. Between 1950 and 1964, United States commodity exports, including the sales of overseas facilities of United States corporations, rose nearly 270 per cent, while commodity sales at home increased only 125 per cent. Expectedly, earnings on foreign investments make up a rising portion of after-tax corporate profits—ten per cent in 1950, and 22 per cent in 1964. In the strategic capital goods sector of the United States economy, military and foreign purchases account for a surprisingly large share of total output—between 20 and 50 per cent in twenty-one of twenty-five industries, and over 80 per cent in two industries. Our second general conclusion is that overseas expansion since World War II has not weakened, but intensified the antagonism between the generation and absorption of the economic surplus.[43]

Close examination of the two modes of surplus utilization overseas is required to substantiate these claims. Foreign commodity trade is the first, and, until the era of monopoly capitalism, the only important way of absorbing the surplus abroad. Contemporary state policies which seek to promote commodity trade encounter a number of crippling handicaps. For one thing, low-cost supplier credits and other forms of export subsidies provided by state agencies such as the Import—Export Bank merely export the surplus absorption problem abroad and hence meet with resistance from other advanced capitalist countries. A comprehensive system of export subsidies is almost guaranteed to result in retaliation in kind. The widely adopted "most favored nation" clause in international trade agreements was an expression of the willingness to "give and take" on the part of the advanced capitalist countries in the immediate post-war period. Second, in recent decades United States commodity exports have run consistently ahead of imports, limiting the ability of the United States to wring tariff concessions from other countries without offering even greater reductions in return. Third, United States penetration of Europe, regions in the sphere of influence of the European imperialist powers, and the semi-independent backward capitalist countries which employ tariffs, import quotas, and exchange controls to conserve foreign exchange by reducing imports is increasingly restricted by a revival of economic nationalism, as well as by the birth of a new economic regionalism—that is, by what Joan Robinson has termed The New Mercantilism.

Private foreign investments and state loans and grants constitute the second, and today far and away the most important, mode of surplus absorption. Capital exports may increase demand in one of two ways: first, by borrowing demand from the future and directly expanding the market for capital goods; second, by raising production and income abroad and therefore indirectly increasing imports in the recipient country or in third countries.

In recent years there have been three new tendencies in capital exporting which support the conclusion that it will become increasingly difficult to find outlets abroad for the investment-seeking surplus generated by the multinational corporations. These tendencies are: first, increased collaboration between foreign and local capital; second, the shift in the composition of foreign investments against primary commodity sectors and in favor of manufacturing and related activities; and third, the shift in the composition of capital exports against private investment and in favor of state loans and grants. All three tendencies are related to the development of anti-colonial and national independence movements in the backward capitalist countries. A brief review of the general implications of national independence for foreign investment opportunities is therefore in order.

Political Independence and Foreign Capital.   Gillman and others have put forward two arguments which support the view that national independence reduces opportunities for the penetration of foreign capital. In the first place, it is asserted that public ownership of the means of production in the ex-colonies encroaches on the traditional territory of private capital and limits investment opportunities available to the international monopolies. This line of reasoning is not only at odds with the facts—in the backward capitalist countries joint state-private ventures are more characteristic than state enterprise—but also pushes aside the critical question of the control of capital. In a number of countries, including many European capitalist nations, the state is the nominal owner of many heavy industrial and infra-structure facilities, but control rests with an autonomous bureaucracy which is highly responsive to the needs of private capital. The vast majority of state and joint enterprises in the backward countries are market-oriented, integrated into the structure of the private market. Far from discouraging foreign investors, one task of state enterprise in many countries is to attract new private investment.

Secondly, there is the argument that anti-colonial sentiment and the urge for an independent field of economic action lead to exchange controls, restrictions on profit remittances, higher business taxes, more costly social legislation, and other policies which are repugnant to foreign capital. Against this view it should be stressed that the economic autonomy of politically independent countries is itself a question for analysis. Military coups in Brazil, Indonesia, and Ghana, to cite only three recent counter-revolutionary movements, provide dramatic evidence for the view that political autonomy must be insured by economic autonomy. Again, seven long-independent Latin American countries with such disparate attitudes toward foreign capital as Chile and Peru—historically the former has been less permissive than the latter—collectively signed the Treaty of Montevideo (1960) which favored foreign investment, and recognized the need for foreign capital in economic development.[44] On the other side, China, Cuba, and other countries which have abandoned the world capitalist system obviously hold little promise for foreign capital.

In reality, there are a number of reasons to believe that politically independent, economically under-exploited countries will continue to welcome private foreign capital. First, and perhaps most important, local financiers and industrialists are eager to participate in profitable economic activities initiated by the multinational corporations based in the advanced countries. Joint ventures and other partnership arrangements are looked upon with great favor by local business interests.[45] Tariff policy is designed to encourage assembly, packaging, and other final manufacturing investments not only to promote the development of national industry but also to increase the flow of foreign capital and open up profit opportunities for the local bourgeoisie.

Secondly, the Latin American countries, as well as the ex-colonies in Asia and Africa, are under great pressure from the masses to initiate and promote economic and social development. In these non-socialist countries local sources of capital are dissipated in luxury consumption and other wasteful expenditures, or cannot be mobilized in the absence of fundamental agrarian and other economic reforms, and hence local governments increasingly depend on foreign capital, private as well as public. Most ex-colonial governments are desperately searching for ways to conserve foreign exchange and actively seek foreign investments and loans. Third, British and French foreign investments are welcome in backward countries which belong to one or the other of these metropoles' currency blocs, where exchange controls are minimal or entirely absent, because there are few if any ways to acquire private foreign capital from other advanced capitalist countries. British investments, for example, are more and more oriented to Sterling Area countries.[46] Fourth, backward countries which have no ambition beyond expanding exports of primary commodities require active foreign participation in the export sector because of the difficulties of independently acquiring and maintaining distribution channels and marketing outlets. After Bolivia nationalized the tin mines, for example, planning of production and sales was partly thwarted because the government "remained beholden to the same big companies for processing and sale."[47]

On the other side, there are at least two reasons for believing that political independence has discouraged some foreign investment, although it is difficult to even guess how much. In the first place, foreign corporations hesitate to invest in the absence of political controls which prevent local firms from using unpatented production processes to invade third-country markets or to pass on to competitors.[48] Second, the ex-colonies have eliminated or reduced in many spheres of the economy the special privileges and exclusive rights which corporations based in the colonial power once took for granted. The increased risk and uncertainty which face foreign capital has discouraged investments by small-scale enterprises which are unable to finance multi-plant, multi-country operations.[49]

The Reduction of Surplus Absorption Capacity: Use of Local Savings. Anti-colonialism, political independence, and the elimination of the colonial powers from many formal economic command posts have contributed to three new tendencies in foreign investment which reduce the surplus absorption capacity of the backward capitalist countries. There is overwhelming evidence of the first tendency, the growing mobilization of local savings and capital by foreign corporations which diminishes the need for capital exports from the advanced countries. In Latin America, local capital is the most important source of financing for wholly-owned subsidiaries of United States corporations.[50] One-half of American and Foreign Power Company's $400 million post-war expansion program in eleven countries was financed from local savings, the other half from retained earnings.[51] A $72 million investment in Argentina by five oil companies illustrates the character of modern overseas finance; the corporations' investment amounted to only $18 million; debentures raised $30 million in Argentina; and the United States government and local investment corporations supplied the remainder.[52] In the capitalist world as a whole, roughly one-third of total U.S. corporate financing overseas in 1964 comprised foreign borrowing or equity financing, and foreign supplies of capital made up two-thirds of the increase in financing over 1963 levels.[53]

The multinational corporations mobilize local savings and capital in a variety of ways: bonds and equities are sold in local capital markets; joint ventures and mixed enterprises mobilize private and state capital, respectively; local development and investment banks acquire local savings directly, and indirectly via local governments;[54] foreign and domestic banks, insurance companies and other financial intermediaries have access to pools of local savings. To cite one example, Morgan Guaranty Trust Company's sixteen correspondent banks in Venezuela hold 55 per cent of privately-owned commercial bank resources, and help foreign firms raise local funds. Morgan is also part-owner of a large Spanish investment bank which in a two-year period raised $40 million for local and foreign companies.[55] The World Bank pioneered in the organization and contributes to the financing of local development banks, develops and integrates capital markets in countries where monetary institutions are weak, and acts as a wedge for private foreign capital into established capital markets.[56]

The growing demand by the international monopolies for local capital is prompted by both political and economic factors. First, and probably most important, both the multinational corporations and the local bourgeoisies are eager to form partnership arrangements, the former to exercise indirect control over, and politically neutralize, the latter; the latter in order to share in the profits of the former.[57] In Nigeria, for example, "foreign investors are beginning to realize that their presence constitutes a political problem and that it is in their interest to encourage Nigerian participation in the structure of their firms to enhance acceptability."[58] Joint ventures and partnerships are up-to-date versions of the colonial policy of creating a dependent, passive local bourgeoisie; British capital, to cite perhaps the most important instance, allied itself with the largest and best organized Indian monopolies, such as those dominated by the Tatas and Birlas, as a hedge against possible discriminatory action by the Indian government.[59]

Second, the alliance between foreign and local capital inhibits potential economic competition and paves the way for the diversification of the foreign operations of the international monopolies, and extends their control over related product fields in the local economy.[60] Even in countries such as Mexico, where the government refuses to extend its cooperation to foreign corporations which compete with local business or displace local capital, foreigners often have "decisive influence" over company policy because domestic equity ownership is dispersed and minority stock ownership is concentrated in the hands of one or two United States corporations.[61] Extending the sphere of corporate operations opens up opportunities for increased profits in the form of royalties and fees for technical services, patents, and brand names. What is more, the use of local capital reduces the risk of conducting operations in foreign countries; local capital is smaller and less diversified than foreign capital and therefore is more vulnerable and assumes a disproportionate risk. In addition, local businessmen are valuable for their knowledge of domestic product and labor markets, government contacts, and other information which insures secure and profitable operations overseas. Finally, the international monopolies profit by spreading their capital thin in branches of production characterized by economies of large-scale operation.

Growth of Investment in Manufacturing.   The growth of private foreign investment in manufacturing industries, with the relative decline of agricultural and mining investments, is the second new tendency in capital exporting. The development of synthetic fibers, the rise in agricultural productivity in the advanced countries, the inelastic demand for foodstuffs, the reduction in the mineral component in production (e.g. non-ferrous metals), and tariff walls erected by the advanced capitalist countries against imports of primary commodities have reduced the demand for investment funds abroad in mining and agriculture. Tariffs, quotas, and other measures to protect manufacturing industries in the backward countries and regional marketing arrangments in Europe and elsewhere have compelled the large corporations in the United States to construct or purchase manufacturing facilities abroad to retain traditional markets. In turn, the expansive impulses of the multi-national corporation have affected world-wide capital flows and the production and distribution of commodities.

Between 1940 and 1964 United States direct manufacturing investments in Latin America (which absorbs about 60 per cent of U.S. manufacturing investments in all backward regions) increased from $210 million to $2,340 million, or from 10 per cent to 25 per cent of total Latin American holdings. In the same period, agricultural investments remained unchanged, mining investments doubled, and the value of petroleum holdings rose from $572 million to $3,142 million. A similar trend is visible in connection with British investments in India. In 1911, about three-quarters of all direct private investments were in extractive industries, utilities and transportation accounted for roughly one-fifth, and the remainder was divided between commerce and manufacturing. In 1956, manufacturing investments made up over one-third of the total, commerce another one-fourth, and plantation investments only one-fifth. As Hamza Alavi has written, "this is a complete contrast from the old pattern" of investment holdings.[62] Of all British direct foreign investments (excluding oil) in 1965, Kemp has estimated that manufacturing investments constituted about one-half, the great part located in other advanced capitalist countries.[63]

Most United States manufacturing investments in backward countries are concentrated in consumer goods fabrication, assembly and packaging, and light chemicals. The pattern is roughly the same in the advanced capitalist economies, with the single exception that investments in industrial equipment facilities are more common. During 1958-1959, of 164 U.S. investments in new or expanded manufacturing enterprises in Latin America, 106 were located in the chemical and consumer good sectors; in other backward regions, the number of facilities were thirty-four and twenty-four, respectively.[64]

In connection with opportunities for capital exporting, and the significance of capital exports for absorbing the economic surplus, nineteenth century and mid-twentieth century imperialism differ in a number of profound respects. In the earlier period, foreign investments were concentrated in raw material and mineral production, and the economic satellites were no more than extensions of the metropolitan economies. Overseas capital expenditures opened up cheap sources of productive inputs, and lowered the costs of production in manufacturing industries in the metropoles. In turn, home and foreign demand for manufactured goods increased, prompting an expansion of output and fresh rounds of foreign investment. To the degree that capital exports were channeled into railroad and other transportation facilities, there were favorable indirect effects on the availability of raw materials, and hence manufacturing costs in the metropoles. For nineteenth century Great Britain, this cumulative, expansive system worked to perfection. Income generated in the satellites by the inflow of capital was expended on British manufactured exports. During periods of rising foreign investment, British exports rose faster than imports, and a consistently favorable balance of payments was maintained.[65]

To be sure, contemporary imperialist powers continue to import many raw materials, and petroleum needs expand at a rapid pace. The economic relationships between the metropolitan economies and their satellites, however, differ in important respects. Petroleum production is concentrated in the hands of a few oligopolists which maintain rigid price structures and fail to pass on reductions in exploration, drilling, and production costs to consumers. The same conclusion can be drawn with regard to other raw materials (iron and copper, for example) for which the ratio of imports to U.S. production is higher than in the pre-war era. Moreover, in comparison with other regions, imports have increased more rapidly from Latin American countries, which have met the expansion of demand for copper, tin, manganese, cocoa, and other commodities largely by diverting sales from other markets, rather than by expanding supplies. The basic reason is that Latin American raw material production is today highly monopolized, and, in addition, operates under conditions of decreasing returns to large-scale production. Thus neither new capital outlays nor modernization investments have significantly reduced the costs of production of primary commodities, and, unlike investments in the earlier period, are not self-perpetuating. What is more, international commodity agreements and regional marketing arrangements reduce competition between raw material producing countries, and tend to maintain prices at relatively high levels.

Manufacturing investments in backward countries fall into one of two categories. Tariff-hopping investments, quantitatively most significant, are defensive moves which enable the international corporations to retain established export markets, and merely change the locale of investment from the metropole to the satellite. These outlays fail to expand commodity demand, and hence do not provide growing outlets for the economic surplus. Opportunities for other manufacturing investments in backward countries are also generally limited to import-substitute activities because domestic markets are typically oriented toward middle and upper class consumption patterns which are imitative of those in the advanced countries. Export markets for satellite manufactured goods are weak because national and regional monopolies operate behind high tariff walls, and, in addition, monopoly controls which the multinational corporations exercise over international distribution systems and marketing outlets place insurmountable barriers to large-scale satellite manufacturing exports. For these reasons, the United States has shown a growing interest in new regional marketing groupings such as the Latin American Free Trade Area and the Central American Common Market. One of the chief objectives of the Common Market during its formative period (1958-1962) was to attract fresh supplies of foreign capital. There are two important barriers, however, to flourishing regional marketing arrangements in economically backward areas. First, less productive, entrenched local monopolies.put up a tenacious struggle to retain their privileged market positions—by contrast with the giant, integrated European cartels and monopolies which promoted the European Common Market. Secondly, the new preferential trading areas in backward regions are too small to compete effectively with Britain's Sterling Area or the European Economic Community. In sharp contrast to the upsurge of United States investment in Canada after the expansion of the Imperial Preference System in 1932, to cite one example, dollar flows of fresh investment to the new trading areas will be limited.[66]

We have finally to consider opportunities for manufacturing investments in other advanced economies. As we have seen, in recent years the great mass of United States manufacturing investments has been in Europe and Canada. Most of these investments have been tariff-shopping operations, or have been channeled into the purchase of existing facilities. Moreover, United States corporations have increasingly been compelled to penetrate lines of production which are competitive with United States exports. Similar to the effect of British reconstruction investments in Europe following World War I, United States capital flows to other advanced capitalist countries tend to be self-defeating in the long run. An excellent illustration is provided by one study of the impact of 112 British subsidiary companies in Europe on British exports; only 5.6 per cent of the subsidiaries' capital outlays was expended on British capital goods.[67] Only investments in distribution facilities, specifically motivated to expand foreign sales, can be expected to significantly increase commodity exports.

These lines of analysis suggest that the surplus absorption capacity of both the advanced and backward countries—in both traditional and newer branches of the economy—will in the future be limited to replacement demand, together with the modest flow of new investments necessary to keep pace with expanding incomes abroad. Reflecting the marginal impact of foreign investments on United States commodity exports is the continuing, although muted, crisis in the United States balance of payments.

State Loans Replace Private.   Roughly the same conclusion can be drawn in connection with public and international loans. The third, and perhaps most striking, tendency in capital exporting is the substitution of state loans for private capital outflows. About two-thirds of all capital exports are on state or international (public) account. Nearly three-quarters of all loans and investments destined for backward capitalist countries originate in the public or international sector. In 1964, the net outflow of resources to satellite countries and multinational agencies (which in turn loans funds to the satellites) amounted to nearly $8 billion, of which less than $2 billion was private.

The relationship between private and public capital flows is highly complex, and a brief analysis inevitably runs the risk of over-simplification. Reduced to essentials, however, state loans serve two main purposes. First, public funds which build up the infra-structure of backward countries frequently complement private capital flows and represent merely a special form of private investment, the costs of which are borne by taxpayers in the lending country. With regard to surplus absorption capacity within the infra-structure sectors of backward countries, the same conclusion reached in our discussion of private investment can be applied *a fortiori*.

Second, the character of United States "aid" programs under-lines their growing importance as projected points of entry for private capital. Many Export-Import Bank loans are made with the purpose of encouraging the flow of private investment; since 1960 the Bank has offered long-term loans of up to five years.[68] Provisions of Public Law 480, the "Food for Peace" program, are "designed almost entirely for the purpose of stimulating the flow of U.S. private investment to the less-developed countries."[69] Under this program, the United States government loans local currencies acquired from the sale of surplus agricultural com-modities to American corporations in order to finance the local costs of investment projects. The greatest portion of both the interest and the principal is reloaned either to private investors or local governments. "How useful to our own foreign aid and foreign development programs could it be," the president of one multinational corporation has written, "if these funds, in local currencies, were to be loaned on an increasing scale to competitive private borrowers—either Americans or others—for local invest-ment . . ."[70] Finally, the United States Agency for International Development grants survey loans to American corporations, paying one-half of the cost of feasibility studies in the event it is decided not to proceed with the investment.

The international agencies, in particular the World Bank, are also beacon lights for private investment. Originally regarded by the leading imperialist nations as a way to restore private international capital movements by guaranteeing private loans, the World Bank has been compelled to centralize and rationalize the world capital market. The Bank has eliminated many of the anarchic features of international capital movements, supervises vast amounts of capital which penetrate the backward countries, and acts as a funnel for private capital in search of safe, profitable returns—banks and investment houses participate in World Bank loans, and the Bank frequently floats bond issues in United States and European money markets. In part dependent on private money market conditions, most Bank activities are financed by subscribed or borrowed government funds. The Bank is thus relatively autonomous, and allocates vast amounts of capital for large-scale infra-structure projects in order to clear the way for private investment flows.

Modern Imperialism's Foreign Policy

Whether or not private capital responds to the incentives held out by national governments and international agencies depends on a host of factors, chief among which are the investment "climate" in the satellite economies and the character of other state political-economic policies. Suffice it for now to note some of the major differences between imperialist foreign policy in the nineteenth and that in the mid-twentieth centuries.

First, and most obvious, modern imperialism attempts to substitute informal for formal modes of political control of countries in the backwash of world capitalism. The methods of establishing political control are varied. The use of old economic and political ties is practiced whenever possible; these include the relationships formed within the British Commonwealth and the French Community, closed currency zones, preferential trading systems, military alliances, and political-military pacts. Economic, political, and cultural missions, labor union delegations, joint military training programs, military grants, bribes to local ruling classes in the form of economic "aid," substitute for direct colonial rule. Only when indirect policies fail are the older instruments of coercion and force brought into play, and the principle of continuity in change applies. An excellent example is the United States-instigated and supported counter-revolution in Guatemala in 1954, the accomplishments of which the State Department listed under four headings:[71]

1. The conclusion of an agreement with a United Fruit Company subsidiary providing for the return of property expropriated by the Arbenz Government.
2. The repeal of the law affecting remittances and taxation of earnings from foreign capital.
3. The signing of an Investment Guarantee Agreement with the United States.
4. The promulgation of a new and more favorable petroleum law.

Within Guatemala, the Armas regime in the post-1954 period was maintained in office via contracts with United Fruit, Bond and Share, and other monopolies.[72]

Secondly, contemporary imperialist states enjoy relatively more financial, and hence political, autonomy. In the nineteenth century, imperialist countries regarded themselves as dependent on the private capital market for raising funds for discretionary state expenditures and were compelled to pursue economic and fiscal policies designed to make it possible for their colonies to meet their private debt service. The dominant state capitalist countries today are financially independent and can follow a more flexible policy toward their satellites. The reason is that both the potential and the actual economic surplus are comparatively large. The potential surplus is large because the normal tendency of monopoly capitalist economies is stagnation and unemployment of labor and capital, attributable to a deficiency of aggregate demand. State expenditures—including military expenditures and foreign loans and grants—normally increase not only aggregate demand but also real income and output, and hence the tax base. A rise in expenditures thus increases revenues, even if tax rates remain unchanged. State expenditures are partly self-financing and virtually costless in terms of the real resources utilized. The actual economic surplus constitutes a relatively large portion of national product because of technological and productivity advances. For these reasons, taxes (and state expenditures) make up a large share of national product with few serious adverse effects on economic incentives, and thus on total production itself.

The significance of the financial independence of the contemporary imperialist state for foreign policy lies in its ability to export capital—or absorb the surplus overseas—without a *quid pro quo*. The Marshall Plan, the extensive program of military aid and grants, and the low-cost loans extended to backward countries by AID are the main examples of this mode of surplus absorption. The surplus absorption capacity of satellite countries which are closely tied to the United States political-military bloc is for practical purposes unlimited. Two factors, however, circumscribe state grants without a *quid pro quo*. First, low-cost state loans and grants-in-aid, or capital exports which are not extended on normal commercial principles, compete "unfairly" with private loans and are resisted by private capitalist interests in the metropolitan economy. Second, metropolitan governments are unable to discipline their satellites effectively unless there are economic strings attached to international loans. Moreover, state bilateral and multilateral loans financed in private capital markets in the advanced countries must earn a return sufficient to cover the cost of borrowing and administration. Opportunities for capital exports extended on commercial principles are limited by the availability of profitable investment projects.

Nineteenth century and mid-twentieth century imperialism depart from each other in a third important respect. In the nineteenth century there were few important antagonisms between Great Britain's role as the leading national capitalist power on the one hand, and her role as the dominant imperialist power on the other. Policies designed to expand Britain's home economy extended capitalist modes of production and organization to the three under-exploited continents, directly and indirectly strengthening the growing British imperial system.[73] For this reason, foreign policy ordinarily served private foreign investors and other private interests oriented to overseas activity. Only occasionally—as in the case of Disraeli's decision to purchase Suez Canal shares in 1875[74]—was foreign investment employed as a "weapon" of British foreign policy. Even less frequently did Britain promote private foreign investments with the purpose of aiding global foreign policy objectives. (It has been suggested by one expert, however, that private investments were made to serve specific foreign policy objectives more frequently than it is ordinarily believed.)[75]

By way of contrast, the national and international ambitions of the United States in the mid-twentieth century are continually in conflict. In the context of the limited absorption capacity of the backward capitalist world and international competition from other advanced capitalist economies and the socialist countries, the United States is compelled to employ a wide range of policies to expand trade and investment. To further national ends, a "partnership" between "public lending institutions" and "private lenders"—with the former "leading the way" for the latter—has been formed.[76] Underlining the role of the state in the service of the multinational corporations, in 1962 Secretary of State Rusk described the newer government policies which extend beyond state loan programs—investment guarantee programs in forty-six backward capitalist countries which cover currency inconvertibility, expropriation, war, revolution, and insurrection; instructions to local embassies to support business interests by making "necessary representations to the host governments . . ."; the creation of a new Special Assistant for International Business in the State Department in order to insure that private business interests receive "prompt representation" in the government.[77] Especially when public loans are disguised or special forms of private loans (see above), the commitment of the United States government to national capitalist interests inhibits state policies which seek to strengthen the industrial bourgeoisie and ruling classes in other advanced countries and the national bourgeoisie in the backward nations. Perhaps this is the most important limit on capital exports on public account.

As the leading international power, the United States is under constant and growing pressure to strengthen world capitalism as a system, including each of its specific parts. Policies which aim to recruit new members for local *comprador* groups, stimulate the development of capitalist agriculture and the middle farmers, reinforce the dominance of local financial and commercial classes, and reinvigorate local manufacturing activities—these general policies pose a potential or real threat to the interests of United States national capital. Alliance for Progress funds destined for the middle sectors of Latin American agriculture, Export-Import bank loans to foreign commercialists, loans and grants to foreign governments dominated by the urban bourgeoisie, loans and subsidies to the Indian iron and steel industry, Mexican industry and agriculture, and other branches of production in countries which are slowly industrializing—these and other stop-gap and long-range measures help to keep the backward countries in the imperialist camp in the short run, but directly or indirectly create local capitalist interests which may demand their independence from United States capital in the long run.

United States private capital increasingly requires the aid of the state, and the state enlists more and more private and public capital in its crusade to maintain world capitalism intact. Specific and general capitalist interests serve each other, finally merging into one phenomenon; a certain one-ness emerges between them. This must have, finally, its institutional reflection. The multinational corporation has become the instrument for the creation and consolidation of an international ruling class, the only hope for reconciling the antagonism between national and international interests.

Surplus Absorption or Surplus Creation?

The preceding analysis supports the conclusion that the surplus absorption capacity of the backward countries, and, probably to a lesser degree, the other advanced economies, and hence oppor-

tunities for utilizing investment-seeking funds overseas, are circum-
scribed in a variety of ways. Opportunities for "enterprise," or
profit-making, however, show few signs of weakening. We have
touched on some of the reasons: first, the multinational corporations increasingly mobilize and utilize local and state savings and
capital, undertake more ambitious investment projects, and profit
from economies of large-scale production and more efficient
intra-corporate planning. Second, a larger share of the retained
earnings of corporation branch plants and subsidiaries is absorbed
by modernization investments, which reduce costs and raise
profits. Third, the multinational corporations monopolize patents,
brand names, and production processes in the greatest demand,
and are able to establish control over national and international
markets via licensing and similar agreements which require
relatively small capital outlays. Fourth, the giant international
corporations are more and more integrated and diversified, and
production and sales are subject to less risk and uncertainty.
Lastly, the international monopolies can count on the active
participation and aid of the state.

For these reasons, the multinational corporations command
growing profit margins on their overseas operations. Small
amounts of capital are sufficient to penetrate, control, and
dominate the weaker, less productive national economies. The
price of disposing of a given amount of economic surplus this year
is the creation of even more surplus next year—hardly a high price
for the individual corporation to pay, but from the standpoint of
the metropolitan economy as a whole, the problem of surplus
absorption becomes increasingly severe.

The United States government, the European powers, and the
United States-dominated international agencies are thus under
growing pressure by the international monopolies to formulate
and implement political-economic policies which will create an
"attractive" investment climate abroad, in particular in the
under-exploited countries. Looked at from another angle, the
imperialist powers are increasingly compelled to "promote
economic development" overseas or, to put it differently, to
integrate the backward areas even more closely into the structure
of world capitalism. In effect, the advanced countries are
desperately seeking to expand outlets for the economic surplus.
To be sure, the imperialist powers view the problem as one of
surplus creation (or profit-realization), rather than of surplus
absorption—their line of vision generally corresponds in this
respect to the perspective of the corporations themselves. These

are merely different sides to the same coin: by promoting profitable opportunities abroad for private capital, the state lays the basis for the absorption of a portion of this year's surplus, and, simultaneously, for the creation of additional surplus next year.

For United States economic, political and foreign policy this line of analysis has a number of important consequences. In the first place, national economic development programs in the backward countries which seek the participation of the socialist countries and other advanced capitalist countries have been and will continue to be opposed by the United States. Secondly, investments in lines of industry which are non-competitive with United States products, especially those which increase demand for United States products, have been and will continue to be encouraged.

Thirdly, the participation of United States capital in the European economy (as well as the participation of European capital in the backward countries) will increasingly be discouraged because these investments will eventually compete with United States commodity exports. Fourth, the United States will continue to initiate anti-socialist, anti-communist military and political pacts and alliances with both backward and advanced capitalist countries—for the international monopolies the basic importance of state loans and aid lies in the long-run impact on the demand for arms, capital equipment, and consumer goods in those satellites which have developed intimate political and military bonds with the United States.

More generally, because the expansion of commodity exports, as well as capital exports, generate even more surplus in the future—because the process of surplus creation and absorption is a cumulative one—the United States is increasingly compelled to follow the policies of a militant, expansive imperialist power, all in the name of economic development for the underdeveloped countries. The task facing the United States in relation to the backward countries is truly Herculean.

At one and the same time, the United States must convince the backward countries that the growing penetration of United States capital, and the growing control of the multinational companies over local economies, are useful and necessary for their economic growth and development, at a time when politically oppressive policies which aim to create more favorable conditions for private investment are followed. Thus economic development is oriented by the multinational companies, and where there are national development plans which on paper assign a certain limited role to private investment, in fact private investment assigns a role to the plan. The underdeveloped world becomes bound up even more closely in a new imperialist system in which investments in consumer goods industries replace investments in raw materials and minerals; in which the backward countries are compelled to deal with a unified private capital-state capital axis; in which political control by the World Bank and the other international agencies, together with the political arm of the official labor movement, the giant foundations, and other quasi-private political agencies, replace colonial rule; and in which the national middle classes in the underdeveloped countries are slowly but surely transformed into a new class of clients and *compradors*, in every important respect equivalent to the old class of traders, bankers, and landlords which for centuries bowed and scraped before their imperial rulers in China, India, Latin America and elsewhere. A new era of imperialism is just beginning, an era which holds out contradictory promises to the imperial powers and their clusters of satellites. Whether or not the advanced capitalist countries can deal with this crisis of their own making depends on two basic factors: first, the power of peoples in the under-exploited continents to resist; and, secondly, the flexibility of the structure of the imperialist system.

Notes

[1] Margery Perham, *The Colonial Reckoning* (London, 1963), p. 1.

[2] Joseph Schumpeter, *Imperialism and Social Classes* (New York, 1951), pp. 98, 128. It should be stressed that the above paragraph fails to capture the subtleties and complexities of Schumpeter's thesis, and aims chiefly to provide a point of comparison with the other two doctrines.

[3] Hans Kohn, "Reflections on Colonialism" in Robert Strausz-Hupe and Harry W. Hazard, editors, *The Idea of Colonialism* (London, 1958). The different kinds of political control are as follows: (1) The metropolitan power can grant the subject people full autonomy, with the exception of foreign relations. (2) Subject peoples can be granted full citizenship, and assimilated into the foreign culture. (3) Indigenous peoples can be annihilated or expelled. (4) Subject peoples can be maintained in an inferior status. (5) The metropolitan power can tacitly claim the right to oust an unfriendly government.

[4] An excellent review of mercantile thought and practice is provided by Eric Roll, *A History of Economic Thought*, 3rd ed. (Englewood Cliffs, N.J., 1957), Chapter 2.

[5] Charles Wilson, *Power and Profit: A Study of England and the Dutch Wars* (London, 1957).

[6] This changeover set the stage for the ruin of Indian manufacturing industries, and can be roughly dated from the abolition of the East India Company's trade monopoly in 1813. The East India Company had provided an umbrella for India's weaving industry, which could not survive the massive importation of British cotton manufactures. (Reference is made to p. 133 of an untitled book published by Richard Pares.)

[7] This is not meant to imply that there are no important conflicts between international-minded capitalists and national-minded power elites.

[8] This of course does not exhaust the motives for colonial conquest. In the conquest of Mexico and Peru, the search for precious metals was of foremost importance. The east coast of Africa was at first seized for strategic reasons. But the characteristic sequence was followed in India and West Africa. In the latter region, Portugal had acquired a monopoly over trade based on coastal fortifications. Cloth, metal, and glass were exchanged on favorable terms for gold, ivory, and, above all, slaves. In the middle of the seventeenth century, Portugal's monopoly was broken by the Dutch, and then by the British and French.

[9] *Capital*, Kerr, ed. (Chicago, 1909), Volume III, pp. 278-279.

[10] Cairncross has shown on the basis of more and better data than those available to Hobson that there was a relative increase in empire trade, most of it, however, with the older colonies such as India (J. Cairncross, *Home and Foreign Investments, 1870-1913* [Cambridge, 1953], p. 189). Cairncross's findings refine but do not contradict Hobson's argument.

[11] V. I. Lenin, *Imperialism: The Highest Stage of Capitalism* (New York, 1926), pp. 71-76. By comparison, Rosa Luxemburg's *The Accumulation of Capital* bases its analysis of capitalist expansion abroad on Marx's models of expanded reproduction which assume a *competitive* economy. Luxemburg saw imperialism as a necessary result of competition between capitalist enterprises which drove capitalism outward in search of new markets in areas which were not incorporated into the world capitalist system. Lenin, as we have noted, stressed the export of capital, not commodity exports. Moreover, Lenin viewed imperialist rivalries over areas already integrated into world capitalism as extensions of the struggles between the European powers over the underdeveloped continents.

[12] In the following paragraph we will rely not only on Lenin's theory of the causes of imperialist expansion, but also on Maurice Dobb's and John Strachey's readings of Lenin ("Imperialism," in *Political Economy and Capitalism* [London, 1937] ; J. Strachey, *The End of Empire* [New York, 1960]).

[13] Dobb, *op. cit.*, pp. 239, 234.

[14] "Long-term Capital Movements" in *Scottish Journal of Political Economy*, Vol. XIII, No. 1, February 1966, p. 137.

[15] R. Koebner, "The Concept of Economic Imperialism," *Economic History Review*, 2nd series, II, 1949, p. 8.

[16] Nevertheless, these historians believe that reasons must be found to explain the *pace* of colonial conquest from the 1880's on. Fieldhouse's explanation—that there was an overriding need for military security after 1870 because Europe had become an armed camp—they consider inadequate by itself. To the spillover from rivalries in Europe, they add the following reasons (R. Robinson and J. Gallagher, *Africa and the Victorians,* [New York, 1961], p. 18): The collapse of Western oriented governments under the strain of previous European influences; the changing importance of Africa for British geo-political strategy; and the need to relieve economic depression, especially relief from tariff increases by Germany in 1879 and France in 1892. As we have seen, the final "reason" itself was explained by Lenin.

[17] D. K. Fieldhouse, "Imperialism: A Historiographical Revision," *Economic History Review*, XIV, 1961, *passim*.

[18] Pares, *op. cit.*

[19] Gabriel Kolko, *The Triumph of Conservatism*, (New York, 1963).

[20] Koebner, *op. cit.*, p. 12. The evidence brought to light by D.C.M. Platt suggests that with regard to Latin American loans only the small lender, not the large financial interests, bore great financial risks ("British Bondholders in Nineteenth Century Latin America—Injury and Remedy," *InterAmerican Economic Affairs*, Vol. XIV, No. 3, Winter 1960).

[21] Cairncross, *op. cit.*, p. 185.

[22] Fieldhouse, *op. cit.*, p. 198.

[23] Robinson and Gallagher, *op. cit.*

[24] *Ibid.*, p. 15.

[25] Kemp, *op. cit.* In 1964, a year of high capital outflow, long-term capital exports amounted to only nine per cent of gross domestic investment.

[26] Palme Dutt, *The Crisis of Britain in the British Empire* (London, 1953).

[27] *After Imperialism*, (London, Heineman, 1963).

[28] Hamza Alavi, "Imperialism Old and New," *Socialist Register*, 1964, pp. 108-109.

[29] *The Theory of Capitalist Development* (New York, 1942), p. 307.

[30] Schumpeter, *op. cit.*, p. 110.

[31] Kenneth J. Twitchett, "Colonialism: An Attempt at Understanding Imperial, Colonial, and Neo-Colonial Relationships," *Political Studies*, Vol. XIII, No. 3 (October, 1965).

[32] "Neo-Colonialism," *Voice of Africa*, Vol. 1, No. 4, April 1961, p. 4.

[33] Pablo Gonzalez Casanova, "Internal Colonialism and National Development," *Studies in Comparative International Development*, Vol. 1, No. 4, Social Science Institute, Washington University, St. Louis, 1965.

[34] J. W. Kratz, "The East African Currency Board," International Monetary Fund *Staff Papers*, July 1966, 13 (2). In 1960 three new members were added to the Board, one from each of the three East African states. The Board was also granted the power to extend credit by fiduciary issues.

[35] C. Y. Thomas, "The Balance of Payments and Money Supplies in a Colonial Monetary Economy," *Social and Economic Studies*, Vol. 12, No. 1 (March 1963), pp. 27, 35; William G. Demas, "The Economics of West Indian Customs Union," *Social and Economic Studies*, Vol. 9, No. 1 (March 1960). According to Thomas, the inability of the Caribbean economies to control their money supply is due not only to their monetary arrangements with Britain, but also to the dependent nature of their "open" economy. The pre-Revolutionary Cuban economy was also characterized by monetary dependence (Henry C. Wallich, *Monetary Problems of an Export Economy, The Cuban Experience, 1914-47*, Cambridge, 1950, *passim*).

[36] K. Brutents, "Developing Countries and the Break-Up of the Colonial System," *International Affairs* (January 1966), p. 67.

[37] Platt, *op. cit.*

[38] James Schlesinger, "Strategic Leverage from Aid and Trade," in David M. Abshire and Richard V. Allen, eds., *National Security: Political, Military and Economic Strategy in the Decade Ahead* (New York, 1963), *passim*. In the past, the United States could discipline a satellite country by threatening to cut off supplies of needed commodities. Today, substitutes from other sources are ordinarily available. Thus the United States must threaten to damage other economies by curtailing access to markets which it controls.

[39] Paul A. Baran and Paul M. Sweezy, *Monopoly Capital* (New York, 1966), *passim*. See also Shigeto Tsuru, *Has Capitalism Changed?*(Tokyo, 1961) *passim*.

[40] The scheme developed below is a greatly modified version of that of Tsuru, *op. cit.*, pp. 197-8.

[41] *Ibid.*, p. 143.

[42] Joseph Gillman, *The Falling Rate of Profit* (London, 1957).

[43] Harry Magdoff, "Economic Aspects of U.S. Imperialism," *Monthly Review* (November 1966), Vol. 18, No. 6, p. 17, Table I; p. 19; p. 25, Table IV.

[44] United Nations, Department of Economic and Social Affairs, Consultant Group Jointly Appointed by the ECLA and the OAS, *Foreign Private Investment in LAFTA* (New York, 1961), pp. 18-19.

[45] *Ibid.*

[46] Kemp, *op. cit.*, p. 145.

[47] Allen Young, "Bolivia," *New Left Review* (September-October 1966), No. 39, p. 66.

[48] Raymond Vernon, "The American Corporation in Underdeveloped Areas," in Edward S. Mason, ed., *The Corporation in Modern Society* (New York, 1966), p. 254.

[49] J. Behrman, "Promotion of Private Investment Overseas," in Raymond Mikesell, ed., *U.S. Private and Government Investment Abroad* (Eugene, Ore., 1962), pp. 174-175.

[50] J. Behrman, "Foreign Associates and Their Financing," in Mikesell, ed., *op. cit.*, p. 103.

[51] H. W. Balgooyen, "Problems of U.S. Investments in Latin America," in M. Bernstein, ed., *Foreign Investment in Latin America*, (New York, 1966), p. 225.

[52] John McLean, "Financing Overseas Expansion," *Harvard Business Review* (March-April 1963), p. 64.

[53] Samuel Pizer and Frederick Cutler, "Financing and Sales of Foreign Affiliates of U.S. Firms," *Survey of Current Business* (November 1965), p. 26.

[54] William Diamond, "The Role of Private Institutions in Development Finance: Service Oriented Profit Making," *International Development Review* (March 1965), p. 10.

[55] *Wall Street Journal*, February 23, 1966, advertisement. Morgan Guaranty has eighteen correspondent banks in Spain with resources equal to 85 per cent of privately owned commercial bank resources.

[56] Industrial finance institutions in East Africa are typical. "National Development Corporations" were established before political independence to promote and direct new ventures and to participate in existing enterprises by subscribing to equity capital issues. "Development and Finance Corporations," in which British and German capital is deeply involved, were established more recently; they specialize in loans and grants, and promote partnerships between African and European capital. —Economic Commission for Africa, Conference on the Harmonization of Industrial Development Programmes in East Africa, "Industrial Financing in East Africa," Lusaka (October 26-November 6, 1965), E/CN. 14/INR/103.

[57] There is some evidence that monopolistic corporations are more interested than competitive firms in acquiring local partners (Wolfgang Friedmann and George Kalmanoff, *Joint International Business Ventures*, New York, 1961).

[58] Douglas Gustafson, "The Development of Nigeria's Stock Exchange," in Tom Farar, ed., *Financing African Development* (Cambridge, Mass., 1965).

[59] Nural Islam, *Foreign Capital and Economic Development: Japan, India and Canada* (Rutland, Vt., 1960), p. 175.

[60] McLean, *op. cit.*

[61] Mario Ramon Beteta, "Government Policy Toward Foreign Investors," *The Statist*, London, January 8, 1965.

[62] Alavi, *op. cit.*, p. 118.

[63] Kemp, *op. cit.*, p. 148.

[64] Behrman, "Promotion of Private Overseas Investment," *op. cit.*, Table VII-I, pp. 168-9.

[65] Kemp, *op. cit.*, p. 139.

[66] Vernon, *op. cit.*, p. 249.

[67] Kemp, *op. cit.*, p. 153.

[68] Raymond Mikesell, *Public International Lending for Development* (New York, 1966), p. 30.

[69] *Ibid.*

[70] Harvey Williams, "New Dimensions for American Foreign Operations," in *Increasing Profits from Foreign Operations*, International Management Association, 1957.

[71] *State Department Bulletin*, No. 6465, April 1, 1967.

[72] Alfonso Bauer Paiz, *Comdopera el capital Yanqui en Centroamerica (El Caso de Guatemala* (Mexico D. F., 1956).

[73] The argument that Britain's home economy suffered because it was deprived of capital which was absorbed abroad is fallacious. On the one hand, given the prevailing distribution of income and industrial organization, there were few profitable opportunities to absorb the surplus at home; on the other hand, the return flow on foreign investments more than offset the original capital exports.

[74] Leland Jenks, *The Migration of British Capital*, (New York, 1963), p. 325.

[75] Herbert Feis, *Foreign Aid and Foreign Policy* (New York, 1963), pp. 33-40.

[76] Mikesell, ed., *op. cit.*, p. 7.

[77] Dean Rusk, "Trade, Investment, and U.S. Foreign Policy," *Department of State Bulletin*, November 5, 1962.

4

PAUL A. BARAN and PAUL M. SWEEZY

Notes on the Theory of Imperialism

The Marxian theory of imperialism—as developed chiefly by Hilferding, Rosa Luxemburg, and Lenin and since accepted with but few modifications by most Marxists—has served at least three major purposes. First, it provides a theory of international relations within the capitalist world, encompassing not only relations between advanced and underdeveloped countries but also among the advanced countries themselves. Second, it contributes to the clarification of the development of social and political conditions within the various capitalist countries, both advanced and underdeveloped. And third, it purports to provide an important part of the explanation of strictly economic tendencies and trends within the advanced capitalist countries. In this third connection, two points have been usually stressed. The unequal relations between the developed and underdeveloped countries result in the establishment of terms of trade which greatly favor the former at the expense of the latter. In this way wealth is transferred from the poor countries to the rich, and the disposable surplus of the rich—which can be used to support parasitic classes, a "workers' aristocracy," as well as for normal purposes of capital accumulation—is vastly expanded. But imperialism, by putting capital export at the very center of the economic stage,[1] is also supposed to provide a crucially important outlet for the surplus of the rich countries. In the terminology of bourgeois economics, capital export expands effective demand and thereby raises income and employment above what they otherwise would have been. It is this last aspect of the traditional theory of imperialism which seems to us to be in particular need of rethinking in the light of conditions existing today, nearly half a century after publication of Lenin's classic work. As we hope to make clear even within the confines of a brief exploratory essay, the problem is very much more complicated than Marxists have been wont to think, and the breadth and depth of its ramifications can hardly be exaggerated.

II

At the outset it must be stressed that the familiar national aggregates—Gross National Product, national income, employment, etc.—are almost entirely irrelevant to the explanation of imperialist behavior. In capitalist societies, there are *ex post* calculations which play little if any causal role.[2] Nor does it make any difference whether the "costs" of imperialism (in terms of military outlays, losses in wars, aid to client states, and the like) are greater or less than the "returns," for the simple reason that the costs are borne by the public at large while the returns accrue to that small, but usually dominant, section of the capitalist class which has extensive international interests. If these two points are kept firmly in mind, it will be seen that all liberal and Social Democratic efforts to refute Marxian—or for that matter any other predominantly economic—theories of imperialism on the ground that in some sense or other it "doesn't pay" have no claim to scientific standing.[3]

All of which is only another way of saying that the relevant actors on the imperialist stage are classes and their subdivisions down to and including their individual members. And this means in the first instance the dominant classes in the most advanced capitalist countries to which the less developed and under-developed countries stand in various relations of subordination. In terms of the total system, these are the classes which have the power of initiative: they are, so to speak, the independent variables. The behavior of other classes—including the subordinate classes in the dominant countries as well as both the dominant and the subordinate classes in the subordinate countries—is primarily reactive. One of the most important tasks of a theory of imperialism is therefore to analyze the composition and interests of the dominant classes in the dominant countries.

At the expense of some oversimplification, we can say that the traditional Marxist view has been that the imperialist ruling classes are made up of industrialists and bankers and that a certain characteristic evolution has taken place in the relations between the two groups. In the first phase—up to the closing decades of the nineteenth century—the industrialists played the leading role. Their interests in the underdeveloped countries were of two kinds: as sources of cheap food and raw materials which would have the effect of raising the rate of surplus value and lowering the organic composition of capital, thus doubly boosting the rate of profit; and as markets for manufactured goods which would help to solve the realization problem. Both these ends would best be served by free trade and free competition which could be counted upon to turn the underdeveloped countries into complementary appendages of the advanced countries.

The second phase, beginning around 1880 or so, is characterized by the dominance of finance capital. Concentration and centralization of capital lead to spread of the corporate form, of stock markets, etc. In this context, bankers (investment bankers in the United States) seize the initiative, promote mergers and monopolies over which they establish their dominance, and thus become the leading echelon of the capitalist class. Since the bankers deal in capital rather than in commodities, their primary interest in the underdeveloped countries is in exporting capital to them at highest possible rates of profit. This end, however, is not furthered by free trade and free competition. Finance capitalists in each imperialist country want to establish an exclusive domain out of which they can keep their rivals and within which they can fully protect their investments. Hence the vigorous revival of empire-building—somewhat in abeyance since mercantile days—in the closing decades of the nineteenth century. There is, of course, no implication that export of capital is in conflict with the aims of the preceding period—raw materials and markets—for, on the contrary, they complement each other nicely. It is only that in the Hilferding-Lenin theory it is the export of capital which dominates imperialist policy.

This theory, taken together with Lenin's very important Law of Uneven Development, worked well in explaining the main lines of development of the world economy and of world politics in the period before the First World War. Since then, however, certain changes in the characteristics of the ruling classes in the dominant countries have taken place which need to be taken into account in the development of the theory.

III

One can no longer today speak of either industrialists or bankers as the leading echelon of the dominant capitalist classes. The big monopolistic corporations, which were formed and in their early years controlled by bankers, proved to be enormously profitable and in due course, through paying off their debts and plowing back their earnings, achieved financial independence and indeed in many cases acquired substantial control over banks and other financial institutions. These giant corporations are the basic units of monopoly capitalism in its present stage; their (big) owners and functionaries constitute the leading echelon of the ruling class. It is through analyzing these corporate giants and their interests that we can best comprehend the functioning of imperialism today.

In size, complexity of structure, and multiplicity of interests the corporate giant of today differs markedly from the industrialist or the banker of an earlier period. This can be most graphically illustrated by an actual case, and for this purpose we can hardly do better than select Standard Oil of New Jersey (hereafter referred to as Standard or Jersey). This corporation was the earliest of its kind anywhere in the world; it is today the second largest industrial corporation in the world (second only to General Motors); and its international ramifications are at least as complicated and far reaching as those of any other corporation. It shows in clearest and most developed form the "ideal type" to which hundreds of other giant corporations, both in the United States and in the other advanced capitalist countries, are more or less close approximations.

Here in brief summary form, are some of the most important data about the size, structure, and operations of Jersey.[4]

Size. As of December 31, 1962, Jersey had total assets of $11,488 million. Its aggregate revenues for the year 1962 came to $10,567 million, and its net income to $841 million (*Form 10-K*).

Geographical distribution of assets and earnings. As of the end of 1958, the percentage distribution of earnings and assets by various regions was as follows (*Notice*):

	Assets	Earnings
U.S. and Canada	67	34
Latin America	20	39
Eastern Hemisphere	13	27
Total	100	100

Rate of return on stockholders' equity. During 1962 the percentage rates of return on stockholders' equity in different regions were as follows (*Annual Report*):

United States	7.4
Other Western Hemisphere	17.6
Eastern Hemisphere	15.0

Number of subsidiaries. As of the end of 1962, Jersey owned fifty per cent or more of the stock in 275 subsidiaries in 52 countries. The following is a list of the number of such subsidiaries by country of organization (*Form 10-K*):

U.S.A.	77	Morocco	2
Canada	37	Switzerland	2
Great Britain	24	Uruguay	2
Panama	17	Venezuela	2
France	12	Algeria	1
Bahamas	8	Danzig	1
Italy	6	Dominican Republic	1
Sweden	6	Egypt	1
Colombia	5	El Salvador	1
Netherlands	5	Finland	1
Australia	4	Hungary	1
Brazil	4	India	1
Chile	4	Indonesia	1
Germany	4	Kenya	1
Philippines	4	Luxemburg	1
Argentina	3	Madagascar	1
Denmark	3	Mexico	1
Ireland	3	New Zealand	1
Japan	3	Paraguay	1
Neth. Antilles	3	Peru	1
Norway	3	Republic of Congo	1

Austria	2	Singapore	1
Belgium	2	South Africa	1
Bermuda	2	Spain	1
Iraq	2	Surinam	1
Malaya	2	Tunisia	1

Recapitulating by regions, we find that Jersey had 114 subsidiaries in the United States and Canada, 43 in Latin America, 77 in Europe, 14 in Asia, 9 in Africa, and 18 in other regions.

Countries marketed in. According to the *Annual Report,* Jersey sold to "more than 100" countries in 1962.

It would obviously be wrong to expect a corporation like this to behave, like a British cotton mill owner interested in getting his raw cotton from abroad at the lowest possible price and in exporting his products to a duty-free India, or like a Rothschild or a Morgan disposing over great amounts of liquid capital and interested in investing it abroad at the highest attainable rate of profit. Standard's interests are much more complicated. Take, for example, the question of exports and imports. Though Standard, through its principal United States affiliate, Humble Oil and Refining Company, is one of the biggest producers in the country, the company is definitely not interested in protectionist measures. Quite to the contrary, it is a strong opponent of the present system of controls which limits the importation of fuel oil.[5] "In the interests of consumers, the national economy, and the international relations of our country," states the *1962 Annual Report,* "we hope that these unnecessary controls not only will be relaxed . . . but will be completely removed." Behind the public-spiritedness, of course, lies Standard's interest in having its relatively low-cost Venezuelan subsidiary, Creole Petroleum, sell freely in the lucrative East Coast fuel-oil market.

Or take the question of capital exports. On the face of it, one might be tempted to conclude from the tremendous magnitude and variety of Standard's foreign operations that over the years the corporation has been a large and consistent exporter of capital. The conclusion, however, would not be justified. From the data presented above, it appears clear that foreign operations are much more profitable than domestic, and this has been the case since the early days of the corporation. Under these conditions, a small initial export of capital could, and undoubtedly did, expand rapidly through the reinvestment of its own earnings. Not only that. So great have been the profits of foreign operations that in most years even after the needs of expansion have been covered, large sums have been available for remittance to the parent corporation in the United States. The year 1962 may be taken as an example: Standard paid out dividends to its shareholders, the vast majority of whom are resident in the United States, a total of $538 million. In the same year, however, operations in the United States produced a net income of only $309 million. It follows that some forty per cent of dividends plus whatever net investment may have been made in the United States during the year were financed from the profits of foreign operations. Far from being an exporter of capital, the corporation is a large and consistent *importer* of capital into the United States.

The foregoing gives hardly more than a hint of the complexity of Standard's interests. It takes no account of the fact that the oil industry as organized by the giant international corporations is in reality a congeries of businesses: extraction of the raw material from the subsoil, transportation by pipe-line and tanker, processing in some of the most technologically advanced plants in the world, and finally selling a variety of products in markets all over the world. Nor is Standard confined to the oil industry even in this comprehensive sense. It is a large and growing supplier of natural gas to the gas pipe-line companies; it is a major producer of artificial rubber, plastics, resins, and other petrochemical products; and it recently entered the fertilizer business with plans which, according to the *1962 Annual Report,* "will make Jersey an important factor in the world fertilizer industry." Finally, Jersey, like other giant corporations, maintains a large research and development program the purpose of which is not only to lower costs and hence increase profits from existing operations but also to invent new products and open up new lines of business. As an illustration of the latter, we may cite the following from the *1962 Annual Report*: "Food from oil through biological fermentation is an intriguing possibility. Esso Research, in a small pilot plant, has produced a white powder that resembles powdered milk or yeast. It is odorless, has a bland taste, and is high in protein and B vitamins. The first goal is to develop food supplements for animals, but it is hoped that the technique may one day help to improve the diet and health of the world's growing population." Quite a promising market, one must admit.

This is, of course, not the place for a detailed examination of the structure and interests of Standard Oil or any other corporation. But enough has been said, we hope, to carry the conviction that such a huge and complicated institutional "capitalist" can hardly be assumed to have exactly the same attitudes and behavior patterns as the industrial or finance capitalists of classical Marxian theory. But before we explore this subject further, we must ask whether Standard Oil is indeed an ideal type which helps us to distil the essence of capitalist reality, or whether on the contrary it may not be an exceptional case which we should rather ignore than put at the center of the analytical stage.

IV

Up to the Second World War, it would have been correct to treat Standard Oil as a sort of exception—a very important one, to be sure, exercising tremendous, and at times even decisive, influence on United States world policy. Nevertheless, in the world-wide scope and ramifications of its operations not only was it far ahead of all others; there were only a handful that could be said to be developing along the same lines. Many United States corporations of course had large interests in exports or imports, and quite a few had foreign branches or subsidiaries. In neither respect, however, was the situation much different from what it had been in 1929. Direct investments of United States corporations indeed declined slightly between 1929 and 1946.[6] Most of the giant corporations which dominated the United States economy were, in the words of *Business Week,* "domestically oriented enterprises with international operations" and not, like Standard Oil, "truly world oriented corporations."[7]

A big change took place during the next decade and a half. To quote *Business Week* again: "In industry after industry, U.S. companies found that their overseas earnings were soaring, and that their return on investment abroad was frequently much higher than in the U.S. As earning abroad began to rise, profit margins from domestic operations started to shrink. . . . This is the combination that forced development of the multinational company."[8] The foreign direct investments of United States corporations increased sharply—from the already cited figure of $7.2 billion in 1946 to $34.7 billion in 1961.[9] While this tremendous jump of course involved actual capital exports by many individual companies, it cannot be overemphasized that for the United States as a whole the amount of income transferred to the United States on direct investment account far exceeded the direct capital outflow. The two series, which can be constructed from official government statistics for the years 1950 and later, are as follows:

Year	Net Direct Investment Capital Outflow ($ Millions)	Direct Investment Income ($ Millions)
1950	621	1.294
1951	528	1.492
1952	850	1.419
1953	722	1.442
1954	664	1.725
1955	799	1.975
1956	1.859	2.120
1957	2.058	2.313
1958	1.094	2.198
1959	1.372	2.206
1960	1.694	2.348
1961	1.467	2.672
Totals	13.708	23.204

Sources: U.S. Department of Commerce, *Survey of Current Business,* November 1954, pp. 9, 13; August 1955, pp. 18, 20; August 1957, p. 25; August 1959, p. 31; August 1961, pp. 22-23; August 1962, pp. 22-23.

From the figures presented it will be seen that from 1950 through 1961, United States corporations were able to expand their direct foreign investments by $27.5 billion while at the same time taking in as income $9.5 billion more than they sent out as capital. Foreign investment, it seems, far from being a means of developing underdeveloped countries, is a most efficient device for transferring wealth from poorer to richer countries while at the same time enabling the richer to expand their control over the economies of the poorer.

But this is not the aspect of the matter which primarily concerns us at the moment. The point is that in the course of expanding their foreign assets and operations in this spectacular way, most of the corporate giants which dominate the United States economy have taken the road long since pioneered by Standard Oil. They have become, in *Business Week's* terminology, multinational corporations.[10] It is not enough that a multinational corporation should have a base of operations abroad; its true *differentia specifica* is that "its management makes fundamental decisions on marketing, production, and research in terms of the alternatives that are available to it anywhere in the world."[11] This, of course, is what Standard Oil has been doing since roughly the beginning of the century. The difference is that what was then the exception has today become the rule.

V

One cannot say of the giant multinational company of today that it is primarily interested, like the industrialist of the nineteenth century, in the export of commodities; or, like the banker of the early twentieth century, in the export of capital. General Motors, for example, produces automobiles for the rapidly expanding European market not in Detroit but in Britain and West Germany; and it probably exports many more from its European subsidiaries to the underdeveloped countries than it does from the United States. In many cases, indeed, the foreign subsidiaries of United States companies are large-scale exporters to the United States market. In 1957, for example, the aggregate sales (excluding intercorporate petroleum sales) of direct-investment enterprises abroad was $32 billion. Of this amount, more than $3.5 billion (11 per cent) was exported to the United States.[12] Considering that aggregate merchandise imports into the United States in 1957 came to $13.2 billion, it is a most striking fact that more than a quarter of this total was supplied by the foreign subsidiaries of United States companies. And as for capital export, we have already seen that United States multinational companies are on balance massive importers, not exporters, of capital.

What all this means is that one must beware of easy generalizations about the specifically economic interests of the leading actors on the imperialist stage. Their interests are in fact variegated and complex, often contradictory rather than complementary. Subsidiaries of a United States company in two foreign countries may both be in a good position to export to a third country. If one gets the business, the interests of the other will be damaged. Which should be favored? Or a certain company produces raw materials through a subsidiary in one country, processes the materials through another subsidiary in a second country, and sells the finished product through yet another subsidiary in the United States. Intercorporate prices can be so fixed as to allocate revenues and profits in any number of ways among the subsidiaries and countries. Which set of prices should actually be selected? These examples illustrate the kind of problem which the top managements of the multinational corporations have to solve every day;

and about the only valid generalization one can make is that in every case they will seek a solution which maximizes the (long-run) profits of the enterprise as a whole. And this of course means that whenever necessary to the furtherance of this goal, the interests of particular subsidiaries and countries will be ruthlessly sacrificed. This is admitted with refreshing candor by the authors of the *Business Week* report already cited: "The goal, in the multinational corporation, is the greatest good for the whole unit, even if the interests of a single part of the unit must suffer. One large U.S. manufacturer, for example, concedes that it penalizes some of its overseas subsidiaries for the good of the total corporation by forcing them to pay more than necessary for parts they import from the parent and from other subsidiaries. Says one of the company's executives: 'We do this in countries where we either anticipate or already face restrictions on profit repatriation. We want some way to get our money out.' "

A whole treatise could—and should—be written about the way the national interests of the subordinate countries fare under the regime of multinational corporations. Here we will have to be content with one illustration—a case which is less known than it deserves to be but which we believe to be fully typical. One of the most important natural resources of the Caribbean area is bauxite. Jamaica, Surinam, British Guiana, and the Dominican Republic are all important producers, with operations being organized and controlled by one Canadian and a few United States corporate giants. Separate figures on the operations of these subsidiaries are not published. However, the United States Department of Commerce does report the profits accruing to United States mining companies on their operations in Western Hemisphere dependencies of European countries, at least 90 per cent of which must be attributable to bauxite production in Jamaica, Surinam, and British Guiana. Adding a conservatively estimated figure for profits of the Canadian company, profits from operations in these three countries in 1961 were between $70 and $75 million on an investment estimated at between $220 and $270 million.[13] This profit rate of between 26 and 34 per cent suggests, in the opinion of Philip Reno, that "this could well be among the most profitable United States investment structures in the world." However, this is only part of the story. Commerce Department figures give current costs of United States aluminum company operations in the three countries for 1957. Of the total of $81 million, no less than $31 million, or almost 40 per cent, are classified under the heading of "Materials and Services." Since it is simply incomprehensible how materials and services could constitute so large a share of the costs of an extractive operation of this kind (more than 50 per cent greater than wages and salaries), one can only conclude that this item is artificially padded to cover excessive payments to United States shipping, insurance, and other interests. In this manner, profits (and hence taxes) can be kept down and funds can be remitted from the colony to the metropolis.

Nor is even this all. The price of bauxite produced in the United States doubled in the two decades from 1939 to 1959, while the price of bauxite imported from Surinam and British Guiana remained almost the same throughout the whole period. This means that profits which should have been realized by the subsidiary companies and been taxed by the Surinam and British Guiana governments were in fact realized in the United States. At length, however, the parent aluminum companies, with one exception, began to alter this price structure, and here we get a revealing glimpse of the kind of considerations that determine the policy decision of the multinational corporation. In Philip Reno's words: "The prices set on bauxite from all the Caribbean countries except British Guiana did finally begin to rise a few years ago. The explanation lies with the law granting tax concessions to United States companies operating in other countries of this Hemisphere through what are called Western Hemisphere Trade Corporations. Instead of a 52 per cent corporate income tax, Western Hemisphere Trade Corporations pay the United States only 25 per cent. By raising the price of bauxite, United States companies could now reduce their total income taxes. The price of bauxite began to rise for the first time in twenty years, except for British Guiana bauxite mined by Altd, Canada-based and unaffected by Western Hemisphere Trade Corporation maneuvers."

If this is a fair sample of how the underdeveloped countries are treated by the multinational companies, it does not follow that these giant enterprises are any more concerned to promote the national interests of the advanced countries, including even the one in which their headquarters are situated. Quite apart from particular actions—like the Ford Motor Company's remittance abroad of several hundred million dollars to buy out the minority interest in Ford of Britain at a time when the United States government was expressing serious concern about the state of the country's balance of payments—a plausible argument could be made that in the last fifteen years United States corporations have developed their foreign operations at the expense of, and often in direct competition with, their domestic operations, and that these policies have constituted one of the causes of the lagging growth rate of the United States economy and hence of the rising trend of unemployment which is now perhaps the nation's number one domestic problem. Whether or not this is really the case—and it would probably be impossible to *prove* either that it is or isn't—it remains true that the decisions and actions of the multinational companies are taken solely with a view to promoting the interests of the companies themselves and that whatever effects, beneficial or injurious, they may have on the various countries in which they operate are strictly incidental.

VI

Does this mean that the giant multinational companies have no interests in common on which they can unite? Are there no *general* policies which they expect their governments—and the governments of the dominant imperialist states are indeed theirs— to follow? The answer is that there are common interests and desired general policies, but that for the most part they are not narrowly economic in nature. The multinational companies often have conflicting interests when it comes to tariffs, export subsidies, foreign investment, etc. But they are absolutely united on two things: First, they want the world of nations in which they can operate to be as large as possible. And second, they want its laws and institutions to be favorable to the unfettered development of private capitalist enterprise. Or to put the point in another way, their ideal would be a world of nations in every one of which they could operate uninhibited by local obstacles to their making and freely disposing of maximum attainable profits. This means not only that they are opposed to revolutions which threaten to exclude them altogether from certain areas—as, for example, the Cuban Revolution excluded all United States corporations from Cuba—but also that they are adamantly opposed to all forms of state capitalism (using the term in its broadest sense) which might tend to hamper their own operations or to reserve potentially profitable areas of economic activity for the nationals of the countries in question.[14] Their attitude is well expressed in the *1962 Annual Report* of Standard Oil on which we have already drawn for illustrative material: "Both at home and abroad, a greater awareness is needed of the importance of private investment to economic progress. Some countries have shown a trend toward state enterprise both through government participation in new commercial ventures and through nationalization of established private businesses. The interest of these nations will best be served, however, by fostering societies that are based on those principles of free enterprise which have produced the outstanding economic development of many other nations. It is reassuring to see steps taken—such as the Hickenlooper Amendment to the Foreign Assistance Act of 1961—to ensure that economic assistance funds from the United States encourage a climate of progress by emphasizing the importance and protection of private investment in nations receiving aid from the United States." It would be wrong to think that the management of Standard Oil opposes government enterprise in the subordinate countries because of a naive belief that state action is identical with socialism. The explanation is much more rational: government enterprise and state action in these countries generally represent attempts on the part of the native bourgeoisies to appropriate for themselve a larger share of locally produced surplus at the expense of the multinational companies. It is only natural that such attempts should be resolutely opposed by the multinational companies.

The general policy which the multinational companies require of their government can thus be summed up in a simple formula: to make a world safe for Standard Oil. In more ideological terms, this means to protect the "free world" and to extend its boundaries wherever and whenever possible, which of course has been the proclaimed aim of United States policy ever since the promulgation of the "Truman Doctrine" in 1947. The negative side of the coin is anti-communism. The necessary complement is the building up and maintenance of a tremendous global military machine.

All the major struggles going on in the world today can be traced to this hunger of the multinational corporations for maximum *Lebensraum.* And the connection usually has a direct, immediate, and visible aspect. We cite just two facts relative to Cuba and Vietnam where the essence of present-day imperialist policy can be seen in its clearest form. Under the heading "Standard Oil Co. (New Jersey)," in Standard and Poor's *Standard Corporate Descriptions,* dated July 24, 1961, we learn that "loss of $62,269,000 resulting from expropriation of Cuban properties in 1960 was charged to earned surplus." And from the same company's *1962 Annual Report* we learn that "Jersey continues to look for attractive opportunities both in areas where we now operate and in those where we do not," and that the following are among the measures being taken to implement this policy: "A refinery in which the company will have majority interest is under construction in Malaya, and affiliates have part interests in a refinery under construction in Australia and one that is being planned for Vietnam."

Losses in Cuba, plans for South Vietnam: what more eloquent commentary could there be on the struggles now going on in and around those two little countries on opposite sides of the globe?

Notes

[1] "Under the old type of capitalism," Lenin wrote, "when free competition prevailed, the export of commodities was the most typical feature. Under modern capitalism, when monopolies prevail, the export of *capital* has become the typical feature." *Imperialism the Highest Stage of Capitalism,* Chapter 4.

[2] To be sure, depressions and mass unemployment have pushed capitalist governments into armaments expansion, aggressive foreign policy, and even war, but the analysis of these crucially important problems is a task of the general theory of monopoly capitalism which is obviously much broader than the classical "pure" theory of imperialism.

[3] It should perhaps be added that in addition to being based on a fatal methodological error, these alleged refutations of economic theories of imperialism usually rely on arguments which can only be described as nonsensical. In this connection a good recent example is Hans Neisser's "Economic Imperialism Reconsidered," *Social Research,* Spring 1960. Neisser would like to compare what the capitalist world is like today with what it would have been like "if western economic penetration of the rest of the world had stopped at the beginning of the nineteenth century" (p. 73). That this involves a wholly fanciful and arbitrary invention of a century and a half of world history does not trouble him in the least.

[4] The sources are the company's *1962 Annual Report,* its *Notice of Special Stockholders' Meeting* (October 7, 1959), and its *Form 10-K for the Fiscal Year Ended December 31, 1962,* filed with the Securities and Exchange Commission pursuant to Section 13 of the Securities Act of 1934. These sources are identified as *Annual Report, Notice,* and *Form 10-K,* respectively.

[5] The existence of these import restrictions is a reflection of the great political power of the oil and gas producing states, especially exercised through the Democratic Party.

[6] The figure was $7.5 billion in 1929 and $7.2 billion in 1946. U.S. Department of Commerce, Office of Business Economics, *U.S. Business Investments in Foreign Countries: A Supplement to the Survey of Current Business,* 1960, p. 1.

[7] "Multinational Companies," A Special Report, *Business Week,* April 20, 1963. It is interesting to note that in the United States, the business press is often far ahead of economists in recognizing, and even attempting to analyze, the latest developments in the capitalist economy.

[8] *Ibid.* The shrinkage of profit margins in the U.S. economy, beginning as early as 1950 and in spite of unprecedentedly rapid technological progress and slowly rising unemployment, is a complete mystery to bourgeois thought, both journalistic and academic. Since it is obviously impossible to pursue this subject within the confines of this essay, we must be content to refer the reader to a forthcoming work, entitled *Monopoly Capital,* by the present authors.

[9] U.S. Department of Commerce, *Survey of Current Business* (August 1962), p. 22.

[10] The term seems to have originated with David E. Lilienthal, Director of the Tennessee Valley Authority under Roosevelt and of the Atomic Energy Commission under Truman, and now Chairman of the Development and Resources Corporation which appears to be backed and controlled by the international banking house of Lazard

Frères. A paper delivered by Mr. Lilienthal at the Carnegie Institute of Technology in April, 1960, and later published by Development and Resources Corporation, bears the title "The Multinational Corporation."

[11] *Business Week's* "Multinational Companies."

12. U.S. Department of Commerce, *U.S. Business Investments in Foreign Countries*, p. 3.

13. All figures are from an article, "Aluminum Profits and Caribbean People," by Philip Reno, *Monthly Review*, October 1963. Mr. Reno spent several months in British Guiana studying the operations of the aluminum companies.

[14] This does not mean, of course, that they oppose foreign governments undertaking public works—roads, harbors, public health and education programs, etc., etc.—of a kind that will benefit their own operations. For such beneficent activities they even favor generous "foreign aid" from their own government.

5

L. MARCUS

The Third Stage of Imperialism

The form of the long-term solution sought by the capitalists is suggested by the runaway shop. Already, capital created by the production of skilled U.S. workers has run away to build shops employing less skilled and much cheaper labor in Europe. In this way the average profit on a world scale is sustained and average profit at home is increased.

There is an abundance of cheap labor below the equator, but a shortage of *labor power.* That is to say, a runaway shop, if it is to be competitive, must find labor with a certain level of skill in general, literate labor, labor that is not only the product of modern education, but also latently educated through *something* of a "Western" standard of living. And plants can not be simply dumped into the middle of an undeveloped savanna or jungle; plants require power, efficient transportation, communications systems, proximity to suppliers and customers, and so forth. The population must also be susceptible to "Western" ways of doing things, to capitalist notions of property relations, family, order, and so forth; it must be assimilable into the modern capitalist culture as reflected in relations between line workers and foremen. That is to say, in addition to the more obvious objective prerequisites for investment, there are, equally important, the subjective preconditions, juridical notions of human relations, etc. All of these conditions together are loosely termed "infra-structure" by brain-trusters in the state bureaucracy.

It is in that direction that imperialists see their longer-term solution to the presently impending economic crisis. Since they move through a bureaucracy, not as scientists, they do not discover such a solution by advancing, discussing, proving some general theory, but pragmatically, through the concepts embodied in the institutions left over from the past. They see the solution not in scientific terms, but through the precedent of the "Marshall Plan" and "Fomento" development of Puerto Rico, in terms of "Food for Peace" and Fulbright funds, in terms of the International Monetary Fund, and through foreign institutions, such as Latin American juntas, or the Nehru bureaucracy or Ky regime, which are their existing institutionalized relations with underdeveloped sectors. They approach something new mainly by attempting to patch up the old instruments, by turning their instrumentalities into a Rube Goldberg device of gadgets affixed hither and yon, each attachment grafted on to "solve" a problem discovered through some particular experience.

Such a new policy was first officially presented to the general public by former President Eisenhower in his 1960 State of the Union address on Foreign Policy. In order to open up the Southern Hemisphere for direct internal market investment, a new "Marshall Plan" would have to be launched, this time with the burden assumed proportionately by Western Europe and Japan. Massive public aid and loans would develop the infrastructure, after which private capital, finding the economic and political climate agreeably air-conditioned for its comfort, would move in. Of course, Eisenhower pointed out that colonial peoples desiring to harvest such largesse from imperialism would have to learn to discipline themselves, a point which was later clarified by the assassination of Patrice Lumumba.

At the instant Eisenhower was delivering this policy statement, Douglas Dillon, then an underling at the State Department, was negotiating a treaty along those very lines with that late great "socialist," Nehru. Under the terms of this treaty, India became, economically at least, in the same relationship to the U.S., Western Europe and Japan as Puerto Rico to the U.S. Under the provisions of this treaty British India investment has stagnated, while West German and Japanese investment has leaped ahead, a process interrupted by the current famine.

Kennedy's abortive "Alliance for Progress" was a miserably inadequate, jury-rigged "fomento" scheme, in all probability hastily scrounged for the occasion from the drafting boards of the left-over Eisenhower bureaucracy. But it was also, in principle, consistent with a policy Kennedy had set forth in a 1958 Senate address. Kennedy's half-baked "land reform" program in Vietnam, continued recipes of the same sort now afoot, and Daddy Bird Johnson's occasional mumblings about a "managed social revolution" for Latin America are aspects of a bureaucratically bungled thrust toward implementation of the policy enunciated by Eisenhower in 1960.

THIRD STAGE

If it could be launched, this policy would represent a third stage of imperialism. The first stage is represented by British colonialist rape of India, by Britain's military effort to push the opium habit on Chinese people, and other picaresque colonial adventures of buccaneering commercial capital. The second stage is that characterized by Lenin and Hilferding, of monopoly capital's investment in the extractive industries, the use of masses of virtually slave colonial labor to work the plantations and mines. Under this second stage of imperialism, under which we have lived to this point, foreigners like the unlamented Leopold of Belgium, or the interests of our own Rockefeller operated abroad with policies which respected not the least how many natives were butchered or worked to death, as long as there remained sufficient "slave" labor to man the imperialist workings. That is the continuing situation, under which our leading press indulges us with its ritual tears of ink over massive misery abroad, without troubling to suggest any alteration in that U.S. policy causing this suffering. In the new stage of imperialism—if it is launched—the lot of colonial peoples will be more fortunate in one respect. It happens that starving illiterates do not represent labor power for today's industrialists. That is to say that U.S. imperialists *will* regard colonial peoples as productive labor, as workers whose human virtues are acknowledged in direct proportion to their qualities of cheapness and servility. The Southern Hemisphere is intended to become the happy hunting ground of the runaway shop in this period as Puerto Rico has been in the last.

COULD IT WORK?

A number of socialist commentators, basing themselves substantially on the "Alliance for Progress" experience, deny that such a "Third Stage of Imperialism" policy could work even if the colonial peoples permitted it. On the contrary, if not prevented, it could work quite well for some period of time, provided only that the imperialists themselves are prepared to undertake the risks, the massive and revolutionary measures required to get such a program under way.

We must grant the cited socialist doubters that, "all things being equal," those very difficulties of starting up would ordinarily prevent imperialists from undertaking such a hazardous venture. The same could be said, of course, for the past two world wars. It happens that, as on the verge of a world war, "all other things" are by no means equal. Imperialism is impelled to any desperate resort the policy demands; it has no other long-term basis on which to predicate its existence.

The first obstacle to industrial development of the Southern Hemisphere is the plantation system. For any sector of the world economy to maintain an industrial working class, it must have a ready and ample supply of cheap food. "Cheap food" is a relative matter; that is to say, there must be a relative abundance at prices which represent only a fraction of the worker's pay for his family's needs. U.S. food "surpluses" do not suffice for this purpose; they are only useful supplemental means or part of an initial "pump-priming" to get local industrialization going under its own power. In order to have local food prices scaled to the wage-levels of local workers, this need must be mainly met out of agricultural surpluses from relatively low-wage areas. It is mainly to ample local food production that the plantation system is an obstacle.

In order to provide plantation owners with cheap labor, there has been created a layer of landless, proletarianized peasants without skills or opportunities for any other kind of employment—as we see in the case of migrant agricultural labor in the U.S. itself. The latifundist is therefore violently opposed to any

"Homestead Act" which will raise the price of agricultural labor by affording peasants the opportunity to take up idle land and put it into modern farm production. In the Southern Hemisphere, the proletarianization of large masses of peasantry is accomplished almost automatically by the draining of the internal economy of the social capital which would be required to develop agriculture. This result of primitive accumulation is augmented by juridical measures including landlordism which prevent peasants from freely occupying and developing fertile plots.

Before stable industrialization can take place, this latifundist *system* must be largely destroyed. This does not mean, generally, a distribution of banana and coffee lands for potato or corn farming. It means mainly a program of distributing *idle* arable plots to peasants, together with technological and financial assistance from the state. This will drive up the price of plantation labor, forcing the plantations to shift from labor-intensive to mechanized methods of production.

The present system is sometimes clumsily called "feudal." In fact, the latifundist system—a system of producing masses of agricultural output for the money market—is a product of capitalism, and has not occurred anywhere in the history of man except through the development of mercantile capitalism (e.g. Hellenism generally, ancient Rome in particular, Southern slave-system). So, the question of social revolution in Latin America, for example, is not a matter of capitalists settling accounts with feudal remnants, but of capitalism reforming itself.

The imperialists' difficulty in Latin America at this point is that plantation interests there are not an isolated group within the capitalist system. Plantations are only the agricultural extremity in that part of the world of the central banking system in the advanced. To institute land reform, to force latifundists to mechanize, etc., is to wipe out a source of profits of the imperialist home countries.

Furthermore, the *comprador* class in these countries, rooted in the latifundist families and system, forms the "loyal" native governing class, the officer cadres of the police and armies servile to imperialist interests. To overturn the present latifundist interests in these countries is to attack major imperialist profits and investments in that sector and also to alienate and impoverish that caste of dons and colonels on which Coca-Cola-ization is presently based.

However, these consequences will ultimately be risked and a solution found, if the need is sufficiently desperate—as it is.

Actually, the latifundists will be offered no more than "psychological" hardships. The procedure to be used is in principle the same as that employed in Northern U.S. cities' slum clearance programs. A tax collection is taken up from wage-earners; these funds are used to compensate slumlords or latifundists at top dollar. "Here's your money; go and invest it in industrial development." The objective transition from serf-owner to financier, like that from gangster to successful businessman, requires only sufficient ready cash.

A VARIATION—THE CASE OF INDIA

One major leg of imperialism's future is India, which requires a slightly different approach than that due for Latin America. The tired soil of that unhappy country does not admit of the land reform solutions feasible in much of Latin America. Decades of soil development, of technological work, must pass before that portion of the subcontinent can feed itself and also provide a surplus to sustain a growing cheap industrial proletariat.

The old British Raj provided for its industrial investment in India with rice imports from Burma. Such resources are insufficient for the collective investment appetites of the U.S., Western Europe and Japan. It is the Southeast Asian rice-bowl as a whole that can provide just such needed agricultural surpluses—that is to speak of such regions as the Mekong River area. (Obviously, there is no direct investment, present or prospective, in Vietnam itself which would explain the present costly war; but when the importance of the rice bowl as a whole is weighed against imperialism's present and future desperate interest in India, the Vietnam war appears in its proper focus in terms of U.S. imperialist interests.)

Planned imperialist investment in the underdeveloped sector is divided into two main parts, *public* and *private*. Massive public assistance, in the form of government grants, World Bank loans, and so forth, are intended to build up what contemporary bureaucrats term the "infra-structure" of the economy. This is to provide education, highways, railways, power, and so forth. These are elements which do not represent profitable investments themselves, but which are indispensable to private investment as they provide labor with skills and otherwise create the facilities on which modern plants depend. Then, private investment follows: the "Marshall Plan" on a larger scale, adapted to the special enormous difficulties of these sectors.

The role of the military should not be overlooked in this process of developing a capitalist infra-structure. Marx remarked on the expression of concentrated production relations in the capitalist army; Engels researched some of the actual connections by which such a result is produced. The organization of a large-scale local army on a U.S. model is the most direct way of educating large numbers of colonial peoples, of drilling them in the customs and technology of capitalist life. The army as an economic entity in its own right also provides, in addition to a massive prostitution industry, a host of camp-followers who soon learn the elements of modern capitalism—cheating, price-gouging, misleading packaging. In the wake of the army appear those wealthy pimps, gangsters, black-marketeers, etc. who have small capital and some knowledge of business, together with a mass of demobilized soldiers who have been drilled in following foremen's orders, in maintaining mechanical tools, etc. (cf. Vietnam today).

With the colonial economies already running at a capital deficit, the public and private capital must come from the product of labor in the advanced countries. To turn India, parts of Africa and Latin America around, from primitive accumulation resources to sectors of industrial development, public aid alone must be advanced on a war-spending scale. Unless financier profits are to be reduced for this purpose, war-economy scale increases in profits and in employee taxes must provide the bulk of these funds.

The general scheme for accomplishing this funding is seen in the "wage guidelines" recipe. Its effect is to hold real wages down to a fraction of the gains in potential real wages attained through productivity, to hold wage increases behind the combined effect of inflation and major increases in productivity. Thus, at best the material standard of living of the worker in the U.S., Europe, etc., may remain about the same while his portion of the product of labor is rapidly reduced.

As for the effect of this scheme on the U.S. economy, it should not be imagined that U.S. foreign aid represents the slightest bit of charity on the part of financiers here. Most U.S. aid dollars need never leave a N.Y. bank; these deposits in U.S. banks will be used to purchase from U.S. corporations the capital goods exported—the U.S. financier will immediately be paid for his *largesse,* while the foreign economy will be in a greater amount of debt to the U.S. bankers! If a small amount of this money does actually leak into colonial native economies, no matter; it will only be used to prime the local pump to further assist U.S. direct investment.

NEO-COLONIALISM

The "Third Stage of Imperialism" should not be confused with "neo-colonialism," a term which only reflects the confusion with which many observers regard U.S. takeover of the colonial world from the old colonial powers. Economically, there is nothing very new in what these observers term "neo-colonialism"; these forms are only a part of the old "Second Stage of Imperialism."

Neo-colonialism signifies chiefly that U.S. imperialism has at last succeeded in extending its 1899 "Open Door To China" policy to the entire colonial world. That "Open Door" policy, it should be remembered, was simply a kind of declaration of war on the old colonial powers, in which a bumptious, nascent U.S. imperialism threw down the gauntlet: "Tear down your customs fences around those colonies we Americans intend to make our property." The granting of national independence to former colonies by old colonial powers—often at the explicit insistence of U.S. imperialism—merely shows that the U.S. has finally compelled those old powers to knuckle under, to turn the colonial world over to the unhampered exploitation of the dollar.

In the case of the Belgian Congo, for example, it was the U.S. which pressured a reluctant Belgium into granting Congo independence, the same U.S. which backed Belgium invasion of that former colony to the hilt immediately thereafter. The White House does not object to Belgian paratroopers shooting down colonial women and children on an Eichmann scale, merely to Belgian customs officials annoying the emissaries of U.S. capital.

Still "neo-colonialism," occurring at the fulfillment of the Second Stage of Imperialism, does represent the point at which the Third Stage begins to emerge. The famous CIA flair shows itself in the recently established counter-revolutionary regimes now in the saddle in Algeria, Congo, Ghana, and Indonesia. U.S. and "allied" agents seek out among the nationalists those who show a proper understanding for the capitalist way of life, just as any slumlord might seek out some ambitious lad to take on the problem of dealing directly with the tenants. As the slumlord "sells" the slum building (with, of course, a usurious second mortgage) to the ambitious lad, assuring him that he is now a "financier," so the U.S. agent or one of his ilk paints the delights of capitalist status to the upcoming "boy." "Of course, this will be your very own native industry; we will be content with no more than a first and second mortgage, plus a fair share of any profits which manage to miraculously survive our financial rates."

6

HARRY MAGDOFF and PAUL M. SWEEZY

Notes on the Multinational Corporation

By now there exists an extensive literature on what have come increasingly to be called "multinational" corporations or companies—that is, corporations with headquarters in one country and a variety of subsidiaries in other countries.¹ Hardly any of it, however, is written from a Marxist point of view, a fact which, given the obvious importance of the subject, casts a revealing light on the state of Marxist social science in the United States (or anywhere else, for that matter). Our purpose in this paper is not to attempt to fill this gap in any comprehensive way but rather to raise a number of key questions and to suggest directions in which answers should be sought.

I

First a few words about the name "multinational corporation." There is no doubt that in much of the literature this is used in a propagandistic and apologetic sense, suggesting the transcendence of national vices and rivalries and the emergence of a new institution with hopeful auguries for the future. That such connotations are nonsensical will appear as we proceed; for the moment we are concerned only with the problem of whether to abandon the name or to attempt to strip it of its apologetic aspects and make use of it for scientific ends.

The problem is by no means a new one and can hardly be said to have a uniquely "correct" solution. For example, the situation is very similar with respect to the expression "Third World" which, in its original usage, was intended to conjure up a picture of a group of countries choosing their own road to economic and social development and standing between the advanced capitalist world on the one hand and the Communist world on the other. Marxists—with the exception perhaps of the official breed in the Soviet bloc—know of course that this picture is as phony as a $9 bill, that the countries in question are really the oppressed and exploited majority of the global capitalist system, and that the only way they can achieve real economic and social development is through socialist revolution. Knowing this, should they have rejected and attempted to discredit the term "Third World," or should they have adopted it and tried to endow it with a new meaning? On the whole it seems that they have followed the second course, presumably on the assumption that the term had caught on and would be used anyway, and that the best that could be done would be to strip it of its apologetic character. And, again on the whole, it seems that this procedure has been reasonably successful. No one finds it paradoxical, for example, that Pierre Jalée should entitle his study of global imperialist exploitation *The Pillage of the Third World:* thanks largely to the work of Marxist scholars and publicists, it is more and more taken for granted that "Third World" is merely a convenient shorthand designation for that large and in many ways diverse collection of colonies, semi-colonies, and neo-colonies which form the base of the global capitalist pyramid.

It seems to us that a similar course is called for in the case of the "multinational corporation." The term is already in such wide use that it will almost certainly survive any attacks that may be launched against it. Moreover, there is no doubt about the reality of the phenomenon to which it refers. We may as well do the best we can to deprive it of its power to mislead and, as in the case of "Third World," make it into a useful term for describing and analyzing the realities of present-day capitalism.

II

First of all, then, we need to understand the precise nature and limits of the multinationality of the multinational corporation. It *is* multinational in the sense that it operates in a number of nations with the purpose of maximizing the profits not of the individual units on a nation-by-nation basis but of the group as a whole. As we shall see, from this characteristic flow some of the most important consequences of the multinational corporation; indeed we can say that it is this alone which constitutes a valid reason for using the term multinational. For in all other decisive respects we are dealing with national corporations. In particular, ownership and control are located in one nation, not dispersed throughout the corporate system. There are two exceptions to this generalization: Royal Dutch Shell and Unilever, in both of which British capital and Dutch capital genuinely share ownership and control through complex parallel headquarters structures. But these exceptions are among the oldest of multinational corporations, and the pattern has not been copied by any of the two to three hundred which have emerged in the half century since the First World War. In particular and contrary to widespread expectation, the European Common Market has not given rise to new multinationals in which ownership and control are shared in two or more countries. There have been mergers and takeovers across national boundaries, and of course many of the European giants have working arrangements with their counterparts in other countries; but we know of no new instance in which a real division of ownership and control has taken place.

Here we meet head-on one of the most persistent themes of the apologetic literature. It is true, these writers say, that up to now the multinationals have been owned and controlled in one of the advanced capitalist countries, but the *trend* is toward a genuine internationalization of both stockholding and management. In support of this contention two sets of facts are cited: the large-scale investment, amounting to many billions of dollars, by foreigners (mainly Europeans) in U.S. stocks; and the hiring by the multinationals of more and more local people at the middle- and even upper-management levels in their foreign subsidiaries. Assuming the continuation of these activities, the apologists argue that in a relatively short time the national grip on the multinational corporations will be broken and they will become, so to speak, citizens of the world rather than of any particular country.

There is no need to quarrel about the facts here, though they are considerably less massive than is sometimes asserted or implied. What is really at issue is their interpretation. As to stockholdings, the following excerpt from a story in the *New York Times* of February 22, 1968, is instructive:

> Experts of the United Nations Economic Commission for Europe say there is a link between the flow of European capital into American equities and the direct investments of the big United States companies in Europe.
>
> "Europeans," the experts say . . ., "buy the stocks of the big United States companies, which are precisely the ones that invest in Europe."
>
> This means, in effect, that European capital joins with United States management to invest in Europe, it is asserted.

Since European stockholders, like their counterparts in the United States, normally have no influence on the composition or policies of managements, what this means is that many European capitalists, instead of investing directly in European industry, put their capital at the disposal of Americans who invest in Europe. "Internationalization" of ownership thus turns out to be one of many ways in which U.S. capital gains control over foreign capital. As far as the hiring of local personnel to staff foreign subsidiaries is concerned, this has absolutely nothing to do with sharing control, which remains undivided in the parent company. Of course if boards of directors and top managements of parent companies began to blossom with foreigners, that would be something else, which would call for serious analysis. But this has not happened. A few foreigners probably sit on the boards of some of the multinationals, but we have not run across a single case of foreigners occupying top management positions. (If there were any such cases, they would almost certainly be mightily celebrated in the apologetic literature.) What John Thackray, U.S. correspondent of the British magazine *Management Today,* has written on this subject seems, if anything, an understatement:

> There are two broad classes of managers in the large international company. One is the national of the parent company, working either somewhere in the domestic operations, abroad, or at headquarters. The second is the indigenous executive manning the foreign outpost.
>
> The existence of these two unequal classes is seldom mentioned by the persons involved; and when admitted, it is softly, softly. Corporate ideology declares that all men have

equal opportunity for advancement and success—every toiling executive has the president's slide rule or the president's nameplate somewhere in the drawers of his desk.

There are good and sufficient reasons as to why there should be these two classes of executives. But their existence presents a serious impediment to the creation of a managerial structure and an executive corps in multinational companies that can be, in the fullest sense, internationalist—where the significance of a man's nationality might be no more important than the color of his tie or the style of his shoes. Because of these two classes, we may never see what would be the acid test of managerial multinationalism: an Italian as president of an American-owned multinational, for example, or a Latin American running a Dutch-owned multinational.[2]

None of this should be taken to imply that the existence of this second and inferior "class" of executives in the multinational company is of no importance. On the contrary these people make up a significant section of the native bourgeoisie in every country where multinationals operate. Their interests (jobs, salaries, bonuses, promotions) lie with the parent company; only to the extent that they serve it well and faithfully can they expect to advance and prosper. But, as we shall see, the interests of the parent company often contradict those of the countries in which they operate. It follows that while multinational corporations do not, as so often claimed, internationalize their managements, they do *de*nationalize a section of the native bourgeoisies in the countries they penetrate. This of course weakens these native bourgeoisies and makes it that much harder for them to resist demands and pressures emanating from more powerful countries.[3]

III

"Capital has its own nationality," says John Thackray in the article cited above. Absolutely true, provided we understand it correctly. The nationality of capital is not that of the nation in which it happens to be located but rather that of the people who control it. Generally speaking, this means that it is also the nationality of those who own it, but this is not necessarily so. If, for example, a German corporation borrows money from a French bank, the amount in question falls under the control of Germans and becomes part of German capital until the loan is repaid. It is thus possible in principle for capital of one nationality to capture and incorporate into itself capital of other nationalities.

But, you may ask, what difference does the nationality of capital make? Isn't capital, like money to which it is so closely related, perfectly homogeneous, and doesn't it function in exactly the same way regardless of the nationality of those who control it? These are difficult questions to which no brief answers can be adequate. But for our present purposes it will be enough to point out that capital, while it does have a quantitative dimension, is fundamentally not a thing or a substance but a *relation*. In the realm of abstract theory which postulates a single capitalist system organized in a large number of small competitive units, the relation in question is between the relatively small class which owns the means of production and the many times larger class which owns nothing and is therefore forced to sell its labor power. Capital is the means of buying labor power and means of production, which are then combined and the product sold in such a way as to replace the value used up and to add a surplus value. This surplus value is produced by the workers and appropriated by the capitalists. The capitalists are capitalists solely because of their ownership of capital, which enables them to exploit the workers. The workers are workers (proletarians) solely because they lack capital and must therefore submit to exploitation on pain of starvation.[4] Ownership of capital is therefore the right to exploit workers pure and simple. All capitalists have this right, and by virtue of it their interests *vis-à-vis* the workers are identical. Capital, in a word, is the relation of exploitation between the owning class and the working class.

In capitalist reality things are more complicated. In particular the conception of a single capitalist system organized in a large number of small competitive units, which implies a homogeneous and undivided capitalist class, is an extreme abstraction—useful as an expository and pedagogic device and approximating the actual situation in one country (Great Britain) during one period (the middle third of the nineteenth century), but requiring far-reaching modification to be applicable to the capitalist system as a whole or to any part of it over long periods of time.

In actual fact competition among capitalists has always been more or less massively obstructed by a variety of natural and man-made barriers—geography, political boundaries, particular conditions of demand and costs, etc. These barriers introduce inequalities into the ranks of capitalists (also into the ranks of workers, but this aspect does not concern us here). Some capitalists enjoy superior rights to exploit workers; more important from our present point of view, some capitalists are able (for example, through monopoly pricing) to transfer surplus value out of the pockets of other capitalists into their own. Under these conditions capital is no longer simply the generalized relation of exploitation between one class and another, though all of it has that quality. It is now split up, with some segments exercising greater power than others to exploit workers and/or power to exploit other capitalists. What was a simple relation between classes now becomes a complex of relations between classes and groups within classes. The conflict between classes remains fundamental, but it is now overlaid with a welter of other conflicts which at some times and in some places occupy the center of the historic stage.

For reasons which reach far back into the origins of capitalism, the deepest and most durable divisions within the global capitalist class have been along national lines. Capitalism did not come into the world fully formed, like Athena from the head of Zeus, but piecemeal and as the result of long and bitter struggles between the rising burghers of the cities and the feudal nobility. In these struggles it was usual for the bourgeoisie to ally itself with the kings or princes who were chronically fighting to assert their authority over their own feudal subordinates. In this way there emerged a series of national monarchical states. As capitalism developed within these national frameworks, the power of the bourgeoisies increased to the point where they were able to reduce the monarchs to the status of figureheads, leaving the capitalists in control not only of the economy but also of the whole state apparatus.

Each national bourgeoisie naturally made use of its control over the state to enhance the profitability of its capital—by measures designed to make it possible to squeeze more surplus value out of workers, by excluding foreigners from national markets, by appropriate taxation and expenditure policies, by forcing unequal treaties on weaker states, by conquering additional territory or annexing colonies, etc. Under these circumstances, it is impossible to speak of capital as qualitatively homogeneous: its power and profitability are functions not only of its magnitude but also of other specific characteristics among which nationality occupies an extremely important position.

One additional point in this connection. The very idea of a unit of capital divorced from any nationality—which, according to some apologetic theories, is what the multinational corporation is in the process of becoming—is a contradiction in terms. Capital is a fundamental part of a particular set of relations of production which, far from being natural and eternal, is historical and alterable. These relations of production, implying as they do the exploitation of some classes and groups by other classes and groups, were established through violent struggles and can be maintained in existence only through a sufficiently powerful apparatus of coercion, i.e., a state. Capital without a state is therefore unthinkable. But in the world as it is constituted today only nations have states: there is no such thing as a supranational state. It follows that to exist capital must have nationality. If, for example, the state of the nation to which it belonged were to collapse, capital would lose its indispensable protector. It would then either be incorporated into the capital of another nation, or cease to be capital, by coming under the jurisdiction of a revolutionary regime dedicated to the abolition of the entire set of relations of production of which capital is one part. Finally, capital of one nationality can operate in other nations only because all the capitalist classes maintain basically similar sets of relations of production and because they find it, on the whole, in their mutual interest to permit this kind of international movement of capital.

IV

As Marx showed—and it was certainly one of his most important contributions—it is of the very essence of capital to expand.[5] There are two basic reasons for this. First, the power and standing of the capitalist (owner or functionary of capital) is proportional to the magnitude of his capital. The way to rise in capitalist society is therefore to accumulate capital. And second, any capitalist who stands still is in danger of being wiped out. As Marx put it in a brilliant passage,

> the development of capitalist production makes it constantly necessary to keep increasing the amount of capital laid out in a given industrial undertaking, and competition makes the immanent laws of capitalist production to be felt by each individual capitalist as external coercive laws. It compels him to keep constantly extending his capital, in order to preserve it, but extend it he cannot except by means of progressive accumulation. (Kerr ed., *Capital*, Vol. 1, p. 649.)

These considerations are as valid for the corporate capitalist as for the individual capitalist of an earlier period. And they are deeply embedded in the ideology of the business world where the worship of growth has attained the standing of a secular religion.

"The only real security for this company or any other company," says the annual report of a major corporation which we have quoted in these pages before, "is through healthy, continuous, and vigorous growth. A company is just like a human being. When it stops growing, when it can't replenish itself through growth, then it starts to deteriorate. . . . There is no security where there is no opportunity for growth and development and continual improvement."[6]

In the abstract terms of Marxist economic theory, growth means that a part of the surplus value accruing to a unit of capital in one period is added to capital in the next period. The larger capital now brings in a greater amount of surplus value which permits a still larger increment of growth, and so on. Marxist theory has traditionally focused on the overall consequences for the whole economy of such behavior by the individual units of capital. What has been unduly neglected are the implications of this spiral process (capital/surplus value/added capital) for what bourgeois economics calls the theory of the firm. The following highly schematic sketch may serve to indicate lines along which fruitful work can advance.

We start—as both Marx and the classical economists did—with the firm in a competitive industry. Its output is small relative to the total, and its product is more or less indistinguishable from that of all the other firms catering to the same market. Under these circumstances each firm will produce up to the point where the cost of turning out an additional unit is equal to the market price (beyond that point cost would exceed price and hence entail a reduction of profit). This is the famous equilibrium position which in textbook economics is too often treated as the end of the subject rather than the beginning.

The profitable course for the capitalist who finds himself in this position is clearly marked: he must bring down his costs and thus increase his profit margin (it is assumed that he can sell whatever he produces at the going price, so he has no sales problem). And cost reduction normally means expanding the scale of production and introducing new and improved techniques. Those who successfully follow this course prosper and grow, while those who lag behind fall by the wayside.

This process, however, cannot continue in this way indefinitely. There comes a time when the expansion in the size of the average firm, brought about by the growth of the successful ones and the elimination of the failures, alters the situation in a fundamental way. The individual firm is no longer one small producer among many, all taking the going price as a datum to which they adjust in the most profitable manner. Instead, each firm now produces a significant proportion of the industry's total supply, and each must take into account the effect of its own output on the market price. This opens up new problems and possibilities which have been more or less adequately studied under such headings as imperfect or monopolistic competition, oligopoly, and monopoly. Here we need only point out that in addition to continuing to seek lower production costs, the rational course for every firm to follow is to get itself as nearly as possible into the position of a monopolist, either individually (through differentiating its product from those of rivals) or collectively (through acting openly or tacitly in collusion with rivals). It follows that for the purposes of theoretical analysis the appropriate assumption is that the typical firm acts like a monopolist, maximizing profits at a level of output which falls well short of the volume at which the cost of producing an additional unit equals market price. When this situation prevails in most of the important industries, capitalism has entered its monopoly stage.

From our present point of view what needs to be stressed is that in the monopoly stage, the problem of growth presents itself to the firm in a radically different light. It is no longer simply a question of progressively reducing costs and expanding output of a homogeneous product. Cost reduction of course remains as important as ever, but now the maximization of profit requires a go-slow policy with respect to the expansion of output. It follows that the monopolistic firm can no longer count on being able to grow while remaining within the confines of the industry of its origin and early development. Not that expansion within the industry is entirely precluded, but it is strictly limited by cost and demand factors which are totally unrelated to the firm's ability and hence desire to grow, that is to say, by its profitability. The monopolistic firm is therefore driven by an inner compulsion to go outside of and beyond its historical field of operations. And the strength of this compulsion is the greater the more monopolistic the firm and the greater the amount of surplus value it disposes over and wishes to capitalize.

Here, it seems to us, we have the fundamental explanation of one of the decisive phenomena of recent capitalist history: the tendency of the corporation as it gets bigger to diversify both industrially and geographically—or, in current terminology, the tendency to become on the one hand a conglomerate and on the other hand a multinational corporation. The great majority of the

200 largest nonfinancial corporations in the United States today—corporations which together account for close to half the country's industrial activity—have arrived at the stage of both conglomerateness and multinationality.

V

In the previous section the thesis was advanced that the self-expansion process of capital goes through two phases, the competitive and the monopolistic. In the competitive phase the individual firm grows by reducing costs, realizing larger profits, and investing in increased capacity to turn out a product which, being essentially indistinguishable from the products of its competitors, can always be sold at—or, more realistically, slightly under—the going market price. Somewhere along the line, as some firms prosper and grow and others lag behind and drop out, the average firm in an industry becomes so large that it must take account of the effect of its own production on market price. It then begins to function more and more like a monopolist for whom the problem of continued growth is radically transformed. Monopoly profits make possible even more rapid growth than in the past, but the need to maintain monopoly prices dictates a policy of slowing down and carefully regulating the expansion of productive capacity. From this conjunction of factors there results an irresistible drive on the part of the monopolistic firm to move outside of and beyond its historical field of operation, to penetrate new industries and new markets—in a word, to go conglomerate and multinational.

This is not to argue that the drive for investment abroad by monopolistic firms is stimulated solely by pressures emanating from the search for investment outlets for surplus funds. For example, capital will move to areas where it is feasible to exploit low wages and other cost advantages. And the monopoly stage adds yet another dimension. Under monopoly conditions in a given industry, it is usual to find not one but several dominant companies. It follows that when one of the leading firms invests in a foreign country, competing giants in the same industry are prompted to follow suit to make sure that they get their "proper" share of the local market. Furthermore, tariff barriers, patent rights, and other local conditions create circumstances in which the corporate giants find that they can best control the market in a foreign country through investment rather than mere exports.

One of the outstanding features of the giant corporation, indeed, is that it has the means to try to control the market over a large part of the world; and, for its own security and profit, it continuously strives to do so.

It is important to understand that under monopolistic conditions the axiom according to which capital always moves from low-profit to high-profit industries and regions no longer holds. Monopoly by definition impedes the free flow of capital into protected high-profit situations; and, as we have already seen, the monopolist sitting inside these bastions is careful not to invest more than the traffic will bear, while seeking outlets elsewhere for his surplus capital. It is therefore not only possible but probably quite common for capital to move in directions opposite to those indicated by traditional economic theory.[7] This fact alone is enough to knock into a cocked hat that supposedly sacrosanct tenet of bourgeois thought according to which any movement of capital in search of maximum profits automatically guarantees a more efficient allocation of resources. (There are other reasons why this idea, considered as a general proposition, is fallacious, but they do not concern us here.) Unless otherwise stated, what follows relates entirely to giant corporations which have reached the monopolistic stage and are in the process of spreading into both new industries and new geographical areas. This is the actual situation of most of the giants that dominate the U.S. economy, and it is increasingly true of the large corporations of Western Europe and Japan.

The spreading process can take two forms. The initiating corporation can establish a new enterprise in the industry or country it is entering, or it can buy up an existing enterprise. We know of no empirical studies dealing with this matter, but it is our impression that the preferred way is generally to buy up an existing enterprise. And there is a good reason for this. Establishing a foothold from scratch in a new field or new place can be costly and time-consuming, while buying one that already exists is quick and easy. In this connection it matters little whether the enterprise in question is doing well or badly; in fact, there is much to be said for a weak company since it can be acquired more cheaply. In any case, the parent corporation usually plans to reorganize the new subsidiary to conform to its own style and to make the most of the advantages which its superior size and strength confer upon it.

What are these advantages? It is usual to think of the large corporation thriving and growing because of its ability to take advantage of the economies of large-scale *production,* and of course there is considerable merit to this line of reasoning. But when it comes to expanding into new fields, the economies of scale may have little or nothing to do with success or failure. For one thing the technology of the new field may be entirely different from that of the base industry and may not lend itself to the development of mass-production methods. And for another, when a corporation sets up shop to produce its accustomed product abroad, it will deliberately tailor its techniques according to the size of the market rather than export its domestically developed mass-production methods.[8] The decisive advantages of the giant corporation lie elsewhere than in production proper. Chief among them are (not necessarily in order of importance, which will vary from case to case) the following: (1) Plenty of capital to invest and almost unlimited access to credit on favorable terms in both domestic and foreign money markets. (2) A pool of experienced managerial talent which can be deployed anywhere in the corporate empire according to need. (3) A large and effective sales apparatus which is similarly available to all units of the corporate empire. And (4) research and development facilities which can be put to work to solve all sorts of technological and marketing problems. The small independent corporation is likely to be deficient in all these respects and hence quite incapable of competing on even terms with a rival which is a subsidiary of one of the giant conglomerate multinationals. It follows that whenever one of the latter enters a new field it tends to forge ahead rapidly until it occupies a leading position along with a few other giants. At this time competitive behavior gives way to monopolistic behavior. The newly matured subsidiary begins to generate more profits than it can safely invest, with the surplus flowing back into the central pool of capital maintained by the parent company. At this time the subsidiary, which began by being an outlet for surplus capital, becomes a source of additional surplus capital and hence a spur for the corporation as a whole to find still new areas into which to expand—in short, to become still more conglomerate and multinational. Logically, this process should come to an end either with all major industries in all capitalist countries dominated by a few hundred giant corporations, or with the overthrow of capitalism on an international scale. At the moment we seem to be moving more rapidly toward the first denouement than the second. Judd Polk of the United States Council of the International Chamber of Commerce is responsible for the following estimates which, at least as far as orders of magnitude are concerned, seem quite reasonable:

> Over the past two decades international investment and its output have been growing about twice as fast as world GNP [Gross National Product]. The effect has been to produce an internationalized sector of production that is now of a very substantial order of magnitude and is continuing to grow in relation to total world output. Already it appears that almost a quarter of all production in the market world is accounted for by the output of international companies. If we look to the end of this century, envisioning the growth of world GNP to continue at its typical pace of the 1960s, and similarly the output of international investment at its typically faster rate of the 1960s we get a picture roughly estimable as follows [table omitted]. The final figure (53 per cent) shows a world economy better than half internationalized.[9]

By "internationalized" Polk of course means gobbled up by a relative handful of U.S., Western European, and Japanese multinational corporations.

As things are going now, this is the realistic prospect. It should be compared with some of the fairy stories of the apologetic literature which tend to give the impression, if they do not openly state, that the multinational corporations can be a great help to the underdeveloped countries in getting their own industries going under their own control. Thus, speaking of Latin America, P.N. Rosenstein-Rodan of M.I.T., by no means an extreme apologist for the big companies, envisages the gradual withdrawal of the multinationals from their Latin American subsidiaries. After pointing out some of the "main conflicts between the host country's and the foreign shareholders' point of view," he proceeds:

> They are serious but not insoluble, and with understanding can be reconciled. The general desirable pattern of future foreign equity investment is a partnership with eventual national majority holding. That amounts to an *ex ante* agreed-upon nationalization up to 51 percent of foreign enterprises. The consequent removal of tensions will improve the climate of investment to such an extent that foreign investors may change their hostile or hesitant attitude toward the new pattern and evolve a new symbiosis in learning to solve the problem of management in a minority holding.[10]

One might be tempted to wonder how this "new symbiosis" would help the multinational corporations to invest the vast amounts of capital which would accrue to them if 51 per cent of their foreign holdings were bought out. But this would be to miss the main point, which is that the whole direction of the *actual* policy of the multinationals is, as distinct from what Dr. Rosenstein-Rodan might like it to be, to *increase,* wherever possible up to 100 per cent, their holdings in their foreign subsidiaries. Even minority holdings by local capitalists are always a source of at least potential conflict of interest (suppose, to take an extreme case, the parent wants to close down all its operations in a particular country and move elsewhere); and of course majority holdings by local capitalists may mean loss by the parent of the crucial element of control—control over sources of raw materials, production processes, prices, and market shares—which is of the very essence and purpose of the multinational structure of the enterprise as a whole. Even when they are *forced* to accept local partners, their aim is always to manipulate local laws and politicians in such a fashion as to maintain decisive control in their own hands, while operating under a façade of partnership. For while the innate expansive drive of capital is the motor force of monopoly corporate growth, the objectives of the process—the realization of profit and the continuous renewal of expansion—can be assured only if the maximum possible degree of control over all relevant variables is guaranteed at every step of the way. The name of the game, as they like to say in the business press, is growth (on a global scale), not retrenchment; and you can be sure that the multinationals are not going to sell out (or get out)—and thereby lose the control which is so important to them—unless or until obliged to do so by *force majeure.* In the meantime, they are buying, not selling, and they are going to do their best to see that it stays that way.

VI

One of the implications of the foregoing analysis is perhaps worth spelling out. The more the giant monopolistic corporations conglomerate and multinationalize, the further removed their top managements become from any particular product or production process. The concerns of headquarters are increasingly purely financial, i.e., profit- and accumulation-oriented; while matters of production, technology, etc., are relegated to the division, subsidiary, and plant managers who are responsible for producing and even to a larger extent selling the corporation's many products. The situation is well reflected, for example, in the corporate structure of General Motors, the biggest of them all, which has its headquarters in New York, the financial center, its main U.S. plants in and around Detroit, popularly known as the automobile capital, and production, assembly, and sales subsidiaries in literally scores of states and countries all around the globe. It is doubtful if the gentlemen in New York know much more about making automobiles than most of the rest of us. But the record speaks clearly that they know a lot more about making dollars!

What this means is that the top companies in the multinational corporate empires, often pure holding companies with no operating functions whatever, are increasingly financial entities receiving and disposing over billions of dollars annually and making their decisions entirely in financial terms. (The relevant business literature is full of anecdotes and references comparing the revenues of the corporations to those of the states and nations they operate in, always tending to show the preponderance of the business entities.) They naturally have the closest relations with banks, insurance companies, and other financial institutions for whom they are by far the most important customers and business partners. As far as "control" is concerned, it is a problem which rarely arises since there are no serious conflicts of interest to interfere with a relationship of smooth cooperation, but our own guess is that, when it comes to *influence,* a General Motors or a Standard Oil can pretty well get what it wants from a Chase Manhattan or a First National City.

The multinational corporation, in brief, is the key institution of finance capital in the second half of the twentieth century; and Lenin's characterization in *Imperialism* (1917) requires little modification to fit it: "The concentration of production; the monopolies arising therefrom, the merging or coalescence of the banks with industry—such is the history of the rise of finance capital and such is the content of this term."

VII

There are of course profound conflicts of interest between multinational corporations and the foreign countries in which they operate. Most of the apologetic literature attempts to play them down as either of little importance or amenable to remedial action, but none can deny their existence. Here is a fairly comprehensive list of such conflicts, cast in the form of "six major fears" felt by the foreign countries:[11]

(1) Fear that the international corporation will take too much and leave too little. The fear is often expressed that the big foreign corporation will take away the national resources (oil, iron ore, foodstuffs, etc.), all the profits, the most able local people (hence the brain drain), and leave only the crumbs in the form of low wages, low compared to the wages the same corporations pay at home.[12]

(2) Fear that the international corporation will crush local competition and quickly achieve a monopolistic dominance of the local market if not the local economy. "Who can compete with the enormous technical resources of a giant corporation whose annual sales are more than the French national budget?"

(3) Fear of becoming dependent on foreign sources for modern technology needed for national defense, and for being competitive in world markets.

(4) Fear that the international corporation's local subsidiary will be used as an instrument of foreign policy by the government of the parent company. For example, in the case of a U.S. subsidiary, fear that the U.S. government will prohibit sales to certain markets (Red China, Cuba, North Korea, North Vietnam, etc.); or that the U.S. government will prohibit the parent from sending certain technology to the subsidiary which technology would be useful locally for national defense or for other purposes; or fear that the U.S. government will prevent the U.S. parent from sending new capital to the local subsidiary, and will require the local subsidiary to remit virtually all of its earnings home thus damaging the balance of payments of the local government.

(5) Fear that the good jobs will be given to nationals of the parent company and not to local nationals.

(6) Fear that decisions will be taken by the parent company in callous disregard for their impact on the local town, province, or even on the national economy. For example—a decision to close down a factory and put thousands of workers out of jobs.

Needless to say, none of these fears is the product of fevered imaginations; all are grounded in much bitter experience. At bottom the conflicts of interest which they reflect are related to the most fundamental characteristic of the multinational corporation, that policies for all the units in the corporate empire are formulated by a central management with a view to benefiting the whole (i.e., the parent corporation) rather than the separate parts. From the point of view of the central owners and managers, this is obviously the correct course to pursue, indeed the only possible course since there could be no other conceivable reason for putting the multinational entity together in the first place. But for the parts—and for the communities and countries in which they operate—it means that they quite literally have no interests which have to be taken into account in the formulation of their own policies. This is not the place for a catalogue of the concrete ways in which the interests of the subsidiaries, considered as separate capitalist enterprises, may be (and at one time or other actually have been) overridden by the interests of the parent. But a couple of examples, taken again from a source friendly to the multinational corporations, will indicate the kind of thing that is involved.

> Every sovereign [nation] is aware that a multinational corporate group which is able to provide export markets for the product of the host country is also capable of withholding such markets and cutting off the jobs that depend on such exports. If Nigeria should eventually become a lower cost producer of widgets than Italy, the corporate group may shift the locus of its operations out of Italy into Nigeria.
>
> Along similar lines, a multinational group that can provide foreign capital to the host government's economy is also thought capable of draining capital away for use elsewhere; hence the perennial accusations of "decapitalization" with which foreign investors are confronted in Latin America.[13]

This last paragraph points to the ultimate conflict of interest between the multinational corporation and the host country. As Paul Baran so eloquently demonstrated, the key to a country's economic development lies in the size and utilization of its surplus. We see now that to the extent that its economy is penetrated by multinational corporations, control over *both* size and utilization passes into the hands of others who are owners or functionaries of capital of a different nationality. Under these circumstances it can be said that multinational corporations are the enemy, perhaps not of *any* development in the host countries but at least of any development which conforms to the interests of any class or group within the country other than those who have been denationalized and coopted into the service of foreign capital.

VIII

The conflicts of interest between multinational corporations and the foreign countries in which they operate generate many-sided political struggles, particularly in the underdeveloped countries where the relative weight of the multinationals is greatest. Here the local bourgeoisies tend to be split and largely incapable of independent action or initiative. An important section works, directly or indirectly, for foreign capital; and much of the remainder is paralyzed by fear of social revolution. Hence the political stance of the local bourgeoisie is generally pro-imperialist and reactionary. Its rule is therefore naturally favored by the countries in which the multinationals have their head-quarters. For practical purposes this means that the chief backer of local bourgeoisies in the underdeveloped countries is the United States, since the great majority of multinationals are U.S. companies. To quote Raymond Vernon again:

> The overwhelming preponderance of these [multinational corporate] groups are headed by a corporate parent of U.S. nationality, and the vast majority of the parent organizations are owned principally by stockholders who are residents of the United States. If one were to list every large U.S. corporation that owns and controls producing facilities in half a dozen or more countries abroad, the roster would contain about 200 names.
> To be sure, a European list of the same sort would include the familiar long-standing names of Unilever, Bowaters, Philips, Olivetti, Nestlé, Ciba, Pechiney, and a few others. But the European list would be considerably shorter, covering only 30 or so cases. And the overseas stakes of the companies on such a roster would not be as much as one fifth of the U.S. commitment.[14]

To complete the picture on the U.S. side, we need only remind ourselves that the government of the United States is controlled by the very same corporations which have spread their tentacles out to every corner of the globe. This is of course not recognized by U.S. political "science," but it is well known, if not often proclaimed, by those who are directly concerned with the business of government. This was refreshingly admitted on a recent television program [Dick Cavett Show, ABC-TV, August 25, 1969] by a high government official, Mr. Nicholas Johnson, a member of the Federal Communications Commission:

> I think basically you have to start with a realization that the country is principally run by big business for the rich. Maybe you have to live in Washington to know that and maybe everyone in the country knows it intuitively; I don't know, but a government of the people, by the people, and

for the people, has become, I think, a government of the people, certainly, but by the corporations and for the rich.

As actual or potential opposition to the local bourgeoisies and their U.S. backers there are various classes and strata in the underdeveloped countries: peasants and workers, petty bourgeoisie, students and intellectuals, some members of the military. Short of making a revolution, which is their ultimate threat and must sooner or later become their goal, the peasants and workers are largely excluded from the political arena, though some elements from these classes may lend support to nationalistic regimes based primarily on the petty bourgeoisie and led by intellectuals and military people. The objective of such regimes, or of those trying to form such regimes, is not to dispossess or oust the multinational corporations, which would involve a life-and-death struggle against imperialism, but to reduce their scope, to limit their freedom of action, and, by applying various economic and political pressures, to force them to operate more in the national interest than they would if left to their own devices. A good example of such a regime is the military dictatorship which seized power in Peru earlier this year. Among its first acts was the taking over of the properties of the International Petroleum Corporation, a subsidiary of Standard of New Jersey, which had been embroiled in a quarrel over taxes with Peruvian governments for more than half a century and in the process had become the chief target of Peruvian nationalism.[15] The regime also embarked on a land reform which impinges on the interests of another multinational, W. R. Grace & Co. But at the same time it has made clear that it intends no large-scale attacks on foreign capital, though the threat (from foreign capital's point of view) always exists that the situation will get out of hand and the regime, or a more radical one that might follow it, will plunge ahead with an all-out nationalization program.

Against this background it can be seen that for the multinational corporation a world of nations is a world full of pitfalls and dangers. Their most fundamental requirement is freedom to do business wherever and whenever they choose, unrestrained by any external authority. In the words of the Business International document quoted above:

> International corporations need the freedom to move capital, materials, technology, and technicians whenever and wherever needed to maximize the growth, competitive strength, and profits of the enterprise. They need the

freedom to make decisions on economic grounds. It is an imperative requirement that they be free to respond to competition, to new opportunities and threats, to pressures from consumers, workers, and investors.

But nations cannot grant these sweeping freedoms without denying their essence as nations, i.e., as collectivities with pretensions to sovereignty, which means simply the right to run their own affairs without interference from those outside the nation. Multinational corporations and nations are therefore fundamentally and irrevocably opposed to each other. The logic of each, carried to its final conclusion, is to destroy the other. Or, to put the point differently, the historic course of the global capitalist system is leading to one of two outcomes: world empire or world revolution.

The *nationalism* of the countries in which the multinationals have their seats is *antinationalism* as far as the rest of the world is concerned.[16] This profound antinationalism, not surprisingly, is ideologically transmuted into the purest and most virtuous *internationalism.* Listen to Business International rhapsodize about the aims and ideals of its clients:

> Utopia for an international corporation would be world government. A world without frontiers. Absolute freedom of movement of people, goods, ideas, services, and money to and from anywhere. No armies, navies, or air forces, only local police. A single global system of patents and trade-marks, of building and safety codes, of food and drug regulations. A single, global currency. A single central bank.
> Nation states would have the same relationship to a world government that the states of the United States have toward Washington, or the cantons of Switzerland have toward Berne [in other words, they would cease to exist as nation states]. Obviously the words "balance of payments" would be found only in history books concerning the savage days before humans learned to live peacefully on the same planet.[17]

"But," the authors lament, "Utopia won't come soon." And while they are less than clear, perhaps on purpose, about what that means, the same cannot be said about the main instrument of the multinational corporations in the world today, the U.S. government. For it shows by its actions, more eloquent than any words, what is considered the only possible substitute for Utopia. Actions, above all, in Vietnam but also in Cuba and Africa and South America and, yes, even in Europe. If it can't achieve a world of states on the U.S. pattern, at least it is determined to do its damnedest to achieve a world of obedient satellites.

Notes

[1] Three leading examples of this literature are the following: (1) Judd Polk et al., *U.S. Production Abroad and the Balance of Payments*, National Industrial Conference Board, New York, 1966. Polk, Economist and Acting President of the United States Council of the International Chamber of Commerce, has continued to produce studies and staff memoranda dealing with foreign investment. (2) Raymond Vernon, "Multinational Enterprise and National Sovereignty," *Harvard Business Review* (March-April 1967). Vernon is Professor of International Trade and Investment at the Harvard Business School and is heading a large-scale Ford Foundation-financed study of the subject of this paper, which is described as an "interim report." (3) Charles P. Kindleberger, *American Business Abroad: Six Lectures on Direct Investment* (Yale University Press, New Haven, 1969). Kindleberger is a professor of economics at M.I.T. whose *International Economics* is perhaps the leading academic textbook in its field. From the footnotes in *American Business Abroad* a useful bibliography can be constructed for further study.

[2] John Thackray, "Not So Multinational, After All," *Interplay* (November 1968), p. 23. (This article forms part of a symposium under the general title "The Multinational Corporation: The Splendors and Miseries of Bigness.")

[3] The section of the native bourgeoisie which identifies its interests with foreign companies rather than with its own class and nation is not limited to those in the direct employ of the foreign companies. It also includes a variety of others such as suppliers, subcontractors, lawyers, etc., who depend on the foreign subsidiaries for the major part of their incomes.

[4] This theme of course runs like a red thread through the entire body of Marxist literature on capitalism. Nowhere is it more powerfully expounded and illustrated than in the last part of the first volume of *Capital* entitled "The So-Called Primitive Accumulation" (Kerr ed., *Capital*, Vol. 1, Part VIII. It should be noted that the division into parts, chapters, and sections is not the same in all editions of *Capital*.) It seems to us that whoever undertakes to study *Capital* would do well to begin with this part before reading Chapter 1 on "Commodities and Money."

[5] See especially, Kerr ed., *Capital*, Vol. 1, Part II, Chapter 4; and Part VII, Chapter 24, Section 3.

[6] From the 1965 annual report of Rockwell-Standard Corporation, since merged with North American Aviation to form North American Rockwell Corporation.

[7] A study of the U.S. automobile industry would provide striking confirmation of these observations. On the one hand it is one of the most highly monopolized and profitable industries in the United States, and on the other hand the Big Three which dominate it are continuous and heavy investors in other industries and abroad.

[8] In an important article Leo Fenster, a veteran member of the United Automobile Workers Union, has shown that for their low-volume Latin American plants the U.S. auto giants design and utilize brand new low-productivity machinery and equipment. ("The Mexican Auto Swindle," *The Nation*, June 2, 1969.)

[9] Judd Polk, "The Internationalization of Production," mimeographed, issued by the U.S. Council, International Chamber of Commerce, May 7, 1969.

[10] Inter-American Development Bank, *Multinational Investment in the Economic Development and Integration of Latin America*, Round Table, Bogota, Colombia, April 1968, p. 78.

[11] "The International Corporation and the Nation State," prepared by Business International, New York, May 1968 (mimeographed).

12 A classic example of the reality underlying this fear—the rape of Cyprus by Cyprus Mines Corporation, a Los Angeles-based multinational—was analyzed in these pages a few years ago. See "Foreign Investment," Review of the Month, *Monthly Review,* January 1965.

13 Raymond Vernon, "Multinational Enterprise and National Sovereignty," *Harvard Business Review* (March-April 1967), p. 163.

14 *Ibid.,* p. 158.

15 For the background of the IPC dispute, see Harvey O'Connor, *World Crisis in Oil, Monthly Review* Press, 1962, Chapter 17 ("Peru: Standard's Province").

16 It is interesting to note that Charles Kindleberger, one of the multinational corporations' best friends in the academic community, actually calls himself an "antinationalist." See his *American Business Abroad: Six Lectures on Direct Investment* (Yale University Press, 1969), p. 144.

17 *Op. cit.*

7

WILLIAM APPLEMAN WILLIAMS

The Vicious Circle of American Imperialism

Modern American imperialism is usually treated as an urban phenomenon. It is analyzed and interpreted as a manifestation of the general drive, among mature industrial countries, for markets for manufactured goods and surplus capital, for raw materials, and for military bases to secure the empire. The evidence supports this view so far as the twentieth century is concerned. And it is likewise apparent that the men who *directed* America's first outward push between 1895 and 1901 acted upon an industrial conception of the economy and its needs.

The weakness of this account is that it ignores a great body of information and the great majority of the population. Once generally accepted, that is to say, the interpretation blocked off a vast preserve of facts: if imperialism was industrial, there was *ipso facto* no need to look at agriculture. The population could not so easily be ignored, however, and hence three general explanations

have been offered to explain why the people supported imperialism.

Radicals and some conservatives argued that the industrial elite
had the power, including control of mass media, to do as they
wished. The majority was ignored when possible and manipulated
when necessary. Most liberals and conservatives concluded that the
majority supported expansion for reasons of humanitarianism and
patriotism, thus entering their ideological caveats against the Hob-
son-Lenin interpretation as they resolved the intellectual problem
involving the majority of the population. The more sophisticated
liberals and conservatives ultimately explained the action of the
majority in psychological terms. The majority opted for imperialism because it was composed of paranoiacs, other pathological
sub-groups, and neurotics who, through the transfer process, dealt
with their domestic frustrations by becoming imperialists.

The only trouble with all these answers is that they are theoretically crude and factually wrong. But two facts, combined with
considerable research, make it possible to offer a closer approxi-
mation to reality. The first fact is a straightforward positivistic bit
of data: the majority of the American population was agricultural
during the period when the country embraced imperialism. Rural
population in 1870 was 28.7 million as compared with 9.9 million
urban; and in 1900 the figures were 45.8 rural and 30.2 urban.

The second fact is theoretical, first seen by Adam Smith: this
rural majority existed in an *internal* colonial relationship *vis-à-vis*
the domestic American metropolis (and the larger Western European metropolis of which New York is a part).

Hence the problem is defined as delineating the way that the
internal colonial majority came either to accept or acquiesce in
imperialism. And the answer lies in understanding that the domestic colonial majority embraced overseas economic expansion as the
best way of improving its relative and absolute position within the
system.

The reason for this is that the domestic colonials were commercial farmers. They did not go on the land to escape the marketplace and live a life of quiet contemplation. They turned the sod
and chopped the cotton to win a healthy share of marketplace
rewards. They intended to be, and they were, men of the marketplace. And they knew that, in order to improve their position,
they had to have either (1) a domestic market capable of absorbing their vast production, (2) a foreign market sufficient unto
their surpluses, or (3) a willingness to change their existing outlook and embrace some form of socialism.

A few of them did move toward socialism. And a good many advocated various reforms of the domestic marketplace. But the vast majority, including the reformers, turned to an expansion of the overseas market as a way of solving their problems. Hence the key to America's external imperialism lies in the way that the dynamic process of internal imperialism, through which the metropolis ruled and shaped the colonial territories south of the Potomac and west of the Appalachians (and the agriculture areas of the northeast itself), ultimately united the domestic colonials and their masters in an imperial outlook and policy that generated a drive for economic supremacy of the world.

It is textbook knowledge, of course, that the Southern cotton producer depended upon the foreign market prior to the Civil War. But it is equally important to realize that Northern and Western farmers were beginning, during the 1850's, to need the same market for their surpluses. The Civil War dramatized this in three ways. They lost their Southern consumers. They parlayed technology and westward expansion into a still greater surplus, and they became accustomed to selling that surplus in the overseas market. The Eastern dairy farmer, as well as the Western sodbuster, came to depend on the export market to provide the crucial differential between subsistence or failure, and entrepreneurial success.

This orientation toward overseas market expansion was reinforced and generalized during the years of reconstruction and the depression of the 1870's. Farmers felt the peacetime pinch within two years, and the birth of the Grange in 1867 documented the persistence of difficulties that increasingly affected more colonials in all regions. As a devasted and occupied society, the South had great difficulty reestablishing its prewar production and market position. In contrast, the Westerners suffered the consequences of their wartime boom. Their good fortune attracted new settlers and more developmental capital and those factors, added to their existing capacity, pushed output even higher. The surplus could not be absorbed even by the restored Southern market and the enlarged requirements of the metropolis, and hence they intensified their efforts to hold and enlarge their foreign markets. And to complicate their problems, they began to export cattle and dressed beef, and to extend their production of pork products.

This pattern of economic development guided the politics of the West and the South between 1865 and 1877. Cattlemen turned to the government for aid in blocking the importation of diseased animals that would ruin their herds and in turn block their exports as well as domestic sales. The Texas Grange launched a campaign for reciprocity treaties to open new markets that preceded comparable efforts by industrial and business groups in the metropolis by at least a decade. The more general agitation led by Grangers for the regulation of railroads, and the improvement of water transportation, was predicated upon the need to improve the competitive position of the colonials in the export market and to win a larger share of the existing return from that market.

These problems led to an increasing awareness of the limits imposed by England's control of the international cereal and cotton markets, and to a blunt confrontation with Britain's imperial economic power in alternate markets around the world. Southerners led the rising agitation by the agrarians for a merchant marine and an Isthmian canal built and controlled by the United States. And from the very outset the campaign by Westerners and Southerners to remonetize silver was predicated as much upon a drive to weaken Britain's world economic power, to penetrate markets dominated by Great Britain, and to enter new markets, as by a concern to increase the money supply at home.

The related aspects of this increasing involvement of the colonials with export markets were equally important. Business, financial, and political leadership in the metropolis recognized (as did the colonials) that the exports of the South and the West were paying the costs of the war, meeting the current balance of payments demands incurred by the metropolis, and rapidly providing the entire economy with a regular net credit in its dealings with the rest of the world. The vaunted turn of the trade balance was the work of the colonials, not the metropolis.

This consciousness of the role and importance of exports in the macroeconomic sense was parallelled and reinforced by a similar, if slower and less general, experience in the microeconomic sphere. Individual entrepreneurs, especially cotton textile manufacturers, turned to foreign markets as a way to survive the depression of the 1870's. The Southern mills, which concentrated from the outset on crude, rough fabrics for the export market, rapidly joined the cotton producers in demanding government action in behalf of market expansion. And the intellectual and political leaders of the metropolis responded to the example provided by the colonials by beginning to generalize that experience to the entire economy, and by concerning themselves with the demands from the Westerners and Southerners for a foreign policy geared to an expansion of the marketplace.

All these patterns of thought and action were reinforced and extended, and in turn generated further consequences, as a result of the export bonanza between 1876 and 1883. On the European side, there was the vast market created by five years of miserable weather, crop and animal diseases, and an increasing population. On the American side, there was the combination of an already sizable crop surplus further increased by immigration and internal migration, railroad expansion, and improved machinery. The result was a fantastic boom in food exports. And, during the same years, the Southerners finally reached and surpassed their prewar cotton production.

This export boom not only pulled the entire economy out of the depression, but it prompted further investments in land, improvements, and transportation, and in the associated processing industries which further increased production. The experience also served to confirm the Southern and Western colonials in their existing belief that agriculture was the foundation of all economic development and thereby reinforced their determination to obtain an equitable share of such progress.

In a similar way, the export bonanza verified the previous experience and analysis which had led the colonials to emphasize market expansion as the solution to their problems. Nor was it simply the field hands who reacted in that fashion. Thinking and acting within the framework of their cotton culture, Southerners increasingly invested capital in mills to produce rough textiles for export, and obtained funds from the North in greater quantities for the same purpose. Meat processors like Nelson Morris and Gustavus Swift launched major drives to penetrate foreign markets. Cattlemen began to pay more attention to overseas markets for beef on the hoof. And the flour companies, including those on the Pacific Coast as well as those in Wisconsin and Minnesota, intensified their efforts, first launched in 1877, to extend their foreign sales.

Watching the statistics, and evaluating the evidence, metropolitan businessmen and intellectuals increasingly devoted more attention to the fortunes of commodity and food exports, and to the relevance of that pattern for their own operations. Politicians began to act within the framework of that new metropolitan concern for market expansion as well as to respond to the colonial agitation and pressure for the same objective. Presidents James Garfield and Chester Arthur, and Secretaries of State James Blaine and Frederick Frelinghuysen, were clearly aware of what was happening; and they approached the issues of diplomacy with one eye on the general expansionist needs of the system dominated by the metropolis, and the other eye on the political consequences of failing to satisfy the demands of the colonials.

The collapse of the export boom made it very difficult to meet those demands and, at the same time, increased the pressures to provide such solutions. The end of the bonanza was caused by two factors: the recovery of European productivity, and the artificial barriers thrown up by European countries against American exports. *The colonials, not the metropolitan manufacturers or bankers, alerted the rest of the world to the challenge and the dangers of the rising power of the American economy.* Great Britain, Germany, France, and other nations retaliated with tariffs, restrictions, and even embargoes against Western commodities that jarred their economic structures and produced serious political and social dissatisfaction and even unrest. Paradoxical as it might appear, the Westerners who were colonials at home had begun to function as overseas economic expansionists who penetrated and changed foreign societies. It gave them a sense of power, and a growing conviction that America could expand without serious difficulties.

These Westerners, including the associated processors of meat and wheat, reacted to the end of the boom and the retaliation in several interrelated and mutually reinforcing patterns. They defined the European powers as enemies because they blocked existing markets and thwarted the drive for alternate markets. Great Britain was considered the chief offender in this respect, but France and Germany were seen as significant and increasingly dangerous opponents. On a broader level, the entire agricultural community saw the imperial expansion of European powers as an extension of their existing opposition to American exports, and as a swelling of their power in the world marketplace.

The fundamental connection made by Southern and Western colonials, both philosophically and psychologically, between the free marketplace and free political and social institutions was likewise applied to world affairs. European infringement upon the free marketplace was not only seen as proof of their domestic autocracy, but also—and in an increasingly important sense—as a growing threat to American freedom. And, in order to preserve and extend their own freedom in the market, which underpinned their political freedom, the colonials increasingly concluded that they had to oppose European expansion while enlarging the American marketplace.

This drive for new and alternate markets was intimately associated with the campaign for the remonetization of silver. On the one hand, Germany and France (and the Latin Union in general) were attacked for demonetizing silver and thus reinforcing Britain's power in the world economic system. For the gold standard was seen as the keystone in England's economic empire. On the other hand, the remonetization of silver was viewed as the way to break London's power. It would destroy England's special and profitable relationship with India, which was considered crucial in the commodity marketplace, and at the same time enable American exporters to deal directly with the silver-using countries of Latin America and Asia. This aspect of the colonial agitation for silver was just as important to the Westerners and Southerners as their concern to increase the money supply. It became a central part of their debate with the goldbugs and illustrates how, from a very early date, the argument concerned the best *means* of economic expansion rather than the issue of whether such expansion was desirable.

The early support by colonials for a merchant marine evolved into active approval of a modern navy. Their early emphasis on commerce destroyers, and on developing the necessary technology on a national basis before undertaking a battle fleet, did not mean they were against a navy. For that matter, the Navy's own building plan called for a very similar escalation in the nature and the size of the fleet, and for mastering the construction problems prior to laying down the keels of any battleships. The crucial point about the role of the colonials in connection with the navy is that their overseas economic activity played a central role in redefining the perimeter of America's strategic security. Their involvement in the world marketplace was vital in transforming the problem from one of continental defense into one of maintaining and extending an American position in a world economic system.

By the end of the 1880's, therefore, the colonials had exerted great influence on American thinking and feeling about foreign policy. Furthermore, they played a key role in the vigorous diplomacy pursued by the administration of President Benjamin Harrison between 1889 and 1893. They exerted direct and militant pressure for action against European market restrictions, and to open alternate markets. Their general dissatisfaction with metropolitan leadership created a serious political problem for the Republicans in particular, and both Harrison and Blaine saw foreign policy as a way to meet that challenge. And through the continuing example they provided, the agrarians steadily. influenced metropolitan thinking about overseas economic expansion.

Blaine was of course concerned with such expansion for industry, and for the economy as a whole, as well as for the colonials; but his fight for reciprocity treaties in 1889-1890 cannot be understood save in the context of this colonial pressure. He had originally formulated his broad policy on the basis of the agrarian example, and his specific campaign in 1890 was clearly a move to keep the Western colonials in the Republican Party as well as a drive for economic expansion in the general sense. In the process of providing the support Blaine needed, moreover, the colonials convinced William McKinley that the time had come to shift his emphasis away from pure protection toward a concern with overseas markets.

It is simply wrong to assert either that the Populists (and associated agrarian protestors) opposed such overseas economic expansion or that they turned abroad only as psychological compensation for their defeat in the election of 1896. Jeremiah Simpson of Kansas, for example, was a vigorous market expansionist who advocated free trade and silver remonetization as means to that end, and who wanted the canal dug and the merchant marine restored to its former place of dominance in world shipping. And when he was confronted with the contradiction between his free trade market expansionism modeled on the British example, and his opposition to a big navy, he admitted that America would have to build such a fleet. When the frontier was gone, he acknowledged, a battle line would become a necessity. In the meantime, moreover, he supported the construction of commerce raiders and other new ships of the intermediate class.

Senator William V. Allen of Nebraska (as well as other Populists in the upper chamber) likewise supported expansion. Allen told his colleagues bluntly that the people of the country wanted more markets and a more forceful and vigorous foreign policy, and that he supported and would act upon that analysis and feeling. When the Hawaiian Revolution offered such an opportunity, Allen stood shoulder to shoulder with Henry Cabot Lodge in demanding that the fleet be used to keep the islands under the control of the United States.

Allen was primarily concerned to establish and maintain access to the world marketplace, and to keep the marketplace itself open and competitive, so that America's great economic power could triumph within that framework. He agreed with Tom Watson that, given such conditions, the American producer could knock the hind sights off any rival. Allen realized that the old territorial colonialism was irrelevant to, if not actually subversive of, the most effective kind of market expansion. For that reason he opposed the acquisition of real estate unless it was absolutely required to establish and maintain America's position in the marketplace.

Allen's differences with other expansionists over whether Hawaii had to be annexed typified the position of the Southerners and Westerners during the entire foreign policy debate of the 1890's. They were generally against taking title to overseas territories, but they were vigorous and militant market expansionists. Allen and other colonials argued among themselves, and with metropolitan expansionists, over the means most appropriate to their common objective, but they did not oppose the creation of an overseas economic empire.

Metropolitan leaders moved rapidly during the 1890's to accept and adopt the outlook and the policy that the colonials had advocated and practiced for more than twenty years. Much of this shift was generated within the metropolitan sector itself by businessmen who needed markets, by politicians who responded to those pressures, and by intellectuals who supplied various arguments (and pressure) for such expansion. And, since the metropolis controlled the central levers of power in the system, such metropolitan leaders came increasingly to formulate and implement the expansionist policy. The diplomacy of the 1890's was conducted by metropolitan leaders, and it was finally and formally cast in terms of industrial rather than agricultural market expansion.

But none of this alters the primary role of the agrarian and colonial sector in evolving the expansionist policy per se. It was their overseas economic expansion, and their agitation in connection with that activity and policy, that defined the problem and the solution. And none of it should be allowed to obscure the continuing and important part played by the colonials during the 1890's in turning the United States into a vigorous imperial competitor in the world marketplace. They sustained their vigorous agitation for such expansion. They made significant contributions to the debate over strategy and tactics. And they were largely responsible for merging economic nationalism with the ideology of political freedom.

For better or worse, the colonials played a major part in combining economics and politics into the heady and explosive brew of expansion for freedom. As early as the 1870's the colonials had defined the world marketplace as part of the frontier which gave them freedom and prosperity, and by the 1890's their demands for sustained and effective action to extend that frontier reached a crescendo. But they were neither unique nor pathological in speaking about empire in terms of freedom. They believed in the inter-relationship between expansion and freedom because their conception of expansion and empire could be demonstrated to offer better conditions than European colonialism, as well as because it could be demonstrated that more markets improved their welfare at home.

They were not flailing about in an irrational response to industrialization, or to their defeat in the election of 1896. They were merely acting on the assumptions of classical marketplace capitalism, and on the basis of an argument concerning its relationship to free and representative government, and they were infused with the kind of nationalistic ardor produced by their competitive experiences in the world marketplace.

Given the assumptions and the practice of the capitalist marketplace, these results can hardly be described as surprising or unusual. And if anything was pathological, it was the system itself rather than one element within it. But accepting what happened with the colonials as part of American history will help provide a more accurate picture of American development in the twentieth century, and of the nation's present predicament. For many present-day attitudes about world affairs derive rather clearly from the attitudes and views that were evolved, agitated, and acted upon by the people of the colonial sector between 1865 and 1901. Such acceptance may also help those who view those American colonials as creators of a tradition appropriate to the contemporary crisis. For it might at the very least suggest that the problem is not so much to find an American tradition as it is to change a set of American assumptions shared by that tradition.

8

HARRY MAGDOFF

Militarism and Imperialism

Peace reigns supreme in the realm of neo-classical economics. War, militarism, and the pacification of natives are treated as merely elements which disturb the harmonious equilibrium models which are to supply us with the universal truths about the allocation of scarce resources.

One of the distinguishing features of Marxist thought, on the other hand, is the conviction that economic processes must be understood as part of a social organism in which political force plays a leading role and in which war is at least as typical as peace. In this context, militarism and imperialism are seen as major determinants of the form and direction of technological change, of the allocation of resources between countries (notably, between rich and poor countries). Accordingly, price and income relations, treated as the ultimate yardsticks of economic efficiency and social justice in neo-classical economics, are viewed, in the Marxist

128   Harry Magdoff

context, as evolutionary products of capitalist institutions in which political force and "pure" economics are intertwined. Rosa Luxemburg put the Marxist case this way:

> Bourgeois liberal theory takes into account only [one aspect of economic development]: the realm of "peaceful competition," the marvels of technology and pure commodity exchange; it separates it strictly from the other aspect: the realm of capital's blustering violence which is regarded as more or less incidental to foreign policy and quite independent of the economic sphere of capital.
> In reality, political power is nothing but a vehicle for the economic process. The conditions for the reproduction of capital provide the organic link between these two aspects of the accumulation of capital. The historical career of capitalism can be appreciated only by taking them together.[1]

The facts of U.S. history provide eloquent testimony to the accuracy of this diagnosis. Thus, Professor Quincy Wright, who directed a major study of war under the auspices of Chicago University, observed in 1942: "The United States, which has, perhaps somewhat unjustifiably, prided itself on its peacefulness, has had only twenty years during its entire history when its army or navy has not been in active operation some days, somewhere."[2]

Professor Wright identifies years of peace as those in which no action of any sort occurred. A more revealing picture is obtained if we measure months of war against months of peace and bring the information up to the present. Adding up the months during which U.S. military forces were engaged in action—starting from the Revolutionary War and including wars against the Indians, punitive expeditions to Latin America and Asia, as well as major wars—we find that the United States was engaged in warlike activity during three-fourths of its history, in 1782 of the last 2340 months.[3] In other words, on the average, there have been three full years in which our armed forces have been engaged in action for every full year of peace. This comparison does not indicate the full extent of the use of military power by the United States to enforce its will. For example, it does not include activities such as those formerly conducted by U.S. gunboats in a "constant patrol in the Yangtze River . . . from the mouth of the river up nearly 2,000 miles into the very heart of China."[4]

It should therefore come as no surprise to discover that war-related expenditures have constituted the dominant sector of the federal budget throughout our history. Omitting the years of the Second World War and the postwar period, where the record is so well known, a tabulation of federal expenditures by decade, from 1800 to 1939, for army, navy, veterans' compensation and pensions, and interest on the debt—prior to the New Deal federal debt incurred was primarily a result of war spending—shows that except for one decade, at least 54 per cent of federal expenditures were for military activities or preparations during the decade or to meet obligations arising from previous military activity.[5] The one exception was the decade of the great depression (1930-1939) when the percentage dropped to somewhat below 40 per cent. In seven of the fourteen decades the war-related share of the federal budget was 70 per cent or more.

This almost continuous preoccupation with military affairs was clearly not inspired by fears of invading barbarians. Of course, the competing colonial and commercial interests of France, England, Spain, and Russia were part of the reality in which the infant and adolescent United States had to operate. At times, self-defense had to be considered. Moreover, resolution of internal tensions, as in the Civil War, exercised a major influence on military aspects of U.S. life. All of this, however, occurred within a context of empire-building. For there has been a continuous thread in U.S. history, beginning with colonial and revolutionary days, of economic, political, and military expansionism directed towards the creation and growth of an American empire. The original expansionism, for which military investment was needed, concentrated on three main thrusts: (1) consolidation of a transcontinental nation, (2) obtaining control of the Caribbean area, and (3) achieving a major position in the Pacific Ocean.[6] It should be noted that this expansionism was not confined to what is now considered the continental territory of the United States: striving for control of the seas, as a shield and promoter of international commerce, has been an ingredient of U.S. policy from its earliest days. In fact, the struggle to incorporate the West Coast into the United States was, among other things, prompted by the desire to control Pacific Ocean ports for the Asian trade.[7]

The experience thus gained in the early stages of empire-building turned out to be most useful when the leading nations of the world entered the stage of imperialism. Several decisive and coinciding developments in the late nineteenth and early twentieth centuries mark off this new stage:

(1) The onset of significant concentration of economic power in the hands of a relatively small number of industrial and

financial giants in advanced nations. Competing interest-groups continued to exist, but now the success or failure of the advanced economies became closely identified with the prosperity of the new giant corporations whose *modus operandi* required control over international sources of supply and markets.

(2) The decline of Great Britain's monopoly position as world trader and world banker. The burgeoning competitive industrial powers—notably, Germany, France, the United States, and Japan—pressed for a reshuffle of established trade relations and a redistribution of world markets.

(3) Industrialization and new naval technology enabled competitive nations to build up their own naval strength to the point where Great Britain could no longer maintain unilateral control over the major sea lanes. As Quincy Wright put it in the study already referred to, "Naval inventions and the spread of industrialization had ended the *pax Britannica.*"[8] Control over sea routes also involved establishing military bases where naval units could be refueled and repaired. The availability of decisive mobile military power on the one hand required acquisition of strategic foreign territory to support bases, and on the other hand provided the means for aggressive pursuit of colonial possessions.

(4) The earliest stage of the new imperialism engendered a race by the major powers for control of available foreign real estate. According to Theodore Ropp, after 1880 "every great power except Austria-Hungary . . . became involved in . . . active, conscious colonial expansionism . . . ."[9] Of the traditional colonial powers—the Netherlands, Portugal, Spain, Britain, France, and Russia—the last four continued to add to their holdings. (Spain, after losing Cuba and the Philippines, proceeded to conquer Spanish Morocco.) And at the same time five new powers entered the race for colonial territory: Germany, Italy, Belgium, Japan, and the United States. As for the United States, it was the Spanish-American War, of course, that placed it with both feet in *the imperialist camp. And it was success in this war, plus the subsequent pacification of the Cuban and Philippine "natives," which satisfied two long-term U.S. expansionist ambitions: a leading position in the Caribbean, broadening the highway to the rest of Latin America, and a solid base in the Pacific for a greater stake in Asian business.

As far as the United States is concerned, there have been three distinct stages in the drive to empire: (1) the period when the United States was the supplier of food and raw materials to the rest of the world, when it was an importer of capital, and when maritime commercial interests were relatively very strong; (2) the period when the United States began to compete with other industrialized nations as an exporter of manufactured goods and an exporter of capital—a time when a small number of industrial and financial giants began to dominate the economic scene; and (3) the period when the United States becomes the major, dominant capitalist economy, the largest manufacturer, foreign investor, trader, the world's banker, and the dollar becomes the key international currency.

The energy and determination with which the expansionist strategy is pursued change from time to time. In the transition from one period to another, and because of internal as well as external conditions, it appears at times as if the United States is "isolationist" and uninterested in further extension of its influence and control.[10] Yet it is especially noteworthy that the drive for business opportunities on a world scale is ever present. Even when, as in New Deal days, domestic solutions were sought for crises, the development of foreign business was high on the agenda of government and private enterprise. Given the structure of the economy, the major operating levers work in such a way as to repeatedly reassert expansionism as the dominant strategy. In this perspective, the history of the years since the end of the Second World War are far from a new departure; instead, they are a culmination of long-term tendencies which profited by and matured most readily in the environment created by the course of the last major war.

The postwar leap forward in empire-building and the transition of U.S. society to rampant militarism are associated with two phenomena: (1) the desire to resist and repress socialist nations and to defeat national liberation movements designed to release underdeveloped countries from dependence on the imperialist network, and (2) the extension of U.S. power to fill "vacuums" created by the decline of Western European and Japanese influence in Asia, Africa, and Latin America.

Combating the rise of socialism is of course not a new objective. The destruction of the Russian Revolution was a top priority of the imperialist powers beginning in 1917. In this connection, Thorstein Veblen's observations on the Versailles Treaty in his 1920 review of Keynes's *The Economic Consequence of the Peace* are most pertinent:

The events of the past months go to show that the central and most binding provision of the Treaty (and of the League) is an unrecorded clause by which the governments of the Great Powers are banded together for the suppression of Soviet Russia—unrecorded unless record of it is to be found somewhere among the secret archives of the League or of the Great Powers. Apart from this unacknowledged compact there appears to be nothing in the Treaty that has any character of stability or binding force. Of course, this compact for the reduction of Soviet Russia was not written into the text of the Treaty; it may rather be said to have been the parchment upon which the text was written.[11]

The failure of the United States to join the League of Nations reflected no slackness in its efforts to contain anti-imperialist revolutions: in Russia, these efforts took the form of armed intervention and support of anti-Bolshevik forces with food and other economic supplies; in Hungary, the manipulation of food supplies to help defeat the Bela Kun government. Surely the issue at that time was not fear of aggressive Russian or Hungarian militarism. Nor can much credit be given to political or religious idealism. The relevant motive, clearly, was recovery of territory lost to free enterprise and prevention of the spread of the contagious revolutionary disease to Western Europe and the colonies. Any such spread, it was recognized, would severely affect the stability and prosperity of the remaining capitalist nations.

Capitalism as an economic system was never confined to one nation. It was born, developed, and prospered as part of a world system. Karl Marx went so far as to claim, "The specific task of bourgeois society is the establishment of a world market, at least in outline, and of production based upon this world market."[12] One might add that it has been the specific task of imperialism to fill out this outline and establish a complex international network of trade, finance, and investment. Given this network, it follows that limitation of opportunity to trade and invest in one part of the world restricts to a greater or lesser extent the freedom of action of private enterprise in other parts of the world. The dimensions of the defense of free enterprise therefore become world-wide.

The United States had long ago accepted its destiny to open and keep open the door for trade and investment in other parts of the world. The obstacles were not only the heathens who wanted to be left alone, but the preference systems established in the colonies of the older nations. The decline of political colonialism and the weakness of the other great powers thus placed upon the United States a primary responsibility for the defense of the

capitalist system and at the same time afforded golden opportunities to obtain special beachheads and open doors for U.S.
enterprise.

With a task of this magnitude, it is little wonder that the United
States now has a larger "peacetime" war machine, covering a
greater part of the globe, than has any other nation in all of past
history. Imperialism necessarily involves militarism. Indeed, they
are twins that have fed on each other in the past, as they do now.
Yet not even at the peak of the struggle for colonies did any of the
imperialist powers, or combination of powers, maintain a war
machine of such size and such dispersion as does the United States
today. In 1937, when the arms race in preparation for the Second
World War was already under way, the per capita military
expenditures of all the great powers combined—the United States,
the British Empire, France, Japan, Germany, Italy, and the Soviet
Union—was $25. (Germany's per capita of $58.82 was then the
largest.)[13] In 1968, the per capita military expenditures of the
United States alone, in 1937 prices, was $132. This was only in
part due to the Vietnam War: in 1964, our most recent "peace"
year, the per capita military expenditures in 1937 prices was
$103.[14]

One of the reasons for this huge increase in military outlays is
no doubt the greater sophistication of weaponry. (By the same
token, it is the advanced airplane and missile technology which
makes feasible the U.S. globe-straddling military posture.) An
additional reason, of course, is the military strength of the
socialist camp. I would like to suggest a third reason: that a
substantial portion of the huge military machine, including that of
the Western European nations, is the price being paid to maintain
the imperialist network of trade and investment *in the absence of
colonialism.* The achievement of political independence by former
colonies has stimulated internal class struggles in the new states for
economic as well as political independence. Continuing the
economic dependence of these nations on the metropolitan
centers within the framework of political independence calls for,
among other things, the world-wide dispersion of U.S. military
forces and the direct military support of the local ruling classes.

Precise information on the dispersion of U.S. forces is kept an
official secret. However, retired General David M. Shoup, former
head of the Marine Corps, who should be in a position to make a
realistic estimate, stated in a recent article in *The Atlantic:* "We
maintain more than 1,517,000 Americans in uniform overseas in
119 countries. We have 8 treaties to help defend 48 nations if they

ask us to or if we choose to intervene in their affairs."[15] The main substance of U.S. overseas power, aside from its present application in Vietnam, is spread out over 429 major and 2,972 minor military bases. These bases cover 4,000 square miles in 30 foreign countries, as well as Hawaii and Alaska.[16] Backing this up, and acting as a coordinator of the lesser imperialist powers and the Third World incorporated in the imperialist network, is a massive program of military assistance. According to a recent study:

> U.S. military aid . . . since 1945 has averaged more than $2 billion per year. It rose to as much as $5 billion in fiscal year (FY) 1952 and fell to as low as $831 million in FY 1956. The number of recipient countries rose from 14 in 1950 to a peak so far of 69 in 1963. In all, some 80 countries have received a total of $50 billion in American military aid since World War II. Except for 11 hard-core communist countries and certain nations tied closely to either Britain or France, very few nations have never received military aid of one kind or another from the United States.[17]

The above factual recital by no means exhausts the international functions of U.S. militarism. Space considerations permit no more than passing reference to (a) the active promotion of commercial armament sales abroad (contributing a sizable portion of the merchandise export surplus in recent years), (b) the extensive training of foreign military personnel, and (c) the use of economic-aid funds to train local police forces for "handling mob demonstrations and counterintelligence work."[18] These are, in the main, additional instruments for maintaining adherence and loyalty of the non-socialist world to the free-enterprise system in general, and to the United States in particular.

The military forces of the politically independent underdeveloped countries frequently perform a very special function. This arises from the relative weaknesses of the competitive elite power groups: large landowners, merchants, industrialists and financiers—each with varying degrees of alliance to interest groups in the metropolitan center. When none of these ruling-class groups has the strength and resources to take the political reins in its own hands and assert its hegemony over the others, the social order is operated by means of temporary and unstable alliances. Under such circumstances, and especially when the existing order is threatened by social revolution, the military organizations become increasingly important as a focal point for the power struggle within the ruling classes and/or as the organizer of political arrangements. Space limitations do not permit a review of this special role of militarism in the underdeveloped world as, one might say, the skeletal framework of the imperialist system in the absence of colonies. It is this framework that is supported and nurtured by the practices mentioned above: military training and advisory services, the widespread military assistance programs, and the stimulus given to commercial sales of U.S. armaments.

This militarism which is working to control the rest of the world is at the same time helping to shape the nature of U.S. society. Some sense of the immensity of this impact can be obtained by noting the relevance of military spending on the employment/unemployment situation. In the first three quarters of 1969, approximately 8.3 million persons were employed as a result of the military program: 3.5 million in the armed services, 1.3 million Defense Department civilian employees, and 3.5 million engaged in producing and moving the goods purchased for the military services.[19] At the same time, there are at least 3.7 million unemployed.[20]

Consider for a moment what it would mean if 8.3 million were not engaged in military affairs. Without substitute employment, this could mean a total of over 12 million unemployed, or a 14.3 per cent rate of unemployment. The last time the United States had such a rate of unemployment was 1937. The percentage of the labor force unemployed in 1931, the second full year of the great depression, was less than 2 points higher, 15.9 per cent.[21]

So far we have not taken into account the multiplier effect. It has been estimated that for every dollar spent on national defense, another $1 to $1.40 of national product is stimulated.[22] If we accept only the lower estimate, and assume for the sake of the argument equivalent labor productivity in the military and civilian sectors, we reach a measure of unemployment in the neighborhood of 24.3 per cent, in the absence of the military budget. Compare this with the unemployment rate of 24.9 per cent at the depth of the depression in 1932.

A counter-argument can, of course, be made to these broad generalizations. Unemployment insurance, for example, would to a limited extent and for a very limited time act as an offset. Conceivably, a sharp decline in military spending, if there were no financial collapse accompanying it, would reduce interest rates and thus perhaps stimulate construction and some types of state and municipal investment. A reduction in taxes would generate consumer demand. A rise in the federal social welfare program would have its effect. But it is by no means obvious that these counteractions would have anywhere near the same impact on the economy as defense spending.

Economists are to a large measure captives of the neat models they create, and they consequently ignore strategic dynamic elements which keep the economy going. For example, they tend to underestimate, if not ignore, the special effects of persistent inflation on business practices regarding inventory accumulation and investment in plant and equipment. Even more important is the almost total neglect of the influence of stock market and real estate speculation on (a) business investment decisions, and (b) the buoyancy of the especially important luxury trades. Inflation and speculation—partners of militarism—have been key triggers of our postwar prosperity, and they are too easily ignored as economists blandly transfer a block of GNP from one category to another, as if such transfers are made in the economy as simply as one keeps accounts.

The experience of the last depression still remains a challenge to economists to come up with an explanation of the way in which the economy operates in reality. For example, consider where we stood in 1939 after ten years of depression. Personal consumption expenditures had finally climbed to a new high—6 per cent above 1929 in constant prices. Yet, at the same time, nonresidential fixed investment expenditures were 42 per cent below the level of 1929, and residential construction was 20 per cent below.[23] Despite six years of rising consumer spending, and the start of orders flowing in from France and England for rearming, the investment community was still in a state of depression, and over 17 per cent of the labor force was unemployed.

In this connection, it is important to recognize that one of the major attributes of the huge military spending in the postwar years is its concentration in the producers durable field and the stimulation it gives to the demand for machinery and equipment. If we combine the spending for producers durable goods resulting from the military with private spending for the same type of goods, we find the following: 36 per cent of the output of the producers durable goods industries is purchased directly or indirectly by the federal government.[24] (These data are for 1963, before the impact of the Vietnam War.) It is here, I suggest, that we find the unique role of military spending in raising and sustaining production and employment at new highs.

There are, to be sure, other impacts of defense spending that help to explain the magnitude and structure of the post-war economy: the unique role of research stimulated and financed by military and space programs; the special place of defense spending in nurturing the growth and prosperity of key giant industrial and financial enterprises; the support given by U.S. military power to acceptance of the U.S. dollar as an international currency;[25] the ease with which military orders can be fed into the economy in spurts which act as adrenalin injections to the private sector.

At the least, it can be concluded, economic theory and analysis which omit imperialism and militarism from their underlying paradigm are far removed from reality. More realistically, it can be said that they operate to obscure the truth about the great problems and dangers of the second half of the twentieth century.

Notes

[1] Rosa Luxemburg, *The Accumulation of Capital* (New York, 1964), pp. 452-453.

[2] Quincy Wright, *A Study of War* (Chicago, 1942), vol. I, p. 236.

[3] Calculated from list in Lawrence Dennis, *Operational Thinking for Survival* (Colorado Springs, 1969), appendix II.

[4] Office of Naval Intelligence, *The United States Navy as an Industrial Asset* (Washington, D.C., 1923), p. 4.

[5] Calculated from data in *Historical Statistics of the United States, Colonial Times to 1957* (Washington, D.C., 1961), pp. 718-719.

[6] Richard W. Van Alstyne, *The Rising American Empire* (Chicago, 1965).

[7] *Ibid.*, chap. 5, "Manifest Destiny and Empire, 1820-1870."

[8] Quincy Wright, *op. cit.*, vol. I, p. 299.

[9] Theodore Ropp, *War in the Modern World* (New York, 1962), p. 206.

[10] The isolation was usually more apparent than real. See William Appleman Williams, *The Tragedy of American Diplomacy* (New York, 1962), chap. 4, "The Legend of Isolationism."

[11] Thorstein Veblen, "The Economic Consequences of the Peace," in *Essays in Our Changing Order* (New York, 1934), p. 464.

[12] In a letter from Marx to Engels, October 8, 1858, in Karl Marx and Friedrich Engels, *Correspondence 1846-1895* (New York, 1934), p. 117.

[13] Quincy Wright, *op. cit.*, pp. 670-671.

[14] The data on military expenditures are the purchases of goods and services for "national defense" and "space research and technology" as used in computing Gross National Product. The 1964 and 1968 data are reported in the *Survey of Current Business*, July 1968 and July 1969. The adjustment for price changes was made by using the implicit price deflators for federal purchases of goods and services, as given in the *Economic Report of the President*, January 1969.

[15] General David M. Shoup, "The New American Militarism," *The Atlantic*, April 1969. The figure of 119 countries seems too large. General Shoup was probably including bases on island locations, which he counted as separate countries. Our guess is that U.S. armed forces to man bases, administer military assistance, and train foreign officers are located in 70 to 80 countries.

[16] *The New York Times*, April 9, 1969.

[17] George Thayer, *The War Business, The International Trade in Armaments* (New York, 1969), pp. 37-38. This is a summary of data presented in *Military Assistance Facts*, May 1, 1966, brought up-to-date through Fiscal Year 1968.

[18] For (a), see *ibid.* (b), see John Dunn, *Military Aid and Military Elites: The Political Potential of American Training and Technical Assistance Programs* (Unpublished Ph.D. dissertation, Princeton University, 1961). (c), see Edwin Lieuwen, *The United States and the Challenge to Security in Latin America* (Ohio, 1966), p. 16.

[19] Data on armed services and Defense Department civilian employment from *Defense Indicators* (Bureau of the Census), November 1969. The estimate of the number employed by private industry for military production is based on Richard P. Oliver's study, "The Employment Effect of Defense Expenditures," *Monthly Labor Review* September 1967. Mr. Oliver estimated 2.972 million employed in private industry in the fiscal year ending June 30, 1967 as a result of Defense Department expenditures. We brought this estimate up to date by (1) assuming no increase in productivity or major change in the composition of production since fiscal year 1967; (2) using the expenditure data for the first three quarters of 1969; (3) adding space research and technology and one half of Atomic Energy Commission expenditures, both of which had been excluded in Mr. Oliver's estimates; and (4) adjusting for price increases in the last two years. The resulting figure of 3.5 million is therefore a broad estimate, but the margin of error is not such as in any way to invalidate our analysis.

[20] Based on data in *Employment and Earnings* (Bureau of Labor Statistics), January to November 1969. The 3.7 million estimate represents the full-time unemployed plus the full-time equivalent of those who were working involuntarily less than a full week. This estimate does not take into account the unemployed who are not counted in the government survey.

[21] *Economic Report of the President*, January 1969 (Washington, D.C., 1969), p. 252.

[22] U.S. Arms Control and Disarmament Agency, *Economic Impacts of Disarmament* (Washington, D.C., 1962).

[23] *Economic Report of the President*, January 1969, p. 228.

[24] Calculated from tables in "Input-Output Structure of the U.S. Economy: 1963," *Survey of Current Business*, November 1969. The per cent of direct and indirect output attributable to (a) gross private fixed capital formation and (b) federal government purchases were used. These percentages were applied to the gross output of each of the industries manufacturing durable goods. It is generally estimated that 85 per cent of federal government purchases are for the military. The figure is probably higher for durable goods manufacturing industries alone.

[25] Given the inadequate U.S. gold reserves, the U.S. dollar can serve as an international currency only as long as foreign banks are willing to keep dollar credit balances in the United States as a substitute for gold payments. It is interesting that former Under Secretary of the Treasury for Monetary Affairs Robert Roosa included the military strength of the United States as a factor in maintaining the present international monetary system: "Moreover, the political stability and enormous economic and military strength of the United States have also increased the desirability of keeping balances here rather than in any other country in the world" (Robert V. Roosa, *Monetary Reform for the World Economy*, New York, 1965, p. 9.).

9

HEATHER DEAN

Scarce Resources: the Dynamic of American Imperialism

> *"That empire in Southeast Asia is the last major resource area outside the control of any one of the major powers on the globe... I believe that the condition of the Vietnamese people, and the direction in which their future may be going, are at this stage secondary, not primary."*

Senator McGee (Wyoming), U.S. Senate, February 17, 1965

FOUR THEORIES OF IMPERIALISM

Lenin's

Lenin wrote at a time when domestic markets in Europe were saturated, leading him to predict that the industrialized countries would war among themselves for overseas outlets for investment capital and for overseas markets. The Social Democrats argued that alternate solutions would be found—the crises of "over-production" would be ended by increasing domestic demand by wage increases, welfare payments, etc. Lenin dismissed with two words (under capitalism!) this notion that the greedy capitalists would give the workers money.

However, the development of capitalist economies has shown an almost limitless capacity for internal expansion. Legalized unions, welfare, public works, defense spending, planned obsolescence, space programs, consumer credit, ad-created markets and fad spending—techniques beyond the wildest dreams of the Social Democrats—lead one to suspect that the last cataclysmic convulsion of capitalism just isn't coming.

Not only have capitalist economies succeeded in expanding internally, but they have observably *not* exploited market and investment opportunities in the underdeveloped countries. The feudal economic and political structures of the Third World provide neither purchasing power nor opportunities for investment in industry and, liberal disclaimers to the contrary notwithstanding, American policies are directed at maintaining such structures. (For example, the Alliance for Progress specifically forbids use of its funds for any sort of land reform program.) There has been no effort to duplicate the European expansion sparked by investment in the industrialization of North America.

Yearly American investment overseas is approximately five per cent of domestic investment, and the major part of that is in Europe and Canada. Only two per cent of American overseas investments is in underdeveloped countries; only a negligible amount on the Asian mainland.

American investors do make a tidy sum each year on their overseas investments, and it would be naive to suppose that the corporations involved would be too altruistic to fight to maintain them. But the degree of expansion has been so limited, the profits so peripheral to the American economy, that it takes a peculiar sort of demonology to believe that they are in themselves adequate justification of the three wars and countless lesser military actions by which the United States has gained and maintained control of the Third World.

Neo-Marxist

Some modern Marxists argue that America's overseas investments are indeed negligible to the survival of the American economy, but that the domestic economic effects of imperial wars are crucial. The figures lend more weight to this argument. American investments in her domestic war industries each year are more than sixty times her investments in underdeveloped countries.

However, there is nothing magical about the kind of economic waste implied in needless war spending. Other forms of waste such as space programs are equally effective sources of investment, and many other forms would be easier to sell politically than wars against fictitious invaders.

Liberal

In response to this sort of argument, the majority of the American liberal-left denies that the Marxist theories of imperialism explain American foreign policy today, although they credit it (when they know it at all) with some degree of accuracy in interpreting the earlier part of the century. Their most common explanation of America's military domination of Asia, Africa and Latin America suggests there is *no* rational motive for it. Imperialism belongs to America's economic past; however, the ideology and bureaucracy that supported these outdated interests have a blind momentum of their own that has made them endure beyond their moment in history.

This understanding leads to a politics of petition—the Quaker "Speak Truth to Power" approach. Its analysis of American power is filled with words like "irrational fear," "blunder," "paranoia," or "fixation." So the solution is seen in effecting a change in the personal qualities of the men at the helm, running peace candidates or helping those in power see the illogic of "the system in which they are trapped."

Scarce Resources

The research for this paper was based on the premise that American policy is rational and successful. It may not be directed at *our* goals, but it is goal-directed, and the goals are not anachronisms of the American system but are essential to the maintenance of existing power relations. I have looked for this motive in that aspect of imperialism that is usually footnoted in considerations of the American economic influence in the Third World—the massive extraction of raw materials.

While not denying the existence of other economic motivations which are stressed by the Marxist left, I would argue that they are secondary to the total dependency of American production on foreign resources, that this dependency is sufficient in itself to explain U.S. policy, and that it leads to a fundamental conflict between the survival of the American economy in its present form and the drive for development in the Third World.

U.S. MATERIALS POLICY STUDIES, 1950-1960

"Has the United States of America the material means to sustain its civilization?"

In 1952, the U.S. President's Materials Policy Commission opened its report with this question. Its answer shattered forever the myth of cornucopian natural resources on the North American continent, and introduced a new alarm into the consciousness of policy makers: the U.S. depended on foreign sources for every significant industrial resource except molybdenum and magnesium.

The Commission, headed by William S. Paley, Chairman of CBS and life trustee of Columbia University, hired a phalanx of experts to predict U.S. demand for natural resources for the next 25 years, and to advise the President on legislation necessary to ensure that these resources would be available.

Its report is far from a dry compilation of statistics; its principal author seems to see himself as something of a philosopher-poet. In the introduction he reflects on the wry workings of fate which makes materials a key factor in the struggle between the Spirit of Man and the Forces of Materialism. The report concluded that the materials would not be lacking. However, it found domestic reserves adequate to meet only a small and shrinking fraction of American needs.

The Third World is expected to supply the bulk of the raw materials used by U.S. industry. In another burst of lyricism the Report details the mutual benefits to arise from this Free World division of labor. Each nation has its appointed role: that of the underdeveloped countries is to produce, that of the U.S. is to consume. (It's highly reminiscent of the speeches on peaceful coexistence that the Russians keep delivering to the Chinese.) By selling to U.S. markets, Third World nations will accumulate the capital necessary to finance their own industrialization. But this eventuality appears only in the rhetoric of the report. Their statistical projections do not allow for a significant increase in consumption of industrial raw materials in the underdeveloped countries.

In response to the Paley Report, defense stockpiling was undertaken on a massive scale to safeguard against such supply shortages as had occurred during the Korean War. Government subsidies (since largely discontinued) encouraged exploitation of inferior domestic ores in hopes of making technological breakthroughs. Government commissions were set up to give early warning of financial or political threats to foreign sources of defense materials.

Most important, and probably most successful, an organization was established with Ford Foundation money to refine and expand the work of the Paley Commission. "Resources for the Future" (RFF) was incorporated to do research, publish, and make policy recommendations. Paley was joined in its administration by such pillars of the American Establishment as George P. Brown (United Shoe Machinery, Boston Herald-Traveller Corp., First National Bank of Boston, New England Tel & Tel, Old Colony Trust Co.), Frank Pace (Time, Inc., Colgate-Palmolive, Continental Oil, Banker's Trust, Eurofund, etc.), and Laurance Rockefeller (Rockefeller Brothers Fund, Rockefeller Brothers, Inc., etc.).

The major publication of RFF is "Resources in America's Future." It is a massive collection of statistics and extrapolations that attempts to predict patterns of American consumption to the year 2000, allowing for substitutions, probable technological innovations, etc. In tone its publications seem to be one half of a debate with Rachel Carson. One feels the presence of an unseen Conservationist Lobby proposing crimps in the style of the barons of the extractive industries, many of them on the board of RFF. This report, too, concludes that the raw materials America needs will be available. But for those of us to whom "America's interests" are not the whole spectrum of concern, the means by which this conclusion was reached are ominous. The introduction warns:

> It should be pointed out clearly, however, that our conclusion that there is no general resource shortage problem for the balance of the century applies specifically to the United States; it cannot be extended automatically to other countries. In many less developed countries, especially in Asia, Africa and Latin America, population presses hard on available natural resources; for them a sustained increase in living levels can by no means be guaranteed with the assurance it can be for the United States and other more advanced industrial countries.

In plainer words, the surpluses of industrial raw materials which America expects to import from Asia, Africa, and Latin America are illusory. They would vanish from world markets if the intolerable stagnation of Third World economies were ended. To ensure their continued availability will require complete political and economic control of Third World countries—a control exercised against the most elemental interests of their populations.

THE EXTENT OF SCARCITY

In 1963, the Minerals Year Book supplied a table of figures for U.S. imports for consumption.

This gives some idea of the magnitude of U.S. reliance on other than domestic sources, but the figures are distorted in two directions. In some cases they minimize the shortage because current needs are being met by uneconomic government-subsidized exploitation of small deposits of inferior ore. In other cases, notably iron, the U.S. imports are of sufficiently high quality to compensate for shipping costs, but apart from the price differential, the U.S. has quite adequate supplies of ore.

Mineral	% of consumption imported	% of world production
Iron	22%	—
Manganese	94%	—
Chromite	100%	14%
Cobalt	98%	—
Nickel	86%	35%
Tungsten	43%	—
Copper	25%	23%
Lead	35%	—
Zinc	44%	—
Uranium	38%	—
Tin	78%	—
Aluminum	—	45%
Bauxite	85%	31%

Taken to the end of the century, the relative significance of the shortages shifts, but the overall picture is sufficiently alarming that it is certain that scarce resources are a significant determinant of government policy. The U.S. has between one per cent and ten per cent of the reserves necessary to meet demand from now to the year 2000, and will require between 50 per cent to 100 per cent or more of known reserves in the "non-Communist world" (the RFF amendent of Paley's "Free World").

All terms and statistics are drawn from the RFF report, 'Resources in America's Future':

USCD—US Cumulative Demand (total demand from 1960 to 2000), often in three projections, low, medium, high;

NCW—non-Communist world;

reserves—minerals contained in ore that can be mined with present technology (this includes ores which are not commercially feasible at current prices but which are technically easy to mine and about 50% less rich than ores currently marketable);

resources—minerals that could be mined if cost were no object, or given a technological breakthrough (such as oil in tar sands).

Electricity and steel will continue to be the irreducible basis of any advanced civilization for at least a century. The imponderables of shifts in consumption patterns, technological innovations and substitutions are held to a minimum in considering the following minerals: the ferro-alloys, and copper and aluminum, the two conductors of electricity.

Manganese is absolutely essential to the manufacture of steel; it strips it of the major impurity, sulphur. There is no possible substitute. Most of the world's reserves of manganese are in the USSR and China. There will probably be discoveries in Africa, however, which could double the figure of 185 million tons in NCW reserves.

USCD—48 million tons (low)—73 million tons (medium)—107 million tons (high)
US reserves—0.9 million tons
Total NCW demand—300 million tons (Medium projection)
Total NCW reserves—185 million tons

Tungsten has the highest melting point of any metal. It is used for high speed steels, and steels that must withstand constant friction like bits and drills. It imparts the necessary hardness to cutting tools, and is a major electrical and electronic component.

USCD—250,000 tons—460,000 tons—800,000 tons
US reserves—71,000 tons (low-grade ore)
NCW demand—1,000,000 tons
NCW reserves—320,000 tons

Molybdenum is a possible substitute for tungsten in steel.

Nickel is the single most important alloy mineral, currently used in over 3000 alloys. It gives steel strength, hardness, and resistance to corrosion or deformation at high temperatures. It is found in quantity only in Indonesia, New Caledonia, Canada and Cuba. Le Nickel of Europe (French Rothschilds) controls the New Caledonia mines, so the North American market is supplied almost entirely from Canada.

USCD—7 million tons—11.7 million tons—19.3 million tons
US reserves—0.5 million tons
NCW demand—37 million tons

NCW reserves—Canada, 6 million tons; New Caledonia, 4.6 million tons; Indonesia, 5-8 million tons total proved—11.3 million tons (+ inferred)

Chrome steels are extremely hard for their weight, and of course are resistant to corrosion.

USCD—40 million tons
US reserves—4 million tons (very inferior ore)
NCW demand—200 million tons
NCW reserves—450 million tons (estimates of reserves are tentative while exploration continues in Africa; reserves in South Africa may run from 80 to 800 million tons, in Southern Rhodesia from 175 to 200 million tons).

Cobalt is used in steels that must resist corrosion at extremely high temperatures. It is used in jets, missiles, gas turbines, and generators. Actual use has been less than the projects so far due to the political instability of the Congo.

USCD—450,000 tons (medium)—700,000 tons (high)
US reserves—45,000 tons
NCW reserves—900,000 tons plus inferred reserves in Africa

The only mineral that conducts electricity as well as copper is silver. However, a more plausible substitute is aluminum, with 60% of the conductivity of copper. Copper shortages are world-wide. Neither the USSR nor China has a potential surplus.

USCD—60 million tons—112 million tons—181 million tons
US reserves—30 million tons; US resources, 20 million tons, Canada, 9 million tons
NCW demand—500 million tons
NCW reserves—200 million tons proved; 200 million tons inferred

Although it is rare in North America, aluminum is a fairly common mineral throughout the world. One major strike was made when a farmer sent a sample of poor soil for analysis. As it is produced by electrolysis, the ore has moved to power; this is why Canada has been a leading aluminum producer. Control of major hydro-electric power projects in the third world is more critical to securing aluminum supplies than is control of the source of the ore.

USCD—140 million tons—255 million tons—480 million tons
US reserves—13 million tons (plus 98 million tons resources)
NCW demand—900 million tons (medium)
NCW reserves—800 million tons

IS THERE ENOUGH TO GO AROUND?

With approximately eight per cent of the NCW population, the United States is presently planning to reserve for her own industries and her own consumption between 50 per cent and 100 per cent of the world's mineral resources. Her assurance that these resources will be available to her use is hard to explain. Even using the figures given for NCW demand, there would appear to be a bitter competition for resources imminent. And those figures are predicated upon continuing desperate poverty for one-half of the world.

NCW demand was calculated by assuming a growth rate of consumption of industrial raw materials of between three per cent and six per cent, most of it to come from Europe. To see these figures in proper perspective, consider the past history of developing nations.

United States

Between 1867 and 1905, steel production increased an average of 25 per cent per annum. This average reflects even higher rates of increase in boom times, followed by severe depressions. After a period of stagnation, World War I sparked another surge in production of 15-20 per cent per annum.

Japan

In arming for World War II, Japan increased her steel production from 2.5 million tons in 1932 to 8 million tons in 1943. Due to deliberate occupation policy, her steel-making capacity was reduced to 3 million tons until 1949. In 1964 she produced 40 million tons—an average rate of growth over 15 years of more than ten per cent.

China

| | Production in Metric Tons | | | |
Commodity	*1952*	*1957*	*1958*	*1959*
Coal	66,000	128,000	270,000	335,000
Oil	440	1,444	2,260	3,500
Copper	10	50	70	80
Iron	4,290	15,000	30,000	45,000
Manganese	191	700	850	1,000
Aluminum	0	20	27	60
Lead	7	45	60	75
Steel	1,350	5,350	8,000	12,000

Based on the U.S. Bureau of Mines Special Supplement #25, March 1960

What surpluses of raw materials would be available to the U.S. if the U.N. undertook a development program designed to bring the Third World to the consumption level of a poor European country by the year 2000? (By which time the U.S. GNP will have quadrupled.) The obvious pattern consumption would follow, from the examples above, would be far from a stately three per cent of nothing increase per annum. For the first few years, reflecting the smallness of the base, production and consumption would increase by 50 per cent to 300 per cent per annum, and then settle to a steady ten per cent growth rate.

What will the year 2000 find in fact? Surely not the world predicted in the U.S. studies, where half the world is swept with plagues and famines as they trudge out to the mines to dig up raw materials for an American affluence of science fiction proportions! The rate of development I have hypothesized is possible. The Third World knows it. They know that the much-vaunted roads, railways and telegraphs that American money has gifted them with lead from the mines to the ports. If they refuse to accept the division of labor on American terms, there will be far too little to go around.

The U.S. represents approximately eight per cent of the "non-Communist world" population. Europe and Canada are approximately twice that. But they need the greater part of all known reserves to maintain their current level of consumption; in some cases they need more than all known reserves, as with copper and tungsten. Is the enemy the U.S. confronts really Communism—or is it in fact industrialization?

IMPLICATIONS FOR U.S. POLICY

It must be a conscious and primary aim of American foreign policy to ensure that the flow of raw materials from the Third World is never interrupted.

Imagine a situation in which pro-Peking Community Parties controlled all overseas sources of raw materials for America's steel industry. They could cripple the U.S. as an economic and military power.

But America runs the risk of political opposition from many strains of political opinion besides the Maoist. And the important conclusion to be drawn from the first part of this paper is that there are economic reasons for any honest and independent government—communist, socialist, liberal democratic or even revolutionary-right—to stop selling raw materials to the United States. An examination of all the possible contingencies that could motivate a government to cut off American supplies makes it quite clear that American dependency on foreign suppliers makes it necessary for her to maintain regimes in power that are under her total control.

First, and most vital, a country may wish to conserve its resource base for its own industrial development. It will not be impressed by arguments that the necessity of containing communism requires economic sacrifices from the underdeveloped countries.

Second, there will be competition for what surpluses they may wish to sell, and they will have no reason to hand America a monopoly of their exports. America will have to compete with capitalist and socialist Europe, and with other Third World countries. Since her competitive position will not be strong, she will probably lose open competitions. Primary producers will sell raw materials in those markets from which they can purchase back finished goods at the lowest prices. This is much more likely to be Japan, for instance, than it is the United States.

Third, there will inevitably be anti-American sentiments associated with any independence Movement, and that may provide a political motive for giving preference to non-American buyers, as a symbol of independence or an expression of a legacy of bitterness.

Fourth, there might be sanctions in protest against American foreign policy in other Third World nations. For example, an independent Asian government such as Sihanouk's in Cambodia would be unlikely to sell war material to the United States while it was engaged in a counter-insurgency war such as in Vietnam.

A military consideration makes it equally imperative, from the American viewpoint, to maintain American puppets in Asia. Any number of Asian countries are located along the shipping routes by which the U.S. obtains strategic materials. If any one of them were to collaborate with a country (guess who) with whom America was engaged in a protracted land war, it could seriously interfere with American war industry.

HOW U.S. SECURITY IS GUARANTEED

There are three dangers against which American policy-makers will guard which arise from reliance on foreign sources of raw materials: political control of strategic locations by potentially hostile regimes, trade sanctions for political reasons, and loss of supplies for economic reasons.

Tactics to forestall these eventualities are varied. The ultimate weapon of government, and perhaps the best understood one, is the military coup, instigated by the CIA and backed by the Marines or the Seventh Fleet.

Short of this, American aid to the armed forces of tottering regimes gives the U.S. *de facto* political control. When Americans train and select the armed forces' officers, and service and repair military equipment, the effective control of such an army lies outside its own territory. This amounts to occupation by proxy.

American aid also means that the capital equipment of a country—its transportation system and industries—rely on American parts, and thus the country is extremely vulnerable in the short run to sanctions.

Stock-piling of scarce resources is used to maintain political and economic orthodoxy in the poor nations, as they are too close to the verge of complete economic collapse to withstand the dislocation of suddenly losing American markets. Since their margin of survival is so slight, they have no bargaining power, even when facing what appears to be a seller's market.

A final barrier to independent development is the lack of any source of development capital that is ear-marked for the priorities of mankind, and not controlled by the handful of great, interlocking financial empires that are most rewarded by the status quo.

HOT SPOTS, OR, GOD SAVE AFRICA

If you make a list of troubled areas around the world—South Korea, Indonesia, Brazil, Congo, Rhodesia, Chile, Ghana, British

Guiana (Guyana), Philippines—you have also made a list of sources of critical raw materials.

At the moment we seem to be trading Africa for Asia, which is cruel for the Africans, but may move us one step from the brink. Africa is particularly valuable, not only for the vast reserves of copper, chromium, manganese, and cobalt, but also for power. The Volta project, whose future has just been taken from Kwame Nkrumah's hands, will generate enough power to take aluminum production out of the hands of the northern hemisphere.

We may expect to see Africa and Asia firmly in the hands of "responsible" leadership, who will stress traditional agriculture and fiscal stability over industrialization. Or else.

THE CORNUCOPIANS

Some economists, known to the Conservationists as "the Cornucopians" see in each exploited raw material not the use of an irreplaceable resource, but the forging of a key to even greater resources. They point to past history and current trends to show that technological innovations have made possible substitutions or mining of inferior ores at lower costs than earlier exploitation of high-grade ores.

In considering the impact of scarce resources on American foreign policy two questions arise. How far can technology deliver us from the Law of Diminishing Returns, and how many of U. S. policy makers are Cornucopians abroad as well as at home?

Theoretically, the whole earth is exploitable as a source of industrial minerals; the barriers are cost in dollars, and cost in time, training and machines. If the U.S. were presented with a *fait accompli,* if all her colonies were denied her and she were thrown back on her own and Canada's reserves, she could probably find ways of surviving as an advanced civilization. She has the knowledge, the training centers, the tax base, the power, the tools.

But short of that, will she do it, or will she continue to loot the poor countries of the earth?

At least three times in man's history, great civilizations have grown stagnant and been destroyed because they lacked the social forms that would realize the potential of their sciences. Steam powered the doors of temples while slaves rowed ships.

The capacity of American technology to solve the resource problem is not in question. It is in the selection of priorities, not the capacity for research, that our civilization is failing.

The space race is everybody's prime example of misallocation of our human and technical resources. Throughout the fifties, reformers cried, "In some countries in the Far East and Africa, 50 per cent of the population is blind! Forget the moon, and find a cure for trachoma." Immunization against the trachoma virus was finally developed through a breakthrough in virological research comparable to the development of the Salk vaccine—by the Chinese.

The system as it is presently structured will not lead to creative alternatives to imperialism as solutions to the resource problem. So long as ownership and control lie in the hands of the great international cartels, and so long as research priorities are determined by market mechanisms, looting will remain the logical solution to a problem with such initial components.

Although the human race as a whole is going to have to find means of using the less accessible and less-easily reduced ores, at any given point, a strong competitive advantage will accrue to whomever has the cheapest raw materials. It is technically feasible for the United States to find ways of mining manganese from the ocean bottom, but as long as Indian coolies are scratching 50 per cent ore out of the ground with wooden spades, it is economically ridiculous to produce it at twenty times the cost. The Russians and the Chinese both possess substantial deposits of most of the minerals America and Europe lack. As long as their low-cost ores are on the market, Americans will purchase on world markets, and keep secondary sources in Asia, Africa, and Latin America "on ice." But since the *status quo* in these countries is a standard of living below subsistence and declining, the *status quo* can only be maintained by force.

VESTED INTERESTS

(no, I am not now, nor have I ever been . . .)

What this phrase means is simply demonstrated. The East India Company made enormous profits out of the maintenance of India as a British colony. It did not make as much in profits, however, as it cost to hold India by means of a vast administrative system, an overseas army and a Pacific fleet. So for Britain as a whole, it was not profitable to hold India, at least by force. *But*, the people who made the profits were not the same people who paid the price. And the people who made the profits, and had a vested interest in maintaining the *status quo,* controlled the foreign policy of Britain against the interests of its people.

The situation may now exist where enclaves of power depend on a productive system that has become obsolete for the nation as a whole. More concretely, it will be possible to substitute agricultural fuels (alcohol) for mineral fuels. So it is no longer in the interests of the American people to support a war for oil, but it may well be in the interests of the Rockefellers.

A parallel and more perplexing problem is the phenomenon of vested psychological interests. If we know enough to make competition for the earth's resources a closed chapter in the evolution of human culture, will the legislators of the great powers undergo the shift in consciousness that will make fear of shortages obsolete in fact as a determinant of policy?

If some of these flying saucers would stop to offer some other-worldly benevolent guidance, they would probably suggest a world-wide program of search, research and development. The needs are obvious; how to get there from here is not.

We need an exhaustive geophysical survey, under U.N. auspices, of Canada, Africa, Latin America, and all areas where reserves are suspected but not proved. With an expanded and scattered reserve base the risks of losing political control over any one country would be minimal.

"Do I understand, Senator, that you are prepared to take those risks with the security of the United States and the Free World?"

The U.N. should also provide development capital, so that owner countries will not run into a credit squeeze in the international capital market, and be forced to sell to the controllers of international credit, who just happen to include the same people who currently own most of the earth's resources (Morgan, Rockefeller, Rothschild).

International aid should be reallocated from currency stabilization to industrial development.

With Russia and China both self-sufficient, and probably able to produce for export, there is probably enough to go around, at least potentially. But we are considering the motivations and probable decisions of groups of men committed to the security, and the competitive advantage, of a particular political and economic system that they wish to preserve unchanged. However great an abundance of raw materials is discovered in this century, the political considerations remain critical as long as one government has political control over the resources necessary to another government. It means that the resource-poor country must control the producing country, or be in some degree dependent on its good will.

A supranational body in control of prices and allocation of scarce resources might lessen the political tensions involved, but there would still be risk, still insecurity, for the developed countries. And a fair allocation would involve surrender of economic advantages that the United States is currently securing by military and paramilitary means.

"Do I understand, Senator, that you are suggesting placing the security of the United States and the Free World in the hands of the one-worlders, Black Africans, communists, and assorted riff-raff who inhabit the United Nations?"

Unfortunately, the economic motives for enforced poverty and economic stagnation in the Third World are easily elided into the "Great Black Blot" theory of communist expansion which U.S. congressmen seem to find so compelling. They overthrow governments to defend freedom, not our inflated levels of consumption. Political unrest in an area of strategic importance is easily rationalized into a military tactic by which the international communist conspiracy is attempting to cut our supply lines. (There's a marshall's baton in every attaché case.) "Our interests" and "our commitments" are logically identical, but psychologically polar opposites.

It is past time that we made the leap in moral imagination that would let us understand that we are rich because they are poor. Guerrilla movements are swelling throughout the Third World, and the lines are becoming clearly drawn. We must commit ourselves to the creation of a system of international distribution that will permit the industrialization of the Third World, or visit more Vietnams on the poor of the earth.

10

Dependency and Imperialism: The Roots of Latin American Underdevelopment

Nine years ago any critic of the Alliance for Progress was dismissed as a cynic, a malicious troublemaker, or worse yet, a Communist. Today such criticism has become so respectable in Washington that disillusioned liberals like Senator Frank Church and corporate hardliners such as Nelson Rockefeller openly acknowledge the bankruptcy of the Alliance policy.

Quite aside from their evaluations, there is far more eloquent testimony to the failure of the Alliance to achieve its stated objective of peaceful social and economic revolution in Latin America:[1]

— annual average growth rates during the 1960's were lower than those of the previous decade, and fell far short of the target (2.5 per cent per capita) established in 1961;

— social problems such as urban poverty, unemployment, and inequality of income distribution have been aggravated rather than resolved: e.g., while average per capita income is $410, the lower half of the population receives an average of $120, and the top 5 per cent of the population receives $2600; U.N. agencies estimate present equivalent unemployment to be about 25 per cent of the labor force;

— the serious agrarian and tax reforms envisioned in 1961 have not been made: e.g., in no country other than Venezuela and Paraguay was more than 10 per cent of the rural population resettled through agrarian reform;

— given the declining value of Latin American exports, and the rising prices of goods imported by the region, Latin America faces an increasingly serious balance of payments crisis and a "virtual commercial deficit" in the coming decade.

These examples indicate the magnitude of Latin America's development problems, and the failure of the Alliance to cope with them in terms of its own rhetoric and *stated* goals.

How can this failure be explained? American policy-makers and social scientists have devised endless *ad hoc* explanations, such as: the U.S. did not send enough aid; the Latin governments failed to carry out their end of the bargain; inefficient use has been made of aid resources; extraneous factors (such as the fall in Latin export commodity prices) counteracted the benefits of the Alliance, and so on *ad infinitum*. But, aside from being factually misleading in some respects (e.g., the U.S. has authorized well over the $1 billion per year pledged in 1961), these sorts of explanations are unsatisfactory because they are based on the very same premises which gave rise to the Alliance in the first place. The possibility is seldom considered that the basic assumptions and theories underlying the Alliance are themselves invalid—that in a very real sense, the failure of the Alliance to resolve the underdevelopment problems of Latin America reflects the bankruptcy of American theories for analyzing those problems.

Rather than listing and criticizing, point-by-point, the various theories devised by American social scientists to explain Latin underdevelopment (as I have done elsewhere),[2] I shall focus here upon the principal distortion underlying all of these theories: the failure—perhaps the refusal—to examine Latin America in terms of its relationship to the advanced industrial nations, particularly the U.S. Most American social scientists have evaded this task either by: 1) treating Latin countries as self-contained units, whose economic, social, or political systems can be analyzed in themselves; or 2) arguing (or assuming) that Latin American development has been stimulated by the region's contact with the advanced industrial nations.[3] The first type of analysis ignores the position of Latin America in an international environment dominated by the developed nations. The second, which maintains or assumes that there has been a net inflow of capital and technology from the developed nations into Latin America (through foreign investment and aid) and that the region has benefitted from that inflow, flies directly in the face of the facts.[4]

It has been shown in a number of studies that foreign investment by the U.S. and other industrial nations in under-developed areas has resulted in a net outflow of capital from the underdeveloped to the developed nations, a decapitalization of the former. In a number of Latin countries and for the region as a whole, the input from foreign private investment has been far exceeded by the outflow of profit remittances abroad. (According to U.S. Department of Commerce figures, the outflow from Latin America was $7.5 billion greater than inflow from 1950 to 1965.) This drain through foreign investment is aggravated by the clear deterioration of the terms of trade for the Latin nations and of their position in world trade. (Between 1950 and 1968 Latin America's share of world trade shrank from 11 per cent to 5.1 per cent.) Foreign aid has become continually more "tied" to conditions imposed by creditor nations to meet their own balance of payments difficulties or to accommodate private business interests. Service (interest and amortization) payments of the foreign debt, as well as the flow of profits abroad, continue to mount in Latin nations, and consume an ever-increasing share of export earnings (now more than 35 per cent for the region as a whole). By the mid-1960's the total paid by Latin countries in debt service payments exceeded the amount of new loans, and at the end of the decade the external debt had doubled since 1960.

Recognition of the distortions in existing theories leads directly to the starting-point for a critical analysis of Latin underdevelopment: *that Latin America is today, and has been since the sixteenth century, part of an international system dominated by the now-developed nations, and that Latin underdevelopment is the outcome of a particular series of relationships to that international system.*

THE DEPENDENCY MODEL

The basic premises of the dependency model, as first elaborated by a group of Latin American social scientists,[5] differ sharply from those of American social science development theories. "Dependency" is conceived as a "conditioning situation," i.e. one which "determines the limits and possibilities for human action and conduct"—in this case, for development in Latin America. We shall accept the definition of dependency as:

> a situation in which the economy of a certain group of countries is conditioned by the development and expansion of another economy, to which their own [economy] is subjected . . . an historical condition which shapes a certain structure of the world economy such that it favors some countries to the detriment of others, and limits the development possibilities of the [subordinate] economies . . .[6]

What does this mean? That Latin America has fulfilled certain definite functions in the "world economy" or world market, and the domestic development of Latin America has been limited or conditioned by the needs of the dominant economies within that world market. To be sure, no nation has ever developed entirely outside the context of the world market. The distinguishing feature of dependent (as contrasted with interdependent) development is that growth in the dependent nations occurs as a reflex of the expansion of the dominant nations, and is geared toward the needs of the dominant economies—i.e., foreign rather than national needs. In the dependent countries imported factors of production (e.g., capital and technology) have become the central determinants of economic development and socio-political life. And while the world market served as an instrument of expansion in European and American development, it restricts autonomous development in the dependent nations. Dependency means, then, that the alternatives open to the dependent nation are defined and limited by its integration into and functions within the world market.

At this point, we must clarify the concrete meanings of the "world market" and the "international system." By itself, the world market encompasses all flows of goods and services among nations outside the Communist trade bloc—all capital transfers (including foreign aid and overseas investment) and all commodity exchanges. But the world market is the core of a broader "international system." This international system includes not only a network of economic (market) relations, but also the entire complex of political, military, social, and cultural international relations organized by and around that market (e.g., the Monroe Doctrine, the Organization of American States, "Free World" defense treaties and organizations, and media and communications networks). The international system is the static expression and outcome of a dynamic historical process: the transnational or global expansion of capitalism.

By focusing on the international system, the dependency model proceeds from a basic concrete fact of Latin American history: that since the Spanish conquest—that is, since its existence as Latin American rather than indigenous Indian society—Latin America has played a certain role in the political economy of one or another dominant capitalist nation (Spain and Portugal in the colonial and early post-independence period, England during most of the nineteenth century, and the U.S. since the beginning of the twentieth century). Thus, unlike *un*developed societies (those few which have *no* market relations with the industrialized nations), the *under*developed Latin economies have always been shaped by the global expansion and consolidation of the capitalist system, and by their own incorporation into that system. In this sense, Latin societies "brought into existence with their birth" their relation to the international system, and hence their relations of dependency.

Although the particular function of Latin America in the international system has varied, the development of that region has been shaped since the Spanish conquest by a general structural characteristic of capitalist expansion: its unevenness. "Unevenness" means that some nations or regions have developed more rapidly than—often at the expense of—others. For Latin America this has entailed increasing relative poverty, as the gap in income and growth rates between the industrial nations and Latin America is constantly widening. (Since 1957, for example, the growth rate of per capita income in Latin America has been less than 1.5 per cent a year, as contrasted with nearly 2.5 per cent in the U.S. and 4 per cent in Europe.[7]) Similar disparities have marked the uneven development of various regions within Latin America.

This unevenness has been manifested through an "international division of labor"; while Western Europe and the U.S. industrialized, Latin America remained for centuries an exporter of primary raw materials and agricultural products. Even the faltering steps toward industrialization more recently have not altered the fundamentally complementary character of the Latin economies: the industrial sectors remain dependent on imports (of capital goods) and, as a result of the increasing foreign control over these sectors, growth is still governed largely by the needs of foreign economies. The international division of labor has persisted (the

1969 *Rockefeller Report* even calls for making it "more efficient"); only its form has changed. This complementarity is not incidental but essential to the underdevelopment of the Latin economies. As is widely recognized, the periods of relative growth and development in Latin America (e.g., industrialization in the 1930's) have occurred during the phases of relative contraction in the world market (during periods of international war or depression), when the region's ties to that market and to the dominant nations have been weakest. Politically as well, Latin American development has been limited by the fact that policy decisions about resource allocation and all aspects of national development are conditioned and limited by the interests of the developed societies.

From the foregoing, it becomes clear that underdevelopment in Latin America is structurally linked to development in the dominant nations. European and American development and Latin underdevelopment are not two isolated phenomena, but rather two outcomes of the same historical process: the global expansion of capitalism.

Insofar as Latin American development has been limited since the sixteenth century by fulfilling one or another function in the international system, the *fact* of dependency has been a constant. But the *forms* of dependency, in particular countries at particular historical moments, have varied according to the specific characteristics of the international system at that time and the specific functions of the Latin country within the system.

Characteristics of the international system:
— the prevalent form of capitalism (mercantile or industrial, corporate or financial);
— the principal needs of the dominant nation(s) in the international system (agricultural commodities, minerals, cheap labor, commodity markets, capital markets, etc.);
— the degree of concentration of capital in the dominant nation(s) (competitive or monopolistic capitalism);
— the degree of concentration internationally (one hegemonic power or rival powers and, if one hegemonic power, which nation [Spain, England, or the U.S.]);
— the typical form of world trade (mercantilism, "free trade," or protectionism).

Characteristics of the Latin country within the international system:

— function primarily as a supplier of raw materials or agricultural products, as a market for manufactured goods, as a supplier of certain manufactured commodities, as an arena for direct foreign investment, or any combination of the preceding;

— the degree of relative autonomy (periods of international war or depression *vs.* "normal" periods of capitalist expansion);

— the degree of foreign control in the principal economic sectors;

— the nature of political tie to the dominant power(s) (colonial or nominal independence).

The specific forms of dependency in Latin America in any given historical period are shaped by the characteristics of the international system and of Latin America's function within it. Latin America was first integrated into the international system in its mercantile phase, under Spanish dominance, and served primarily as a provider of raw materials and agricultural commodities. Thus dependency during the colonial period and during much of the nineteenth century was manifested primarily through the development of export-import "enclaves." The conditions which shape Latin dependency today are quite distinct. The international system today is characterized by: advanced industrial capitalism (corporate integrated with financial capital); the dominant nations' need for raw materials and, more important, for commodity and capital markets; monopolistic concentration of capital; American hegemony (*vis-à-vis* Latin America); and increasing international integration of capital. Trade within the international system is increasingly protectionist (tariffs or quotas imposed by the dominant nations) and is increasingly incorporated within the structure of the multinational corporations. Latin America's function within the system is shifting from a supplier of raw materials and agricultural commodities to an arena where certain phases of industrial production are carried out—but still under the auspices of foreign corporations.[8] The degree of foreign control in the principal economic sectors is increasing, and Latin America's integration into the orbit of the dominant capitalist nations is becoming more complete, despite nominal political independence.

These characteristics of the international system and of Latin America's function within it impose definite limitations on the possibilities for Latin development. Nevertheless, it would be an oversimplification to say that the international system causes underdevelopment directly; it does so *indirectly,* by generating and reinforcing within Latin America an *infrastructure of dependency.* What is the infrastructure (internal structures) of dependency? The international system affects development in Latin America by means of certain institutions, social classes, and processes (industrial structure, socioeconomic elites, urbanization, and so on). These aspects of Latin society become part of the infrastructure of dependency when they function or occur in a manner that responds to the interests or needs of the dominant powers in the international system, rather than to national interests or needs. It is through the infrastructure of dependency that the international system becomes operative within Latin America. And it is through the infrastructure of dependency that the legacy of Latin America's integration into the international system is transmitted and perpetuated within Latin America, thereby limiting the possibilities for development.

Let us take two examples of the infrastructure of dependency. *(a)* Industrialization in the broadest sense implies far more than the construction of new factories and the production or processing of commodities. In most Latin nations the industrial sectors lie at the heart of the entire national economy. In addition the quality of industrialization is integrally related to, among other things, political decision-making, social structure, and urbanization. Industrialization is not by nature dependent; it becomes so when the industrial structure is integrated into and complementary to the needs of foreign economies. Some specific characteristics of dependent industrialization are: 1) increasing foreign control over the most dynamic and strategic industrial sectors through direct ownership and control over production, control of marketing and distribution, or control of patents and licenses (in many sectors foreign corporations have been buying out formerly national industries); 2) increasing competitive advantages for (often monopolistic) foreign enterprises over local firms, particularly in industries of scale; 3) as a result of foreign ownership, outflow of capital (profits) abroad; 4) despite some production for the internal market, adaptation of the entire economic structure to the needs of the buyers of Latin exports in the dominant nations; 5) introduction of advanced, capital-intensive foreign technology, without regard to size or composition of the local labor market, and consequent aggravation of unemployment (which in turn results in restriction of the domestic market): in several countries (e.g. Chile, Colombia, Peru) employment in manufacturing industry actually declined as a percentage of total employment between 1925 and 1960 ; 6) also as a result of foreign control over technology, its restriction to those sectors in which foreign capital has a direct interest; 7) lack of a domestic capital goods industry in most countries, and consequently an increased rather than reduced dependence on imports and rigidities in the composition of imports. In short, dependent industrialization has aggravated rather than resolved such basic problems as balance of payments deficits, unemployment, income disparities, and an insufficient domestic market.

(b) Intersecting the process of dependent industrialization is another, equally fundamental, dimension of dependency: the creation and/or reinforcement of clientele social classes. Clientele classes are those which have a vested interest in the existing international system. These classes carry out certain functions on behalf of foreign interests; in return they enjoy a privileged and increasingly dominant and hegemonic position within their own societies, based largely on economic, political, or military support from abroad. In this sense the clientele classes come to play in Latin America today the role historically performed by the *comprador* bourgeoisie (export-import mercantile elites, whose strength, interests, and very existence were derived from their function in the world market). Like their behavior, the ideologies of these classes reflect their dual position as junior partners of metropolitan interests, yet dominant elites within their own societies. The clearest example of clientele classes today are those elements of the Latin industrial bourgeoisie which "expand and thrive within the orbit of foreign capital . . . [whether as] wholesalers . . . or as suppliers of local materials to foreign enterprises or as caterers to various other needs of foreign firms and their staffs. . . ."[9]

The state bureaucracy and other sectors of the middle class—for example, the technical, managerial, professional or intellectual elites—become clientele when their interests, actions, and privileged positions are derived from their ties to foreign interests. Particularly with the expanded role of the state in the national economy, the state bureaucracy (including the military in many countries) has been viewed by some as the key to national autonomy. Nevertheless, when the primary function of the state is to stimulate private enterprise, when the private sector is largely controlled by foreign interests, and when the state bureaucracy itself relies on material and ideological support from abroad (as in Brazil today), the "autonomy" of the state bureaucracy must be illusory.

The alliances and conflicts of clientele classes with other domestic classes are shaped to a considerable extent by their previous and present alliances with foreign interests. Thus, for example, no less important than the alliances or conflicts of a São Paulo industrialist with the Brazilian proletariat or coffee-growing interests are his economic and ideological alignments with Wall Street bankers or foreign industrial interests; indeed the former are often shaped by the latter. The existence of these clientele classes in the dependent nation, whose interests correspond to those of the dominant classes in the dominant nations, is the kingpin and the *sine qua non* of dependency.

From the preceding discussion, it may be seen that dependency does not simply mean external domination, unilaterally superimposed from abroad and unilaterally producing "internal consequences." The internal dynamics of dependency are as much a function of *penetration* as of domination. It is in this way that dependency in Latin America differs from that of a formal colony: while the chains binding the latter to the mother country are overt and direct (administrative control), those of the former are subtler and are internal to the nation—and for that reason are much more difficult to break. In this sense, the infrastructure of dependency may be seen as the functional equivalent of a formal colonial apparatus—the principal difference being, perhaps, that since all classes and structures in Latin society have to a greater or lesser degree internalized and institutionalized the legacy of dependency, that legacy is much more difficult to overcome.

From this analysis follow certain political implications. Even if the U.S. and every other dominant capitalist nation were to suddenly disappear, Latin American dependency would not be immediately ruptured. And thus, by implication, Latin nations cannot break the chains of dependency merely by severing (or attempting to sever) their ties to the international system. A total rupturing of dependency as an internal condition of underdevelopment requires simultaneously—and indeed as a precondition for lasting autonomy or independence from the international system—a profound transformation, an anticapitalist, socialist transformation, of their own socio-economic order.

Thus, as experience has demonstrated, the various efforts to build "bourgeois nationalist" or "national capitalist" or, more recently, "state capitalist" solutions must fail in the end because the social classes on whom such solutions are based (the bourgeoisie) are themselves limited by their role in the international system. They may advocate a foreign policy "independent" of the U.S. (as in Brazil during the early 1960's); or they may successfully expropriate foreign holdings in some sectors, as has been done in Peru and as may be increasingly the case in other countries. But so long as they follow the capitalist road of development, they will continue to depend upon foreign investment, and thus will eventually have to make their compromises with and cater to foreign interests. And regardless of their intentions to implement far-reaching domestic reforms, they will be limited in practice by the legacy of dependency as institutionalized within their own class interests and alliances, within the existing industrial base, and so on. To break out of dependency means, then, to break out of the capitalist order whose expression in Latin America is dependency.

THE PREDECESSORS OF THE DEPENDENCY MODEL

The dependency model was not the first attempt to relate Latin American underdevelopment to the region's function in the world market. Why, then, was this model in some sense "necessary?" In order to understand both the continuities and the differences of the dependency model with respect to its predecessors, we shall deal briefly with two previous "international system" analyses of Latin underdevelopment: the classical model of the U.N. Economic Commission for Latin America (CEPAL) and that of André Gunder Frank.

The starting-point of the CEPAL analysis[10] is Latin America's "peripheral" status *vis-à-vis* the advanced industrial "centers," as manifested primarily in the region's historical evolution as an exporter of primary commodities. Until the 1930's, when some Latin nations began to industrialize, their economies (and the economy of the region as a whole) typified *desarrollo hacia afuera* (externally-oriented development), geared to the needs of the then-industrializing nations which dominated the world market, rather than to the needs of their national markets. This historical condition finds its contemporary expression in the unfavorable position of the "peripheral" nations in world trade, stemming from the low income elasticity of demand for Latin American exports and the high income elasticity of demand for the industrial imports into those countries. As a means of overcoming Latin America's inherent disadvantage in the world market and excessive dependence upon one or a few primary exports, and as a means of stimulating internally rather than externally-oriented development, the CEPAL solution has been import-substituting industrialization. Import-substitution was expected to lessen dependence on foreign trade, transfer the "centers of decision-making" to Latin America, and expand production for the internal market. The rise of a national industrial bourgeoisie would weaken the traditional oligarchies (mainly landed and import-export interests). And, if coupled with an agrarian reform, import-substitution could lead to income redistribution and incorporation of the lower classes into the national economy. Since industrialization required far more capital than was currently available from domestic sources, foreign investment and foreign aid on terms favorable to Latin America were seen as necessary and desirable.

Although the CEPAL thesis (which has been grossly over-simplified here) was fruitful when first put forth, in that it linked Latin American underdevelopment to the international economic system, it is limited in several respects. First, its explanation of why Latin America has been at such a disadvantage in the world market relies too heavily on the nature of traditional Latin exports, and pays insufficient attention to the conscious policies and the specific needs of the developed nations. As has been seen above, it is no natural accident that the Latin countries have remained, until recently, exporters of primary products and importers of manufactured goods. Second, CEPAL's class analysis places the entire responsibility for retarded industrialization upon "traditional" or "feudal" oligarchies within Latin America. But the characterization of Latin society as having been "pre-capitalist" or "feudal" or dominated by feudal oligarchies is misleading, since Latin American society and modes of production since the sixteenth century have been mercantile, that is, geared toward exporting to an international capitalist market. In addition the CEPAL theorists assumed that an indigenous industrial bourgeoisie would be developmentalist, progressive, and nationalistic—a premise which clearly requires reexamination, in view of the actual behavior of that bourgeoisie.

Third, and perhaps most important, the CEPAL analysis has been partially invalidated by facts: specifically, the increasing dependence upon the international system of those countries which have been import-substituting for more than 30 years (e.g., Chile, Argentina, Brazil), and the stagnation plaguing those nations in recent years, which is a symptom of the exhaustion of import-substitution possibilities. To mention only three examples: since beginning to industrialize, Latin America has become more dependent than ever upon certain critical imports (heavy capital goods for industrial facilities); foreign ownership and control of industry have increased, thus contradicting the expectation that decision-making would be transferred to Latin America; and growth rates for the entire region and for some of the most industrialized nations were lower during the 1960's than during the 1945-60 period. In short, the CEPAL diagnosis took insufficient account of the built-in limitations of the import-substitution solution, arising from Latin America's historical dependency.

Faced with the by now obvious bankruptcy of import-substitution during the 1960's, CEPAL has avoided a thorough reappraisal of its analysis by discovering yet another panacea: regional economic integration. But, in the absence of a transformation of the national economic structures, this panacea (supported by U.S. and international aid agencies as well as CEPAL) promises to be no more viable than import-substitution: first, because, unless accompanied by strict regulations on foreign investment, economic integration will benefit foreign rather than local firms, the former having the capital and advanced technology to support regional enterprises which are beyond the capacity of local firms; second, because the increased scale and advanced technology of regional enterprises aggravate national development problems such as unemployment unless these negative effects are counteracted through deliberate policies; third, because regional integration of markets removes the pressure for drastic social reforms which would normally be created by industries of scale requiring large markets. Instead of enlarging the consumer base within each country by improving the economic status of the majority of the population, it is possible to combine middle and upper class consumer bases of several nations (as is currently happening in Central America). These factors do not imply the invalidity of the *idea* of integration, but rather the illusory nature of integration under present conditions as a substitute for basic structural changes.

Fourth, on the grounds that capital shortage has been one of the main obstacles to industrialization, CEPAL recommends increased foreign investment and aid. But this recommendation flies in the face of considerable evidence that foreign investment and aid have served as channels for the outflow of capital from Latin America rather than the inflow. Thus the CEPAL analysis calls for the intensification rather than the rupturing of ties to the dominant world powers—and (unintentionally) for the intensification of dependency.

In short, the CEPAL model provides at best a partial explanation of Latin underdevelopment; it confronts the symptoms rather than the basic causes. Perhaps this is more understandable in the light of its socio-economic roots. The CEPAL strategy is the expression of a Latin bourgeoisie trying to be national, but confined by the contradictions of the national capitalist "solution" to dependency, and forced, in the end, to call for additional foreign capital as a requisite for development. The inadequacy of the CEPAL model represents the failure of a particular social class, with particular interests, to offer a long-range alternative to Latin America.[11]

The second "international system" analysis, which goes considerably beyond the classical CEPAL model, is André Gunder Frank's Marxist model of relations between "metropolitan" and "satellite" nations. Frank traces the underdevelopment of Latin America and all the manifestations of that underdevelopment to the global expansion of capitalism and its penetration of the non-Western nations: "Underdevelopment [in Latin America] was and still is generated by the very same historical process which also generated economic development [in the U.S. and Europe] : the development of capitalism itself."[12] This process has resulted in a hierarchical chain of metropolis-satellite relations, in which each metropolis appropriates the economic surplus generated in its satellites, and "each of the satellites . . . serves as an instrument to suck capital or economic surplus out of its own satellites, and to channel part of this surplus to the world metropolis of which all are satellites." Within Latin America power has always rested with the subordinate metropolises, particularly the bourgeoisie, intimately tied to foreign interests, yet dominant at home.

Frank addresses the major weaknesses of the CEPAL model. He provides a causal explanation for Latin America's unfavorable position in the world market, specifying clearly the role of the dominant classes in the developed societies as well as of the local metropolises (dominant classes and regions) in the Latin nations. He refutes the myth that Latin America is currently emerging from a feudal social order, which must be destroyed by the triumph of the national bourgeoisie over the feudal oligarchy. He suggests why industrialization, import-substituting or otherwise, will not rupture the cycle of underdevelopment and dependency unless the existing structure of metropolis-satellite relations, both domestic and international, is overthrown. Thus he projects no hopes as to the "positive contribution" which might be made by foreign investment and aid; these are, in Frank's model, instruments for the extraction of capital from Latin America, rather than for its infusion into the region.

There remain, however, several problems in Frank's analysis. For our purposes it is necessary to mention only the most relevant one. It is just because his theory is so sweeping and "elegant" (in the sense of reducing complex phenomena to one basic set of principles and relationships) that it tends to be one-dimensional. Although the extraction of economic surplus may be the basis for all metropolis-satellite relations, both international and internal, it is not the only important dimension of those relations or of Latin dependency. The concept of dependency calls attention to many other aspects of Latin America's relation to the international system which cannot be reduced to the extraction of economic surplus. It is for this reason (among others) that the dependency theorists did not simply adopt Frank's model as it stood, but developed a somewhat different version of the same basic thesis: that Latin underdevelopment and dependency are an expression and a consequence of the global expansion of capitalism. Thus the dependency model has incorporated the important theoretical contributions of its predecessors, while attempting to avoid their problems and limitations.

THE LIMITS OF THE DEPENDENCY MODEL
AND ITS INTEGRATION WITH A THEORY OF IMPERIALISM

Insofar as the international system lies at the heart of dependency, that system must be understood in its entirety—not only at its point of impact on Latin America, but also at its origins in the dominant nations. It is at this point that we reach the limits of the dependency model. While providing the basis for an analysis of the impact of capitalist expansion and the functioning of the international system in Latin America, by itself it is not very explicit about the reasons for the expansion of capitalism or the roots of the international system in the dominant nations (for our purposes, the U.S.). Furthermore, (although a certain conception is implicit within the writings of a number of the dependency theorists) it does not make explicit the relation between the state and private capital in the American political economy. Private capital remains the driving force in the international system; nevertheless, the state or public sector of the dominant nations plays an important role in relations with Latin America and even in the operations of private capital. It is in terms of the relation between the state and private capital in the dominant nations that we may understand why the international system perpetuates underdevelopment in Latin America—and ultimately why policies such as the Alliance for Progess cannot resolve the underdevelopment problem.

In attempting to fill the "gap" left by the dependency model, we may choose from among several alternative theories which presume to explain U.S. relations with Latin America. For our purposes these theories may be classified in three groups: international relations theories, non-Marxist theories of imperialism, and Marxist theories of imperialism. After suggesting the insufficiencies of the first two bodies of theory for the specific problem at hand, I shall indicate why the third provides an appropriate complement to the dependency model.

In most conventional international relations theories[13] the international context is depicted as an arena in which independent (though not necessarily equal) players bargain about competing or conflicting national interests, and in which war occasionally erupts when the bargaining process breaks down. In the case of U.S. relations with Latin America this model is inappropriate. It assumes that Latin American nations are separate units, led by autonomous decision-makers. It implicitly or explicitly postulates a clear dichotomy between internal and international structures, thus ignoring the reality of Latin American dependency. In addition, international relations theories tend to deal with "policy choices," the implication being that Latin governments, acting autonomously, could make alternative decisions. In fact, so long as they remain within the international capitalist system, the range of alternatives open to these governments is limited to changing certain minor aspects of their relation to the dominant nations (for example, gaining trade concessions, more economic or military aid). This restricted range of options is, in fact, a principal feature of Latin American dependency. Moreover, the autonomy of Latin American decision-makers is not to be taken for granted; while they may go through the motions of deciding policy, the substance of their decisions often reflects foreign interests more nearly than national interests.

From the standpoint of the U.S. as well, international relations theories tend to obscure the essentials of U.S.-Latin American relations. They generally treat those relations in terms of policies and policy-choices, which presumably could have been or could be changed by more "enlightened" policy-makers. (Thus, for example, the Alliance for Progress and, thirty years earlier, the Good Neighbor Policy were seen as real departures from previous U.S. policies.) To be sure, American strategies and policies toward Latin America *do* change; but these changes represent variations of a less flexible underlying relationship between the U.S. and Latin America, rather than alterations in the basic relationship. The exclusive focus on U.S. policy also precludes attention to the institutions and social groups within the U.S. socio-economic system which shape these policies. Given the dichotomy between domestic and international politics, foreign policy is seen as part of the state (public) apparatus, is assumed to reflect the "public interest," and hence is seldom examined in terms of dominant private interests within the U.S. By obscuring the essential relationship between public policy and private interests, international relations theories must devise *ad hoc* explanations—or excuses—for the failure of policies such as the Alliance for Progress; their own assumptions preclude a real understanding of its roots, and thus of its consequences.

The basic assumption of most international relations theories, that there exists at least a minimal autonomy and freedom of action for all nations as actors in the international arena, is challenged by all theories of imperialism. The notion of an imperialistic relation between two or more nations implies (regardless of the particular theory of imperialism) a decisive inequality between those nations, an exploitative relationship (that is, one which serves the interests of the dominant nation at the expense of the subordinate nation), and the crippling of the latter's autonomy. The subordinate nation becomes, to one degree or another, the object of the needs and interests of certain groups in the dominant nation. Beyond the very general notion of imperialism as exploitative, however, Marxist theories differ sharply from most non-Marxist theories in analyzing the nature and causes of imperialism.

Given the great diversity of non-Marxist theories of imperialism, these remarks must be limited to those tendencies which have direct bearing on Latin American dependency.[14] First, there is a tendency to associate imperialism with expansionism (territorial expansion or protracted political domination) and/or the military aggression and intervention generally accompanying such expansion. By associating imperialism with a phenomenon that has characterized international political relations since the beginning of time, this conception is so broad as to deprive the term "imperialism" of any specific meaning. Nor does it contribute toward an explanation of dependency in Latin America: for dependency is not created by occasional military interventions or even gunboat diplomacy (which historically involved prolonged occupation and/or overt political control by the U.S. or other hegemonic powers). Rather, dependency has been a chronic condition of Latin development, maintained by the day-to-day and for the most part peaceful relations between Latin America and the dominant nations. The very identification of imperialism with physical or direct coercion projects an oversimplified image of overt domination, and almost automatically excludes from examination the subtler mechanisms through which dependency has been internalized and perpetuated in Latin America.

Second, non-Marxist theories tend to dissociate imperialism from the economic system (for our purposes, capitalism) in the dominant country. Thus they may resort to ideological-political-military explanations (such as the obsessive anti-Communism of American leaders, the doctrine of the "American responsibility" held by the "national security bureaucracy," independent of economic interests, and the needs of the defense establishment). Or they may argue that imperialism is "unprofitable" or "irrational" in a capitalist society, basically a "vestige" or "atavism" surviving from a pre-capitalist era. By conceptualizing imperialism too narrowly in terms of the actions of the state, or implicitly distinguishing *a priori* the interests of the state ("national security") from those of the dominant socio-economic classes, these theories do not consider imperialism to be systemically related to capitalism. But if imperialism is dissociated from capitalism, then it must be regarded as little more than a policy; in this respect the logical conclusions of many non-Marxist theories of imperialism almost converge with those of international relations theory. And if imperialism is dissociated from the global expansion of capitalism on the international level, the concept loses its potential as an explanation of dependency in Latin America.

In contrast to the above, a Marxist theory of imperialism[15] addresses itself directly to the economic basis (as well as the political-military aspects) of American policies and to the causes of dependency and underdevelopment in Latin America. For our purposes the adoption of a Marxist framework implies an integral relation between the actions of the U.S. government abroad and the structure of the American socio-economic system; it analyzes U.S. relations with Latin America as one aspect of American capitalism. In this sense American imperialism is not "irrational" or "accidental," but rather is a necessary extension of capitalism. It is not a fleeting policy, but *a stage in the development of capitalism as a world system.* Moreover, while recognizing the importance, necessity and inevitability of military or coercive actions abroad, a Marxist analysis understands these not as the essence of imperialism, but rather as the ultimate recourse, when the subtler mechanisms of imperialism are insufficient to contain a threat to the existing international system. This analysis is appropriate to a specific feature of contemporary U.S. relations with Latin America: namely, the attempt to avoid and to obviate the need for overt military intervention or direct political control wherever possible. To accept a theory of economic imperialism as a general hypothesis does not imply the necessary reduction of every *specific* political or military action by the state to pure economic motives; there are occasions (such as the Cuban missile crisis) when "security" considerations are decisive. This theory insists, however, that isolated military or political actions be understood in their over-all context, which is the preservation of capitalism as an economic order.

To introduce the model of contemporary imperialism, we begin with a skeletal description of the main units of contemporary capitalism and imperialism. This sketch is based on a particular Marxist model which takes *monopoly capital* as the defining feature of the U.S. political economy today:

> Today the typical unit in the capitalist world is not the small firm producing a negligible fraction of a homogeneous output for an anonymous market, but a large-scale enterprise producing a significant share of the output of an industry or even several industries, and able to control its prices, the volume of its production, and the type and amounts of its investments. The typical economic unit, in other words, has the attributes which were once thought to be possessed only by monopolies.[16]

The outstanding features of these economic units are, briefly: 1) increasing concentration of capital and resources under the control of fewer units, through the traditional forms: horizontal integration (increasing concentration of control over the production of a commodity or class of commodities) and vertical integration (increasing concentration of control over all phases of the production process, from the supply of raw materials to the marketing and distribution of the commodity to consumers); 2) a growing tendency toward conglomeration or diversification—that is, the control by a smaller number of corporations over production in various different and often unrelated sectors, thus augmenting the corporation's strength, and simultaneously minimizing the risks of production or marketing, in any one sector; 3) increasing "internationalization" or "multinationalization" of the operation (*not* the ownership or control) of capital. Multinational corporations are: plants that purchase inputs from one branch of a corporation located in the same or a different country and sell outputs to another branch of the same corporation located elsewhere. . . . [They] are able to mobilize, transform, and dispose of capital on a regional or even world-wide scale—in effect constituting themselves as extra-territorial bodies.[17] —in short, the (non-Communist) world has replaced the nation as the arena for their operations in both production and marketing; 4) the progressive shift from rivalry among the capitalist powers (such as prevailed, for example, during the heyday of colonialism, from 1870 to 1914) toward closer integration of the capitalist world, and inability of the secondary capitalist powers thus far to offer a serious challenge to American hegemony. (This is especially the case *vis-à-vis* Latin America.)

These characteristics of contemporary capitalism give rise to certain generally shared interests of the multinational corporations with respect to their overseas operations.[18] First, there arises a need to control all aspects of the production process, including the sources of supply and processing of raw materials, as well as the markets or outlets for commodities. Second, as the scale, monopolistic concentration, conglomeration, and internationalization of private capital increase, the dependence upon immediate profit returns from overseas investments is reduced. The emphasis shifts toward long-range planning, maximum security and avoidance of risk, and preservation of a favorable climate (ideological, political, and social as well as economic) for the *perpetuation* of corporate operations and for long-range profits —a concern frequently expressed by U.S. businessmen themselves.[19] To insure against sudden changes in the "rules of the game," controls over the political situation in Latin America— generally informal and indirect—must be tightened. And in the international environment there is need of an apparatus to guarantee not only the rationalization of international capital flows and monetary transactions, but also maximum political stability. "Hemispheric security" comes to mean protection not against interference by non-hemispheric powers or even "International Communism," but rather against the threat of truly independent regimes of any type in Latin America.

Third, corporate capitalists acquire an interest in a limited measure of "development" in Latin America. A moderate redistribution of income in Latin America provides a larger market for U.S. exports, as well as a safeguard against potential political instability. A relatively healthy Latin economy improves the climate for investment and trade. In this sense modern imperialism has an element of "welfare imperialism." Under these conditions, however, Latin development responds primarily to the needs of the foreign corporations, rather than national needs; it is, in short, fragmented, dependent, and ultimately illusory development. Fourth (and partly as a response to the failure to achieve real income redistribution or expansion of the domestic market in Latin countries), there is an interest in regional integration of markets. As *Fortune* (June, 1967) points out, the advantages of integration are that it not only eliminates tariff barriers, but it also provides "the chance to move to the broader, more competitive, and potentially more profitable task of supplying a market big enough to be economic on its own terms . . ."

Finally, the nature of private corporate operations overseas is such that they require protection by the (imperialist) state. Thus the multinational corporation has an increasing stake in consolidating its influence over "public" or (U.S.) government decisions, that is, over the apparatus of the state. This implies not only a strong influence over government foreign policies, but also the active participation of the state in international economic relationships which serve their interests. As the interests of the state come to overlap with those of the multinational corporations, "the state enlists more and more private capital in its crusade to maintain world capitalism intact," and there arises a "partnership" between public and private capital.[20] For our purposes, the significance of this partnership is that the state performs certain services which are essential to the overseas operations of the multinational corporations.

To take only a few examples of the ways in which state agencies service U.S. corporate interests abroad: the CIA, the State Department, and the Pentagon exercise numerous forms of political pressure, provide training for local military "civic action" and counter-insurgency programs, military assistance, and ultimate direct protection of U.S. investors—and in extreme cases of noncooperation by Latin governments, they have played decisive roles in overthrowing those governments. The in-country U.S. embassies provide crucial information to the corporations, represent their interests to the local governments, and influence local government policies. The U.S. Treasury Department exerts pressures for tariffs and quotas on imports from Latin America which are competitive with U.S. goods, and so on.

Foreign aid agencies perform a variety of services for the corporations:[21] they socialize the indirect operating costs of the multinational corporations (transferring those costs from the corporations to the American—ultimately the Latin American—taxpayers); they create advantages for U.S. firms over existing or potential local competitors; and they facilitate long-range planning and minimize the risks of foreign investment for the corporations, principally by stabilizing the local investment climate. In addition to these services for specific corporations, foreign aid fulfills more general functions for the preservation of U.S. capitalism (e.g., keeping Latin America in the capitalist orbit and gaining cooperation of Latin governments by offering loans as rewards or threatening to withhold aid; and providing markets for and in effect subsidizing U.S. exports through such mechanisms as "tied aid").

This analysis is not to imply that the state *never* acts independently of, or even in direct opposition to, private corporate interests in particular situations. Indeed there have been notable instances. Moreover, the state is sometimes faced with conflicting interests among the multinational corporations. In short, the state (and even the corporations themselves) are sometimes forced to sacrifice specific interests in order to serve the "higher interest"—the preservation of the capitalist system as a whole. In this sense the overriding task of the modern capitalist state is the stabilization and rationalization of world capitalism and imperialism as a socio-economic order.

We may now draw together the two parts of the analysis. By itself the dependency model provides a view "from below." It traces Latin American underdevelopment to that region's function in the world market and international system, which is governed by the interests of the dominant nations. The theory of imperialism provides a view "from above"—an explanation of the specific nature of the international system and its roots in the dominant nations. Through it the principal force which has conditioned Latin development—the global expansion of capitalism, which is the engine of the international system—is personified. For the theory of imperialism specifies *whose* particular needs or interests in the dominant nations—that is, those of the corporate and financial capitalists—are served by the international system. And on the basis of the ties between the state and private interests in the dominant nations, the theory offers an account of U.S. relations with Latin America, thus converging with the dependency model. Dependency and imperialism are, thus, two names for one and the same system.

INSTABILITIES AND CONTRADICTIONS IN THE SYSTEM

Let us return briefly to the starting-point: the failure of the Alliance for Progress. The Alliance was billed as a massive infusion of capital to promote a peaceful social and economic revolution in Latin America. From the preceding analysis, it becomes evident that the Alliance could not have succeeded: first, because, contrary to the assumption that foreign aid and investment make a positive capital contribution to Latin development, the evidence shows that these have served as mechanisms for the *extraction* of capital; and second, because the cumulative effect of Latin America's contact with the dominant capitalist nations has been and remains the generation of dependency as an internal condition. Thus the Alliance was merely one more means of integrating Latin America into the international system which creates dependency and hinders development in that region.

From this perspective we must also reconsider the original objectives of the Alliance. The stated goal was to promote development through reform. This may have been a partial motivation for the Alliance. Far more important, however, was the *unstated* objective: to stabilize Latin America, and to make the region perpetually safe for private U.S. investment. Some reform would be desirable—but only insofar as it was perceived as a necessary precondition for stability in Latin America and for preservation of the international capitalist system in the Western Hemisphere. (In case there is any doubt about this hidden agenda of the Alliance, let us recall that it was initiated simultaneously with the Bay of Pigs invasion and with the establishment of counterinsurgency campaigns wherever a threat to stability existed in Latin America).

But this stability is precisely what was not, and could never have been, achieved by strengthening Latin America's ties to the international system and thereby intensifying Latin dependency. For the international system and Latin American dependency are fraught with serious contradictions, of which we can mention only a few here. First, because it is dependent—because it is controlled by monopolistic foreign corporations and adapted to imported capital-intensive technology—industrialization has generated not employment but unemployment. Those very social classes which were to have been incorporated within the national economy have been progressively marginalized. Not only does this create the usual threat from an increasing reserve army of the unemployed. It also limits the expansion of the domestic market, which is a necessary condition for the expansion of foreign investment in Latin America (as well as for Latin development). Thus the multinational corporations are creating the conditions which will limit their own expansion in Latin America.

Second, because it is a dependent bourgeoisie—one which is closely allied, yet a junior partner in that alliance, with foreign capital—the once-national industrial bourgeoisie loses whatever potential it had for mobilizing a nationalist united front within Latin America. With its internationalization, the Latin industrial bourgeoisie loses its ideological hegemony and control over other popular nationalist forces. Thus the international system is reinforcing a bourgeoisie which will in the long run be incapable of maintaining Latin America within the orbit of the international capitalist system.

Third, as underdevelopment is intensified and new sectors of the population are radicalized, dependent or *comprador* governments, subservient to foreign interests, are forced to employ overt repression, not only against revolutionary movements but also against popular movements (peasant land invasions as in Chile, resurgent labor movements as in Argentina, and students). When these movements spread and, in response, the measures of repression are generalized to the entire nation, opposition to the government increases (even, as in Brazil, among sectors of the middle class which initially brought it to power), and the repression-resistance cycle becomes chronic. Or, as in the case of the Dominican Republic, the imperialist power is finally forced to intervene directly, thereby transforming a reformist movement into a potentially revolutionary force.

The real and ultimate failure of the Alliance for Progress then— and of any other policy designed to intensify Latin America's integration into the international system—was the failure to stabilize Latin America. It had to fail, because dependency is not a stable or stabilizing condition for Latin American development. As one Latin American put it,

> The process of internationalization has two faces: one dependent face (the present) and one liberating face (that of the future). The dependent face and the liberating face present themselves in one and the same process . . . .[22]

Notes

[1] The following figures are taken from: U.N. Economic Commission for Latin America (CEPAL), *El Segundo Decenio de las Naciones Unidas para el Desarrollo: Aspectos Básicos de la Estrategia del Desarrollo de América Latina* (Lima, CEPAL, April 14-23, 1969); Keith Griffin, *Underdevelopment in Spanish America* (London, Allen and Unwin, 1969); U.N. figures cited by André Gunder Frank, "The Underdevelopment Policy of the United Nations in Latin America," *NACLA Newsletter*, Dec. 1969; Simon Hanson, "The Alliance for Progress: The Sixth Year," *Inter-American Economic Affairs*, Winter, 1968; CEPAL, *Los Déficit Virtuales de Comercio y de Ahorro Interno y la Desocupación Estructural de América Latina* (Santiago, CEPAL).

[2] "The Ideology of Developmentalism: American Political Science's Paradigm-Surrogate for Latin American Studies," *Berkeley Journal of Sociology*, 1970.

[3] The first approach is exemplified in the work of structural functionalists such as Gabriel Almond; the second argument, that foreign investment and aid stimulate development, is made in W. W. Rostow, *The Stages of Economic Growth* (London, Cambridge Univ. Press, 1962), pp. 142-3; Rostow and Max Millikan, *A Proposal* (N.Y., Harper & Bros., 1957), p. 56; Claude McMillan and Richard Gonzales, *International Enterprise in a Developing Economy* (Lansing, Mich., 1964); selections by Frederic Bonham and others in Gerald Meier, ed., *Leading Issues in Development Economics* (N.Y., Oxford Univ. Press, 1964), pp. 131 ff.

[4] These figures are taken from: Frank, "Sociology of Development and Underdevelopment of Sociology," *Catalyst*, Summer, 1967, pp. 46-9; Frank, *Capitalism and Underdevelopment in Latin America* (N.Y., Monthly Review Press, 1967); Keith Griffin and Ricardo French-Davis, "El Capital Extranjero y el Desarrollo," *Revista Económica*, 1964, pp. 16-22; Luis Vitale, "Latin America: Feudal or Capitalist?", James Petras and Maurice Zeitlin, eds., *Latin America: Reform or Revolution?* (Greenwich, Conn., Fawcett, 1968); Maurice Halperin, "Growth and Crisis in the Latin American Economy," in Petras and Zeitlin, eds., *op. cit.;* Griffin, *op. cit.,* pp. 144-5; CEPAL, *Estudio Económico de América Latina* (annual) (Santiago, CEPAL); U.N. Dept. of Economic and Social Affairs, *Foreign Capital in Latin America* (N.Y., U.N., 1955), p. 15; Harry Magdoff, "Economic Aspects of U.S. Imperialism," *Monthly Review*, Nov., 1966; U.S. Department of Commerce data (*Balance of Payments Statistical Supplement, Survey of Current Business*); CEPAL, *El Segundo Decenio,* p. 9; Miguel Wionczek, "El Endeudamiento Público Externo y la Inversión Privada Extranjera en América Latina" presented to Consejo Latinoamericano de Ciencias Sociales, Lima, Oct. 1968, p. 6 (mimeo).

[5] The principal ones are: Theotonio Dos Santos, Fernando Cardoso, Enzo Faletto, Aníbal Quijano, Osvaldo Sunkel, José Luis Reyna, Edelberto Torres, Tomas Vasconi, Marcos Kaplan, Pablo González-Casanova, and Dale Johnson.

The specific impetus for the dependency theorists was their increasing dissatisfaction with an earlier Latin American model, that of the U.N. Economic Commission for Latin America (CEPAL), and particularly its failure to explain the economic stagnation and aggravation of social problems in Latin America during the 1960's. (See below.) They also incorporated some of the principal theoretical contributions of André Gunder Frank's analysis of underdevelopment. Although my account of the dependency model is taken largely from the work of these Latin Americans, they should not be held responsible for those elements (e.g. the infrastructure of dependency) which I have added here.

[6] Dos Santos, "Crisis de la Teoría del Desarollo y las Relaciones de Dependencia en América Latina," reprint from *Boletin de CESO*, Oct.-Nov. 1968, pp. 26, 29.

[7] Griffin, *op. cit.,* pp. 62, 265.

[8] According to CEPAL, *External Financing in Latin America* (N.Y., U.N., 1965), p. 215, the proportion of U.S. private investment directed toward the industrial sector in Latin America has risen from 35 per cent in 1951 to 60 per cent in 1962.

[9] Paul Baran, *The Political Economy of Growth* (New York, Monthly Review Press, 1957), pp. 194-5.

[10] For a good example of the classical CEPAL model, see Raúl Prebisch, *Toward a Dynamic Development Policy for Latin America* (N.Y., U.N., 1963). Good critiques of the classical CEPAL assumptions and analysis have been presented by A. G. Frank, "Latin America: A Decrepit Capitalist Castle with a Feudal-Seeming Facade," *Monthly Review*, Dec., 1963, and "The Underdevelopment Policy . . ."; Dos Santos, "Crisis de la Teoría . ." and "Dependencia Económica . . "; Vitale, *op. cit.*; Sergio Bagú, "La Economia de la Sociedad Colonial," *Pensamiento Crítico*, April, 1969.

[11] The irony is that much of the empirical evidence which contradicts (and is used to refute) the classical CEPAL analysis and strategy comes from the very thorough annual and periodic studies made by CEPAL itself.

[12] A. G. Frank, "The Development of Underdevelopment," *Monthly Review*, September, 1966; see also *Capitalism and Underdevelopment* and other works cited above.

[13] Examples of international relations theory may be found in several selections in Stanley Hoffmann, ed., *Contemporary Theory in International Relations* (Englewood Cliffs, N.J, Prentice-Hall, 1960), e.g., Frederick Dunn, "The Scope of International Relations."

[14] The main theorists discussed here are: Joseph Schumpeter, *Imperialism; Social Classes* (N.Y., Meridian, 1955); John Strachey, *The End of Empire* (N.Y., Praeger, 1964); Richard Barnet, *Intervention and Revolution* (N.Y., World Publishing Co., 1968); Juan Bosch, *Pentagonism, A Substitute for Imperialism* (N.Y., Grove Press, 1968); Franz Schurmann, "On Imperialism" (mimeo, 1967); Bernard Semmel, *Imperialism and Social Reform* (Garden City, N.Y., Anchor, 1968). A notable non-Marxist exception to the following discussion is J. A. Hobson, *Imperialism* (Ann Arbor, Univ. of Michigan Press, 1965).

[15] The theory presented here is Marxist in the sense of remaining within the Marxist tradition—even though Marx himself left little in the way of an explicit *theory* of imperialism. This does not necessarily imply blanket acceptance of the works of Lenin, Luxemburg, or any other individual Marxist. Even among Marxists there is considerable controversy as to the specific nature of modern imperialism. See: V. I. Lenin, *Imperialism, The Highest Stage of Capitalism* (Peking, Foreign Languages Press, 1965); Rosa Luxemburg, *The Accumulation of Capital* (N.Y.,Monthly Review Press, 1964); Victor Perlo, *The Empire of High Finance* (N.Y., International Publishers, 1956); Heather Dean, "Scarce Resources," (Ann Arbor, Radical Education Project); Michael Barrat-Brown, *After Imperialism* (London, Heinemann, 1963); Baran, *op. cit.*) Moreover, many of the classical Marxist writings on imperialism are specific to a particular historical era (e.g., the late nineteenth and early twentieth centuries).

[16] Paul Baran and Paul Sweezy, *Monopoly Capital* (N.Y., Monthly Review Press, 1966), p. 6. Other works based on the monopoly capital model include: James O'Connor, "The Meaning of Economic Imperialism," "Notes on the Multinational Corporation," (elsewhere in this volume), and other writings; Harry Magdoff, *The Age of Imperialism* (N.Y., Monthly Review Press, 1969) and "Economic Aspects of U.S. Imperialism," David Horowitz, *Empire and Revolution* (N.Y., Random House, 1969). The emphasis given here to the monopolistic corporations is not meant to detract from the importance of the institutions of financial capital (particularly banks) nor to underestimate the extent to which corporate and financial capital have been integrated. In a sense the entire dispute about financial *vs.* corporate capital is distorted: Lenin himself defined "financial capital" as "the concentration of production; the monopolies arising therefrom; the merging or coalescence of the banks with industry" (*Imperialism* p. 52).

[17] O'Connor, "The International Corporations and Economic Underdevelopment," *Science and Society*, Spring, 1970, pp. 45-6.

[18] The following account of generally shared interests of the multinational corporations should not be taken to imply the absence of conflicting interests between individual corporations (or even within one conglomerate); indeed such conflicts exist

and remain important. But given the essentially monopolistic (rather than competitive) nature of contemporary capitalism, particular interests are often superseded by the overriding common interests of corporate capital.

[19] A recent article in *Fortune* (Juan Cameron, "Threatening Weather in South America," Oct., 1969) stated: "[U.S. investors in Latin America] find the rules that govern foreign investment constantly changing, almost always in what, from the American investor's point of view, is an undesirable direction. Day-to-day operations are becoming more and more difficult, and planning for the future uncertain and sometimes futile . . ." This concern is also frequently expressed by organizations representing U.S. business, such as the Council for Latin America.

[20] O'Connor, "The Meaning of Economic Imperialism"; see also Raymond Mikesell, ed., *U.S. Government and Private Investment Abroad* (Eugene, Ore., Univ. of Oregon Press, 1962).

[21] For more details on the functions of aid (whose importance to American corporations overseas has been repeatedly confirmed by U.S. corporate and aid officials), see: John Montgomery, *The Politics of Foreign Aid* (N.Y., Praeger, 1962); Mikesell, ed., *op. cit.*; Mikesell, *Public International Lending for Development* (N.Y., Random House, 1966); Hamza Alavi, "Imperialism, Old and New," *Socialist Register*, 1964; William Caspary, "American Economic Imperialism" (Ann Arbor, Radical Education Project); and even Congressional testimony and reports such as "New Directions for the 1970's: Toward a Strategy of Inter-American Development," Subcommittee on Inter-American Affairs of the House Committee on Foreign Affairs (Washington, Government Printing Office, 1969).

[22] Dos Santos, "El Nuevo Carácter de la Dependencia," revised and reprinted in Matos Mar, ed., *op. cit.*, p. 24.

11

FIDEL CASTRO

On Underdevelopment

There are still many people among the masses who are unaware of one of the most worrisome and serious of contemporary problems: the problem of underdevelopment—this word that is heard so often. What does underdevelopment consist of? What is the significance of the underdeveloped world? How can this be explained clearly and precisely?

The world is divided into developed countries and countries termed "underdeveloped." The euphemism of calling them "developing" countries is also used; in the argot of international organizations they are called developing countries. And we would like to call attention to some data that may help our masses to situate the problem of Cuba within the context of the present world situation.

Many of the developed countries embarked on their development more than a hundred years ago. They developed slowly and, in many cases, with the aid of the resources of their colonies, which were plundered mercilessly, and with resources amassed from the sweat of their masses, who were exploited to an incredible degree. Written testimony exists; there are the chapters written by Marx and Engels concerning the plight of the working class in England: workers who labored 15 or 16 hours a day, children under ten years of age who worked full time under the worst material conditions. In other words, the resources which enable those countries to accumulate investment capital and on which they based their development were extracted from the sweat of their colonies and from the sweat of their workers.

Industry was mainly developed in Europe, the United States, and Canada in such a way that nowadays these countries of developed economies have an extraordinary head start in relation to the underdeveloped world, which they exploited yesterday and which they exploit today in many ways, either directly, via new institutions, or indirectly.

But let's take a look at the figures on the gross product of the developed countries, what their production was in 1960 and what it is expected to be in 1975. The United States with a population of 180 million inhabitants, had a gross national product of 446,100 million dollars—we'll say pesos. This was the gross national product of the U.S. economy in 1960, and it should reach $865,400 million for a population of 235 million in 1975. Western Europe had a gross product of 394,659 million pesos in 1960 for a population of 353 million; it is estimated that this figure will reach $750,748 million in 1975 for a population of 402 million inhabitants. Japan, in 1960, had a gross national product of $55,604 million for a population of 93 million inhabitants and it is estimated that this figure will rise to $138,350 million for a population of 106 million inhabitants in 1975. Canada had a gross national product of $31,530 million for a population of 17 million; it is estimated that this figure will rise to $63,527 million for a population of 23 million in 1975.

These are the major developed capitalist countries of the world. We should also include the Republic of South Africa and Australia.

So that all these countries—the United States, the Western European countries, Japan, and Canada—had a total gross national product of 927,893 million pesos in 1960. It is estimated that this figure will rise to 1,818,025 million pesos in 1975. That is, almost 2 billion—the Spanish billion, at least in my time, was a million millions; I believe the U.S. billion is a thousand millions; here I'm talking about Spanish billions.

So. What was Latin America's gross product in 1960? It was 61,750 million pesos for a population of 204 million inhabitants. That is, 61,750 million pesos in all of Latin America as opposed to $446,100 million in the United States. According to optimistic estimates, which, it appears, will not be borne out, in 1975, Latin America will have a gross product of 117,800 million for a population of 299 million inhabitants.

Africa: a gross product in 1960 of 21,720 million for a population of 240 million. For 1975, an estimated gross product of 40,500 million for a population of 338 million.

The Middle East: a gross product in 1960 of $7,300 million for a population of 51 million inhabitants. For 1975, an estimated gross product of $13,700 million for 76 million inhabitants.

Asia (excluding China): a gross product in 1960 of $68,750 million for a population of 797 million. For 1975, an estimated gross product of $129,300 million for a population of 1,140 million.

In 1960 all of the countries of the underdeveloped world together produced a total of $159,520 million for a population of 1,294 million. That is, all the underdeveloped world together produced a third of what the United States produced and less than half of what Western Europe produced. And it is estimated that this will reach $301,000 million in 1975. That is, in 1975 the entire underdeveloped world's gross product will be very much lower than the U.S. gross product for 1960.

The entire underdeveloped world, now with 1,294 million inhabitants, will reach 1,853 million by 1975. So that today the developed world produces, or rather produced in 1960, twelve times as much per capita as the underdeveloped world, and in 1975 this per capita production will be fourteen times as great.

While the developed world will increase its production by almost a billion, its population will only increase by some 122 million. That is, 122 million new inhabitants but $890 thousand million increase in production. Meanwhile, the underdeveloped countries' population will increase by some 559 million, but their total production will increase by only $142 thousand million.

So that from 1960 to 1975, in developed countries, production will increase by $7,300 a year for every additional inhabitant, while in the underdeveloped world the increase for each new inhabitant will be just $250 a year. That is, for each new birth in developed countries production will increase 29 times as much as it will increase for each new birth in the underdeveloped world.

Translated into available income, this means the following: the per capita available income in the USA in 1960 was $1,762; in

1975 it will be $2,564, an increase of $802. As a whole, the underdeveloped world's available per capita income in 1960 ranged from $70 to $85, while in 1975 it will range from $90 to $110. If in 1960 the average increase, or rather, the per capita available income in the USA, for example, was 22 times as much as that of the underdeveloped countries, in 1975 it will be 25 times as much.

The imbalance—that is, the deficit in the balance of payments between the underdeveloped nations and the developed capitalist countries in world trade—was $4,640 million in 1960, and it will come to $10,500 million in 1970 and $18,900 million in 1975.

To this incredible situation of poverty, we must add the siphoning off of profits from investments. That is, the amount siphoned off by consortiums and monopolies must first be subtracted from the profits that would have corresponded to the underdeveloped countries. And there's still an even more subtle—although quite evident—method of exploitation: the fact that the developed world imposes its own conditions upon the underdeveloped world; the prices paid for the products of the underdeveloped world are ever lower, while the articles manufactured in the developed world are sold at ever higher prices. It is estimated that tea, for example, will drop some 6 per cent in price by 1975; wool, 6 per cent; cotton, 6 per cent; cacao, 9 per cent; skins and hides, 9 per cent; jute fiber, 14 per cent; rubber, 32 per cent.

That is the situation. Does it have any solution? Is there a way out? How was this situation created? Can any underdeveloped country today repeat the history of those countries when they began their industrialization? If not, why not? What factors constitute the major obstacles? One factor is population increase.

Let's see just how the population of the world is increasing. In 1967 the world's population increased by 70 million persons. It will reach a total of 3,500 million in 1968. In 1968 there will be 118 million births and 49 million deaths.

At this rate of population increase, by the year 2000 the world's population will reach 7,000 million. And for many of you, especially the students, the year 2000 is not so far off.

Earlier FAO estimates had set the figure at 6,000 million, but at the present rate of increase the world's population will reach 7,000 million by the end of this century.

And what is the situation in Latin America? Let us look at what the United States Demographic Office states in information received on March 10: "The Demographic Office today predicted that within 32 years the population of Latin America will increase by 157 per cent, the highest rate of increase in the world.

"The present population of this region, some 268 million, will increase to 690 million by the end of the century.

"In contrast, the U.S. agency states that the populations of North America and the Soviet Union will increase by 42 per cent, and that of Europe by just 25 per cent."

That is, Europe—whose population of 353 million produced some $400,000 million in 1960—will increase its population by 25 per cent, in 32 years. In contrast, Latin America, whose population of 204 million produced a total of $61,750 million in 1960—that is, less than one-sixth as much as Europe—will have a population of 690 million in 32 years.

"The U.S. Demographic Office warns that, with the exception of Argentina, Chile, and Uruguay, Latin America is, in only a slightly better position than Africa, the region with the highest infant mortality and illiteracy rates and the lowest per capita income and life expectancy in the world.

"The most rapidly-increasing rates of population growth in the world are those of El Salvador, 3.7 per cent; the Dominican Republic, 3.6 per cent; and Venezuela, 3.6 per cent.

"At the same time, this agency observes that the area from Mexico to Panama is the part of the world with the highest rate of population growth, where the population will double in twenty years if the present rate of growth continues."

The report goes on: "Almost invariably, the countries having the greatest population increases are those in which the great number of cases of needy and unprotected children creates serious social and economic problems."

The report goes on to say that a "shocking aspect" of the present demographic situation is the growing gap between the rates of food production and human reproduction.

"Every day there are more than 190,000 new mouths to feed," the research group asserts." Yet, of the thousand million additional calories needed to provide this human mass with even a starvation diet, less than one-third is being produced."

This is affirmed by the Demographic Office of an imperialist country, the most imperialist of all imperialists.

Constantly, almost daily, news dispatches come in concerning this tremendous problem of the increase in world population with which the increase in food production does not keep pace.

"New Delhi, India, March 12, REUTER: The mass sterilization drive which has been put into effect to date in India will prevent the birth of 10 million children in the next ten years, it was stated today in Parliament.

"The Minister of Family Planning, Sripati Chandrasehar, told the Council of States (Upper Chamber) that a total of 3,500,000 persons have been subjected to sterilization operations to date.

"Surgical operations are voluntary in India, whose population of 515 million is increasing, according to recent official statistics, by 13 million every year. In November, following a virtual storm of questions brought in Parliament, a plan for the compulsory sterilization of parents who already have three children was thrown out.

"Chandrasehar also said today that the Indian Government plans to introduce laws this year which will raise the legal age for marriage from 15 to 18." Perhaps one of our "rumormongers" read this dispatch and got his wires crossed!

But, in reality, this is something that will require ever greater attention, since it truly constitutes one of the most serious problems of today's world. And let us see how this is related to the problems of development.

You all can see what the imperialists propose: formulas for birth control, including sterilization and practically forced sterilization. In other words, their solution for this situation is sterilization of the human race.

Not long ago, the U.S. Secretary of State declared in alarm that, if science and technology fail to find a solution to this problem, the world will find itself exposed to a thermonuclear explosion. These people are so frightened by these unsolved realities that they're beginning to see thermonuclear bombs exploding everywhere. And presumably this other bomb that is now in the process of gestation is indeed going to continue to develop, and it cannot be subjected to agreements or controls of any kind. Now, then, how and why does this phenomenon—together with other factors—have a tremendous influence on the problem of the development of the underdeveloped world?

The countries that began the Industrial Revolution in the last century were—among others—England, France, Belgium, Germany and Italy.

What was the rate of population growth in England when that country began its industrial development? It was 0.6 per cent a year. At that time, various plagues, illnesses and epidemics still provided a kind of natural balance. Plagues appeared and wiped out large parts of the population. Modern developments, modern-type medicines which have practically eradicated many of those epidemics, were then nonexistent.

So, the rate of population growth in England was 0.6 per cent; in France, 0.4 per cent; in Belgium, 0.7 per cent; in Germany, 0.8 per cent; and in Italy, 0.8 per cent.

With a 0.7 per cent increase the population could grow 40 per cent in 50 years. That is, on the basis of a 0.7 per cent growth, the population could increase 40 per cent every 50 years.

During the first 60 to 100 years of their development, these countries achieved only a one per cent increase in gross product per inhabitant per year. That is, these countries, that initiated the era of the Industrial Revolution, succeeded in increasing their gross product per inhabitant, per year, by only one per cent in the first 60 to 100 years of their development. This was true in spite of the fact that, in many cases, they had colonies to exploit and ruthlessly exploited workers, children, women—everyone. They managed to increase their annual gross product by one per cent.

To do this, they invested only six per cent of their gross national product. That is, by investing six per cent of the gross national product, and with a population growth of 0.7 per cent, their economy grew at the rate of one per cent per annum.

They raised the amount of their investment of the gross national product to 12 per cent only after their income had grown to be three or four times greater than the mean per capita income of today's underdeveloped countries—that is, when they had a four-times-greater available income, per capita, than that of a person living in an underdeveloped country today. In other words, once they had reached a level four times higher than that of any underdeveloped country today, they raised or a raise occurred—since this was not the product of specific planning but rather what resulted from the prevailing reality—of 12 per cent in the amount of gross product invested in furthering their economic development.

Now that is the story of how development began, what the population increase was, what per cent of the gross product they invested, what per cent of growth they got, and how much they grew in a period of 60 to 100 years.

If, on the other hand, a country's population grows at a rate of 2.2 per cent, in 50 years it will be tripled. So whereas the developed countries' population in the beginning of their development increased by 40 per cent in 50 years—or could have increased by 40 per cent—the countries that are now underdeveloped, any underdeveloped country that increases its population by 2.2 per cent, will triple its entire population in 50 years and will need to invest no less than 12 per cent of the gross product to compensate for the population increase.

This means that, while the countries that we were talking about compensated for the population growth by investing 6 per cent and increased production by one per cent annually, an underdeveloped country with a 2.2 per cent population growth at present needs to invest double that, just to compensate for the population increase, without augmenting its annual per capita production.

If, because of that enormous population growth, such a country wants to increase its gross product per inhabitant by one per cent annually, it must invest no less than 16 per cent of its gross product. Thus a country with a 2.2 per cent rate of growth, investing 16 per cent of its gross product, will compensate for the population increase, and its production will grow by one per cent annually. Thus, in 80 years it would only double its income, and that income is today ten times less per capita than Europe's and 20 times less than that of the United States.

That means that a country whose population grows by 2.2 per cent, by investing 16 per cent of its gross product, will increase its annual production by one per cent and in 80 years will double its present income, which is one-twentieth of the per capita income in the United States.

In order to increase the per capita gross product by two per cent, a country whose population grows by 2.2 per cent should invest twenty per cent of its national gross product.

None of those developed countries reached an investment of 20 per cent until its income was already five or six times as high as the present income of the underdeveloped world.

Now then, in the case of Latin America, as we see it, the population growth rate is not 2.2 per cent. So where does that 2.2 per cent come from? It was taken by the United Nations as an average population increase in the underdeveloped world. But an underdeveloped country with that per cent annually does not reflect reality.

Thus, Latin America, with a 3.2 per cent population growth rate, would need to invest 25 per cent of its national gross product in order to achieve a two per cent annual per capita increase in its gross product. It would need to invest 25 per cent of its national gross product, which it doesn't invest, nor can it invest, nor under the present political conditions will it ever be able to invest.

Even with an incomparable higher per capita income, no currently developed country ever invested such amounts.

Now, let's look at another problem related to this population increase. Don't get scared; we're not promoting family planning or birth control. Those are the measures that the imperialists are proposing for the underdeveloped world. The only measures that we believe will solve the problem are different. In countries with a 2.2 per cent population growth and a low average life expectancy—that is, where there is a high birth rate and the people die younger—more than thirty per cent of the population is under ten years of age and cannot participate in production. That is, another factor related to this enormous annual increase is that more than thirty per cent of the population is under ten years of age, while in the developed countries the percentage of children under ten years of age fluctuates between 15 and 18 per cent of the population. This means that the rich countries, that have much more, much more income available, have much less population under ten years of age—about half of the same population category as the poor country with a very low per capita income. The percentage of the population under ten years of age in an underdeveloped country is double that of a developed country.

In the developed countries per capita food production increases nearly two per cent a year, the slow increase of their population notwithstanding; with all their technology, the developed countries achieve an increase of two per cent, more or less.

In Latin America as a whole—when I say as a whole I mean the average, because some have more, others less—with a population growth of over three per cent, the per capita food production in 1961 was two per cent lower than what it had been prior to the Second World War.

The United Nations Yearbook for 1967 states: "Both in Africa and in Latin America, where there has not been any increase in food production since 1965, food production decreased in 1966. This loss of level cannot be easily made up, because it would require an increase of seven per cent in 1967 in order to equal the 1964 level per person."

In this desperate race against time, a year when the population increases three per cent, when there is a production stagnation or a decrease, the effort needed to reach the previous level is almost impossible to make. That is, this conduces to a phenomenon of progressively decreasing per capita food production. The problems of the development of food production are very serious, very serious. Above all, when much of the best land nearest to the cities is already used for agriculture, the problems posed by the requirements of transportation, roads, technology, irrigation and fertilization are very serious. You can increase production incredibly, above all when you begin with a very poor technology, but the difficult part is the effort necessary to reach the application of higher levels of technology.

What factors facilitated development in the times of those early developing countries which today are obstructing it? We have already spoken of the population, of the increase of population, of the percentage of the population under ten years of age. One factor is modern technology, which involves an investment incomparably higher than in that earlier period. You understand that, in the period of the horse-drawn carriage, in the period of the first textile machines, in the period of the first machinery with low technological requirements, low cost, low levels of investment, men who had practical experience would invent certain machinery. The necessary investment per active worker—that is, investment in machinery necessary to keep a worker active—was equivalent to a worker's salary for five to eight months in that period. The necessary financial investment was the same as that earned by a worker in five to eight months.

Today, in order to construct an industrial plant with modern technology in an underdeveloped country, it is necessary to invest in machinery the equivalent of a worker's salary for 350 months— that is, for thirty years. Therefore, take any example, any of the cement factories, or if you wish, the nitrogenous fertilizer plant in Cienfuegos, that will cost more than 40,000,000 dollars in foreign exchange alone, and, in all, more than 60,000,000, and will employ fewer than a thousand workers. Naturally, this fertilizer cannot be produced in any other way than with a really modern industrial plant; otherwise it means wasting fuel, wasting all sorts of things. That production of nitrogen, if it is to be economical, must be carried on with very modern machinery, and that factory will cost the country some 60,000,000 dollars, more than 60,000 dollars per worker to be employed there. That is, the complexity of modern technology demands an enormous investment—that is, sixty times as great as that needed when the Industrial Revolution began in those industrialized countries.

Another question: almost all the rudimentary machines with which the Industrial Revolution began could be produced in the country, so that England and France imported approximately 1.5 per cent of the machinery they used. They imported only 1.5 per cent.

The underdeveloped countries, given the technical complexity of modern machinery, have to import no less than ninety per cent of the machinery they need—it is obvious that there is a difference between manufacturing a carriage and manufacturing a locomotive.

That is, the first machines with which the Industrial Revolution began were constructed within the country. Today when an underdeveloped country needs an industrial plant, it must import machines at a high cost because those machines are necessarily and unavoidably costly, and the equipment costs the country sixty times more than it used to cost per worker employed. And not only that: that same technical complexity demands skilled workers and specialists who must be trained over a long period of time, in costly training programs.

Naturally, these are not the only problems, not at all. But I am pointing out some that serve as examples to explain the present phenomenon, the unavoidable difficulties that the countries of the underdeveloped world face.

There is another question that has to be taken into account, and it is that many underdeveloped countries have sectors of the population devoted to many unproductive activities, such as bureaucratic and commercial activities, so that a very high percentage of the population and the resources are invested in these activities.

This is speaking about the objective problems, the objective difficulties. Now, then, the subjective ones: the social system, political regime, feudal exploitation of the land, strong-man oligarchical governments imposed by imperialism or neocolonialism, control of the economy by imperialist monopolies, sacking of natural resources, even sacking of technical resources. And one of the most serious problems is illiteracy. In 1950, ninety per cent of the countries of the underdeveloped world had an illiteracy rate of over fifty per cent, more than fifty per cent.

Of course, an understanding of these things can make us more clearly aware of the monstrous crimes the imperialists are committing the world over, the monstrous crime implicit in imperialism's policy of repression of the revolutionary movement, a policy which unleashes aggression and war and manufactures all kinds of puppet regimes. For what purpose? So as to keep the world in this situation. And why? To satisfy the interests of the financial oligarchies in those countries.

Because, once a country has become industrialized, its standard of living largely depends, or will depend, on the productivity of the labor force and the type of equipment used in industry, which will permit it to achieve a high per capita production. And, of course, even if all privileges and the exploitation of man have not been eliminated, the standard of living of a worker in a developed capitalist country is different from that of a farmer or worker in an underdeveloped capitalist country.

The United States not only possesses up-to-date technical equipment and a high rate of productivity, it not only is able to extract natural resources, cheat and exploit a large part of the world through its monopolies, through unequal terms of exchange, but in addition it drains technical personnel from the underdeveloped world.

As an example, we can cite that, of the 43,000 engineers who emigrated to the United States between 1949 and 1961, 60 per cent came from underdeveloped countries. Underdeveloped countries! Remember the statistics cited: increasing population, the amount of gross product, the incredible current difficulties of an underdeveloped nation. And, to make matters worse, of the 43,000 engineers who emigrated to the United States in a period of twelve or thirteen years, 60 per cent were from underdeveloped countries. Of the 11,206 emigrants from Argentina who entered the United States between 1951 and 1963, 50 per cent were qualified engineers. Half of the 11,206 Argentine emigrants were qualified engineers.

Of course in such countries, where there has been no revolution, those who are permitted to go to the United States are selected from personnel who will benefit the U.S. financially. It is not the same as here, where they have taken the lumpen elements, the bourgeoisie, the latifundists, the thugs, all types of persons. Here they have not had a chance to make much of a selection. They permit a limited number from Latin America and give preference to highly qualified technical personnel.

In 1950 the number of engineers and scientists who emigrated to the United States from all over the world was 1,500. By 1967 the rate at which engineers and scientists emigrated to the U.S. was 6,000 a year. So the United States, with its enormous economic resources, drains the world—especially the underdeveloped world—of scientific and technical brains.

And this is a situation which is resented not only in the underdeveloped world. Europe, too, in spite of its standard of living and development, despite its advanced technology, is beginning to resent this trend, because it is beginning to fall behind the United States. Because the United States drains technicians and buys out any European enterprise it can. They even invest a mere ten per cent of the value of an enterprise. For they do not invest just U.S. money in Europe, but, controlling the most advanced methods of technology, they raise the capital in Europe itself for their investments.

And we have observed that this has been occurring quite frequently. That they buy up an Italian factory here, a Spanish factory there, or a French or British plant, or that of any other country. And, at times, as in the matter of the rice harvesting combines, this can virtually cause a social problem. When we attempted to purchase a certain type of rice combine in Europe, we discussed this purchase with a Belgian firm, and it turned out to be an impossibility. Even though the workers were idle, they would not sell us any equipment. The workers favored the sale, but it was impossible because a U.S. company held stock in that plant. And when a U.S. company holds stock in a European firm, the one who gives orders concerning that plant is not the government of that country, but the U.S. Department of State or the Department of Commerce, the U.S. Government.

And Europe resents the fact that the United States is taking over its industry, infiltrating, draining off each nation's best technicians and carrying out a policy of penetration which threatens to leave Europe far behind the United States.

We have been observing, or trying to observe, attempting to gain an overall picture of such matters, which are not discussed in any manual, just as they do not deal with a number of very important matters, such as the problem of unequal terms of exchange, by which the developed world contributes to, or in one way or another takes part in, the plunder of underdeveloped countries.

12

JOSUÉ DE CASTRO

Colonialism, Hunger and Progress

Hunger, the most tragic expression of the economic complex of backwardness, is the most terrible and the most widespread disease in our world. It takes an enormous toll of human lives. Hunger is the reason for the demographic differences between the poor and rich countries, differences so pronounced that I would describe the highly developed countries as a world in which people are born to live upon the earth, whereas the poor countries are the kingdom of starvation and misery, a world in which people are born only to ascend to the heavens like the angels. Over half the population in these countries dies in childhood. This mortality rate creates a new geography, a geography in which not the earth feeds man but man feeds the earth with his body.

Why is it that in the world of today two-thirds of mankind go hungry? And why is it that hunger reigns in those parts of the world which we refer to as underdeveloped? In my view the main reason for hunger in the world is colonialism. Here I would like to make an explanation. Someone may say that people went hungry long before the colonialist era was opened by the voyages of Vasco da Gama in 1498. Yes, hunger has raged at all times in history. But judge for yourselves. In the past people went hungry because they didn't have the technical and scientific means with which to combat it. In the non-colonial countries, in countries which are highly developed and where the achievements of science and technology find practical application, mass starvation has been abolished. It continues to reign in the underdeveloped countries precisely because the colonialist economic structure there has not permitted the use of scientific and technical achievements to solve the problem of hunger.

Only twenty per cent of the land which could be cultivated by man, considering the present level of technical development, is being tilled in the world today. Why is this so? Because agriculture is viewed through the prism of possible profit. Agriculture is frowned upon because its raw materials and foodstuffs are much cheaper than manufactured goods. This is the first consequence of colonialism. It was colonialism that led to the gap between industrial and agricultural prices and, consequently, damped down the interest in agricultural advancement and rational utilization of the land. Second, surely it is possible to enlarge agricultural production even if all the crop areas have already been tilled and the soil exhausted. Yes, this can be done. Provided the necessary capital, machinery, and labor are concentrated on a definite area of land, yields can be increased five- to six-fold.

So it is a lie to say that the land and the resources needed to ensure the food are lacking. Given the present level of technology it would be possible to feed a population ten times larger than that inhabiting our planet today. And with the advance of technology it will be possible to feed one hundred times as many people because right now we can foresee the discovery of an artificial synthesis of organic substances. No longer shall we be bound by the biological world which makes us wait until the fruits have ripened. In the future we shall obtain them through synthesis in a brief space of time. And even without making any utopian plans, and by sticking to reality, we can affirm, on the basis of the latest scientific achievements, that Malthus was wrong.

The Malthus doctrine appeared at the time of the Industrial Revolution when the British ruling class, then pursuing a brutal policy in India, badly needed a salve for its conscience, that is, if it had such a thing. Its aim was to either conquer or destroy the

Indians, do away with their textile industry and, consequently, condemn them to starvation. At the same time it wanted to find justification for its actions, to demonstrate that it was not the British who were to blame but the Indians who "were multiplying at a rate beyond control." Malthus rendered a good service to the colonialists. His name was given to the pessimistic theory which has proved so useful to the rulers of this world and which is as old as social injustice. Malthus was generously rewarded for his service: he was given a professorship in the East India Company's college.

It is now customary to say that colonialism is in its death agony; but I think that as yet it would be more correct to say that it is not in its agony but that it is suffering from a grave illness. The fact that forty countries have gained political independence does not yet signify the death agony of colonialism. Political independence has existed for over a century in Latin America, but economically these countries still are colonies. Fortunately, we are living now in the atomic age when progress in all spheres is proceeding at a rapid rate, and I hope that in Africa the agony of colonialism will be of shorter duration.

The colonialists have the means with which to cause a state of hunger and maintain it; they can do this by means of a mechanism which I shall try to explain by the example of India. When the British first came to India that country was emerging from the medieval phase of its history. The Middle Ages in Europe also witnessed considerable outbreaks of famine because the economic life of those days was based on autarchy, while means of communication were poorly developed. In the eighteenth century when India was emerging from her medieval stage, her handicraft industry was highly developed and attracted the rural population. What we now know as agrarian overpopulation was non-existent. The foundations of a modern economy were beginning to take shape, in which agriculture used only the labor power needed for production. But it was exactly at this moment that the British arrived and disrupted everything. They destroyed the handicraft industry, strangled industry at its birth, and forced the Indian to return to his village, which was now overpopulated in relation to technique and capital.

Then, as was the case in all colonies, a colonial type of agriculture was introduced in India, an agriculture based on crops for export, i.e., not the crops the country needed but crops that were profitable for the colonialists. Thus it was that production of these "colonial goods" became the occupation of the inhabitants of the tropical countries; occupation was simply the hypocritical covering for their subjugation and enslavement. The colonial peoples, forced to produce for the enrichment of the metropolitan countries, could hardly be enthusiastic. And then it began to be said of them, especially of the Indians in Latin America, that they did not like agricultural work, and that rather than engage in it they would prefer death. There is some logic in this statement. For in substance they were faced with the choice: either slow death from starvation or a quick death of their own free will. And not infrequently they chose the latter. It was more practical to do so than to die for the sake of work. Such kinds of economic activity as growing sugar, cotton, rubber, and coffee for export are destructive rather than productive—and all for the sake of exporting goods at cheap prices, with the receipts going into the pockets of a tiny minority.

To this day there are tribes in Black Africa for whom agriculture is the sole occupation. And while it cannot be said that they live in affluence, they at least vary their diet. This safeguards them against a shortage of vitamins, and meager though their diet is, it keeps life going. But the moment Africans migrate to the towns and begin to work in industry, they begin to suffer from malnutrition. What is the reason for this? The reason is that in the towns they are used as machines which are given only the fuel needed to keep them going—rice and manioc. But they are denied the fresh victuals containing vitamins and proteins. And as we know, the essential thing for metabolism is that the intake of vitamins should correspond to the intake of carbohydrates. And the human organism quickly becomes run down, like a machine abundantly provided with fuel to make it work at high speed but never repaired. And just as the hog is fed with corn to turn the latter into pork, the worker is fed with manioc and beans in order to turn them into sugar and coffee. The process is exactly the same as that of raising pigs: if the most profitable way of marketing corn is to sell it in a bag of pigskin, the most profitable way of marketing manioc is to sell it in the form of sugar in the skin of a Negro or, to be more precise, distilled from his sweat. This, then, was the mechanism which upset and worsened the food balance of various peoples.

But even with this kind of agriculture things could be improved if the growers were paid more for the raw materials. But here major powers resort to another method by means of which the nations dependent on them are kept in poverty. The prices paid for the raw materials are steadily falling. Latin America is now exporting three times more raw materials than it did before the war, but is getting much less money for them. In 1958, for example, Brazil exported millions of sacks of coffee more than in 1948, but received a million dollars less. So what is the use of working? The more you work the less you get. Here, then, you have the explanation for the "laziness" of the tropical peoples.

One of the profit-making mechanisms used by the Americans is payment for not producing. In an indirect way this device is used also in Latin America. The only difference is that in the United States the farmers are generously compensated for not growing crops, whereas in Latin America they are not. But in either case money is paid for not producing, and here we have a contradiction of capitalism expressed in a glaring colonialist form and providing no incentive for progress, for real economic development.

The United States concentrates in its hands seventy per cent of the raw materials of the Western world. This enables it to dictate prices for raw materials. And because of this the other countries find it impossible really to develop their economies. Long-term planning is essential if there is to be any economic and social progress; but, it may be asked, how is it possible to plan for five or ten years when even in the course of a single year the prices of your products and your raw materials are likely to change in terms ranging between fifty per cent and two hundred per cent? Maybe it's only the top politicians who can foresee these price oscillations: when they find out that a particular country is determined to vote in the U.N. in accordance with its own interests and not at the whim of its creditors, then the prices paid for the country's products fall. See what happened to Cuba. The United States bought her sugar, "generously" paying her more than she could get on the world market; the result was that Cuba became a country with a monoculture economy. Sugar filled everything there, just as in Venezuela where the unwholesome smell of oil has penetrated into every pore of her entire culture; one is conscious of it in the streets and even in the houses. Cuba was turned into a "sugar island" suffering from diabetes in exactly the same way as people suffer from it. The United States used to say to the Cubans: We will guarantee you a high export quota, so please be obedient and accommodating.

But there are always patriots who yearn for freedom and for its sake are prepared to sacrifice the sugar. For example, in 1932 Cuba made some efforts to free herself from foreign domination, and so the U.S.A., which prior to this annually bought 5 million bags of Cuban sugar, reduced the quota for the following year to 2 million. As a result, a crisis broke out in the country and its economy was disorganized. Sugar made up two-thirds of Cuba's exports; in Bolivia it was tin, in Venezuela oil, in Brazil coffee; this kind of economic specialization is the second melancholy consequence of colonialism. The concentration on a single product makes the country's economy unstable and dependent. And so long as this is the case, it will never get rid of hunger.

But this state of affairs can be changed. And the example of the selfsame Cuba is proof of this. In 1948 Cuba produced only sugar and imported $140 million worth of beans and rice. One should not overlook the "noble" gesture of the United States in this respect. In 1958 it paid Cuba $60 million more for her sugar than it would have paid had it bought the sugar at world prices. But then with the same "noble" gesture it sold Cuba $140 million worth of beans and rice. In effect, what the Americans paid Cuba was not the price of the sugar but the price of the beans and rice paid to the American farmers. Two years later, after the revolution, Cuba grew on her own soil beans and rice to the value of $40 million and $50 million respectively. She is now gaining for herself economic liberation. But the land is the same land, and she has the same tropical climate. There has been no change in her natural conditions. What has changed is the economic structure, and she has liberated herself from colonialism.

A few words about the International Monetary Fund. This organization is "international" in the sense that it represents various countries, but the seats on the Board and the votes are distributed in proportion to the contribution made by each country. Each vote signifies $100,000. But since the United States makes the biggest contribution, the Fund, from the standpoint of its decisions, is one hundred per cent a United States organization. For this reason there is always a certain amount of mistrust of the reports which the Fund submits to the United Nations. So that this, too, is a form of colonial oppression. My own country, Brazil, has been one of the victims of this oppression. On various pretexts it has been forced to halve the prices of its products. This kind of action deprives the underdeveloped countries of the possibility of buying industrial plants. Being exporters of raw materials, these exports are the only means with which they can buy the machines and develop their industry. But while raw material prices have been falling steadily, prices for the equipment purchased by the Latin American countries have doubled, in the same way as the purchasing power of the dollar has doubled at the behest of the International Monetary Fund. This safeguards U.S. industry against possible competition. Money is available for expanding agriculture and the production of raw materials for export, but it is never found for industrial expansion.

An obsolete economic structure is artificially maintained in the colonial countries. Their population is denied access to education and to health services, because both education and medical service are commodities, and access to them depends wholly on purchasing power, and purchasing power is extremely low. In each of these countries there is a tiny privileged group, the elite; this elite, associated with the big international trusts and the colonialists, cares nothing for the national interests. It makes no demands, and merely bends the knee in obedience.

The economic development which one can observe in these countries is but a fig leaf. Take, for example, Latin America. The per capita income in Venezuela is $700, i.e., the same as in France. But can Venezuela's cultural standards and social welfare be likened to those in France? By no means, because account should be taken not of *per capita* income, which is an abstraction, but the distribution of income. The $700 per head in Venezuela, an abstract figure, is the mean obtained by adding up the $700 million of the seven families and the poverty of the hungry masses.

The major powers have never been interested in including the economy of the colonies in the world economic system on an equal footing. Yet economic integration is a necessity. All the plans worked out for the colonies will remain a fiction unless they provide for equal economic cooperation.

Industrialization is the only way to end poverty and hunger. It is only in industrial countries that people eat well; in the purely agrarian countries starvation is greatest. But what kind of industrialization will it be? There is a colonial type of industrialization which creates an industry, national in the geographic sense but international in the economic sense, i.e., it does not belong to the country. But there is also the genuine kind of economic development, one that unites the masses. The colonial type of industrialization enriches only the "elite" and makes the bulk of the population poorer than ever. In point of fact there always has been in the underdeveloped countries an insignificant segment of the population with a very high standard of living, whereas the overwhelming majority live under pre-capitalist, feudal, and even pre-feudal conditions. That is why the peoples of Latin America, Africa, and Asia know that their hunger and poverty are not engendered by Nature but are the products of social injustice.

The hunger of the poor and the fear of the rich *vis-à-vis* the hungry must be abolished, and for this there is needed a revolutionary change in the existing system. Financial and technical aid alone to the countries with backward economic and social systems will be of little avail in this respect. All men of good will, all who are anxious to step out along the one road on the earth that belongs to all, should ponder over the problem of hunger.

13

EDUARDO GALEANO

Latin America and the Theory of Imperialism

While Lenin was writing his fundamental work on imperialism in the spring of 1916, the imperialist powers were locked in a bloody conflict for control of the world. This century of ours is passing with the speed of several millennia. In the second imperialist war to redivide the world, it was possible, thanks to the progress that had been made in killing our fellowmen on the earth and in the sky, to reap an even more awesome harvest—the survivors were able to count ten times as many corpses as in the First World War. And today their past feats are being over-shadowed by even greater accomplishments. More bombs have been dropped in an undeclared war on a small, poor country ·in Southeast Asia than fell on Germany, Italy, and Japan in the 1940's. The same giant that is conducting the bloodbath in Vietnam is simultaneously sending astronauts to the distant surface of the moon. Wernher Von Braun is worried about raw materials. "In 1970," he announced, "we intend to orbit a space laboratory at an altitude of 400 kilometers. . . . We will be able to explore all the riches of the earth from this marvellous observation platform: the unknown oil deposits, the copper and zinc mines. . . ."

More than half a century after Lenin wrote his book, monopoly capitalism has shown that it has more than the proverbial nine lives; and imperialism, its logical extension, has survived with unsuspected vigor, centered now around a single great power. But the instruments of this universal system of exploitation are no longer simply the ones Lenin described. Imperialism has evolved and has become more effective, both in robbing as well as in killing. It has polished its methods, extended into new areas, and constructed new models of domination that were unknown on the eve of the Russian Revolution. In this era of electronic computers, the "multinational" corporations do not count their profits on their fingers, to put it mildly.

The goal of this brief paper, a very modest tribute to Lenin's brilliant work and exemplary life, is to provide some data and ideas that may help to clarify certain new features in the system of seizing the world's markets and national resources. We are concerned above all with imperialism in Latin America at the present time—an interlocking system of conquest, domination, extortion, and pillage, in which deceptive characteristics are not lacking.

COLONIALISM AND DEPENDENCE

In *Imperialism, the Highest Stage of Capitalism,* Lenin warned, in refuting Kautsky, that the domination of finance capital not only does not lessen the inequalities and contradictions present in the world economy, but on the contrary accentuates them. Time has passed and proven him right. The inequalities have become sharper. Historical research has shown that the distance that separated the standard of living in the wealthy countries from that of the poor countries toward the middle of the nineteenth century was much smaller than the distance that separates them today. The gap has widened. In 1850 the per capita income in the industrialized countries was fifty per cent higher than in the underdeveloped countries. To have an idea of the progress that has been achieved in the *development of inequality,* we have only to listen to President Richard Nixon: ". . . and I think about what this hemisphere, the new world, will be like at the end of this century. And I consider that if the present growth rates of the United States and of the rest of the hemisphere have not changed, at the end of this century the per capita income in the United States will be fifteen times higher than the income per person of our friends, our neighbors, the members of our family in the rest of the Hemisphere."[1]

The oppressed nations will have to grow much more rapidly just to *maintain* their relative backwardness. Their present low rates of development feed the dynamic of inequality: the oppressor nations are becoming increasingly rich in absolute terms, but they are richer still in relative terms. The overall strength of the imperialist system rests on the necessary inequality of its component parts, and that inequality is achieving ever greater proportions. Capitalism is still capitalism, and unequal development and widespread poverty are still its visible fruits. "Centralized" capitalism can afford the luxury of creating and believing its own myths of opulence, but myths cannot be eaten, and the poor nations that constitute the vast capitalist "periphery" are well aware of this fact. Imperialism has "modernized" itself in its methods and characteristics, but it has not magically turned into a universal philanthropic organization. The system's greed grows with the system itself.

Nowadays imperialism does not require the old-style colonial administrations. The archaic Portuguese model of control over Angola and Mozambique is no longer the most "convenient." Lenin described the reality of his time, saying that "naturally . . . finance capital finds it most 'convenient,' and is able to extract the greatest profit from a subordination which involves the loss of the political independence of the subjected countries and peoples." In his report to the Twenty-second Congress of the CPUSSR in 1961, Nikita Khrushchev reached the conclusion that "imperialism has irrevocably lost its control over most of the peoples of the world." According to his report, 40.7 per cent of the population of the world, without counting the socialist countries, had won their independence after 1919, and the total number of people living in colonies, semi-colonies, and dominions included, at the beginning of the 1960's, less than three per cent of the world's population. "The revolutions of national liberation have dealt a demolishing blow to the colonial Bastille," Khrushchev said. "Forty-two sovereign states have emerged on the ruins of the colonial empires."

In this connection, it can well be said that Latin America is a prophetic zone within the Third World. The political independence of almost all of the Latin American countries dates back to the beginning of the nineteenth century. *It was as a result of that independence, however, that Latin America consolidated its dependence.* Power passed from the "foreign" viceroys to "national" merchants advocating free trade, but it was precisely then that all obstacles were removed for the total incorporation of the entire region into the international division of labor that was centered in England. The words "sovereignty" and "independence" were not then, and still are not in most cases, more than the lip service that vice pays to virtue. In reality, most Latin American countries have never controlled their own internal markets nor the destination of the economic surplus generated by their productive forces. The control of their basic resources has always been in foreign hands, either through direct appropriation of the sources of the production of raw materials and food, or through the monopoly of demand in the foreign markets. The humiliating conditions under which they have received "foreign aid" have always facilitated the penetration of foreign products and capital. Exactly one century after Argentina achieved its "independence," Lenin was able to describe that country as a British semi-colony, and he warned that "finance capital is such a great, it may be said, such a decisive force in all economic and international relations, that it is capable of subordinating to itself, and actually does subordinate to itself, even states enjoying complete political independence." Subsequently this Latin American nation, perhaps the most fortunate in its relations with imperialism, passed through a rather intense process of industrialization and accelerated urbanization: Buenos Aires is one of the largest and most attractive capitals in the world. But this does not keep Argentina from being today a U.S. semi-colony, at least in regard to its oppressive financial dependency on Washington and the omnipotence that direct investments by U.S. corporations enjoy in its internal market.

The threads that make up the dense web of imperialist power have multiplied and become more subtle. It is not by chance that the world-wide process of capitalist integration under the hegemony of the United States, a process filled with tension and conflict, has coincided with the irreversible decline of the old colonial powers and their methods of control. The eminent Brazilian anthropologist Darcy Ribeiro described the new situation in America as follows:

Hegel, in his classic study on the philosophy of history, foresaw the war between the Latin and Anglo-Saxon peoples of the Americas. This war is already taking place. However, instead of troop movements and pitched battles, it is being waged by conspiracies, bribery, contracts, intimidation, coups, programs of sociological studies, economic plans, and publicity campaigns. Through these means of pressure and compulsion, the United States is implementing, extending, and strengthening its own plan for exploiting our resources, organizing our societies, regulating our political life, determining the size of our population, and determining our destiny.[2]

THE INVESTMENTS CHANGE THEIR DIRECTION

The First World War was followed by the well-known withdrawal of European interests from certain underdeveloped areas of the world. In Latin America, due to obvious geopolitical reasons, the devastating advance of U.S. imperialism took place before and with greater speed than it did in other regions; already by the end of the nineteenth century the Caribbean was the *Mare Nostrum* of the United States. When Lenin wrote his book on imperialism, however, U.S. capital still represented less than a fifth of all private, direct, foreign investment in Latin America; today it represents close to three fourths. What concerns us most here is to point out that after the Second World War there was an important change in the direction of these investments. The tendency is clear. Capital invested in public services and mining has been losing its relative importance, while the proportion invested in petroleum and, above all, in manufacturing industries is increasing. Forty years ago U.S. investments in manufacturing represented only six per cent of the total value of U.S. capital in Latin America; in 1960 the proportion had come close to 20 per cent; and at present almost a third of total U.S. investments is in manufacturing.

The three largest countries in Latin America—Argentina, Brazil, and Mexico—are the ones that offer the most attractive markets for foreign industrial capital. The Organization of American States (OAS), the United States' traditional "Ministry of Colonies," describes the process as follows:

Latin American enterprises are beginning to achieve superiority over already established industries and technologies of lesser sophistication, and private North American investments and probably also investments from other industrialized countries are rapidly increasing their participation in certain dynamic industries that require a relatively high degree of technology and are more important in determining the course of economic development.[3]

The penetration has been successful; the potential of U.S. factories located south of the Rio Grande is much greater than that of Latin American-owned industry in general. It can be seen from data released by the U.S. Department of Commerce and the Inter-American Committee of the Alliance for Progress that, based on an index of 1961 = 100, industrial production in Argentina rose to 112.5 in 1965, while during the same period sales by U.S. subsidiaries in Argentina rose to 166.3. The respective figures for Brazil are 109.2 and 120; and for Mexico, 142.2 and 186.8.

Of the fifty largest Argentinian businesses (those with a sales volume in excess of 7 billion pesos annually), half of the sales volume originates in foreign businesses, a third in state enterprises, and only a sixth in private Argentinian businesses.[4] In 1962, two enterprises operating with private Argentinian capital ranked among the five largest industrial enterprises in Latin America; by 1967 both of them had been taken over by foreign capital.[5] A study carried out by the Institute of Social Sciences of the Federal University of Rio de Janeiro and published in 1965 revealed that of the fifty-five multi-billionaire private groups in the Brazilian economy, twenty-nine were foreign, twenty-four Brazilian, and two of mixed foreign and Brazilian capital; of the Brazilian groups, only nine had no links through stockholders with foreign groups or enterprises. A subsequent study by the Brazilian Congress provided new data which spoke eloquently of the denationalization process that is proceeding at breakneck speed in that country's industry.[6] A minister of the Brazilian government said publicly in 1969 that "with a few honorable exceptions, the only strong sector in Brazil, besides the government itself, is foreign capital."[7] His statement is valid not only for Brazil. According to figures published in 1962, fifty-six of the hundred most important enterprises in Mexico are totally or partially controlled by foreign capital, twenty-four belong to the state, and twenty to Mexican private capital.[8] These twenty private Mexican concerns account for barely 13.5 per cent of the total sales volume of the one hundred enterprises under consideration.

Except in the case of petroleum and some public services—activities in which the state clearly predominates in Argentina, Brazil, and Mexico—almost all of the other enterprises included in the above-mentioned studies are manufacturing industries, and it is precisely in this sector that foreign capital is most prominent. If this is the situation in the strongest countries in Latin America, it would be redundant to offer examples of foreign penetration of the few industries in the weaker countries. By far the largest part of these investments in manufacturing belongs to U.S. corporations, although there are European enterprises with quite considerable interests in Latin America. For example, Volkswagen in Brasil; the largest manufacturer of automobiles in Latin America is a German concern.

The interest of imperialist corporations in appropriating the fruits of Latin American industrial growth for themselves and capitalizing it for their benefit does not imply, certainly, a lack of interest on their part in all the other traditional forms of exploitation. It is true that the railway which used to belong to United Fruit in Guatemala was no longer profitable and that Electric Bond and Share and the International Telephone and Telegraph Corporation made a splendid profit when their properties were nationalized in Brazil and they were paid indemnities in gold for outmoded installations. But this abandonment of public services in search of more lucrative activities does not occur in the case of many raw materials and foodstuffs. While a relative decline has been registered in the total volume of new investments in minerals, the U.S. economy cannot do without the supply of vital materials coming from the southern part of the hemisphere. In *The Age of Imperialism*, Harry Magdoff has shown that the United States' need for iron, copper, and a long list of strategic materials is steadily increasing; the proportion of imports is growing as the internal production of the United States declines. This is also the case with petroleum. After all, the splendid iron deposits in the Brazilian valley of Paraopeba caused the fall of two Presidents before the deposits were graciously ceded to the Hanna Mining Company; copper certainly has something to do with the disproportionate amount of military aid that Chile receives from the Pentagon; bauxite was certainly a factor in the conspiracy to overthrow Cheddi Jagan in Guyana; Cuban nickel explains the blind fury of the Empire even better than sugar; while the largest U.S. military mission in Latin America is located in Venezuela, the great oil preserve of Standard Oil and Gulf.

But all of this should not keep us from emphasizing the importance of this new phenomenon, which has occurred long after Lenin's period: the capture of markets *from within*. The affiliates of U.S. and European corporations jump at a single leap over Latin American tariff barriers, paradoxically erected against foreign competition, and seize control of the internal processes of industrialization. They export factories or, frequently, take control of and devour the already existing national factories. For this they can count on the enthusiastic aid of the majority of the governments of Latin America.

UNDER THE SIGN OF PROGRESS?

"The export of capital," wrote Lenin, "greatly affects and accelerates the development of capitalism in those countries to which it is exported." Historical experience has demonstrated that this is not so. The imperialism that Lenin knew—the greed of industrial centers in the search for world markets for their excess production and the capture of all the possible sources of raw materials; the extraction of iron, coal, and oil; the railways cementing their control of the areas under exploitation; the usurious loans made by the financial monopolies; the military expeditions and the wars of conquest—certainly did not accelerate anything except "the development of underdevelopment," as Andre Gunder Frank expresses it so well. Contrary to Midas, imperialism has turned everything it touched into scrap. But now some are tempted to deny this, basing themselves on the supposedly different situation that exists today. It is possible that Lenin was mistaken when he attributed an accelerated effect on development to the "old model" of imperialist exploitation, they argue, but this is not the case with the "new model." There is no lack of technocrats today prepared to demonstrate that foreign capital, in its new positive guise, benefits the areas it penetrates. To the degree that the model of exploitation has changed, they tell us, its consequences have also changed. Previously, imperialism razed the places where a colony or a semi-colony might have dared to erect its own factories, but now the rich countries stimulate the industrialization of the poor nations. This "industrializing imperialism" of our day, they maintain, contrary to the imperialism of past times, has an inevitable civilizing effect on a universal scale. Now guilty consciences no longer need alibis, since they are no longer guilty; modern imperialism radiates technology and progress, and it is even in bad taste to use that hateful word to describe it.

What actually are the effects of the increasing shift of foreign investment toward manufacturing industries in Latin America?

In the first place, it is necessary to note that this process of industrial denationalization has not required a large influx of capital. After all, direct investments of U.S. origin in 1966 in Argentinian, Brazilian, and Mexican industry, so important for the virtual monopolization of "key" manufacturing industries, were barely 3, 3.8, and 3.6 per cent respectively, of the total amount of U.S. capital invested on a world-wide basis. And it must be noted that even those investment figures are inflated. In effect, since the rapidity with which technology is advancing is shortening at an ever increasing rate the length of time needed for the amortization of fixed capital in the advanced economies, the vast majority of the manufacturing installations and equipment exported to Latin America has already passed through a complete productive life cycle in its country of origin and has been completely or partially amortized before it is exported. This "detail" is not considered for the purposes of calculating the amount of foreign investment—the value placed on the machinery is fixed at an arbitrarily high level and would not be even remotely so expensive if the frequent cases of prior depreciation were taken into account. But why should the parent company incur expenses to produce in Latin America goods which were previously sold there after being manufactured in the home country? The Latin American governments them-selves make sure that the foreign companies do not incur these expenses, by extending aid to the affiliates that are being installed, they say, to redeem the Latin American countries from their condition of underdevelopment. The affiliates have access to local credit from the moment they first post a sign on the land where the factory is to be built; they can count on foreign exchange privileges for their imports—imports which the companies usually purchase from themselves—and in some cases (such as Brazil) they can even count on special exchange rates for the payment of their foreign debts, which frequently are debts that they owe to the financial branch of the same corporation. The affiliates are also exempted from numerous taxes over long periods of time, and it is even common for them to receive guarantees against the risk of expropriation and monetary devaluation. They finance their subsequent expansion by reinvestment of part of their juicy profits and, above all, by means of the credit they receive in the country where they are operating. According to the OAS, an unimpeachable source in this respect, barely twenty cents of every dollar that U.S. industrial affiliates use for their operations and expansion come from the United States. The remaining eighty cents come from Latin American sources, through credits, loans, and the retention of profits. U.S. affiliates employ Latin American capital almost exclusively to finance their various operating needs.[9] This channeling of national resources into foreign enterprises is due in large part to the proliferation of U.S. bank branches spread throughout Latin America in order to pour national savings into foreign hands. There were 78 branches of U.S. banks in the area in 1964; in 1967, the number had risen to 133.[10] The Bank of New York acknowledges publicly that the most important among its new goals in Latin America is the capture of domestic savings for the benefit of the multinational corporations, so as to meet their production and sales needs.[11] It is worthy of note that the number of national banks which, without change of name, are coming under foreign banking control is growing. Even those Latin American banks which have not been infiltrated or captured find it highly convenient to satisfy the credit requests of foreign affiliates, which are solidly backed and have a very considerable sales volume. The mobilization of local resources does not have, of course, the slightest effect on the capital structure of these enterprises. In general, 99 per cent of the affiliates' stock is controlled by the parent corporation.[12]

A form of foreign penetration which does not require any investment at all is becoming increasingly common in Latin America. Even the OAS itself recognizes in the above-cited document that the development of U.S. companies in Latin America is due to a great degree to "the acquisition of Latin American industrial enterprises by U.S. interests, a phenomenon that has been observed over the last few years." Every method of financial coercion is employed for this purpose, including dumping, financial blackmail, and the infinite possibilities for exerting financial pressure provided by an overwhelming technological superiority. The old mechanism by means of which the creditor acquires the debtor's property, for example, is employed on a large scale. Debts acquired through the purchase of supplies, the use of patents and trademarks, etc., complicated by monetary devaluations that force the national enterprise to pay more pesos for the same amount of dollars, frequently lead to bankruptcy. Since the end of the 1950's, economic recessions, monetary instability, tighter credit, and the drop in the buying power of the internal market have all facilitated the task of bringing national enterprises to their knees before the large foreign corporations. Besides, since the affiliates of these corporations are no more than cogs in a world-wide system, they can afford the luxury of losing money for a year or two or indeed for whatever time is necessary.

Consequently, they lower their prices and wait for their victim's demise. The siege begins. The banks collaborate, and the national enterprise is found not to be as solvent as it seemed—it is therefore denied assistance. The national enterprise, completely surrounded, soon raises the white flag. Both sides then merrily celebrate the surrender. The Latin American "national bourgeoisie," which was produced by the old agricultural exporting system, rediscovers its destiny—the local capitalist becomes either a junior partner or a functionary of his conquerors. Or he gains the most coveted prize of all: he receives the ransom of his goods in stocks in the foreign parent corporation and ends his days living the soft life of a shareholder.

The great corporations, then, do not need to bring many dollars along with them. Quite to the contrary, they take them out of the country. "Under modern capitalism, when monopolies prevail, the export of *capital* has become the typical feature," wrote Lenin. In our days, as Baran and Sweezy have pointed out, imperialism imports capital from the countries where it operates. In the 1950-1967 period, new U.S. investments in Latin America totaled, without including profits which were reinvested, $3,921 million. In the same period, $12,819 million were repatriated by those enterprises in profits and dividends. The earnings which have been drained off are more than three times as much as the total amount of new capital invested in Latin America. But this is a conservative estimate. A good part of the money which was sent back to the U.S. as amortization was really profits, and the figures also do not include payments abroad for patents, royalties, and technical assistance; nor do they reveal other invisible transfers that usually appear under the heading "errors and omissions"; nor do they take into account the profits that the corporations receive when they inflate the prices of supplies sold to their affiliates and when they inflate, with equal enthusiasm, their operating costs. The negative flow of capital reflects increasingly greater profits, above all in the most underdeveloped areas: Latin America, Africa, and, to an even greater degree, Asia.

The profound structural deformations in the Latin American economy, which can be seen everywhere and at all times, like a bone laid bare by a wound, are also reflected in the simple and terrible fact that half of all investments in Latin America are of an unproductive nature.[13] The "internationalization" of the industrial process has only increased this waste, allowing the economic surplus produced in the region to be drained off by foreign interests. It is becoming more and more evident that the bread of the oppressive minorities in Latin America is the poison of the oppressed majorities; south of the Rio Grande private interests coincide less and less with public interests. Foreign investment in industry does not alter this picture of things; it only confirms it in a dramatic fashion.

When they remove more dollars than they bring, the foreign enterprises help increase the growing deficit in the balance of payments; *the region that is "benefited" is decapitalized instead of capitalized. The loan mechanism then begins to function.* And it is important to observe that the international credit organizations play a very important role in dismantling the defensive citadels of Latin American industry. Lenin rightly emphasized the fact that the export of finance capital is, for the imperialist countries, a means of stimulating the export of goods. In this sense, the conditions attached to loans made by the Alliance for Progress, "tied" to the purchase of goods and services in the United States, are instructive. This holds true to such an extent that the portion of *real* aid in official U.S. financial assistance to Latin America is less than half the amount of *nominal* aid, again according to unimpeachable sources,[14] as a result of the conditions under which it is given. The changes announced by President Nixon do not significantly alter the situation. But it is still more important to note the importance of international credit in "clearing the way" for direct investments by the large corporations. "The characteristic feature of imperialism," wrote Lenin, "is *not* industrial capital, *but* finance capital." The evolution of capitalism since then implies an evolution of imperialism. In the last half century changes have taken place within the capitalist system; in the United States banks no longer control industrial corporations, but are instead integral parts of the same system.[15] And just as the multinational corporations are multinational because they operate in the four corners of the capitalist globe, while their property is in no way international, so the international monetary organizations are in no way at the service of the numerous countries that provide the capital with which they operate, but instead fulfill the designs of the great integrating power of world capitalism—the United States. The death of the system based on the gold standard, which signaled the definitive decline of the British Empire, enormously increased the international supply of finance capital and made possible the appearance of organizations such as the World Bank, the International Monetary Fund, and, on the regional level, the Inter-American Development Bank, which reserve for themselves the right of governing the Third World and of determining the course to be followed by the countries that benefit from the credit they extend. The presence of the marines is becoming less and less necessary; the international technocrats disembark instead (tears flow, not blood) and mount assaults on the central banks and the key ministries of the poor nations.

With its direct investments, imperialism bleeds dependent economies. With its loans, it administers the drug necessary to keep them on their feet and takes control, in an increasingly arrogant way, of the internal power structure. Imperialism first makes its subject ill, and then it constructs the hospital in which the patient lies imprisoned and without any possibility of being cured. Latin America is now living through what economists call the "debt explosion." It is a vicious circle of strangulation: loans and investments increase, and as a result the payments of amortizations, interests, dividends, and other services also increase. In order to make these payments, new injections of foreign capital that generate greater obligations are needed, and so on successively. According to the World Bank, payments for services in 1980 will completely cancel out the influx of foreign capital to the underdeveloped world. In the decade 1956-1965, Latin America's public foreign debt climbed from $4 billion to close to $11 billion. In 1965, the influx of credit was already less than the capital leaving the region to meet commitments previously contracted.

The World Bank, the Alliance for Progress, and U.S. private banks make their loans contingent on approval by the International Monetary Fund (IMF). The IMF uses the magic phrase "monetary stabilization" to impose on Latin America the policies of liberalization of trade, tightening internal credit, freezing wages, discouraging state activities, and monetary devaluations that are theoretically intended to stimulate exports but that in fact only stimulate the internal concentration of capital in the hands of the large landowners, the bankers, and the big speculators. This is a policy intended to destroy national defenses against the omnipotent penetration of foreign private capital. *The terrain is prepared in advance for the conquerors.*

All these imperialist organizations for international philanthropy insist on the struggle against internal and external imbalances in the Latin American economy. Their prescriptions correspond to the diagnosis. We cannot, given the brevity of this study, demonstrate the many ways by which the policy imposed by them aggravates those imbalances instead of lessening them. What interests us here is simply to observe the effect that imperialist investments in the field of industry have on one of the most important factors in Latin American economic imbalance—foreign trade. The "trade gap" is becoming wider and wider because the need to import products is growing steadily in relation to the financial resources generated by exports. Only a tenth of Latin American exports are provided by manufactured products. The region depends on sales of unprocessed or hardly processed primary products that have very unstable prices on international markets controlled by the rich countries and their powerful corporations. Latin American exports grow in volume but their prices tend to fall—or, in the best of cases, they remain stagnant—while the prices of industrialized products imported by the region rise. Buying power is diminishing. Taking 1950 prices as a base and adding data from various documents published by the United Nations Economic Commission for Latin America and the UN itself, it can be seen that Latin America lost, due to the deterioration of its terms of trade, more than $18.5 billion in the ten years from 1955 to 1964. Now then, *imperialist investments in the industrial sector have had absolutely no effect on these terms of international trade. Latin America continues to exchange its primary products for specialized articles produced in the metropolitan economies.* The importance of "traditional" exports is actually growing within the total picture rather than diminishing, and the proportion of foreign sales by foreign affiliates is steadily decreasing within the total volume of sales.

The head of a U.S. technical mission to Brazil, John Abbink, announced prophetically in 1950: "The United States must be prepared to 'guide' the inevitable industrialization of under-developed countries if it wants to avoid the blow of very intense economic development outside of U.S. influence. . . . Industrialization, if it is not controlled in some way, will lead to a substantial reduction in U.S. export markets."[16] There was absolutely no reduction in the Latin American market for U.S. goods. One of the paradoxes of industrialization to *reduce* imports is that it forces an *increase* in imports. Certain goods that previously were imported are produced internally, but such internal production generates a "derivative" demand for intermediate products and capital goods, the magnitude of which goes far beyond the original saving in foreign currency. The United States now sells Latin America a greater proportion of more sophisticated products requiring a higher level of technology. "In the long run," says the U.S. Department of Commerce, "as Mexican industrial production increases, there are greater opportunities for additional exports from the United States. . . ."[17] The affiliates of great corporations have leaped the tariff barriers to supply Latin American markets from within, and they obtain additional benefits to the degree that they make purchases abroad, buying materials from their parent corporations or from other affiliates at prices set deliberately high.

This imperialism that even exports entire factories corresponds to the highest stage in the development of monopoly capitalism. In Lenin's time, free competition was already a museum piece. Today the corporations comfortably enjoy the control of prices in the countries where they operate. In Latin America they protect themselves behind a Chinese Wall of protective tariffs to produce, at prices two or three times higher, products that they used to export to our countries from abroad. Investments are low, manpower is as abundant as it is cheap, and the state subsidizes the financing of installment buying. Nevertheless, everything is more expensive. Control over the market is facilitated by the complete freedom which these enterprises enjoy, by the magic prestige of U.S. trademarks and advertising slogans in English, benefiting from an unparalleled and effective international publicity campaign, and from the fact that foreign industrial investments control the "modern sector" of the dependent economies which, by its own dynamics, subordinates all the other sectors to it.

The internal markets, then, provide juicy profits, even though the significant consumers in Latin America represent only a very small part of the total population. Barely one out of every four Brazilians can be considered a real consumer. The population is growing at a dizzy rate, and yet the development of dependent capitalism—a voyage with more disasters than survivors—leaves more people on the margin of the economy than it integrates into it. In the majority of Latin American markets there is only an elite with buying power. Foreign industry is aimed, above all, at that elite, and it does not show the slightest interest in expanding the consumption of the masses beyond a certain limit. The market could only be expanded both horizontally and vertically if profound changes were made in the entire socio-economic structure. Fernando Henrique Cardoso has noted[18] that national capital in Argentina and Brazil is strongest in the "traditional" industrial sectors, those with a low technological level which depend to the greatest degree on a mass market, while the foreign affiliates or the national capitalists subjected to "structural dependency" only "require the strengthening of economic links between the islands of development in the dependent countries and the international economic system, and subordinate internal changes to this primary objective."

The studies that have been carried out concerning the need for agrarian reform are very instructive in this regard, above all if one takes into account the fact that the agrarian question is the main bottleneck in Latin American development. In Argentina as well as in Brazil, "the managerial sector shows a marked tendency to oppose agrarian reform,"[19] and the studies that have been made show clearly that the more dependent the managerial sector is on the "international mode of production," the sharper is its opposition to changes in the agrarian structure. The industrially less complex sectors are the ones that favor drastic broadening of the market. The most complex sectors, when they represent national capital, are usually bound to foreign interests by their technological or financial dependency, and the payment on account of patents, profits, interest, royalties, stock dividends, or "know-how" is accompanied by an attitude of resistance to possible structural changes. There is a direct relationship between the manager's degree of dependency and his political panic when there is the slightest possiblility of change in the power structure from which he benefits. The *latifundium* continues untouched—it is his ally.

The continued existence of the rural *latifundium* generates a constant and growing flow of workers moving from the countryside to the cities, but the factories do not provide employment for the surplus workers. On the contrary, industrial productivity is increasing in the face of ever-diminishing job opportunities—and Latin America has the highest demographic growth rate in the world. The "internationalized" industrialization has an exclusive character; the enterprises bring a technology along with them to save on manpower in countries where manpower has no employment. *The proportion of workers in manufacturing industry is diminishing in relation to the total active population in Latin America.* Factory workers represented 14.5 per cent in the decade of the fifties, but only 11.6 per cent in the decade of the sixties.[20] A fourth of the active population is currently unemployed or underemployed; in the large cities a growing multitude is crammed into the *favelas*, the *villas miserias*, the *ranchos*, the *cantegriles*, and the *callampas*, broad belts of poverty around the wealth of the urban centers. The system vomits forth men, but industry gives itself the luxury of sacrificing manpower to an even greater degree than European industry does.[21] In contrast to the "classical" models of capitalist development, there is no coherent relationship between available manpower and applied technology. Rich lands, vast underground wealth, and very poor people—that is the panorama presented by this realm of abundance and need. Great numbers of workers are abandoned by the roadside by the system which condemns them to a marginal existence and frustrates the development of the internal market and lowers the wage level. The eruption of the urban bourgeoisie onto the stage of history has not provoked, in contrast to Europe and the United States, any agrarian revolution; dependent industrialization functions on the structure just as it is. It is true that "poles" are developing around which the production and wealth of each country are being concentrated, but they do not share the benefits of their growth. They are oases of prosperity in the desert, the shining cities that feign their existence amid the desolate landscape of widespread poverty. The new type of foreign capital, which raises smokestacks in underdeveloped areas, is concentrated around these poles in such a way that it not only sharpens social contradictions by segregating the labor force and polarizing wealth still further, but also sharpens regional contradictions within the borders of each country and within the overall limits of Latin America. The efforts that are being made to form a Latin American Common Market reflect, in this sense, the desire to lay the basis for a new division of labor that would benefit the most developed urban centers, thus broadening the markets for the denationalized industry, while leaving intact the structure each country must endure.

The native Latin American bourgeoisie, a bourgeoisie of merchants without creative spirit, connected by its umbilical cord to the power of the land, is on its knees before the altar of the goddess technology. It is in the name of technological progress that national enterprises pass into the hands of foreign interests, sometimes in the most direct and brutal fashion and at other times through the consolidation of multiple hidden forms of dependency. Raúl Prebisch himself warns that "U.S. enterprises in Europe install laboratories and engage in research that helps strengthen the scientific and technical capacity of those countries, something which has not occurred in Latin America." And he reveals a very serious fact. "National investors," he says, "due to their lack of specialized knowledge (know-how), carry out most of their transfer of technology by receiving techniques *that belong to the public domain and that are imported as though they were licenses of specialized knowledge. . . .*"[22] This "national" bourgeoisie with its clipped wings is defeated in advance. The great multinational corporations, which stand at the controls of technological progress, obviously also hold the keys to the Latin American economy. The transfer of power to foreign interests is, when things are seen in their proper perspective, much more serious than the statistics indicate. It is also necessary to keep in mind that the large imperialist investments in the most dynamic sectors of the Latin American economy provide those corporations with limitless power to manipulate the consumer market, which is increasingly attracted by U.S. advertising, to channel national savings and the economic surplus produced by our countries, to use advertising and the various other ways of creating public opinion, and, also, to exert that political pressure required by imperialism's digestive needs.

The new type of imperialism does not make its colonies more prosperous, even though it enriches its "enclaves"; it does not alleviate social tensions, but on the contrary sharpens them; it extends poverty and concentrates wealth; it takes over the internal market and the key parts of the productive apparatus; it appropriates progress for itself, determines its direction, and fixes its limits; it absorbs credit and directs foreign trade as it pleases; it does not provide capital for development, but instead removes it; it encourages waste by sending the greatest part of the economic surplus abroad; it denationalizes our industry and also the profits that our industry produces. Today in Latin America the system has our veins as open as it did in those distant times when our blood first served the needs of primary accumulation for European capitalist development.

(Translated by William Rose)

Notes

[1] Richard M. Nixon, speech to the OAS, April 14, 1969. Of course, it is also necessary to take into account the rate at which the gap separating the poor from the rich widens *within* Latin American countries—per capita income is a deceptive average.

[2] Darcy Ribeiro, "El dilema latinoamericano," unpublished.

[3] General Secretariat of the OAS, *El financiamiento externo para el desarrollo de la América Latina* (Washington, 1969). A document of limited distribution presented to the sixth annual meeting of the Inter-American Economic and Social Council.

[4] Quoted by the United Nations Economic Commission for Latin America, (*Estudio Económico de América Latina,* 1968).

[5] Rogelio García Lupo, *Contra la ocupación extranjera* (Buenos Aires, 1968).

[6] See Eduardo Galeano, "The De-nationalization of Brazilian Industry," in *Monthly Review*, December, 1969.

[7] Speech by Minister Hélio Beltrão before the Commercial Association of Rio de Janeiro, *Correio do Povo*, May 24, 1969.

[8] José Luis Ceceña, *Los monopolios en México* (Mexico, 1962).

[9] OAS, *op. cit.*

[10] International Banking Survey, *Journal of Commerce*, New York, February 25, 1968.

[11] Robert A. Bennett and Karen Almonti, *International Activities of United States Banks* (New York, 1969).

[12] Celso Furtado, *La economía latinoamericana desde la Conquista Ibérica hasta la Revolución Cubana* (Santiago de Chile, 1969).

[13] Aldo Ferrer, "Distribución del ingreso y desarrollo económico," *El trimestre económico*, Mexico, April-June, 1954.

[14] OAS, *op. cit.*

[15] Paul Baran and Paul M. Sweezy, *Monopoly Capital* (New York, 1966).

[16] *Jornal do Comercio*, March 23, 1950.

[17] *International Commerce*, a U.S. Department of Commerce weekly, April 24, 1967.

[18] Fernando Henrique Cardoso, "Política e desenvolvimento em sociedades dependentes: ideologias do empresariado industrial argentino e brasileiro," unpublished thesis, São Paulo, 1968.

[19] *Ibid.*

[20] United Nations Economic Commission for Latin America, *op. cit.*

[21] OAS, *op. cit.*

[22] Raúl Prebisch, "La cooperación internacional en el desarrollo latinoamericano," *Desarrollo*, Bogota, no. 12, January, 1970. (Emphasis added.)

14

THEOTONIO DOS SANTOS

The Structure of Dependence

The objective of this paper is to demonstrate that the situation of dependence to which Latin American countries are subjected cannot be overcome without a qualitative change in their internal structures and external relations. We shall attempt to demonstrate that the relations of dependence to which these countries are subjected conform to a type of international and internal structure which leads them to underdevelopment, or more precisely to a dependent structure that deepens and aggravates the fundamental problems of their peoples.

*This work, presented at the annual meeting of the American Economics Association (1969), expands on certain preliminary work done in a research project on the relations of dependence in Latin America, directed by the author at the Center for Socio-Economic Studies of the Faculty of Economic Science of the University of Chile. In order to abridge the discussion of various aspects, the author was obliged to cite certain of his earlier works. The author expresses his gratitude to the research of Orlando Caputo and Roberto Pizarro for some of the data used, and to Sergio Ramos for his critical comments on the paper.

WHAT IS DEPENDENCE?

"By dependence we mean a situation in which the economy of certain countries is conditioned by the development and expansion of another economy to which the former is subjected. The relation of interdependence between two or more economies, and between these and world trade, assumes the form of dependence when some countries (the dominant ones) can expand and can be self-starting, while other countries (the dependent ones) can do this only as a reflection of that expansion, which can have either a positive or a negative effect on their immediate development."[1]

The concept of dependence permits us to see the internal situation of these countries as part of world economy. In the Marxian tradition, the theory of imperialism has been developed as a study of the process of expansion of the imperialist centers and of their world domination. In the epoch of the revolutionary movement of the Third World, it has become incumbent upon this system of thought to develop the theory of laws of internal development in those countries that are the object of such expansion and are governed by them. To take this theoretical step means to transcend the theory of development which seeks to explain the situation of the underdeveloped countries as a product of their slowness or failure to adopt the patterns of efficiency characteristic of developed countries (or to "modernize" or "develop" themselves) and which, while admitting the existence of an "external" dependence, is unable to perceive underdevelopment in the way our present theory perceives it, as a consequence and part of the process of the world expansion of capitalism: a part that is necessary to and integrally linked with it.

In analyzing the process of constituting a world economy that integrates the so-called national economies in a world market of commodities, capital, and even of labor power, we see that the relations produced by this market are unequal and combined. *Unequal* because development of parts of the system occurs at the expense of other parts. Trade relations are based on monopolistic control of the market, which leads to the transfer of surplus generated in the dependent countries to the dominant countries; financial relations are on the side of the dominant powers, based on loans and the export of capital, which permit them to receive interest and profits, thus increasing their domestic surplus and strengthening their control over the economies of the other countries. On the part of the dependent countries these relations signify an export of profits and interest which carries off part of the surplus generated domestically and leads to a loss of control over their productive resources. In order to permit these disadvantageous relations, the dependent countries must generate large surpluses, in such a way as to create not a higher level of technology but rather super-exploited manpower. The result is to limit the development of their internal market and their technical and cultural capacity, as well as the moral and physical health of their people. We call this *combined* development because it is the combination of these inequalities and the transfer of resources from the most backward and dependent sectors to the most advanced and dominant ones which explains the inequality, deepens it, and transforms it into a necessary and structural element of the world economy.

HISTORIC FORMS OF DEPENDENCE

Historic forms of dependence are conditioned by: (1) the basic forms of this world economy which has its own laws of development; (2) the type of economic relations dominant in the capitalist centers and the ways in which the latter expand; and (3) the types of economic relations existing inside the peripheral countries which are incorporated into the situation of dependence within the network of international economic relations generated by capitalist expansion. It is not within the purview of this paper to study these forms in detail but only to distinguish broad characteristics of development.

Drawing on an earlier study, we may distinguish: (1) Colonial dependence, in which commercial and financial capital in alliance with the colonialist state dominated the economic relations between the Europeans and the colonies, by means of a trade monopoly complemented by a colonial monopoly of land, mines, and manpower (serf or slave) in the colonized countries. (2) Financial-industrial dependence, which consolidated itself at the end of the nineteenth century, characterized by the domination of big capital in the hegemonic centers, and its expansion abroad through investment in the production of raw materials and agricultural products for consumption in the hegemonic centers. A productive structure grew up in the dependent countries devoted to the export of these products, which Levin labelled export economies, producing what ECLA has called "foreign-oriented development" (*desarrollo hacia afuera*).[2] (3) In the post-World War II period a new type of dependence has been consolidated, based on multinational corporations which began to invest in industries geared to the internal market of underdeveloped countries. This is basically technological-industrial dependence.[3]

Each of these forms of dependence corresponded to a situation which conditioned not only the international relations of these countries but also their internal structures: the orientation of production, the forms of capital accumulation, the reproduction of the economy and, simultaneously, their social and political structure.

In forms (1) and (2) of dependence, production is geared to those products destined for export (gold, silver, and tropical products in the colonial epoch; raw materials and agricultural products in the epoch of industrial-financial dependence); i.e., production is determined by demand from the hegemonic centers. The internal productive structure is characterized by rigid specialization and mono-cultivation in entire regions (the Caribbean, the Brazilian Northeast, etc.). Alongside these export sectors there grew up certain complementary economic activities (cattle-raising and some manufacturing, for example) which were dependent, in general, on the export sector to which they sold their products. There was a third, subsistence economy, which provided manpower for the export sector under favorable conditions and toward which excess population shifted during periods unfavorable to international trade.

Under these conditions, the existing internal market was restricted by four factors: (1) Most of the national income was derived from export, which was used to purchase the inputs required by export production (slaves, for example) or luxury goods consumed by the hacienda- and mine-owners, and by the more prosperous employees. (2) The available manpower was subject to very arduous forms of super-exploitation, which limited their consumption. (3) Part of the consumption of these workers was provided by the subsistence economy, which served as a complement to their income and as a refuge during periods of depression. (4) A fourth restricting factor was to be found in those countries in which land and mines were in the hands of foreigners (cases of an enclave economy): a great part of the accumulated surplus was destined for overseas in the form of profits, limiting not only internal consumption but also possibilities of reinvestment.[4] In the case of enclave economies the relations of the foreign companies with the negemonic center were even more exploitative and were complemented by the fact that purchases by the enclave were made directly abroad.

THE NEW DEPENDENCE

The new form of dependence (3), which is in process of developing, is conditioned in various ways by the exigencies of the international commodity and capital markets. The possibility of generating new investments depends on the existence of financial resources in foreign currency for the purchase of machinery and processed raw materials not produced domestically. Such purchases are subject to two limitations: the limit of resources generated by the export sector (reflected in balance of payments, which includes not only trade but also service relations); and the limitations of monopoly on patents, which leads monopolistic firms to prefer to transport their machines in the form of capital rather than as commodities for sale. It is necessary to analyze these relations of dependence if we are to understand the fundamental structural limits that they place on the development of these economies.

1. Industrial development is now dependent on the existence of an export sector which brings in the foreign currency that makes it possible to buy the inputs used by the industrial sector. The first consequence of this dependence is the need to preserve the traditional export sector, which limits economically the development of the internal market by the conservation of backward relations of production, and signifies, politically, the maintenance of power by the traditional decadent oligarchies. In the countries where these sectors are controlled by foreign capital, it signifies the remittance abroad of high profits, and the political dependence of those interests. We must point out that only in rare instances does foreign capital not control at least the marketing of these products. In response to these limitations, dependent countries in the 30's and 40's developed a policy of exchange restrictions and taxes on the national and foreign export sector; today they tend toward the gradual nationalization of production and toward the imposition of certain timid limitations on foreign control of the marketing of exported products. Furthermore they seek, still somewhat timidly, to obtain better terms for the sale of their products. In recent decades, they have created mechanisms for international price agreements, and today UNCTAD and ECLA press to obtain more favorable tariff conditions for these products on the part of the hegemonic centers. It is important to point out that the industrial development of these countries is dependent on the situation of the export sector, the continued existence of which they are obliged to accept.

2. Industrial development is, then, strongly conditioned by fluctuations in the balance of payments. This leads toward a deficit due to the relations of dependence themselves. The causes of the deficit are three:

(a) Trade relations take place in a highly monopolized international market, which tends to lower the price of raw materials and to raise the price of industrial products, particularly inputs. In the second place, there is a tendency in modern technology to replace various primary products with synthetic raw materials. Consequently the balance of trade in these countries tends to be less favorable (even though they show a general surplus). The overall Latin American balance of trade from 1946 to 1968 shows a surplus for each of those years. The same thing happens in almost every underdeveloped country. However, the losses due to deterioration of the terms of trade (on the basis of data from ECLA and the International Monetary Fund), excluding Cuba, were $26.383 million for the 1951-1966 period, taking 1950 prices as a base. If Cuba and Venezuela are excluded, the total is $15.925 million.

(b) For the reasons already given, foreign capital retains control over the most dynamic sectors of the economy and carries off to its country of origin a high volume of profit; consequently, capital accounts are highly unfavorable to dependent countries. The data show that the amount of capital leaving the country is much greater than the amount entering, which produces an enslaving deficit in capital accounts. To this must be added the deficit in certain services which are virtually under total foreign control—such as freight transport, royalty payments, technical aid, etc. Consequently an important deficit is produced in the total balance of payments, thus limiting the possibility of importation of inputs for industrialization.

(c) The result is that "foreign financing" becomes necessary, in two forms: to cover the existing deficit, and to "finance" development by means of loans for the stimulation of investments and to "supply" an internal economic surplus which was decapitalized to a large extent by the remittance of part of the surplus value generated domestically and sent abroad as profits.

Foreign capital and foreign "aid" thus fill up the holes created by themselves; that is, by the monopoly of world trade, by the freight transport monopoly, etc. The reality of this aid, however, is very doubtful. If from the total flow of these grants is subtracted the extra prices, due to the financial conditions imposed by the aid, in respect to the international market, an average net flow is obtained of approximately 54.5 per cent of the gross flow, according to calculations of the CIES.[5]

If other aspects are examined, such as the fact that a large part of these credits are payable in local currency, the contributions of Latin American countries to international financial institutions, the effects of "tying" these credits, we find a "real component of foreign aid" of 42.2 per cent on a very favorable hypothesis, and of 38.3 per cent on a more realistic one.[6] The gravity of the situation is even more clearly seen if we take into account that the purpose of these credits is in large part to finance North American investments, to subsidize foreign imports which compete with national products, to introduce technology not adapted to the needs of underdeveloped countries, and to invest in sectors not necessarily of high priority. The hard truth is that the underdeveloped countries have to pay the full amount, 100 per cent for the "aid" they receive. All this has generated an enormous protest movement on the part of the governments of Latin American countries in their search for at least partial relief from such negative relations.

3. In the third place, industrial development is strongly conditioned by the technological monopoly exercised by imperialist centers. We have seen that the underdeveloped countries depend on the importation of machinery and raw materials for the development of their industries. However, these goods are not freely available in the international market; they are patented and usually belong to the big companies. The big companies do not sell machinery and processed raw materials as simple merchandise: they demand either the payment of royalties, etc., for their utilization or, in most cases, they convert these goods into capital and introduce them in the form of their own investments. This is how machinery, replaced in the hegemonic centers by more advanced technology, is sent to dependent countries as capital for the installation of affiliates. Let us pause and examine these relations, in order to understand their oppressive and exploitative character.

The dependent countries do not have sufficient foreign currency, for the reasons given. In the second place, local businessmen have financing difficulties. In the third place, they must pay for the utilization of certain techniques that are patented. The combination of these factors obliges the national bourgeois governments to facilitate the entry of foreign capital in order to supply the restricted national market, which is strongly protected by high tariffs in order to promote industrialization. Thus, foreign capital enters with all the advantages: in many cases, it is given exemption from exchange controls for the importation of machinery; financing of sites for installation of industries is provided; government financing agencies are available to facilitate industrialization; loans from foreign and domestic banks, which prefer such clients, are available; in many cases, foreign aid for the strengthening of industrialization is available, etc.; after installation, high profits obtained in such favorable circumstances are available to it and can be reinvested freely. Thus it is not surprising that the data of the U.S. Department of Commerce reveal that the percentage of capital coming in from abroad for these companies is such a small part of the total amount of invested capital. These data show that in the period from 1946 to 1967 the new entries of capital into Latin America for direct investment amounted to $5.415 million; the sum for reinvestment of profits was $4.424 million. On the other hand, the transfers of profits from Latin America to the United States amounted to $14.775 million. If we estimate total profits as approximately equal to transfers plus reinvestments we have the sum of $18.983 million.

In spite of enormous transfers of profits to the United States, the book value of the United States' direct investment in Latin America went from $3.045 million in 1946 to $10.213 million in 1967. From the data presented it is clear that:

(1) Of the new investments made by U.S. companies in Latin America for the period 1946-1967, 55 per cent corresponds to new entries of capital and 45 per cent to reinvestment of profits; in recent years, the trend is more marked, with reinvestments between 1960 and the present, excluding 1967, representing more than 60 per cent of new investments.

(2) The remittance rate (remittance of capital with respect to book value) remains, for each year of this period, at about 10 per cent.

(3) The ratio of remitted capital to new flow is around 2.73 for the period 1946-1967; that is, for each dollar that enters $2.73 leaves. In the 1960's this ratio roughly doubled, and in some years was considerably higher.

If we take the *Survey of Current Business* data on sources and uses of funds for direct North American investment in Latin America in the period 1957-1964, we confirm the fact that, of the total sources of direct investment in Latin America, only 11.8 per cent comes from the United States. The remainder (88.2 per cent) corresponds in large part to sources that are a product of the activities of North American firms in Latin America (46.4

per cent net income of the companies, 27.7 per cent under the heading of depreciation and wear-and-tear), and from "sources located abroad" (14.1 per cent). It is significant that the funds obtained abroad that are external to the same companies are greater than the funds originating in the United States.

The relative participation of funds from the United States dropped in this period from 35 per cent in 1957 to 0.9 per cent in 1964. Although the period is a short one for indicating precise trends, what is clear is that funds coming from the United States have tended to decrease.

EFFECTS ON THE PRODUCTIVE STRUCTURE

It is easy to grasp, even if only superficially, the effects that this dependent structure has on the productive system itself in these countries, and the role of this structure in determining a specified type of development, characterized by its dependent nature.

(a) The productive system that is developing in the underdeveloped countries is essentially determined by these international relations—in the first place, by the need to conserve the agrarian or mining export structure. The conservation of these structures generates a combination among more advanced economic centers that extract surplus value from the more backward sectors, and also between internal "metropolitan" centers and internal interdependent "colonial" centers.[7] The unequal and combined character of capitalist development at the international level is reproduced internally in an acute form. In the second place, because of the need to create an industrial and technological structure responding more to the interests of the multinational corporations than to internal developmental needs (conceived of not only in terms of the overall interests of the population, but also, if one prefers, from the point of view of the interests of a national capitalist development). In the third place, the technological and economic-finanacial concentration of the hegemonic economies is transferred without substantial alteration to very different economies and societies, giving rise to a highly unequal productive structure, a high concentration of incomes, under-utilization of installed capacity, intensive exploitation of existing markets concentrated in large cities, etc.

(b) The accumulation of capital in such circumstances assumes its own characteristics. In the first place, it is characterized by profound differences among domestic wage-levels, in the context of a local cheap manpower market, combined with the utilization of a technology of intensive-use of capital. The result, from the point of view of relative surplus value, is a high rate of exploitation of labor power.[8]

This exploitation is further aggravated by the high prices of industrial products enforced by protectionism, exemptions and subsidies given by the national government, and "aid" from hegemonic centers. Furthermore, since dependent accumulation is necessarily tied into the international economy, it is profoundly conditioned by the unequal and combined character of international capitalist economic relations, by the technological and financial control of the imperialist centers, by the realities of the balance of payments, by the economic policies of the state, etc. The role of the state in the growth of national and foreign capital merits a much fuller analysis than can be made here.

(c) Using the analysis offered here as a point of departure, it is possible to understand the limits that this productive system imposes on the growth of the internal markets of these countries. On the one hand, allowing the survival of traditional relations in the countryside is a limiting factor, which is very serious, if we take into account the fact that the new industrialization does not offer hopeful prospects. The productive structure created by dependent industrialization limits the growth of the internal market for various reasons.

First, because it subjects the labor force to highly exploitative relations, limiting its purchasing power. Second, because in adopting a technology of intensive capital use it creates very few jobs, relatively speaking, in comparison with population growth, and limits the creation of new sources of income. These two limitations affect the growth of the consumer-goods market. Third, the remittance abroad of profits carries away part of the economic surplus generated within the country which cannot be utilized, in part because of the above-mentioned limitations on the domestic market, in part because it does not find new outlets with equally high rates of exploitation and prefers to move to those areas where they can be found, in part so as not to open new industries which would compete with goods imported from imperialist centers. In all these ways limits are put on the possible creation of a national basic industry which could provide a market for the capital-goods this surplus value would constitute if it were not remitted abroad.

From this cursory analysis we can see that the most serious phenomena faced by these economies do not come from an alleged backwardness due to a lack of integration with capitalism but that, on the contrary, the most powerful obstacles to their full development come from the way in which they are joined to this international system and its laws of development.

SOME CONCLUSIONS: DEPENDENT REPRODUCTION

In order to understand the system of dependent reproduction and the socio-economic conformations created by it, we must see it as part of a system of world economic relations based on monopolistic control of large-scale capital, on control of certain economic and financial centers over others, on a monopoly of technology that is highly complex and that leads to unequal and combined development at a national and international level. Attempts to analyze the reality of these countries, as the result of backwardness in assimilating more advanced models of production or in modernizing themselves, are nothing more than ideology disguised as science. The same is true of the attempts to analyze this international economy in terms of relations among elements in free competition, such as the theory of comparative costs which seeks to justify the inequalities of the world economic system and to conceal the relations of exploitation on which it is based.[9]

In reality we can understand what is happening in the underdeveloped countries only when we see that they develop within the framework of a process of dependent production and reproduction. This system is reproduced as a dependent one when it reproduces a productive system whose development is limited by those world relations which necessarily lead to the development of only certain economic sectors, to trade under unequal conditions to competition within its borders with international capital under unequal conditions, to the imposition of relations of super-exploitation of the domestic labor force with a view to dividing the economic surplus thus generated between internal and external forces of domination.[10]

In reproducing such a productive system and such international relations, the development of dependent capitalism reproduces the factors that prevent it from reaching a nationally and internationally advantageous situation; and it thus reproduces backwardness, misery, and social marginalization within its borders. The development that it produces benefits very narrow sectors, encounters unyielding domestic obstacles to its continued economic growth (with respect to both internal and foreign markets) and leads to the progressive accumulation of balance of payments deficits, which in turn generate more dependence and more super-exploitation.

The political measures proposed by the developmentalists of ECLA, UNCTAD, BID, etc., do not appear to permit destruction of these terrible chains imposed by dependent development. We have had occasion to examine in another paper the alternative forms of development presented for Latin America and the dependent countries in such conditions.[11] Everything now indicates that what can be expected is a long process of sharp political and military confrontations and of profound social radicalization which will lead these countries to a dilemma: governments of force which open the way to fascism, or popular revolutionary governments which open the way to socialism. Intermediate solutions have proved to be, in such a contradictory reality, empty and utopian.

Notes

[1] Theotonio dos Santos, *La crisis de la teoría del desarrollo y las relaciones de dependencia en América Latina,* Boletín del CESO, 3, Santiago de Chile, 1968.

[2] ECLA (U.N. Economic Commission for Latin America) is abbreviated CEPAL in Spanish. See its publication *La CEPAL y el Análisis del Desarrollo Latinoamericano* (Santiago de Chile, 1968). See also V. I. Levin, *The Export Economies* (Harvard University Press, 1964).

[3] Dos Santos, *El nueve carácter de la dependencia,* CESO, Santiago de Chile, 1968.

[4] Paul Baran, *The Political Economy of Growth* (New York, 1967).

[5] Consejo Interamericano Económico Social (CIES), *El Financiamiento Externo para el Desarrollo de América Latina* (Washington, D.C.: Unión Panamericana, 1969).

[6] *Ibid.,* II-33.

[7] Andre G. Frank, *Development and Underdevelopment in Latin America* (New York, 1967).

[8] On the measurement of forms of exploitation, see Pablo Gonzalez Casanova, *Sociología de la explotación* (Mexico, D.F.: Siglo XXI, 1969).

[9] Cristian Palloix, *Problèmes de la Croissance en Economies Ouvertes* (Paris: Maspero, 1969).

[10] For a recent analysis of unequal exchange, see A. Emmanuel, *L'Echange Inégal* (Paris: Maspero, 1969). On economic surplus and its utilization in the dependent countries, see Baran, *op cit.*

[11] Dos Santos, *La dependencia económica y las alternativas de cambio en América Latina.* Report to the IX Congreso Latinoamericano de Sociología, Mexico, D. F., November, 1969.

15

ANDRÉ GUNDER FRANK

On the Mechanisms of Imperialism: the Case of Brazil

THE FLOW OF CAPITAL FROM BRAZIL TO THE UNITED STATES

It is widely believed that the United States and other developed capitalist countries contribute more capital to the underdeveloped countries than they receive from them. Nonetheless, all available statistics, including those compiled by the official agencies of the developed countries themselves, show precisely the opposite. Between 1947 and 1960, the flow of investment funds on private capital account from the United States to Brazil was $1,814 million while the capital flow of amortization, profits, royalties, interest and other transfers from Brazil to the United States totaled $3,481 million. For the seven largest Latin American countries (Argentina, Brazil, Chile, Peru, Venezuela, Colombia, Mexico), the United States Department of Commerce's conservatively calculated figures for the years 1950 to 1961 indicate $2,962 million of investment flows on private account out of the United States and remittances of profits and interest of $6,875 million; adding in American public loans and their Latin American servicing between the same years still leaves a conservatively calculated net capital flow of $2,081 million *to* the United States. My present purpose, however, is not to dwell further on the amount of this capital transfer from Brazil and other countries to the United States. Instead it is proposed to inquire into some of the reasons for and sources of this, for Brazil and others, so prejudicial capital flow. When the facts finally force American business, political, and unfortunately also academic, spokesmen for American capital to admit the existence of this capital flow from the poor underdeveloped countries to the rich developed ones, they often try to defend it in the following terms: Either it is said that the direction of the flow is the result of the accidental or deliberate choice of a year or set of years in which the return flow on past investment happens to be greater than the outflow of new investment; or it is said instead (and sometimes in addition) that this drainage of capital from the poor underdeveloped countries really helps them to develop and that it is normal and logical that the capital flow into the investing and lending country—in this case into the United States—should be greater than the capital flow out of it because, after all, profits and interest legitimately earned abroad must be added to the amortization and repayment of the original investment.

The facts of economic life completely vitiate this American logic. If the disparity between capital inflow from and outflow to Brazil is as normal and legitimate as its defenders claim, then why is it that according to the late President John F. Kennedy the capital inflow to the United States from the underdeveloped countries in 1960 was $1,300 million and the capital outflow from the United States to the same countries $200 million, while in respect to the advanced countries of Western Europe the outflow from the United States ($1,500 million) exceeded the inflow ($1,000 million) by a wide margin? (Cited in *O Estado de Sao Paulo,* April 12, 1963.) Why does *U.S. News & World Report* (December 25, 1961), using Department of Commerce data, find the same pattern to obtain for the five-year period 1956-1961, that is, a ratio of inflow to the United States to outflow from the United States of 147 per cent for Latin America, 164 per cent for the underdeveloped world as a whole, and 43 per cent for Western Europe? To eliminate still further the possibility that this disparity may be due to accidentally comparing years of low current outflow and high return flow of previous outflows, we may add up (as the Department of Commerce never does) the officially registered capital flows into and out of the United States for each year from 1950 to 1961 as reported in the *Survey of Current Business* and find that the total capital outflow is $13,708 million and the "corresponding" inflow $23,204 million, or an inflow/outflow ratio of 177 per cent.[1] Are we to believe that it is normal and legitimate that profits and interest earned by the United States in weak underdeveloped countries are very much greater than in the strong developed ones, the United States included?

The disparity between capital inflows and outflows is more realistically explained by examining, as I propose to do in the paragraphs following, the source and composition of these flows than by appeal to any simplistic theories. In the first place, the argument that it is only logical for capital inflows to the United States to exceed outflows because, after all, the latter must earn a profit is premised on the unstated but erroneous assumption that official capital inflows into the United States are earnings on capital the United States previously sent abroad. As a matter of fact, much of the capital on which Americans "earn" profits in Brazil is Brazilian in origin and American only in ownership, control, and earnings. The Brazilian origins of "American" capital are manifold. We here take note only of those which fall under the titles of loans, concessions, and foreign exchange privileges.[2]

Direct loans from the government's Bank of Brazil to American firms and to mixed American-Brazilian consortia are common in industry, commerce, and agriculture. The two giant American world-wide cotton merchants, SANBRA and Anderson & Clayton, in 1961 received $54 billion cruzeiros in loans from the Bank of Brazil, or 47 per cent of that bank's entire agricultural and industrial loan portfolio (reported by Congressman Jacob Frantz in Congressional debate and cited in *Semanario*, May 30-June 6, 1963). By re-loaning this money (at higher interest rates of course) to wholesalers and producers of cotton whom they thereby control; by buying up harvested stocks, storing them in government provided bins, and speculating with them later; by monopolizing important sectors of organization and distribution—these American firms use *Brazilian* capital to control much of the Brazilian domestic and export cotton market (as they also do that of many other countries) and to ship the profits therefrom home to the United States. Swift, Armour, and Wilson (recently involved in a public scandal for having partly exported and partly held back for a higher price the meat consigned to them by the government for storage and sale to the public), the A. & P.'s subsidiary American Coffee Company, and other American monopolies similarly derive fat profits from using Brazilian capital to monopolize critical sectors of the domestic and export markets. American banks like the ubiquitous National City Bank of New York, insurance companies, and other financial institutions evidently work almost entirely with Brazilian capital, loan much of it to American non-financial firms in Brazil, and then serve as a channel to send their own and others' profits on this Brazilian capital "back" home.

In the public utility sector especially, the ownership and earnings of so-called American capital are based, not on original investment of capital, but on concessions, exorbitant use rates, and other privileges. The capital is provided by Brazil. The Sao Paulo Light Co. (now merged with the Rio Light, Rio Gas, Brazilian Telephone and other companies in the Brazilian Traction Co.) in 1907 took over a concession already granted to two Brazilian individuals until 1950 and then got it extended to 1990. By engaging an ex-President as its lawyer to fight a legal battle through several courts up to the Supreme Court—still staffed by the ex-President's appointees—the company in 1923, contrary to the stipulations of its contract, obtained an extension of the concession for its telephone subsidiary. Later the concession of the gas subsidiary was also extended. For its starting capital the Sao Paulo Light issued bonds for $6,000,000. It then took over the already existing streetcars and associated properties. Following the usual procedure, the various light companies financed expansion of service to new areas by assessments on, and more recently by loans from, the communities to be served, while equipment was purchased out of earnings from exorbitant public utility rates. Even so, as any user can testify, service always lags far behind demand (electricity rationing is now normal in Rio and sometimes reaches blackouts of five hours daily). Through political influence and bribery, the company managed to delay the construction of competing facilities for 15 years at one site. In 1948 the company received $90 million in loans from the International Bank for which it obtained a guarantee from the Brazilian government. Part of this foreign exchange was used, of course, not to import new equipment, but to convert cruzeiro earnings into dollars for remittance to the United States. To avoid showing exorbitant profits, the company increased its registered capital base by issuing stock dividends to its owners. Between 1918 and 1947, Brazilian

Traction made profits of $550 million of which $165 million were sent home. Now that public utilities have become unprofitable relative to other industries and that the Brazilian government wants to take them over in order to permit the expansion of needed service, the American owners bring all possible diplomatic and other pressure to bear in usually successful attempts to obtain once again the remaining equipment's value several times over through "expropriation." (Sources: Paulo F. Alves Pinto, *Antologia Nacionalista,* vol. 2, cited in Barbosa Lima Sobrinho, *Maquinas para transformar cruzeiros em dolares* and Sylvio Monteiro, *Como Atua o imperialismo ianque?*)

Addressing the Brazilian Senate in 1953, President Vargas' Treasury Minister said, "I have to declare that foreign capital . . . demands guarantees to enter the country, greater guarantees to remain in it, and still greater ones to withdraw from it. Therefore, it does not seem desirable for any country and still less for Brazil." (Quoted in Osny Duarte Perira, *Quem faz as leis no Brasil?*, p. 97.) After the establishment of a state petroleum company and threatening to do the same with electric power, the government of Vargas was, owing to foreign and domestic pressure, replaced by one which proposed the "creation of a climate favorable for the investment of foreign capital in the country." To this end the Superintendency of Money and Credit (SUMOC) issued Instruction 113 according to which, in the words of the President of the Federation of Industries of the State of Sao Paulo, "foreign firms can bring their entire equipment in at the free market price . . . national ones, however, have to do so through exchange licenses established in import categories. In this way there was created veritable discrimination against national industry. We do not plead for preferential treatment but for equal opportunities." (Quoted in Jocelyn Brasil, *O Pao, O Feijao, e as Forcas Ocultas,* p. 125.) Moreover, foreign firms were permitted to import used equipment (often already depreciated for tax purposes at home), while Brazilians could import only new machinery. As a result, Brazilians, who on this basis were unable to compete with foreign firms and/or who were unable to get assignments of foreign exchange from the Central Bank, were forced to combine with non-Brazilians who, though they might not contribute much of any capital to the common enterprise could contribute and capitalize on special privileges as foreigners. Ten years after Vargas, President Goulart was still forced to observe (*O Semanario,* September 26, 1963): "In fact it is incomprehensible—and much less justifiable—that in this time of renewed heavy burden for the people, innumerable superfluous or easily dispensable products which are consumed mainly by the richer classes continue to enjoy the benefits of an exchange rate of 475 cruzeiros [the market rate was then 800 cruzeiros]. The same exchange rate as for petroleum products and other basic goods is enjoyed by extract of whisky and of Coca-Cola. . . . The disappearance of our scarce foreign exchange resources occurs not only through imports. The concession of exchange privileges to remit foreign exchange destined for the payment of unessential services causes the same harmful effects to our balance of payments." It is worthy of note that, "fascist" or "communizing" or not, as Presidents Vargas and Goulart respectively have been termed by the foreign press, the effective power of these Presidents was evidently insufficient to combat the forces, inside and outside their own governments, which benefit from and fight to maintain those privileges which accrue to small but powerful foreign and domestic interests at the cost of national development. There are, of course, influential Brazilian interests which willingly cooperate in this provision of Brazilian national capital to American firms so long as, in association with this powerful ally from the North, they can participate in some of the spoils.

EFFECTS ON BRAZILIAN ECONOMIC AND INDUSTRIAL STRUCTURE

Spokesmen for the supposed advantages for Brazil of American investment often claim that the distribution of American investments and loans among productive sectors in the receiving country contributes to that country's economic development, and that the resulting import substitution is converting the Brazilian economy into one capable of self-sustained overall economic growth. The facts support neither of these contentions.

We have already noted in part what kind of contribution American owned, *but not supplied,* capital makes to Brazilian development in the trade and public utilities sectors which according to the Department of Commerce, absorb 43 per cent of the total. Of the 791 American firms in Brazil in 1960, we must certainly call into question the allegedly essential contribution to the development of its economy made by the 125 import, export, and other commercial houses; the banking, insurance, real estate, and other financial institutions, which are 64 in number; petroleum distribution (by the world-wide petroleum monopoly of notorious fame); retailing (such as Sears and Roebuck which outside the United States is a luxury chain); and publishing, advertising, hotels, cinema, and other services (including towel supply), which account for 77 more dubious contributions to a solid basis for Brazilian economic development (Barbosa Lima Sobrinho citing Editora Banas, in *Semanario,* September 26, 1963). Coca-Cola at least built or equipped a manufacturing plant. As for the 54 per cent of American capital which the Department of Commerce attributes to manufacturing, no detailed breakdown is given. In 1959, light consumer goods industry accounted for 48 per cent of foreign, including American, manufacturing in Brazil, of which approximately 20 per cent was in the food and beverage sector, including 17 bottling and ice cream firms (Editora Banas, *Capital extranjero no Brasil*). Even the 40 per cent of United States investment which the Department of Commerce attributes to basic industry is not telling. To serve as a base for self-sustained industrialization and growth, investment must, all will agree, produce the materials and equipment—steel, machinery, trucks, tractors—necessary for expanded production. But the bulk of this investment is in the automotive industry, and there it does not produce primarily trucks and tractors which are needed for development purposes but which are not immediately profitable; rather, it seeks maximum profits in the production of passenger cars for the high-income market.

In general, then, American enterprises in Brazil tend to produce non-essentials, and they do so largely with Brazilian capital.

But this is not all. The composition of foreign investment and its effects on the structure of the Brazilian economy are crucial to the maintenance of underdevelopment there. It is often claimed that American investment in Brazil results in import substitution which creates Brazilian capacity for autonomously-directed and self-sustained economic development. Examining only American investment in the most basic sectors, we find, unfortunately, that the facts demonstrate largely the opposite. It is characteristic of American investment in Brazil and elsewhere that the giant investing corporations set up only a part of a particular productive process abroad and keep a critical, though it may be a smaller, part under their immediate control at home. The archetype of this arrangement is the Brazilian assembly plant of an American corporation which is made to depend on the import from the parent corporation of the basic equipment needed, later of its spare parts and replacements, often of critical components, especially the highly tooled ones, of critical raw materials, associated patents, technicians, transport, insurance, and above all, of the technical and organizational schema of the productive process.[3] Significantly, this arrangement also serves to eliminate any existing or potential Brazilian markets for inventive engineering and ties Brazilian technological development to the American economic structure; the reason is, of course, that the solutions to technical problems are already engineered into the productive process in the United States and are exported to Brazil in the form of the technological organization established there.

The Brazilian economy is tied still further to the stronger American economy when American interests "cooperate" with Brazilian capital in joint enterprises, or when American firms farm out part of the productive process to local suppliers of components. While the propaganda has it that the United States is stimulating private enterprise and economic development, the reality is that American corporations use Brazilian capital for their own purposes, transferring part of the risk and cost of demand fluctuations to the local supplier, channeling Brazilian capital into the provision of goods and services which maximize the American corporations' profits, and binding the Brazilian economy increasingly to themselves in particular and the American economy in general. Moreover, American influence thus increases not only in the Brazilian economy but also in Brazilian political life; and, interestingly, in view of the claims about import substitution, this process results in increasing American determination of the composition even of Brazilian imports. Brazilian exports, of course, have been largely in American hands. Thus, what to Americans may appear as "the natural process of import substitution" appears to Brazilians, other than those directly cooperating in the process, as what it is: the progressive domination of the Brazilian economy and the strangulation of its capacity for national development.

The problem of imports is compounded by that of exports which are not keeping pace. The United Nations Economic Commission for Latin America (ECLA) notes that, subtracting petroleum, Latin American exports have risen only 40 per cent since 1938, while world trade has doubled and the trade of the developed countries has tripled. ECLA notes further, "that the deterioration of Latin America in world trade is one of the most important points of strangulation of its economic and social development" (*Jornal do Brasil*, January 22, 1964). Add to this the drain of capital out of Brazil and the misuses of its own resources engendered by foreign investment, and the result is Brazil's chronic balance of payments deficit. Now come the foreign loans.

These loans, we are asked to believe, are also development-producing. The fact is that to an increasing extent they are deposited in New York banks to cover the dollar needs of Americans in Brazil. As Simon Hanson has repeatedly pointed out in his *Latin American Letter* (for American businessmen) and in *Inter-American Economic Affairs* (Summer 1962), Alliance for Progress dollars are destined to serve as the source of the foreign exchange needed by Brazil to buy out American owned (but as we saw, not supplied) capital in Brazilian public utilities, and to pay for imported equipment, materials, technicians, and service "needs" that (as we also saw above) American corporations have built into the Brazilian economy's underdeveloped structure. As these loans come with economic and political strings attached, Brazil thus loses control of critical sectors of her economy to foreign interests on foreign investment, domestic production, export, import, and loan accounts. These levers of control integrate the weaker Brazilian economy ever more into the stronger American economy, render the oligarchic Brazilian allies of American interests ever more dependent on the United States, and structure *under*development all the more firmly into the very foundations of Brazilian society.

Beyond these considerations, some observations about recent features of American aid in Brazil may be illuminating. It is well to note that, though included in the dollar totals of aid, loans under Public Law 480, euphemistically called "Food for Peace," do not supply a single dollar but consist rather of cruzeiros derived from the sale in Brazil of American surplus wheat which, like all other "dumping," competes unfairly with and inhibits the development of Brazilian wheat production.

The major American-financed capital project in Brazil, the Volta Redonda steel mill was, in fact, built by the United States during the Second World War to provide steel in Brazil for the United States' own wartime needs: Brazilians have been paying for the mill ever since. As for the much heralded aid for the development of the "depressed Northeast," the governor of one of its states has publicly pointed out that with a population of 25 million and one of the world's lowest standards of living, this area received $13 million from the Alliance for Progress while the state of Guanabara (including the city of Rio de Janeiro) with 4 million inhabitants and the highest per capita income among Brazil's 22 states was allocated $71 million. The governor of this latter state, it just so happens, is the presidential candidate of the ultra-right economic interests, the Brazilian Barry Goldwater, who spends his American-supplied dollars on parkways marked "works of the government of Carlos Lacerda" and on other projects such as forcing slum dwellers to move out to "John Kennedy village" located twenty miles out of town, while burning down their houses in the center of town to make room for a new tourist hotel. That's development!

UNDERDEVELOPMENT, INDUSTRIALIZATION, AND FOREIGN INVESTMENT

Finally we may briefly broach what is undoubtedly the most difficult but the most important matter of all, the economic history of underdevelopment and development, and the role of foreign trade and investment therein. The events in this history which are critical for the understanding of the problems under discussion are universally known albeit all too conveniently forgotten in certain circles.

The expansion of metropolitan mercantilism and capitalism to Latin America, Africa, and Asia wrought the destruction of productive and viable agricultural and also industrial economies on these continents and most notoriously in Mexico, Peru, West and East Africa, and India. Arriving mostly by force of arms and establishing alliances in these societies (and in newly established ones such as Brazil) with old and newly created exploitative oligarchies, the metropolitan economies reduced the large bulk of the world's people to levels of abject poverty that they had never suffered at the hands of their previous own or foreign masters. In our times, it has become fashionable to call these societies "underdeveloped," as though they have always been this way. The developing metropolitan powers pillaged the peoples in these political and economic colonies of capital which they used to industrialize their own economies. By incorporating them into what is now known euphemistically as the world market, they converted these now *underdeveloping* economies into appendages of their own. As we have seen above, this process continues unabated in our day.

Lest it be thought that the United States is only a newcomer to this exploitative process which produces development for some at the expense of underdevelopment for others, it is well to remember that the initial industrial capital of the Northeastern United States was derived largely from the slave trade and from the products of Southern slavery. Though the forms have been modernized, the content and the effects of the expansion of capitalism in contemporary times remain essentially what they always have been; the level of living of the majority of the people is still *falling*. The United Nations Food and Agricultural Organization (FAO) supplies part of the evidence. Taking per capita food production in 1934-1938 as 100, in the three crop years 1959/60, 1960/61, and 1961/62, it was 99, 100, and 98 in Latin America, Africa, and Asia (excluding the socialist countries) respectively; while it was 113 for the world as a whole, and 145 for the countries universally known for the failure of their agriculture, the Soviet Union and Eastern Europe (FAO, *The World State of Agriculture and Nutrition,* 1962, p. 15 of the Spanish edition). But these figures tell only part of the story. The other part lies in the combination of low or negative economic growth rates with the increasing *inequality* of the distribution of income in countries for which estimates are available, such as Brazil, Argentina, Mexico, and India. The result is that while foreign and domestic exploiters enrich themselves, the masses of the people in the underdeveloping countries are suffering an absolute decline in their per capita incomes.

This article has been an attempt to report on a few of the mechanisms of imperialist exploitation of underdeveloped countries. It is not, and is not intended to be a substitute for inquiry into the structure and transformation of the imperialist system. But even these structurally derived mechanisms of imperialism in action, though no doubt familiar to practicing imperialist and allied businessmen and diplomats, are all too unfamiliar to many of those who would combat imperialism. Yet an understanding of contemporary imperialism in action is essential to the theoretical base necessary for any successful struggle against the system. And there are many more such mechanisms of imperialism in action. (Hamza Alavi has recently reported on some others in his "U.S. Aid to Pakistan," *Economic Weekly,* Bombay, Special Number July, 1963, reprinted in French as "Pakistan: le fardeau de l'aide américaine" in *Revolution,* Paris.) But even where reports of economic mechanisms of imperialism exist, they are usually studies of individual firms, industries, incidents, etc. Not only do these make tedious, if necessary, reading, as those who have followed this report this far will have found out; but in the absence of more inclusive and quantitative information on such matters as real profit rates and totals, concessions, financial control, imperialist-nationalist joint ventures, etc., we can reach only a very inadequate understanding of even these mechanisms of imperialism. It is hoped, therefore, that students in the underdeveloped countries, as well as in underdeveloped regions and sectors of the industrialized nations, will increasingly report on the hard facts of imperialism.

Notes

[1] These totals can be computed from the following issues of the *Survey of Current Business*: November 1954, pp. 9, 13; August 1955, pp. 18, 20; August 1957, p. 25; August 1959, p. 31; August 1961, pp. 22, 23; August 1962, pp. 22, 23.

[2] The reader should note that the author thus omits entirely the largest single source, namely, the plowing back of profits by American branches and subsidiaries of a large part of the profits realized on their Brazilian operations.—The Editors [*Monthly Review*].

[3] Much the same pattern was noted and criticized by the American observer John Gerassi (*The Great Fear*, 1963) in Latin American petroleum, mining, steel, automotive, machine building, and other industries.

16

DAVID TOBIS

Foreign Aid: the Case of Guatemala

Experience has proven that foreign influence is one of the most pernicious enemies of republican government.
—George Washington

At one time Guatemala was called a "Banana Republic." The United Fruit Company owned the only railroad, the only public telegraph system, Puerto Barrios (the only Atlantic sea port), and 460,000 acres of arable land in the country.[1] But today the situation is very different. The railroad and port have been sold to another United States company, the telegraph system is now owned nationally, and most of the Fruit Company's land has been sold. Criticism can no longer be leveled against one "imperialistic" foreign company.

Today there are many foreign investors in Guatemala. Conditions in the country have been made favorable for these investors.

There are no transfer restrictions of any kind on foreign owned assets, dividends, and interest. There is no fixed amount of profit which must be re-invested in industry.[2] The industrial laws of 1952, which gave preferential treatment to domestic capital over foreign capital, were repealed in 1959. Today new foreign industries are exempt for ten years from payment of duties on imports of construction materials, factory machinery and equipment, raw materials, and automotive vehicles for industrial use. These industries receive exemption from payment of taxes for five years and a fifty per cent reduction of taxes for the following five years.[3]

The United Fruit Company no longer controls all the foreign investment in Guatemala. But 92 per cent of the $117 million of foreign investment still comes from the United States;[4] and three United States companies, IRCA (International Railroad of Central America), Empresa Eléctrica; and United Fruit Company (UFC) own 43 per cent of the total.[5]

In addition to what United States companies already have invested in Guatemala, International Nickel is beginning a mining project in the eastern part of the country. In a few years the investment will be $60 to $80 million.[6] This will be the largest single investment in Guatemala. The nickel, however, will not be processed in the country and therefore will not lead to earnings for Guatemala but only for the North American company.

One of the basic problems of United States manufacturing investment in Guatemala is that it has gone exclusively into the production of consumer goods, luxury items, and only to the assembly of durable goods. This type of investment does not lead to the industrialization of the country but merely provides the means for distributing North American products.

The United States seems destined by providence to plague Latin America with miseries in the name of liberty.

—Bolívar

To perpetuate the favorable position the United States has as the principal foreign investor in Guatemala, an elaborate system of loans, called "aid," has been developed. The United States Agency for International Development (USAID) loans money to Guatemala for industrial development. The requirements for receiving loans are few. The industries which are eligible are: (1) those which are not in competition with products from United States companies, and (2) those which will increase the sales of products imported from the United States.[7] In addition, if a Guatemalan industry can be developed which will stop the import of a foreign product, other than from the United States, that industry can receive a loan.[8]

Besides making loans to Guatemalan industries, the United States foreign "aid" program also makes loans to United States companies to invest in underdeveloped countries. As reported by USAID, Washington "will finance up to fifty per cent of the cost of pre-investment surveys undertaken by United States investors."[9] The government also provides as part of foreign aid a program of investment guarantees for United States companies abroad. The aggregate of such loans is well over $2 billion.[10]

The trade relations of Guatemala with the United States have also been detrimental to the development of the country. In 1964 Guatemala imported $38 million more than it exported, and $36 million of this unfavorable balance was with the United States.[11] It is interesting to note that from 1947 to the present there have only been three years when Guatemala has had a favorable balance of trade—from 1952 to 1954, the years when Jacobo Arbenz was the President of Guatemala.[12] It was, of course, the reformist Arbenz government which was overthrown in 1954 by the joint effort of the CIA and the United Fruit Company.[13]

In an attempt to diversify the international markets with which Guatemala trades, the Central American Common Market (CACM) has been developed and is now being promoted by the United States aid program. The basic problem with the CACM is that the five Central American countries essentially produce the same commodities—raw materials and agricultural products. The goods which are traded between the Central American countries in the Common Market are primarily machinery, industrial items, and processed foods. It is on these items that tariffs have been eliminated in the Common Market. United States corporations are the main producers of these items in the five Central American countries. Furthermore, any producer who can provide fifty per cent or more of the trade for any industry will have free-trade privileges.[14] This allows large United States firms to have near monopoly rights and makes it more difficult for new or small industries to enter the Market. Today, 48 per cent of all the trade in the Central American Common Market is from United States companies.[15]

The Deputy Chief of the United States Embassy in Guatemala was asked if he felt that the CACM was a greater benefit to the United States than to the Central American countries. He replied:

"The Central American Common Market is in the self-interest of the United States but fortunately our selfish interests coincide with those of the Central American countries."[16]

The United States government claims that it is attempting to help Guatemala and other Latin American countries to "develop." To this end it has organized what is called in Spanish the *Alianza para el Progreso*. In English this can be translated, the "Alliance *for* Progress" or the "Alliance *Stops* Progress." Unfortunately it is not only the name of this program that has a double meaning.

Last year, through the Alliance, the United States provided $220 million for development loans in Latin America—a truly impressive figure.[17] Most of this "aid," however, does not lead to the development of Latin America. In a booklet distributed by USAID it is reported that "about 85 per cent of the United States bilateral aid is 'tied' . . . so that the money would be spent on United States goods and services."[18] Such "aid" only leads to increased markets for United States-produced goods and makes it more difficult for Latin American producers to compete in their own countries.

An example of how this "aid" works is seen in the road-building project sponsored by USAID in Guatemala. USAID and the Export-Import Bank are each providing about $6 million for the Rio Hondo Road Project. This road will connect Puerto Barrios (the major Atlantic port, owned by IRCA) with Honduras. The $12 million principal plus roughly $5 million in interest has to be paid back to the United States in dollars, which puts a heavy burden on Guatemala's balance of payments. The machinery for the construction must all be bought in the United States. The engineers, the contractors, and the supervisors are all from United States companies. Three United States firms—Nelloteer, Poteshnick, and Harrison—are paving and constructing the road. Brown & Root Overseas, Inc., are the supervisors of the construction. When the road was begun in 1961 under an Ex-Im Bank loan, the United States company Thompson-Cornwall, Inc. had the original contract.[19] It is interesting that Thompson-Cornwall is the same company that constructed the United States airbase at Retalhuleu. This was the base from which United States planes left Guatemala for the Bay of Pigs invasion in that same year.[20]

What the United States government essentially has done through the Export-Import Bank and USAID is to use taxpayers' money to subsidize the exports of large United States companies. By the Export-Import Bank's own figures, the Bank is currently "financing ten per cent of all United States exports."[21]

The United States government claims that the road which is being built to connect Puerto Barrios with Honduras will aid Guatemala and Central America in two ways. First, the project will create jobs in the *Oriente* portion of the country where the *guerrilleros* are concentrated and "will show the *campesinos* in that area that we are doing something to help them."[22] But the money which will be spent to pay Guatemalan salaries is only a small percentage of the total loan.

Second, the United States claims that the road will increase Common Market trade between the Central American countries. But Puerto Barrios is primarily used as the port of entry for United States products which are to be sold in the Central American countries. The other Central American countries have little use for the Atlantic port in Guatemala. The road will therefore be of greatest benefit to the United States companies that export to Central America.

Another way in which United States foreign "aid" helps Central American countries is seen in a project sponsored by ROCAP (United States Regional Office for Central America and Panama).[23] An important ROCAP official related this story:

> The project was to build highway CA-12 in Nicaragua. It is an unimportant road except for the fact that it leads to one of Somoza's *fincas*. ROCAP officials were opposed to the project because they felt that it would not help the development of the Central American Common Market. They changed their minds, however, when representatives from the CIA told them that the road was part of Somoza's payment for allowing United States pilots who flew in the Bay of Pigs to leave from Nicaragua.[24]

Because of projects like this and because of the CIA involvement in the 1954 overthrow of Arbenz to protect the interests of the United Fruit Company, the CIA has become known as the Corporation for Investment Abroad.

A recent USAID project is also of interest. The United States lent $200,000 to Guatemala to purchase 54 Ford cars to be used by the police in fighting *guerrilleros*.[25] In addition 300 bullet proof vests were given by USAID to the Guatemalan police.[26] When the cars arrived, they were publicly blessed in the Central Plaza by the Archbishop. USAID tried to avoid publicity about its participation in this project, since the United States government does not want to be openly connected with any counter-insurgency operations. But all the Guatemalan papers carried articles about the loan, and USAID's role is widely known.

In addition to the economic assistance which the United States lends Guatemala, the United States also provides equipment and money for military development. This aid, however, is not as generous as one would think. Most military "assistance" is in the sale of equipment. The Chief of the United States Military Mission in Guatemala, Colonel John Webber, reported that seven per cent of the entire Guatemalan budget each year is used to buy United States military equipment, some of which is new but most of which is used, out of date, and useless to the United States.[27] This seven per cent comes to well over $12 million a year. The United States then, through its "aid" program, sends technicians to train the Guatemalans to use the equipment they have bought. But total military aid and grants to Guatemala for the last fifteen years ($9,100,000)[28] is less than the amount of money which Guatemala spends each year to buy our surplus equipment.

The reason for this military program was summarized by Colonel Webber: "There is hardly any business of this sort with third nations. These other countries would like to get their foot in the door and make some of these sales, but they can't. There's a lot of money involved."[29]

The sale of United States military equipment is going on throughout the world. About $2 billion of United States military equipment is sold abroad annually.[30] This military build-up not only increases the possibility of international wars but also leads to internal repression within the receiving countries. And finally, the money which, for example, Guatemala spent last year for United States military equipment could have been used to decrease the 75 per cent illiteracy rate, or to lower the ten per cent infant mortality rate, or to raise the average per capita yearly wage of $200.

If the United States were truly interested in developing Central and South American countries, it would pay equitable prices for the mineral and agricultural products of Latin America. In the past ten years there has been a ten per cent *increase* in the import price of United States products. In the same time period there has been a 25 per cent *drop* in the export price of Latin American products.[31]

If the development of Latin America were the sincere desire of the United States, it would listen to the requests of the Latin American countries and eliminate "tied" loans, substituting instead tariff preferences for Latin American exports.

But this is not in the interest of United States corporations. They need consumers. If Latin America develops her own industries, their markets will be restricted. If the prices of Latin American raw materials are increased, the United States industries which are dependent on these commodities will be hurt.

Peter Valky, the Deputy Chief of the United States Mission in Guatemala, stated that "The United States basically has a foreign policy based on self-interest."[32] If this be the case, do not call "tied" loans aid; do not call "the sale of military equipment" assistance; do not talk about the Alliance *for* Progress. Do not call it the United States Agency for International Development; rather call it the Agency for International Development of the United States.

Notes

[1] *La Empresa Estadounidense en el Extranjero* (La United Fruit Company, 1958), p. 86.

[2] *Investing in Guatemala*, Banco de Guatemala, 1966, pp. 1, 19.

[3] *Industrial Laws: Economic Restrictions*, compiled by the United States Embassy, Guatemala, 1966.

[4] *Sector Externo: estadisticas*, Banco de Guatemala, 1966, p. 36.

[5] *Ibid.*, p. 40.

[6] *Guatemala, International Development Manufacturers*, 1966, p. 23.

[7] *La Empresa Privada y La Alianza para el Progreso*, USAID.

[8] Interview with the manager of a large United States company in Guatemala.

[9] *Foreign Aid Through Private Initiative*, USAID, p. 14.

[10] *Ibid.*, p. 16.

[11] *Sector Externo*, p. 19.

[12] *Ibid.*, p. 3.

[13] *The Invisible Government*, David Wise and Thomas Ross, 1965, ch. 11.
President Arbenz attempted a moderate land reform program which involved 200,000 acres of idle land owned by the United Fruit Company. This land would be paid for with 20-year bonds. That John Foster Dulles, the United States Secretary of State at the time, was the legal representative of the UFC; that his brother Allen Dulles, Director of the CIA at the time, had been president of the UFC; that Henry Cabot Lodge, the United States Ambassador to the United Nations at the time, was on the board of directors of the UFC; that John Moors Cabot, then Assistant Secretary of State for Inter-American Affairs, was a large shareholder of the UFC; that Walter Bedell Smith, Director of the CIA before Dulles, became president of the UFC after the 1954 venture—probably had no relation to the United States involvement in the overthrow of Arbenz. See John Gerassi, *The Great Fear in Latin America*, p. 241.

[14] Interview, USAID official (Industrial Section), Guatemala, 1967.

[15] *World Business*, The Chase Manhattan Bank, July, 1966, p. 24.

[16] Interview, Peter Valky, DCM, Guatemala, March, 1967.

[17] Paul Montgomery, *New York Times*, June 22, 1967.

[18] *Foreign Aid Through Private Initiative*, USAID, p. 27.

[19] Interview with USAID official, and *Prensa Libre* (Guatemalan daily paper), Dec. 16, 1966.

[20] *The Invisible Government*, p. 27.

[21] *Export-Import Bank Fact Sheet*, 1967, p. 1.

[22] Interview, USAID official, Jan., 1967.

[23] ROCAP is similar to USAID but is for the entire Central American region.

24 Interview, ROCAP, Nov. 1966.
25 *El Gráfico,* Feb. 9, 1967.
26 *Impacto* (Guatemalan daily paper), Feb. 19, 1967.
27 Interview, Colonel John Webber, Oct. 1966.
28 USAID, Chart of Direct United States Assistance to Guatemala, 1953 to 1966.
29 *Ibid.*
30 *New York Times,* July 21, 1967.
31 *The Great Fear in Latin America,* John Gerassi, p. 30.
32 Interview, Peter Valky, DCM, Guatemala, March 1967.

17

ERNEST MANDEL

Where is America Going?

Today, profound forces are working to undermine the social and economic equilibrium which has reigned in the United States for more than twenty-five years, since the big depressions of 1929-32 and of 1937-38. Some of these are forces of an international character, linked with the national liberation struggles of the peoples exploited by American imperialism—above all the Vietnamese Revolution. But from the point of view of Marxist method, it is important in the first place to stress those forces which are at work inside the system itself. This essay will attempt to isolate six of those forces—six historic contradictions which are now destroying the social equilibrium of the capitalist economy and bourgeois order of the United States.

THE DECLINE OF UNSKILLED LABOR AND THE
SOCIAL ROOTS OF BLACK RADICALIZATION

American society, like every other industrialized capitalist country, is currently in the throes of an accelerated process of technological change. The third industrial revolution—summarized in the catchword "automation"—has by now been transforming American industry for nearly two decades. The changes which this new industrial revolution has brought about in American society are manifold. During the fifties, it created increased unemployment. The annual growth-rate of productivity was higher than the annual growth-rate of output, and as a result there was a tendency to rising structural unemployment even in times of boom and prosperity. Average annual unemployment reached 5,000,000 by the end of the Republican administration.

Since the early sixties, the number of unemployed has, however, been reduced somewhat (although American unemployment statistics are very unreliable). It has probably come down from an average of 5,000,000 to an average of 3,500,000 to 4,000,000: these figures refer to structural unemployment, and not to the conjunctural unemployment which occurs during periods of recession. But whatever may be the causes of this temporary and relative decline in structural unemployment, it is very significant that one sector of the American population continues to be hit very hard by the development of automation: the general category of unskilled labor. Unskilled labor jobs are today rapidly disappearing in U.S. industry. They will in the future tend to disappear in the economy altogether. In absolute figures, the number of unskilled labor jobs in industry has come down from 13,000,000 to less than 4,000,000, and probably to 3,000,000, within the last ten years. This is a truly revolutionary process. Very rarely has anything of the kind happened with such speed in the whole history of capitalism. The group which has been hit hardest by the disappearance of unskilled jobs is, of course, the black population of the United States.

The rapid decline in the number of unskilled jobs in American industry is the nexus which binds the growing Negro revolt, especially the revolt of Negro youth, to the general socio-economic framework of American capitalism. Of course it is clear, as most observers have indicated, that the acceleration of the Negro revolt, and in particular the radicalization of Negro youth in the fifties and early sixties, has been closely linked to the development of the colonial revolution. The appearance of independent states in Black Africa, the Cuban Revolution with its radical suppression of racial discrimination, and the development of the Vietnam War, have been powerful subjective and moral factors in accelerating the Afro-American explosion in the U.S.A. But we must not overlook the objective stimuli which have grown out of the inner development of American capitalism itself. The long post-war boom and the explosive progress in agricultural productivity were the first factors in the massive urbanization and proletarization of the Afro-Americans: the Northern ghettos grew by leaps and bounds. Today, the average rate of unemployment among the black population is double what it is among the white population, and the average rate of unemployment among *youth* is double what it is among adults, so that the average among the black youth is nearly four times the general average in the country. Up to 15 or 20 per cent of young black workers are unemployed: this is a percentage analogous to that of the Great Depression. It is sufficient to look at these figures to understand the social and material origin of the black revolt.

It is important to stress the very intimate inter-relationship between this high rate of unemployment among black youth and the generally scandalous state of education for black people in the ghettos. This school system produces a large majority of drop-outs precisely at the moment when unskilled jobs are fast disappearing. It is perfectly clear under these conditions why black nationalists feel so strongly about the problem of community control over black schools—a problem which in New York and elsewhere has become a real crystallizing point for the black liberation struggle.

THE SOCIAL ROOTS OF THE STUDENT REVOLT

The third industrial revolution can be seen at one and the same time as a process of *expulsion* of human labor from traditional industry, and of tremendous *influx* of industrial labor into all other fields of economic and social activity. Whereas more and more people are replaced by machines in industry, activities like agriculture, office administration, public administration and even education become industrialized—that is, more and more mechanized, streamlined and organized in industrial forms.

This leads to very important social consequences. These may be summed up by saying that, in the framework of the third industrial revolution, manual labor is expelled from production while intellectual labor is reintroduced into the productive process on a gigantic scale. It thereby becomes to an ever-increasing degree alienated labor—standardized, mechanized, and subjected to rigid rules and regimentation, in exactly the same way that manual labor was in the first and second industrial revolutions. This fact is very closely linked with one of the most spectacular recent developments in American society: the massive student revolt, or, more correctly, the growing radicalization of students. To give an indication of the scope of this transformation in American society, it is enough to consider that the United States, which at the beginning of this century was still essentially a country exporting agricultural products, today contains fewer farmers than students. There are today in the United States 6,000,000 students, and the number of farmers together with their employees and family-help has sunk below 5,500,000. We are confronted with a colossal transformation which upsets traditional relations between social groups, expelling human labor radically from certain fields of activity, but reintroducing it on a larger scale and at a higher level of qualification and skill in other fields.

If one looks at the destiny of the new students, one can see another very important transformation, related to the changes which automation and technological progress have brought about in the American economy. Twenty or thirty years ago, it was still true that the students were in general either future capitalists, self-employed or agents of capitalism. The majority of them became either doctors, lawyers, architects, and so on, or functionaries with managerial positions in capitalist industry or the State. But today this pattern is radically changed. It is obvious that there are not 6,000,000 jobs for capitalists in contemporary American society: neither for capitalists or self-employed professionals, nor for agents of capitalism. Thus a great number of present-day students are not future capitalists at all, but future salary-earners, in teaching, public administration and at various technical levels in industry and the economy. Their status will be nearer that of the industrial worker than that of management. For meanwhile, as a result of automation, the difference of status between the technician and the skilled worker is rapidly diminishing. U.S. society is moving towards a situation in which most of the skilled workers for whom there remain jobs in industry will have to have a higher or semi-higher education. Such a situation already exists in certain industries even in countries other than the United States—Japanese shipbuilding is a notorious example.

The university explosion in the United States has created the same intense consciousness of alienation among students as that which is familiar in Western Europe today. This is all the more revealing, in that the material reasons for student revolt are much less evident in the United States than in Europe. Overcrowding of lecture halls, paucity of student lodgings, lack of cheap food in restaurants and other phenomena of a similar kind play a comparatively small role in American universities, whose material infrastructure is generally far superior to anything that we know in Europe. Nevertheless, the consciousness of alienation resulting from the capitalist form of the university, from the bourgeois structure and function of higher education and the authoritarian administration of it, has become more and more widespread. It is a symptomatic reflection of the changed social position of the students today in society.

American students are thus much more likely to understand general social alienation, in other words to become at least potentially anti-capitalist, than they were 10 or 15 years ago. Here the similarity with developments in Western Europe is striking. As a rule, political mobilization on the U.S. campus started with aid to the black population within the United States, or solidarity with liberation movements in the Third World. The first political reaction of American students was an anti-imperialist one. But the logic of anti-imperialism has led the student movement to understand, at least in part, the necessity of anti-capitalist struggle, and to develop a socialist consciousness which is today widespread in radical student circles.

AUTOMATION, TECHNICIANS AND THE HIERARCHICAL STRUCTURE OF THE FACTORY

The progress of automation has also had another financial and economic result, which we cannot yet see clearly in Europe, but which has emerged as a marked tendency in the United States during the sixties. Marxist theory explains that one of the main special effects of automation and the present technological revolution is a shortening of the life-cycle of fixed capital. Machinery is now generally replaced every four or five years, while it used to be replaced every ten years in classical capitalism. Looking at the phenomenon from the perspective of the operations of big corporations, this means that there is occurring a shift of the centre of their gravity away from problems of *production* towards problems of *reproduction.*

The real bosses of the big corporations no longer mainly discuss the problems of how to organize production: that is left to lower-echelon levels of the hierarchy. The specific objective in which they are interested is how to organize and to ensure reproduction. In other words, what they discuss is future plans: plans for replacing the existing machinery, plans for financing that replacement, new fields and locations for investment, and so on. This has given the concentration of capital in the United States a new and unforeseen twist. The process of amalgamation during the last few years has not predominantly consisted in the creation of monopolies in certain branches of industry, fusing together automobile, copper or steel trusts, or aviation factories. It has instead been a movement towards uniting apparently quite *unconnected* companies, operating in completely heteroclite fields of production. There are some classical examples of this process, widely discussed in the American financial press, such as the Xerox-CIT merger, the spectacular diversification of the International Telephone and Telegraph Corporation, or the Ling-Temco-Vought empire, which recently bought up the Jones and Loughlin Steel Corporation.

What this movement really reflects is the growing pre-occupation with 'pure' problems of accumulation of capital. That is to say, the imperative today is to assemble enough capital and then to diversify the investment of that capital in such a way as to minimize risks of structural or conjunctural decline in this or that branch—risks which are very great in periods of fast technological change. In other words, the operation of the capitalist system in the United States today shows in a very clear way what Marxists have always said (and what only economists in the Soviet Union and some of their associates in East European countries and elsewhere are forgetting today), namely that real cost reduction and income maximization is impossible if profitability is reckoned only at plant level. In fact, it is a truth which every big American corporation understands, that it is impossible to have maximum profitability and economic rationality at plant level, and that it is even impossible to achieve it at the level of a *single branch of industry.* That is why the prevailing capitalist tendency in the U.S.A. is to try to combine activities in a number of branches of production. The type of financial empire which is springing up as a result of this form of operation is a fascinating object of study for Marxists.

But the more Big Capital is exclusively pre-occupied with problems of capital accumulation and reproduction, the more it leaves plant management and organization of production to lower-echelon experts, and the more the smooth running of the economy must clash with the survival of private property and of the hierarchical structure of the factory. The absentee factory-owners and money-juggling financiers divorced from the productive process are not straw men. They retain ultimate power—the power to open or to close the plant, to shut it in one town and relaunch it 2,000 miles away, to suppress by one stroke of their pens 20,000 jobs and 50 skills acquired at the price of long human efforts. This power must seem more and more arbitrary and absolute in the eyes of the true technicians who precisely do *not* wield the decisive power, that of the owners of capital. The higher the level of education and scientific knowledge of the average worker-technician, the more obsolete must become the attempts of both capitalists and managers to maintain the hierarchical and authoritarian structure of the plant, which even contradicts the logic of the latest techniques—the need for flexible co-operation within the factory in the place of a rigid chain of command.

THE EROSION OF REAL WAGE INCREASES THROUGH INFLATION

Since the beginning of the sixties and the advent of the Kennedy Administration, structural unemployment has gone down and the rate of growth of the American economy has gone up. This shift has been generally associated with an increased rate of inflation in the American economy. The concrete origins and source of this inflation are to be located not only in the huge military establishment—although, of course, this is the main cause—but also in the vastly increased indebtedness of the whole American society. Private debt has accelerated very quickly; in the last fifteen years it has gone up from something like 65 per cent to something like 120 per cent of the internal national income of the country, and this percentage is rising all the time. It passed the $1,000,000,000,000 (thousand billion) mark a few years ago, in 1966, and is continually rising at a quicker rate than the national income itself. The specific price behavior of the monopolistic and oligopolistic corporations, of course, interlocks with this inflationary process.

This is not the place to explore the technical problems of inflation. But it should be emphasized that the result of these inflationary tendencies, combined with the Vietnam war, has been that, for the first time for over three decades the growth of the real disposable income of the American working class has stopped. The highest point of that disposable real income was reached towards the end of 1965 and the beginning of 1966. Since then it has been going down. The downturn has been very slow—probably less than one per cent per annum. Nevertheless it is a significant break in a tendency which has continued practically without interruption for the last 35 years. This downturn in the real income of the workers has been the result of two processes: on the one hand inflation, and on the other a steep increase in taxation since the beginning of the Vietnamese war. There is a very clear and concrete relation between this halt in the rise of the American working class's real income, and the growing impatience which exists today in American working class circles with the U.S. Establishment as such, whose distorted reflection was partly to be seen in the Wallace movement.

It is, of course, impossible to speak at this stage of any political opposition on the part of the American working class to the capitalist system as such. But if American workers accepted more or less easily and normally the integration of their trade union leadership into the Democratic Party during the long period which started with the Roosevelt Administration, this acceptance was a product of the fact that their real income and material conditions, especially their social security, improved during that period. Today that period seems to be coming to an end. The current stagnation of proletarian real income means that the integration of the trade union bureaucracy into the bourgeois Democratic Party is now no longer accepted quite so easily as it was even four years ago. This was evident during the Presidential Election campaign of 1968. The UAW leadership organized their usual special convention to give formal endorsement to the Democratic candidates, Humphrey and Muskie. This time they got a real shock. Of the thousand delegates who normally come to these conventions, nearly one half did not show up at all. They no longer supported the Democratic Party with enthusiasm. They had lost any sense of identification with the Johnson Administration. All the talk about welfare legislation, social security, medicare and the other advantages which the workers had gained during the last four years was largely neutralized in their eyes by the results of inflation and of increased taxation on their incomes. The fact was that their real wages had stopped growing and were even starting to decline a little.

It is well known that dollar inflation in the United States has created major tensions in the world monetary system. Inside the U.S.A., there is now a debate among different circles of the ruling class, the political personnel of the bourgeoisie, and the official economic experts, as to whether to give priority to restoring the U.S. balance of payments, or to maintaining the present rate of growth. These two goals seem to be incompatible. Each attempt to stifle inflation completely, to re-establish a very stable currency, can only be ensured by deflationary policies which create unemployment—and probably unemployment on a considerable scale. Each attempt to create full employment and to quicken the rate of growth inevitably increases inflation and with it the general loss of power of the currency. This is the dilemma which confronts the new Republican administration today as it confronted Johnson yesterday. It is impossible to predict what course Nixon will choose, but it is quite possible that his economic policy will be closer to that of the Eisenhower Administration than to that of the Kennedy-Johnson Administrations.

A group of leading American businessmen, who form a council of business advisors with semi-official standing, published a study two weeks before the November 1968 election which created a sensation in financial circles. They stated bluntly that in order to combat inflation, at least 6 per cent unemployment was needed. These American businessmen are far more outspoken than their British counterparts, who are already happy when there is talk about three per cent unemployment. Unemployment of 6 per cent in the United States means about 5,000,000 permanently without work. It is a high figure compared to the present level, to the level under 'normal' conditions, outside of recessions. If Nixon should move in that direction, in which the international bankers would like to push him, the American bourgeoisie will encounter increased difficulty in keeping the trade-union movement quiescent and ensuring that the American workers continue to accept the integration of their union bureaucracy into the system, passively submitting to both bosses and union bureaucrats.

THE SOCIAL CONSEQUENCES OF PUBLIC SQUALOR

There is a further consequence of inflation which will have a growing impact on the American economy and especially on social relations in the United States. Inflation greatly intensifies the contradiction between "private affluence" and "public squalor." This contradiction has been highlighted by liberal economists like Galbraith, and is today very striking for a European visiting the United States. The extent to which the public services in that rich country have broken down is, in fact, astonishing. The huge budget has still not proved capable of maintaining a minimum standard of normally functioning public services. In late 1968, the *New York Times Magazine,* criticizing the American postal services, revealed that the average letter travels between Washington and New York more slowly today than it did a hundred years ago on horseback in the West. In a city like New York street sweeping has almost entirely disappeared. Thoroughfares are generally filthy: in the poorer districts, streets are hardly ever cleaned. In the richer districts, the burghers achieve clean streets only because they pay private workers out of their own pockets to sweep the streets and keep them in more or less normal conditions. Perhaps the most extraordinary phenomenon, at any rate for the European, is that of certain big cities in the South-West, like Houston or Phoenix, which have half a million inhabitants or more and yet do not have any public transport system *whatsoever*: not a broken-down system—just no system at all. There are private cars and nothing else—no buses, no trains, no subways, nothing.

The contradiction between private affluence and public squalor has generally been studied from the point of view of the consumer, and of the penalties or inconveniences that it imposes on the average citizen. But there is another dimension to this contradiction which will become more and more important in the years to come. This is its impact on what one could call the "producers," that is to say of the people who are employed by public administration.

The number of these employees is increasing very rapidly. Public administration is already the largest single source of employment in the United States, employing over 11,000,000 wage earners. The various strata into which these 11,000,000 can be divided are all chronically underpaid. They have an average income which is lower than the income of the equivalent positions in private industry. This is not exceptional; similar phenomena have existed or exist in many European countries. But the results—results which have often been seen in Europe during the last 10 or 15 years—are now for the first time appearing on a large scale in the United States.

Public employees, who in the past were outside the trade union movement and indeed any form of organized social activity, are today becoming radicalized at least at the union level. They are organizing, they are agitating, and they are demanding incomes at least similar to those which they could get in private industry. In a country like the United States, with the imperial position it occupies on a world scale, the vulnerability of the social system to any increase in trade union radicalism by public employees is very great. A small example will do as illustration. In New York recently both police and firemen were, not officially but effectively, on strike—at the same time. They merely worked to rule, and thereby disorganized the whole urban life of the city. Everything broke down. In fact, for six days total traffic chaos reigned in New York. Drivers could park their cars anywhere without them being towed away. (Under normal conditions, between two and three thousand cars are towed away by the police each day in New York.) For those six days, with motorists free to park where they liked, the town became completely blocked after an hour of morning traffic—just because the police wanted a ten per cent rise in wages.

The economic rationale of this problem needs to be understood. It is very important not to see it simply as an example of mistaken policy on the part of public administrators or capitalist politicians, but rather as the expression of basic tendencies of the capitalist system. One of the main trends of the last 25 to 30 years of European capitalism has been the growing socialization of all indirect costs of production. This constitutes a very direct contribution to the realization of private profit and to the accumulation of capital. Capitalists increasingly want the State to pay not only for electrical cables and roads, but also for research, development, education, and social insurance. But once this tendency towards the socialization of indirect costs of production gets under way, it is obvious that the corporations will not accept large increases in taxation to finance it. If they were to pay the taxes needed to cover all these costs, there would in fact be no "socialization." They would continue to pay for them privately, but instead of doing so directly they would pay indirectly through their taxes (and pay for the administration of these payments too). Instead of lessening the burden, such a solution would in fact increase it. So there is an inevitable institutionalized resistance of the corporations and of the capitalist class to increasing taxes up to the point where they would make possible a functional public service capable of satisfying the needs of the entire population.

For this reason, it is probable that the gap between the wages of public employees and those of private workers in the United States will remain, and that the trend towards radicalization of public employees—both increased unionization and even possibly political radicalization—will continue.

Moreover, it is not without importance that a great number of university students enter public administration—both graduates and so-called drop-outs. Even today, if we look at the last four or five years, many young people who were student leaders or militants three or four years ago are now to be found teaching in the schools or working in municipal social services. They may lose part of their radical consciousness when they take jobs; that is the hope not only of their parents but also of the capitalist class. But the evidence shows that at least part of their political consciousness is preserved, and that there occurs a certain infiltration of radicalism from the student sector into the teaching body—especially in higher education—and into the various strata of public administration in which ex-students become employed.

THE IMPACT OF FOREIGN COMPETITION

The way in which certain objective contradictions within the United States economy have been slowly tending to transform the subjective consciousness of different groups of the country's population—Negroes, especially Negro youth; students; technicians; public employees—has now been indicated. Inflation has begun to disaffect growing sections of the working class. But the final, and most important, moment of a Marxist analysis of U.S. imperial society today has not yet been reached—that is the threat to American capitalism now posed by international competition.

Traditionally, American workers have always enjoyed much higher real wages than European workers. The historical causes for this phenomenon are well known. They are linked with the shortage of labor in the United States, which was originally a largely empty country. Traditionally, American capitalist industry was able to absorb these higher wages because it was practically isolated from international competition. Very few European manufactured goods reached the United States, and United States industry exported only a small part of its output. Over the last forty years, of course, the situation has slowly changed. American industry has become ever more integrated into the world market. It participates increasingly in international competition, both because it exports more and because the American domestic market is rapidly itself becoming the principal sector of the world market, since the exports of all other capitalist countries to the United States have been growing rapidly. Here a major paradox seems to arise. How can American workers earn real wages which are between two and three times higher than real wages in Western Europe, and between four and five times higher than real wages in Japan, while American industry is involved in international competition?

The answer is, of course, evident. These higher wages have been possible because United States industry has operated on a much higher level of productivity than European or Japanese industry. It has enjoyed a productivity gap, or as Engels said of British industry in the nineteenth century, a *productivity monopoly* on the world market. This productivity monopoly is a function of two factors: higher technology, and economy of scale—that is a much larger dimension of the average factory or firm. Today, both of these two causes of the productivity gap are threatened. The technological advance over Japan or Western Europe which has characterized American imperialism is now disappearing very rapidly. The very trend of massive capital export to the other imperialist countries which distinguishes American imperialism, and the very nature of the so-called "multi-national" corporation (which in nine cases out of ten is in reality an American corporation), diffuses American technology on a world scale, thus equalizing technological levels at least among the imperialist countries. At the same time, it tends, of course, to increase the gap between the imperialist and the semi-colonial countries. Today, one can say that only in a few special fields such as computers and aircraft does American industry still enjoy a real technological advantage over its European and Japanese competitors. But these two sectors, although they may be very important for the future, are not decisive for the total export and import market either in Europe or in the United States, nor will they be decisive for the next ten or twenty years. So this advantage is a little less important than certain European analysts have claimed.

If one looks at other sectors, in which the technological advantage is disappearing or has disappeared—such as steel, automobiles, electrical appliances, textiles, furniture, or certain types of machinery—it is evident that a massive invasion of the American market by foreign products is taking place. In steel, something between 15 and 20 per cent of American consumption is today imported from Japan and Western Europe. The Japanese are beginning to dominate the West Coast steel market, and the Europeans to take a large slice of the East Coast market. It is only in the Mid-West, which is still the major industrial region of the United States, that imported steel is not widely used. But with the opening of the St. Lawrence seaway, even there the issue may be doubtful in the future. Meanwhile, automobiles are imported into the United States today at a rate which represents 10-15 per cent of total annual consumption. This proportion too could very quickly go up to 20-25 per cent. There is a similar development in furniture, textiles, transistor radios and portable television sets; shipbuilding and electrical appliances might be next.

So far, the gradual disappearance of the productivity differential has created increased competition for American capitalism in its own home market. Its foreign markets are seriously threatened or disappearing in certain fields like automobiles and steel. This, of course, is only the first phase. If the concentration of European and Japanese industry starts to create units which operate on the same scale as American units, with the same dimensions as American corporations, then American industry will ultimately find itself in an impossible position. It will then have to pay three times higher wages, with the same productivity as the Europeans or the Japanese. That would be an absolutely untenable situation, and it would be the beginning of a huge structural crisis for American industry.

Two examples should suffice to show that this is not a completely fantastic perspective. The last merger in the Japanese steel industry created a Japanese corporation producing 22,000,000 tons of steel a year. In the United States, this would make it the second biggest steel firm. On the other hand, in Europe the recent announcement that Fiat and Citroën are to merge by 1970 has created an automobile corporation producing 2,000,000 cars a year; this would make it the third largest American automobile firm, and it would move up into second place, overtaking Ford, if the momentum of its rate of growth, compared with the current rate of growth in the American industry, were maintained for another three or four years.

These examples make it clear that it is possible for European and Japanese firms, if the existing process of capital concentration continues, to attain not only a comparable technology but also comparable scale to that of the top American firms. When they reach that level, American workers' wages are certain to be attacked, because it is not possible in the capitalist world to produce with the same productivity as rivals abroad and yet pay workers at home two or three times higher wages.

THE WAGE DIFFERENTIALS ENJOYED BY
AMERICAN WORKERS

The American ruling class is becoming increasingly aware that the huge wage differential which it still grants its workers is a handicap in international competition. Although this handicap has not yet become a serious fetter, American capitalists have already begun to react to it in various ways over the past few years.

The export of capital is precisely designed to counteract this wage differential. The American automobile trusts have been investing almost exclusively in foreign countries, where they enjoy lower wages and can therefore far more easily maintain their share of the world market, with cars produced cheaply in Britain or Germany, rather than for higher wages inside the United States. Another attempt to keep down the growth of real wages was the type of incomes policy advocated by the Kennedy and Johnson Administrations—until 1966, when it broke down as a result of the Vietnam war. A third form of counter-action has been an intensification of the exploitation of labor—in particular a speed-up in big industry which has produced a structural trans-formation of the American working class in certain fields. This speed-up has led to a work rhythm that is so fast that the average adult worker is virtually incapable of keeping it up for long. This has radically lowered the age structure in certain industries, such as automobiles or steel. Today, since it is increasingly difficult to stay in plants (under conditions of speed-up) for ten years without becoming a nervous or physical wreck, up to 40 per cent of the automobile workers of the United States are young workers. Moreover, the influx of black workers in large-scale industry has been tremendous as a result of the same phenomenon, since they are physically more resistant. Today, there are percentages of 35, 40 or 45 per cent black workers in some of the key automobile factories. In Ford's famous River Rouge plant, there are over 40 per cent black workers; in the Dodge automobile plant in Detroit, there are over 50 per cent. These are still exceptional cases—although there are also some steel plants with over 50 per cent black workers. But the average employment of black workers in United States industry as a whole is far higher than the demographic average of ten per cent: it is something like 30 per cent.

None of these policies has so far had much effect. However, if the historic moment arrives when the productivity gap between American and West European and Japanese industry is closed, American capitalism will have absolutely no choice but to launch a far more ruthless attack on the real wage levels of American workers than has occurred hitherto in Western Europe, in the various countries where a small wage differential existed (Italy, France, West Germany, England and Belgium, at different moments during the sixties). Since the wage differential between Europe and America is not a matter of 5, 10, or 15 per cent, as it is between different Western European countries, but is of the order of 200-300 per cent, it is easy to imagine what an enormous handicap this will become when productivity becomes comparable, and how massive the reactions of American capitalism will then be.

It is necessary to stress these facts in order to adopt a Marxist, in other words a materialist and not an idealist, approach to the question of the attitudes of the American working class towards American society. It is true that there is a very close inter-relation between the anti-communism of the Establishment, the arms expenditure which makes possible a high level of employment, the international role of American imperialism, the surplus profits which the latter gets from its international investments of capital, and the military apparatus which defends these investments. But one thing must be understood. The American workers go along with this whole system, not in the first place because they are intoxicated by the ideas of anti-communism. They go along with it because it has been capable of delivering the goods to them over the last 30 years. The system has been capable of giving them higher wages and a higher degree of social security. It is this fact which has determined their acceptance of anti-communism, and not the acceptance of anti-communism which has determined social stability. Once the system becomes less and less able to deliver the goods, a completely new situation will occur in the United States.

Trade-union consciousness is not only negative. Or, to formulate this more dialectically, trade-union consciousness is in and by itself socially neutral. It is neither reactionary nor revolutionary. It becomes reactionary when the system is capable of satisfying trade-union demands. It creates a major revolutionary potential once the system is no longer capable of satisfying basic trade-union demands. Such a transformation of American society under the impact of the international competition of capital is today knocking at the door of U.S. capitalism.

The liberation struggles of the peoples of the Third World, with their threat to American imperialist investment, will also play an important role in ending the long socio-economic equilibrium of

American capitalism. But they do not involve such dramatic and immediate economic consequences as the international competition of capital could have, if the productivity gap were filled.

As long as socialism or revolution are only ideals preached by militants because of their own convictions and consciousness, their social impact is inevitably limited. But when the ideas of revolutionary socialism are able to unite faith, confidence and consciousness with the immediate material interest of a social class in revolt—the working class, then their potential becomes literally explosive. In that sense, the political radicalization of the working class, and therewith socialism, will become a practical proposition in the United States within the next ten or fifteen years, under the combined impact of all these forces which have been examined here. After the black workers, the young workers, the students, the technicians and the public employees, the mass of the American workers will put the struggle for socialism on the immediate historical agenda in the United States. The road to revolution will then be open.

18

MARTIN NICOLAUS

Who Will Bring the Mother Down?

Messengers of revolution are always welcome. Ernest Mandel's thesis in "Where Is America Going?" that a socialist revolution within the United States is on the agenda of the next decade or two is an important corrective to the more gloomy theses being advanced from other quarters. Nevertheless, false hope is as wrong as false despair. The grounds for confidence which Mandel outlines are not tenable. They must be exposed to criticism so that those who occupy them do not fall into disillusion. Beyond hope and despair there are better premises. The most important of Mandel's theses is contained in his points six and seven, in which he holds that the impact of European and Japanese competition on the world market will precipitate a major structural crisis in United States industry. This question will be discussed at length below. The article also commands attention, however, for its first five points, which outline an equal number of "forces or contradic-

275

tions" arising, Mandel holds, from "forces which are at work inside the system itself" by which he means, within the domestic sector of the U.S. capitalist economy. Since most of the content of these five points will be more or less familiar to people in or around the U.S. movement, I don't propose to deal with them here separately or in detail. The more important problems of Mandel's viewpoint lie not within each of these five points separately, but in the manner in which he attempts to tie them together.

TECHNOLOGY AND INFLATION:
ETHER AND PHLOGISTON

The experience and literature accumulated over the last decade regarding radicalization of blacks, students, technicians, state employees and the industrial working class are considerable. To a greater or lesser extent, each of these groups, categories or classes of people seems to have become radicalized spontaneously, and except for blacks and (white) students—where ties existed almost from the beginning—independently of one another. So, for example, the great majority of wild-cat strikes or of intra-union protest waves have occurred and still occur without the knowledge or participation, much less initiative, of student radicals or of revolutionary black organizations; such radicalism as exists among technicians and scientists moves in virtual ignorance of the militancy of municipal employees; and so on.

Arriving in the U.S. with more or less fresh eyes, Mandel's view was not tied down, as can happen, within the horizon of one or the other sphere of specific movement work, nor (despite his position as leader of the Fourth International, with which the Young Socialist Alliance in the U.S. is affiliated) was he a gut-level participant in the factional in-fighting of the last year. Ernest Mandel has almost naively—in the good sense—hit upon an important truth, namely that these five forces are—or ought to be—part of a single movement. He has omitted a couple of the strongest forces, the women's movement and the movement within the Army, but has nevertheless drawn an unmistakable circle around a number of hitherto apparently separate phenomena and pointed out that they are in some way related to one another.

This is a step forward. Mandel's often perceptive summary brings these forces together on paper in an easily accessible form. **But** anyone who has had the experience of making contact with radicals in a different segment, for example, a student trying to talk to workers, or a technician trying to talk to black revolutionaries, knows that bringing these forces together by listing them on paper one-two-three-four-five, and actually making contact, even if only on the talking level, are very different things. Even so apparently simple a step as identifying a common enemy can prove difficult.

One usefulness of good theoretical writing is to make this process of making contact easier, by showing and explaining the common roots of separately experienced oppressions. Unless he gets drafted, and not necessarily even then, the college student doesn't know from his own experience that the causes of his discontent and the causes of the NLF's fight have a common root; the young white factory worker doesn't know *from his own experience* that he and the black street organizer are fighting against the same system. It has to be shown and explained. On that level, it has to be noted, Mandel's article does not go very far forward; in some respects, it even goes backward.

What are the common roots of these separately-experienced oppressions? In Mandel's view, the first three (blacks, students, technicians) are jointly derived from "an accelerated process of technological change" which he calls "the third industrial revolution." Thus he claims automation has thrown black workers out of unskilled jobs; it has further created a demand for more educated people and thus led to the use of industrial methods in education; and finally, it has led technicians into conflict with financiers. As for points four and five (industrial workers, government employees), their problems are rooted, he says, in "inflation."

Not one common root, but two separate ones. And neither of them, unfortunately, extremely enlightening. For nearly a decade, the entire official spectrum of analysts, critics and columnists has been pointing to "technology" and "inflation" as the root causes of one or another troublesome phenomenon. These are the "ether" and "phlogiston" of contemporary socio-economic criticism, the residual, fictional categories into whose murky depths escape all those who fear the sunlight of critical, radical thought. There are a dozen analyses of "technology" and its social and political effects; at least that many of "inflation." They range from right to left. The problem with "technology and inflation" is that as explanations they include *too much*; they can be used to explain everything, and therefore end up explaining nothing.

Imagine a conference called to assemble forces for an attack on the oppressive effects of "technology." Who would *not* be able to participate? Imagine another conference to protest "inflation."

Whom would it exclude? Now put the two conferences together and you have a committee to draft a platform for both the Democratic and the Republican parties. Whatever these "common roots" may sprout, it is not a revolutionary movement. Especially when both of these common roots are themselves internally split. A closer examination of Mandel's theory of his "third industrial revolution" and of "inflation" yields some curious statistical and logical problems within each of them.

In point number one, for example, the "third industrial revolution" has allegedly eliminated ten million unskilled industrial jobs from the labor market. Since their occupants presumably did not all become students or emigrants, this massive exodus from industry should have made a sizeable bulge in the unemployment figures. Although Mandel is right to accuse the unemployment statistics of being notoriously unreliable, they are not so unreliable as to dip downward consistently if there is a ten million-strong upsurge in reality. A countercheck on the side of the employment figures—percentage of people in given occupations—shows only a minute decline in the proportion, and no decline at all in absolute numbers, of people employed as "operatives" or "laborers other than farm and mine," the chief "unskilled industrial" categories. In short, either there is a massive conspiracy by the Bureau of Labor Statistics, or these ten million unskilled industrial jobs disappeared only in Mandel's imagination.

Leaving the statistical question aside does not end the problem, for the contradiction goes further. Whereas there was, in point one, a massive exodus from industry, which "hit hardest" at the black population, suddenly in point number seven there is "a tremendous *influx* of black workers into large-scale industry." Since we knew that the great majority of black workers are not being employed as skilled workers, this is an impossible contradiction. Either there is an exodus or there is an influx. Black workers in the millions cannot be coming and going at the same time.

Mandel's analysis of "inflation" is hardly more satisfactory. Responsibility for this phenomenon, he writes, lies mainly with the huge military establishment. This is true but superficial. On what does responsibility for the huge military establishment lie? Responsibility further lies, he says, with the vast increase in private indebtedness, i.e., on instalment buying. This is not even superficial, it's slanted. Inflation doesn't happen because people go into debt; people go into debt because of inflation. At the very least, there is a circular process. The net effect of Mandel's analysis is to deposit blame for inflation courageously on the doorsteps of Pentagon wastefulness and consumer recklessness, precisely where we see it deposited almost daily in the editorial pages of the average metropolitan newspaper. And as for the corporations: they do not have a stake in the inflationary process one way or the other, they are merely "interlocked" with it. As they, of course, claim themselves.

This is what calls itself Marxist political economy? Incredible. The high respect which Mandel's work has earned makes such lapses particularly astonishing. These are not merely "technical problems," as Mandel, retreating, claims. They are very much on the political agenda of the movement, and their correct solution is one of the tasks to which Marxist political economy ought to be contributing. These are problems, moreover, which cannot be understood by drawing a dividing line between forces or contradictions "within the system itself"—meaning within the domestic sector of U.S. capitalism itself—and forces or contradictions of an "international" character, as if the latter were outside the system. They have to be understood as "international" problems from the beginning—as problems arising from imperialism—if they are to be understood at all. Unfortunately, Mandel's view of the international scene, next to be examined, only adds to the problem.

USA, EUROPE AND JAPAN

We come then to "the final and most important moment of a Marxist analysis," points six and seven, which feature the subversion and overthrow of U.S. capital by the bourgeoisies of Europe and Japan. These latter powers, Mandel holds, have risen from their position of almost complete dependence on the U.S. immediately after the war to a condition of near-equality with the U.S. in the commercial sphere. The growth in scale and productivity of European and Japanese industry, combined with the relatively lower wages which they enjoy, permits the exports of these nations to compete favorably against U.S. exports on the world market, and even allows an increasing degree of penetration into the U.S. domestic market.

Mandel foresees that sooner or later (and his formulations vary widely) the commercial superiority of European and Japanese export products will provoke a "huge structural crisis" in U.S. industry. Presumably—Mandel's formulations are not conceptually clear—this "huge structural crisis" will provide the major impetus for "deneutralization" of the trade unions on the side of revolution.

There is no denying that the last decade has brought an increase in export competition between U.S. industry and those of Europe and Japan, and a steep rise in the level of friction in nearly every other sphere of these inter-capitalist relations as well. Particularly has this been the case in U.S.-European relations, and not only in regard to France under de Gaulle. The formation of the six-member European Economic Community (Common Market) with the express intent of creating a European economy comparable to that of the U.S. in scale and power, has forced U.S. capital to reconsider its global strategy in a number of respects. The fortification of the "free world" which this measure promises on the European front has permitted a relative reduction of U.S. military strength there, and a correspondingly greater U.S. potential in the Pacific, a development finalized with the retreat of Britain from "east of Suez."

On the other hand, the notion of an independent European capitalism, an ideal which has agitated Europeans of a variety of political persuasions for many years, provokes anxiety among U.S. "Atlantic" strategists, who fear an eventual alliance between Europe and the U.S.S.R. It appears that no clear consensus on the question of strategy has yet emerged in the U.S. ruling class, nor among the national bourgeoisies of the European states or the "European" bourgeoisie proper. There are sharp divisions on all aspects of the problem, which deserve close attention in the future.

The aspect of Mandel's thesis to which objection must be taken is the cause-and-effect relationship he tries to establish between these phenomena of trade competition and the "huge structural crisis" awaiting U.S. industry. It is possible to challenge this thesis on two levels. One method would be to show empirically that the competition is not as significant as he claims, that it is restricted to certain non-vital industries, that additional U.S. labor is employed in processing or finishing some types of imported goods, that the productivity gap is widening rather than diminishing, as he claims, that the wage gap, instead of widening, as he claims, is actually narrowing, and that in any case, foreign trade is of far less importance to the U.S. economy than to those of Europe and Japan.

Mandel has assembled some of these data in a longer work addressed to a German audience,[1] whose conclusions, interestingly enough, do not always coincide with those of his (foregoing) article. He writes there, for example, that U.S.-Japanese competition is negligible, and that competition between Japan and Europe is sharper than competition between either or both of them and the U.S. These divergences illustrate the extreme complexity of the question, which involves the whole of world relationships, and point to the need for further systematic empirical research.

A second line of objections to the thesis, however, arises on the basis of structural information which Mandel leaves out of account, and on the basis of historical experience which he chooses to ignore. While granting an increase in trade competition as an established fact, I regard the analysis which sees this phenomenon as the cause of a crisis in U.S. industry, a crisis with revolutionary implications, as mistaken and misleading on the following grounds:

1. The predominance of U.S. banking capital. In order to provoke a "huge structural crisis" in U.S. industry, European capital would first have to provoke a huge crisis in U.S. banking. The role of banks in competitive battles is crucial, and becomes more so as the production advantages of one antagonist over the other diminish. Given parity in wages and productivity, such as obtains, for example, between the major U.S. auto producers, the outcome of sales wars is decided by financial strength. That side which can afford to make the largest new investments, spend the most on distribution costs, and hold out longest in the face of losses, will win. The internally-generated reserves of individual corporations also weigh in the outcome, but ultimately the volume of credit which can be obtained through banks is determinant. The ability of European industry to force a crisis on U.S. industry thus depends on the relative strength of the respective privately-controlled capital reserves and credits.

While Mandel acknowledges, indeed underlines, the importance of the financial sphere in the domestic sectors (in point three), he is guilty of neglecting, indeed obfuscating it with some fancy footwork as regards the international sector. In point four he suddenly introduces the anonymous figures of "international bankers," who appear at the side of the chief executive of the U.S. and urge decisions with worldwide consequences upon him, and then disappear never to be heard from again. Unless Mandel wishes to resurrect on the finance level the capitalist unity which he denies on the industry level, an alternative which is open to him but which would require a serious modification in his analysis, he must be more specific as to the identity of these figures. Of course the major banks all operate internationally, and none of them can be accused of patriotism, but through their ties and interlocks

with major corporate clients, the banks nevertheless retain a
national *base*. In the capitalism of which nation are these
international bankers grounded? In the German book already
referred to, Mandel provides fairly persuasive evidence for the
conclusion that these financial powers are based in U.S. capitalism.
He points out that (a) U.S. firms operating in Europe are treated
as preferred customers by European bankers, with the result that
U.S. firms raise nearly all the capital required for operation and
investment in Europe itself, instead of importing it from the U.S.
This produces the further consequence that European firms find
themselves at a disadvantage, singly, in borrowing back the capital
which they themselves generated collectively. They thus turn to
the branch offices of U.S.-based banks in Europe, who are eager to
acquire new customers, with the consequence (b) that an
increasing amount of European capital falls under the control of
U.S.-based banking houses, who then use their domestic reserves
to purchase increasing degrees of control in European banks, (c)
thus completing a cycle of financial takeover.

The evidence on this score, which is supported by Harry
Magdoff in his book *The Age of Imperialism,* tends to the
conclusion that in case of a serious export crunch, it is European
industry which will in the long run be forced to undergo the more
severe crisis. The "international bankers" to which Mandel refers
are Chase Manhattan, Bank of America, Morgan Guaranty, etc.

In this connection, the question of the recurrent monetary
crises deserves brief consideration from two aspects. First, it is
clear that the European states find the vast holdings of inflated
U.S. dollars which they have been forced to accept to cover the
U.S. payments deficit a burden, and that they have been bringing a
variety of pressures on the U.S. to make good the deficit and
redeem the undesirable holdings in trade or gold. The U.S. dollar is
thus acknowledged as a weak currency, and an official devaluation
is repeatedly suggested and as repeatedly denied by U.S.
authorities; the political consequences of such a move domestically are unforeseeable.

But (and this is, in the midst of all the crises, even more
important to keep in mind) the dollar remains the international
capitalist monetary unit, as was the pound sterling in the era of
British imperial supremacy, and hence a devaluation of the dollar
(not to speak of its collapse, which is what a major structural crisis
in U.S. industry would mean) would create the profoundest shocks
in the entire structure of world capitalist finance and trade. The
chief overseas victims would be precisely those European and

other states and banks who are stuck with huge dollar holdings. If the dollar poses dilemmas for U.S. capital, therefore, it poses even greater problems for the European bourgeoisie. They would like to cut the dollar down but find themselves sawing the branch on which they sit.

Thus, partly unwilling and almost wholly unable to bring the dollar down, such European giants as France and Britain have been forced into repeated devaluations of their own currencies. While such moves improve their chances in the export trade by cheapening their products relative to dollar products, devaluations also weaken their domestic economic sovereignty, since, by lowering the relative price of their capital assets, they permit U.S. corporations to buy into and buy out their domestic firms at bargain rates.

2. *The role of U.S. direct investments in Europe, Japan and the Third World.* By direct investments are meant those which consist of ownership of and control over productive installations, as opposed to, e.g., portfolio investments, which give the right only to participate in yields. The point is that direct overseas investments by U.S. corporations are a form of "export"—which is, however, a misleading term, as the capital is raised locally— through which whatever disadvantages U.S. capital may suffer in export *trade* are bypassed.

Mandel's procedure of equating the economic sphere of U.S. capital with the territorial area of the U.S.A. is highly misleading. The impression is created that U.S.-European competition is analogous to two grocery stores on opposite corners. The fact is that one of the "grocery stores" also owns a very large interest in the other. The sphere of U.S. capital is not confined to the territorial nation, but of course extends in varying degrees throughout Canada, Japan, the states of Europe, and the Third World. The term "third Europe" has been coined by European capitalist-independentists to signify that sector of the European economy which is neither socialist nor European capitalist, but under U.S.-capital control. By some estimates, that sector is now larger than any of the European states' economies singly.

It follows that the wage-comparisons Mandel makes to show the alleged growing disadvantage of U.S. capital in the export trade are not very relevant to phenomena on the order of "huge structural crisis."

The major U.S. capitals have no need whatever to "compete" against European and Japanese capitals on the basis of U.S. wage rates; on the contrary, through their direct investments, they compete against European capital on the basis of European wage rates, and against Japanese capital on the basis of Japanese wage rates. In other words, U.S. capital is not merely national, it is imperial; and a comparison of wage rates which confines itself to the U.S. domestic or national sector tells little; what needs to be compared is the prevailing wage rate within the entire U.S. imperial sphere, on the one hand, and that prevailing within the entire European-Japanese "imperial spheres"—but that measurement would be very largely redundant.

It should further be pointed out that at least some of the "competition" now faced by U.S. industry originates not with "foreign" capital, but with the imperial branches of U.S. corporations themselves. This is particularly graphic in the auto industry, where major U.S. producers own major European producers (GM-Opel; Ford-Vauxhall; Chrysler-Simca) whose products they then import into the U.S. to compete not only against European-owned imports (e.g., Volkswagen) but also against U.S.-domestic economy models (e.g., Ford's Maverick). Similar "foreign" competition which is actually competition among U.S. capitals themselves occurs to an as-yet-undetermined extent in other branches of industry. Since there is no first-glance way of telling which "foreign import" is actually a U.S.-imperial "re-import," caution should be exercised in drawing political-economic conclusions from "made in Japan" or "made in Germany" labels.

This phenomenon of imperial re-imports, or "captive imports" as they are also referred to, suggests that a serious conflict of interests exists between the giant U.S. corporations (and their banks) on the one hand, and the lesser manufacturers on the other. The latter cannot afford to "compete" on the basis of direct overseas investments; if they wish to enter the European market, they must stick to the by now old-fashioned mechanisms of the export trade in finished goods, where indeed they may be at a disadvantage. The major corporations, on the other hand, because they enter overseas markets through direct investments, are not so hampered.

There is emerging in U.S. politics a revival of the debate between "free-traders" and "protectionists," in which the latter represent the U.S. domestic manufacturers who do not operate on an imperial scale. The "competition" thesis with all its nationalist overtones, alas, fits perfectly into the latter's public relations outlook. While opposed to protectionism in practice, U.S. imperial capital is not averse to borrowing pages from the protectionist ideology for domestic social purposes, inasmuch as "foreign competition" is a convenient scapegoat explanation for a rise in unemployment. We should at all costs avoid getting sucked in by these maneuvers.

A further misleading implication of Mandel's wage-comparisons surfaces when it is kept in mind that the U.S. imperial corporations not only operate on the basis of European and Japanese wage levels, but can take advantage of even lower wage levels than these in their Third World operations. An example is the Singer corporation, which competes successfully against Japanese products—on the basis of Taiwanese and South Korean wages. Again it must be emphasized, in the face of Mandel's theoretical retreat into capitalist-nationalist analysis, that the U.S. economy in its dominant sectors has a thoroughly imperial structure; that the *average* wage level in the U.S. economy as a whole, i.e., in the U.S. imperial economy, is far lower than it is in the metropolis, and is probably one of the lowest in the world; and finally that the contradiction between "Europe" and the "U.S." which Mandel outlines is to a very great extent a contradiction not between capitalisms but within U.S. imperialism itself. This becomes a little more graspable when we turn to the military question.

3. The role of the U.S. military.   No major power of whatever internal economic structure sits idly by while another power masses its forces for an attack on its industry. The threat of a "huge structural crisis in U.S. industry" which Mandel sees emerging from the growth of European and Japanese capital, if it were real, would necessarily provoke on the U.S. side the most energetic reaction. On the two previous occasions in this century when major national capitalisms have entered into major export conflicts, the "competition" between them necessarily rapidly escalated into protectionism, embargos, financial blockades, colonial wars, and finally the First and Second World Wars. (The "huge structural crisis" which U.S. industry suffered in the 1930's, incidentally, was decidedly *not* due to foreign competition.) The threat which Mandel depicts, if it had the magnitude he ascribes to it, would clearly be a *casus belli.*

Or, put in other terms, European and Japanese capital would be in a position to follow through on such a threat only if they were prepared to contest the matter also on the military level. It is axiomatic that a nation which cannot prevail militarily cannot maintain or achieve commercial hegemony. But there is little question at present or in the foreseeable future that Europe and

Japan are in no condition whatever to cut themselves off from the control which the U.S. imperial armed forces directly and indirectly exercise over their respective military postures.

There is, however, a further dimension. The one undoubted commercial advantage which European and Japanese capital enjoy over U.S. capital is in their relationships to the U.S.S.R., Eastern Europe, and China. The trade which they maintain with these countries, particularly the EEC-Eastern Europe-USSR sector, is a significant expansion of the capitalist market which accounts for much of the dynamism and hence the competitive capacity of European capital. Even here U.S. capital begins to enter behind the scenes, as part-owner of the firms which carry on this trade, but it is probably justified to regard this as still largely a European capitalist preserve.

These commercial relations, because mutually profitable, have so far led to a significant reduction in "East-West" tensions in Europe, from which the U.S. has been able to draw benefit by being able to display a relatively stronger force in the Pacific, as mentioned. But, should these tensions relax too far, then the entire U.S. military presence in Europe would be from the European capitalist standpoint a useless burden, and popular grounds would exist for the disbanding of NATO. The "pacification" of the USSR, which U.S. policy has allegedly been pursuing for several decades, would then reveal its other face: a peaceful Soviet Union implies an independent European capitalism. Extend this line of reasoning, which of course bears the Gaullist stamp, into a military alliance between European capital and the USSR, so that European industry would in effect "compete" under the Soviet umbrella, and *then* the Mandel thesis makes sense! But that the head of the Fourth International and the sworn opponent of the Old Nose would agree to this extension of the conditions of his argument, I doubt. That, nevertheless, is what his explanation of the origins of the threat to U.S. capital presupposes. Beneath the appearance of the "competition" doctrine lies the very essence of "peaceful coexistence", beneath the appearance of Mandel's European "internationalism" lies de Gaulle. Is it not proverbial that we learn most from our enemies?

The export trade in manufactured commodities is only one aspect of European-U.S.-Japanese relations; and these relations are only one aspect of the power and contradiction of capital. When he places the responsibility for the collapse of U.S. capital on "foreign competition," on this aspect of an aspect, Mandel is looking at the world not through a telescope, objectively from afar, but through a microscope. The consequences are necessarily regressive.

Either we understand the structural crisis confronting capital as a *general* crisis, as rooted in the *entire* system itself, as an international system with an imperial structure, or we have to abandon the Marxist endeavor and relapse into the methods and concepts of Adam Smith. What happens when we make a cut between "forces of an international character" and "forces which are at work within the system itself," between world developments on the one hand and the "objective stimuli which have grown out of the inner development of American capitalism itself" on the other? These Mandelian phrases mentally reconstitute a universe divided into independent and mutually hostile national capitalisms, each of which behaves toward the other as individual manufacturing firms behave toward one another in Adam Smith's economic theology: the same image on a larger screen. Suddenly the stuff of empire evaporates; banking, currency, investments and war count for nothing; imperialism is merely an idea, a figment; history crawls the seas in the holds of freighters; neither China nor the USSR are so much as conceived of; and Commodore Perry has not yet set sail.

THE INTERNATIONAL LIMITS OF CAPITALISM

We will not get a socialist revolution out of a capitalist world divided into petty-capitalist nationalisms. Instead of viewing the changes upon us through the narrow eyes of the smaller capitals on either side, who are given to sudden enthusiasms alternating with spells of nervousness—and whose reasons for wishing a socialist revolution upon the other are, incidentally, transparent—we should chart the process as it affects Capital with an upper-case *C*. If we are to make a theoretical case for the objective possibility of socialist revolution in the U.S., we must grant the opponent the strongest possible hand. "No social order ever disappears before all the productive forces for which there is room in it have been developed" (Marx).

Assuming the dominance of the giants of capital, an attempt to chart the revolutionary process would have to take the following into account:

(1) The integration of capitals. From the viewpoint of the major corporations in industry and finance, national boundaries

have long ceased to be obstacles. Although the different rates of profit obtaining in different national spheres guide their investment behavior, and while they engage in exchange-rate speculation with portions of their liquid capital—and thus benefit from national divisions—they cannot send their factories, mines and lands similarly chasing across the boundaries. They themselves created, and depend on, the integration of the capitalist world. They naturally resist the pressures toward protectionism and capitalist nationalism emanating from the non-imperial or backward industries, chiefly from the smaller manufacturers among them.

Capitalist integration of the industrial capitalist nations has already advanced so far in the spheres of banking, currency, investment and war that a "huge structural crisis" in any of the major capitalist nations would entail a huge structural crisis in all of them. This was already the case before the Second World War, as the 1930's depression showed: the crash in the U.S. brought every other capitalist industrial economy down with it. Today, any major national sector of capitalism could embark on a course of provoking a huge structural crisis in another sector, particularly that of the U.S., only as a suicide measure. Whether in banking, currency, investment or war, a serious crisis in the U.S. becomes a serious world capitalist crisis.

In Mandel's own terms, in which the export market in finished commodities counts for everything, this is clearly visible. A U.S. crisis would deprive European and Japanese capital of a major market, and thus immediately entrain their own collapse.

(2) The impossibility of further capitalist expansion. The present boundaries of the capitalist world, already greatly reduced from what they were before 1917, cannot move further outward. Both the USSR and China having become nuclear powers, and the Third World having been thoroughly penetrated already, there remain no further areas into which capitalist-imperialist expansion could drive by military conquest. A degree of peaceful penetration into the states of Eastern Europe and into the USSR itself is apparent, but short of a general Soviet capitulation to capitalist investment penetration, and short of a collapse of the Chinese revolution, both improbable, capitalism has reached its limits and has no place to go but inward, in the direction of greater intensification of all exploitation within its boundaries. In the face of increasing Third World attacks, the cost of maintaining the existing boundaries of the capitalist world rises steeply.

(3) Development of a general crisis of over-production. The backlog of unfulfilled demand created by the devastation of the Second World War having been exhausted, the limits of imperial expansion having been reached, no epoch-making technological innovations on the order of railroads and automobiles having materialized, and the ratio of profits relative to wages having risen, the entire capitalist world finds itself presently in the initial stages of a slowly-unfolding general crisis of overproduction. The long—unprecendently long—period of postwar capitalist growth is over.

In every capitalist nation, general productive capacity far exceeds output; military and other governmental expenditures, instead of spurring business growth, have begun to exhaust both people and governments, reducing private demand on the one hand and state fiscal power on the other, without yielding major new areas of investment; in nearly every country, technological advances have improved upon previous capital only quantitatively, without rendering major sectors obsolete, and thus providing a new major field of investment; in all capitalist industrial countries, while the long-term rate of profit is both equalizing internationally and levelling off historically, it has been out-accelerating wages at a pace where both investment and demand become problematic without the artificial and necessarily temporary stimulus of inflation; nearly all industrial capitalist nations face a rise in unemployment and various degrees of recession.

(4) Concentration and centralization of capital on an international scale. In times of crisis within a "national" sphere, the marginal, weaker, financially shallower enterprises get shaken out of the market; they either merge with others to save themselves, or are bought out at a bargain price by the larger, financially more solid concerns. Given the interdependence, and even more, the interpretation and integration of all national capitalisms since the Second World War, the same process repeats itself on a worldwide scale.

Corporations operating internationally have a serious advantage over nationally-confined firms in this shakeout process. The additional strength they derive from imperial investments gives them the edge in the struggle against domestic competition. At the same time, the home-office backing received by their overseas branches gives the latter an edge against competition in the foreign sphere. The result is the familiar process of "huge structural crises" confronting the smaller, nationally-confined, and marginal or backward industries *in all countries,* who then fall prey to the imperially-organized capitals who are strong in all countries.

The wave of mergers, bankruptcies, acquisitions and other forms of concentration and centralization of capital which has been visible within Europe, Japan and the U.S., as well as between them and among them, for a number of years, is only the prelude. The higher interest rates obtaining throughout the capitalist world are a further part of the process, since they hinder small capitals more than large. The U.S.-produced drain on European capital-markets is one international aspect of the process, as is the increasing voluntary flight of European capital to the U.S. Instead of increasing capitalist independence in Europe and Japan, we are likely to see their increasing subjection to U.S. capital. The examples of Britain and France, whose economies are virtually subject to U.S. financial dictates, rather than that of the Federal Republic of Germany, which still displays at least a vestige of economic autonomy if no other, are likely to become more typical. The re-opening of the Japanese door to U.S. investment capital, probably dictated to Japanese capital via the Pentagon (Japan depends vitally on trade, but has no independent navy), although ostensibly on a 50-50 basis with Japanese management, is reminiscent of French-Algerian or U.S.-Venezuelan arrangements. Whether through its military monopoly or through its control of the international monetary system, through banking or investments, U.S. capital seems likely to concentrate and centralize an increasing proportion of the entire capitalist world's business in its hands, thereby reducing the other industrial capitalist states to the status of satellites, junior partners in imperialism but themselves imperialized; colonized metropoles.

A line of continuity is thus drawn between the states of the Third World and the smaller industrial nations, even while the contradictions between them sharpen. Official British actions toward the people of the Third World, as an example, have never been as openly hostile and racist as they are today; yet never in modern history has British capital been as thoroughly under foreign control, and Britain itself as thoroughly colonized, as it is today. The Third World shows the way to the smaller capitalist powers; as exploitation sharpens in intensity throughout the capitalist world, the line of military coups stretching from Argentina, Brazil, Ecuador, etc., to Ghana, Indonesia, etc., has drawn its knot around Greece, seems coiled and ready to tighten on Italy (birthplace of the EEC), and (in the form of the emergency laws) is visible even in the Federal Republic of

Germany and elsewhere. Capital "socializes costs" (Mandel) not only on a domestic but also on an imperial scale; each step in this monstrous "socialization" reduces the peripheral bourgeoisies further to the rank of vice-consuls, and the peripheral working classes to the condition of colonial working classes; relative impoverishment is followed by absolute impoverishment.

(5) *"Import" of colonial conditions into the U.S. metropolis; re-emergence of the contradiction between capital and labor.* The process of intensification in all exploitation, of imperial "socialization" of costs, of reduction of all labor to the status of colonial labor, does not stop at the U.S. boundaries, but spreads from its established base among black, brown and Asian internal minorities to engulf the working class as a whole. The return of absolute impoverishment (decline in real wages) is only part, and only the beginning of the process. The probably increasing proportion of the working class which is black, brown or Asian, also noted by Mandel, is another. Here we are still dealing with developments which would fall within the economistic and civil-libertarian purview of trade-unionism, if the union power structure had the desire or the political credibility to organize effectively around them. But the process goes farther in the U.S.A.

First, impoverishment comes not via the traditional path of reduced paychecks from the direct employer, which allows wage-disputes to be confined within the "private" economy up until the critical moment of open confrontation when federal troops enter against strikers. Rather, impoverishment comes from the beginning via the State, as taxation, and from Capital in general, as inflation; thus a wedge is driven from the beginning between workers and the State—the wage conflict acquires from the beginning a political dimension. Neither able nor willing to fight on this front, the trade unions themselves get driven into reaction by this wedge.

Second, the increasing insecurity and instability of employment undermines unionism's entire base and invalidates its operating procedures, leading to a widespread working class search for alternative forms of organization with an *a priori* political content.

Third, the increasingly involuntary conscription of U.S. workers during their youth into foreign wars polarizes the ranks of the army into an outright fascist officer corps and a growingly anti-imperialist, *internationally*-educated element among the common soldiers.

Fourth, the repression against internationally-conscious elements of the student movement drives "theoreticians, propagandists, agitators, organizers" (Lenin) down into the working class to leaven the *political* ferment.

Fifth, as the spread of poverty forces more women to work, the male's domestic lordship, hearth of imperialist consciousness, is subverted and eliminated.

Sixth, the increasing internationalization of the labor process, visible in runaway shops as well as in imported materials, advances the international consciousness of part of working-class leadership.

Seventh, the erosion in governmental and trade-unionist legitimacy requires increasing resort to police and army power in the settlement of labor disputes, as well as all other conflicts, and brings the question of self-defense to the fore.

Eighth, a long process of political education by welfare authorities at all levels of government makes the army of the unemployed and unemployable less amenable to becoming unwitting instruments of reactionary maneuvers.

Ninth, the absence of a politically credible and nationally organized Social Democracy in the post-1914 sense, thanks to the total bankruptcy of liberalism since the New Deal, removes a number of illusions from the path of consciousness and permits a more rapid development.

Tenth, the virtual disappearance of the small family farm removes a traditional ·base both of reaction and of Populist-chauvinist tendencies.

Eleventh, the industrialization of the South and the improvement of imperial communications equalizes political conditions in all regions of the States, gradually creating a firmer base for truly nationwide organizations.

Twelfth, the collapse of municipal, state, and other intermediate fiscal authorities increasingly polarizes all political conflicts directly against the *federal* (national and imperial) government.

Thirteenth, the links between the all-sided impoverishment of the U.S. working class and the maintenance of the capitalist empire become increasingly visible in concrete manifestations such as runaway shops, special taxes, and the import of coffins.

Fourteenth, the impossibility of further capitalist progress drives the ruling class and all its hangers-on farther into political, moral, cultural and intellectual rot, severing the last bonds of respect and legitimacy . . .

It is possible to continue the list, but better halt and summarize.

CONCLUSIONS

In this day and age of imperialism, more than in any previous epoch, the contradiction between labor and capital emerges in a universal form. The days when it was *possible* for that contradiction to show itself *only* within a national, much less regional, local, or single-shop sphere, are far behind us; only the most withered mind could imagine it as arising from purely local causes and merely in the boundaries of a dispute over wages. Contrary to what many writers think, working people—in the U.S. as elsewhere—are not merely a peculiar kind of nickelodeon that will play any tune so long as coins are fed into the slot; capitalism is not merely a scattering of microscopic islands, each governed by a separate Robinson Crusoe and his bag of nickels; and the contradiction of labor *v.* capital is not merely what happens on any one island when the nickels run out.

The entire world has had to be explored, charted, crisscrossed, paved, railed, mined, sown, flown, piped, riveted and wired; every human being upon this earth has had to be uprooted, transplanted, educated and re-educated, pushed and pulled, organized and reorganized; every idea and invention has had to be thought and invented, tested and discarded, picked up and reformulated, sifted through a hundred languages and applied a million different ways—before one single person could insert bolt *A* into nut *B* for the 479th consecutive time in one day and say "Basta! Enough of this!" There are no more "local" contradictions, and no more "economic" contradictions, in the sense that is usually meant; all of our contradictions, and the deeper they are, the truer this is, have universal causes and universal effects: one baby in one room in one town who cries from hunger throws the entire history of the world into question.

It takes a peculiarly arid perspective, then, to imagine the re-emergence of the contradiction between labor and capital as a re-run of some textbook accounts of the contract-bargaining sessions between Reuther and G.M. This contradiction has (a) penetrated the entire capitalist world, (b) fought and lost the battle for ultimate expansion, (c) turned in upon itself, sharpening every discord within it, (d) overthrown and subjugated every nationality, including the former imperial sovereignties. When it finally comes home to roost again, the whole world comes with it, not as a single beeping of a tin whistle, but as the *tutti fortissimo* of a mammoth intercontinental orchestra.

Let others speculate whether a decade or two, or three or five, are required before a recognizable facsimile of the stereotyped image of what might have been a revolutionary situation in times and conditions past and gone will show its face again. The course of history over the past quarter century inspires the profoundest revolutionary confidence. No longer does capital labor in narrow confinement at its dissolution; it has made the whole world into the workshop of its overthrow. If we are to assist in the process, we cannot retreat into the provinces of our nationalist or disciplinary specialties; our analysis and our action must be at the least—at the minimum—as universal as the power of Capital itself.

Notes

[1] Ernest Mandel, *Die EWG und die Konkurrenz Europa Amerika* (Europäische Verlagsanstalt, 1968). Shortly to be published in English, as *Europe versus America?—Contradictions of Imperialism*. NLB.

19

PETER IRONS

On Repressive Institutions and the American Empire

The repressive nature of domestic social institutions in the United States flows directly from the demands of the imperialistic foreign policy of the American Empire in the twentieth century, which in turn is a consequence of the structure of monopoly capitalism. Any effective attack on these institutions, any attempt to construct a new society which meets human needs rather than repressing them, necessarily depends on the destruction of American imperialism. The nexus of domestic repression and imperialism is so tightly woven that each becomes the product of the other; no critical analysis can separate one from the other. This essay is based on the assertion that the emergence of the United States as an imperialistic power, especially since the enunciation of an overtly imperialist foreign policy in the Open Door Notes of 1899-1900, has thwarted any effective movement to reform and restructure our domestic institutions.

Although I will describe the links between domestic repression and imperialism, our ultimate concern is with the developing consciousness of these links and the transformation of this consciousness into action and involvement. This analysis is based on the foundation laid by Marx and Engels, who stated in *The German Ideology* that "The production of ideas, of conceptions, of consciousness, is at first directly interwoven with the material activity and the material intercourse of men, the language of real life. Conceiving, thinking, the mental intercourse of men, appear at this stage as the direct efflux of their material behavior. The same applies to mental production as expressed in the language of the politics, laws, morality, religion, metaphysics of a people."[1]

Marxism acutely perceived the direct relationship between the structure of social institutions and "the material intercourse of men." Ideas and institutions do not develop in a vacuum; they are products of the material world and reflect the most basic division in society, upon which all social institutions are built, that of social class. Classes, the historic product of the clash of interests between those who control property and those controlled by it, provide each of us with a world-view and broadly control our place in the social institutions which shape and mold us. In a fragmented, repressive society such as ours, it is difficult to perceive the inseparable links between repression and imperialism without a form of political "gestalt" which looks under the surface of liberal rhetoric and uncovers the essential unitary nature of a social system we have been trained to see as a collection of discrete, unrelated events and processes.

Most of us consider ourselves members of a huge, amorphous "middle class" that includes all but a marginal residue of the very poor and the very rich. This "declassification" is rooted in the myths of Equal Opportunity and the Great American Melting Pot which our schools and corporate propaganda inculcate in us. This propaganda has been quite successful; it has resulted in a widespread "false consciousness" that ignores the reality of class conflict and replaces it with the ideology of "pluralism," the concept of political scientists who presuppose a basic congruence of interest between social groups in this country. This congruence, based on a common acceptance of the "rules of the game," emphasizes the stability and "equilibrium" of the social system. In crude form, it states that all contending groups—business and labor, black and white, rich and poor—all must recognize that although each may desire a larger slice of the national pie, it is against the rules to grab the knife and demand the whole pie.

The pluralists, riding the wave of several decades of "false consciousness," are increasingly being shaken by the upheavals and tremors caused by the growing crisis of the system of monopoly capitalism. Trapped by their ideology, they fail to see that the basic "stability" of the system is founded on repression at home and imperialism abroad, and that the revolts they attribute to such causes as "the generation gap" and "communist agitation" are in actuality based on the development of revolutionary consciousness among those who have been subjected to the domestic and foreign repression of the American Empire.

We will return to the concept of consciousness and its revolutionary implications. At this point, our development of a political "gestalt" turns to an analysis of the imperialist nature of American foreign policy, the emergence in the twentieth century of the American Empire. Although scholars such as R. W. Alstyne have asserted that "The concept of an American empire and the main outlines of its future growth were complete by 1800,"[2] I have chosen the issuance of the Open Door Notes by Secretary of State John Hay in 1899-1900 as a starting point because by this time the British had relinquished their role as the dominant imperial power to the United States, and conscious imperialism and massive foreign intervention were most directly articulated and legitimized by the Hay notes.

During the decade preceding the Hay notes, the United States had recovered from severe domestic economic depression and had begun the subjugation of Latin America as an economic dependency. The Spanish-American War had loosed a flood of desire for foreign expansion and intervention which turned to the Orient. Hay, in warning the world community that American business intended to grab the lion's share of trade in the Orient, especially the burgeoning market in China, set forth in his notes what historian William A. Williams has called "a classic theory of non-colonial imperial expansion."[3] As we completed our internal expansion and came to consider ourselves a Great Power, our foreign policy became characterized by rapacity, ethnocentrism, xenophobia and Christian "missionaryism."

Leading up to Hay's pronouncements was a campaign by leading politicians, capitalists and ministers seeking not only to open the door to the Orient, but to wrench it off its hinges. Senator Albert J. Beveridge, in April, 1897, put the imperialist ethic in classic summation: "American factories are making more than the American people can use; American soil is producing more than they can consume. Fate has written our policy for us; the trade of the world must and shall be ours."[4]

Lest it be thought that the flowering of imperialism was nurtured solely by reactionaries who shared the outlook of Standard Oil, it should be noted that leading domestic reformers such as Senator La Follette joined the imperialist movement with fervor. Putting his reformist missionary zeal at the service of capital, La Follette hailed American acquisition of the Philippines as allowing America "to conquer (its) rightful share of that great market now opening (in China) for the world's commerce."[5] Imperialism was given his Progressive sanction in the same statement, because "it has made men free." That imperialism stems from the basic drives of monopoly capital was clearly understood by Woodrow Wilson: "Our industries have expanded to such a point that they will burst their jackets if they cannot find a free outlet to the markets of the world. . . . Our domestic markets no longer suffice. We need foreign markets."[6] Wilson also, in a moment of candor, once stated that "The masters of the government of the United States are the combined capitalists and manufacturers of the U.S."[7]

Imperialsim, of course, does not begin and end at the doors of the Custom House. It permeates the whole society, and as the American Empire has grown and expanded, the structural unity of all of our social institutions in the service of imperialism has grown stronger. Although every American president in this century has asserted what Wilson said above, the links between domestic capitalism and an aggressive, Cold War foreign policy based on paranoid anti-communism and domestic militarism were most clearly stated in 1944 by Charles E. Wilson, then executive vice-president of the War Production Board. In a speech to corporate and military leaders at a meeting of the Army Ordnance Association, Wilson (later president of the General Electric Company) said that the end of the war must signal an alliance of the large corporations, the military establishment and the executive branch of the government. Outlining a Permanent War Economy that would be "a continuing program and not the creature of an emergency," he said that "the burden is on all of us to integrate our respective activities—political, military and industrial—because we are in world politics to stay, like it or not."[8]

In the two-thirds of a century since Hay's firing of the starting pistol, our capitalist traders have spread out around the globe and taken with them, as protection, a Praetorian Guard of soldiers, planes, tanks and ships. More than a million and a half Americans, civilian and military, serve in the branch offices of the American Empire and those of us living in the home office spend much of our energy in their support. The magnitude of the American Empire has become staggering: as of 1967, there was $60 billion in direct U.S. investment abroad, and the output of American-owned production facilities abroad totaled $120 billion.[9] This made the American Empire the third largest economy in the world, exceeded only by our domestic economy and that of the Soviet Union. Some 4,200 American corporations are now in control of over 14,000 foreign businesses.[10]

Documentation is hardly needed for the assertion that the Permanent War Economy envisioned by Wilson has become a fact. It consumes more than half of the federal budget and employs, directly or indirectly, more than ten percent of the work force. The impact of the "military-industrial complex," as we now call it, extends into every local, state and federal office, as President Eisenhower ruefully noted in his Farewell Address. To protect our foreign investment, we have spread the cloak of the "Free World" wide enough to cover every dictatorship and authoritarian government which will allow American capital to extract profit from the soil and sweat of its people. We have provided the ruling classes of these countries with some $32 billion in arms in the last quarter-century, arms whose functions are the perpetuation of the rule of a privileged elite. Although Congress every year salves the liberal conscience with a meager dose of foreign aid, much of this "aid" is military and most of it (about 85 per cent) is actually spent in the United States. The essential nature of American imperialism has recently been best exemplified by a study, initially entitled "Pax Americana," conducted for the Department of Defense by Boeing Aircraft, which was designed, according to *The New York Times,* to show how America can "maintain world hegemony in the future."[11] In spite of pressure from Senate doves, this study remains classified.

Imperialism not only exploits our foreign subjects, but it also, and necessarily, exploits and represses all of us and our basic social institutions. It is this linkage which is essential to our political "gestalt." Our major attention will focus on the educational system, although the family and the state, as basic components of the institutional triumvirate which monopoly capital most depends on, will also be examined. But it is our schools which are the factories in which the raw material, children, are transformed into the finished product, "citizens." This may seem a crude analogy, but it was chosen simply because it is not an analogy but a fact. Schools are factories, and the process involved in turning out mass-produced "citizens" is no different than that by which General Motors turns out cars. The end result is standardization, and the foremen and managers of the schools are as alert to product defect as the engineers in Detroit.

Our schools, from the primary to the graduate level, enroll some 70 million people, a third of the total population. Teachers make up the largest occupational group in the work force, and the vast majority of them are employed by the state and are subject to the constraints placed upon them by the conservative schoolboard mentality. Although the teaching "profession" absorbs a large number of the children of the working class and provides one of the major avenues of upward mobility in our class-stratified society, the political demands of the system and the status-quo orientation of teacher-training schools insures that most teachers share the values of their conservative, capitalist employers.

That schools are repressive needs little documentation; everyone who has gone through them intuitively recognizes this. Teachers demand order, obedience and docility. The "rules and regulations" would do credit to most prisons. Instruction in the social sciences involves uncritical presentation and acceptance of the capitalist system and current foreign policy. Not every student is fooled, of course, since a good proportion is brighter and more perceptive than its teachers. One high school student, analyzing the content of his textbooks in *Liberation* magazine, wrote that "As might be expected of textbooks written for future managers of the Empire, these reflect all the chauvinistic, anti-communist and counter-revolutionary assumptions which have underpinned American foreign policy for the past twenty years."[12] The point is not that the schools are uniformly successful in producing "good citizens," but that on the whole they attempt to stifle the kind of critical spirit expressed by this young man.

Schools not only serve to repress the instinctive expressiveness of children and indoctrinate them with the virtues of the capitalist system; they also serve the more direct need of maintaining the class basis of this system and channeling students into the American Empire at home and abroad. The process of separating students to serve the varying needs of capitalism is not an openly-acknowledged function of the educational system, but it lies at its heart. Business needs a certain number of operatives and menial workers to fill the factories and mop the floors, and a certain number to become the administrative and intellectual elite, replenishing the upper echelons of the imperialist institutions. It is this function that the schools perform admirably, in spite of the liberal myth of social mobility and equality of opportunity. Upward social and economic mobility do exist, enough to keep alive the

Horatio Alger credo, but, as Kenneth Clark has said,". . . there is concrete evidence which demonstrates beyond reasonable doubt that our public-school system has rejected its role of facilitating social mobility and has become in fact an instrument of social and economic class distinction in American society."[13]

Monopoly capitalism is based on class division, and the schools perpetuate the existing class divisions in American society. The majority of working-class youth, both white and black, ends its education in the secondary schools and becomes absorbed into the factories, menial service occupations and Armed Forces, while the majority of middle-class youth continues on to colleges and universities. Although race and color are primary components of class division, it is their class-linked nature that concerns us here. Black, Puerto Rican, Chicano and Indian children receive inferior education; that hardly needs proof. Working-class white children also receive inferior education. The crucial point is that poor schools are *necessary* as part of the process of ruthlessly weeding out and channeling into manual and menial work those not destined to become part of the capitalist elite. Those who believe in the inherent goodness of the system may balk at this point, but the reality of the educational system in performing this function is beyond dispute. If a child is not exceptionally bright, those who provide "counseling" in the public schools discourage any aspirations to higher education.

The repressive nature of the educational system is less evident in our colleges and universities, but it is obvious in the subordination of higher education by monopoly capital to the training of the elite necessary to staff the American Empire at home and abroad. Our 2,000 colleges and universities, both public and private, are governed by some 50,000 trustees, invested with state-granted power to formulate and execute basic policy. These trustees, most often a self-perpetuating group, are overwhelmingly conservative, white, Anglo-Saxon businessmen, and their values flow from their place at the apex of the capitalist system.

For example, the men who are directors of General Motors also serve as trustees of fourteen colleges and universities, including such elite institutions as Dartmouth, M.I.T. and Duke. This is not to imply that such institutions should be seen as subsidiaries of General Motors, but rather as an indication of the "community of interest" link between corporate power and higher education.

Liberal myth has enshrined the college as the impregnable bastion of reason and rationality. Unlike public primary and secondary schools, colleges shelter a significant minority of liberal and radical critics of the existing social order, which leads to periodic witch-hunts and howls of outrage from legislative super-patriots, corporate donors and conservative alumni. Nevertheless, faculty radicals are disproportionately concentrated in departments which are not vital to the functioning of the American Empire. Most dissident faculty are found in the humanities and social sciences, with a sprinkling in the pure sciences. But departments of business, economics and the applied sciences, in which is trained a majority of the managers and technicians of the American Empire, are distinctly inhospitable to radicals.

It seems probable that the toleration of academic radicals is actually advantageous to the system, since such toleration hardly threatens the recruitment process of the system and allows the perpetuation of the myth of the university as a "marketplace of ideas." In spite of the annoying prick of criticism, the corporations and Armed Forces continue to train an adequate supply of elite personnel in the colleges and universities. For example, there are Reserve Officer Training Corps units on 365 campuses, with a 1968-1969 enrollment of 218,000 students. These programs turn out more than 20,000 commissioned officers each year, more than half of the Navy's line officers and well over half of the Army officers serving in Vietnam.

The ROTC program has been under sporadic attack by student and faculty radicals for years (it was a prime target of students in the 1930's), and during 1969 major outbreaks of student opposition forced several of the prestige universities, most notably Harvard, to reduce ROTC to the status of an extra-curricular activity. This ferment has unsettled the Pentagon officials responsible for ROTC. In April, 1969, the chief of the Army's ROTC division said that "It would be disastrous for the Army if there were no ROTC." He was echoed by the Navy's director of officer education, who added that "We bank on ROTC for our officers. I don't know what we'd do without it." But fears of the demise of ROTC do not really bother the Pentagon; it is still firmly entrenched on the campuses of the major state universities and hundreds of small, conservative colleges as yet untouched by major student protest. In fact, *The New York Times* reported after the Harvard action to remove ROTC from the campus (still permitting the Army to train cadets in its own facilities) that the Army plans to establish new ROTC units at 30 additional schools by 1972.[14] The point here is that the colleges, not only through ROTC but also by virtue of their increasing subsidization by government aid and research funds, remain a crucial institution in the maintenance of the

American Empire, a role they have filled for at least a hundred years.

The family is the basic institutional unit of the social system. As such, it is of importance to the American Empire that it perform its functions in the service of the Empire. Through it, the child learns his fundamental values and patterns of behavior. It is our most conservative institution, because it recapitulates and reinforces the patterns of dominance and submission required by every other institution. It is in the family that class position is learned, respect for hierarchical authority instilled and patterns of consumption so necessary to capitalism established. The repressive nature of the family is grounded in the class divisions which capitalism perpetuates. The necessity for children to absorb the "work and consume" ethic of the capitalist system forces parents to treat their children as repressively as they are treated by the system.

The family has its beginning in the private-property contract issued by the state to the husband and wife. At this point the joint accumulation of property and the molding of the family into a unit of consumption begin. The legal system, a product of the necessity of capitalism to preserve and protect existing property relationships, effectively turns the wife into a servant of the husband (who can usually secure a divorce if she refuses to perform the duties of a servant) and the children into the property of the state as well as the parents. The family, an increasingly "closed" system as rapid geographical mobility breaks down extended kinship relations, excludes "others" and fosters ethnic and class prejudice. Property is passed on to children by inheritance. In middle-class families, children learn deference and the necessity to "get along with others," and respect for the authority of teachers, policemen and other agents of the state is instilled. Working-class families have much the same child-rearing patterns, although methods of discipline vary; corporal punishment is more characteristic of the working-class, and the withholding of affection prevalent in the middle-class.

The repressive nature of family structure seems to many an historic continuity unconnected to any particular economic system. It seems probable, however, that the characteristic features of the family in capitalist society, even if molded in the context of pre-capitalist society, necessarily have continued their repressive functions because of the quite specific demands of monopoly capitalism. In a system which demands a work force willing to submit to domination, the family, as the bedrock institution of socialization, cannot deviate significantly from the repressive nature of the system as a whole. In the face of rapid technological change, the crisis of values and deepening global conflict, the family has served capitalism perhaps better than any other institution. We are still, as Sartre said, trying to stuff the live bodies of our children into the dead skins of our ancestors.

If the family serves capitalism by inculcating basic values necessary for the system, the state insures that these values will be placed at the service of the American Empire. The repressive nature of the state is based on two crucial functions: first, it defines our nationality and structures our whole view of ourselves as opposed to "the rest of the world"; and second, it offers all of the other institutions in society the instruments of coercion and force necessary to repress conflict and enforce compliance. The state, most simply, was defined by Max Weber as "a human community that (successfully) claims the *monopoly of the legitimate use of physical force* within a given territory."[15] Weber preceded that definition with the statement that "If no social institutions existed which knew the use of violence, then the concept of 'state' would be eliminated."[16] This is an illuminating insight, which makes the functioning of all other social institutions more clearly visible in their repressive nature.

The state, first of all, by defining nationality provides legitimacy for the use of force in "defending" that nationality. To protect the American Empire, the state compels military service of males, and jails or exacts forced labor from those who refuse such service. The state enforces the compulsory attendance laws for the educational system. Even the family is dependent on the state's "monopoly of the legitimate use of physical force." Children who run away from home as an act of rebellion are hunted down and returned to their parents by the police forces of the state.

The state, as the servant of monopoly capital in the American Empire, is inhospitable to the demands of the world's poor that this Empire stop exploiting them. Lyndon Johnson put it plainly and aggressively: "There are three billion people in the world and we have only 200 million of them. We are outnumbered 15 to 1. If might did make right, they would sweep over the United States and take what we have. We have what they want."[17] A franker expression of nationalism and xenophobia would be hard to invent. But what Johnson stated in his crude Texas manner is merely the philosophy which undergirds the whole repressive American Way of Life. Imperialism, racism, class conflict: all of these hard-to-swallow concepts are concisely defined between the lines of that quotation.

The repressive nature of the state is an every-day fact of life to those at the bottom of the class ladder. The state thrusts into the front lines of its imperialist wars a disproportionate number of the poor and the black; the state allows the very rich virtual exemption from taxation; the state trains as criminals in its prisons mainly those lawbreakers who are poor and black; the state subsidizes the housing of the middle-class and leaves the poor rotting in slums; the state teaches its children the virtues of "democracy" and representative government and operates so corruptly in the service of class interests that from a third to a half of the eligible voters do not bother to exercise their franchise; the state advertises "freedom of speech and assembly" but prosecutes those who use it effectively to attack domestic repression and imperialism. Increasingly, monopoly capital assists the state in protecting class interests by diminishing the scope of free expression; for example, there are only 45 cities with competing daily newspapers, and the concentration of the mass media into a few corporate hands has been facilitated by the "regulatory" agencies of the state.

The state masks its repression behind the facade of "due process" and the Bill of Rights, but its basic attitude was well stated by Richard Kleindienst, Nixon's Deputy Attorney General, speaking about dissenting students: "If people demonstrated in a manner to interfere with others, they should be rounded up and put in a detention camp."[18]

Let us return at this point to our discussion of consciousness. I have argued that the repressive nature of our domestic social institutions is organically related to the imperialist nature of the capitalist system, which has its current form in the Permanent War Economy, the alliance of politics, militarism and industry outlined twenty-five years ago by Charles Wilson. This analysis is only persuasive to the extent that a "gestalt" apprehension of the organic unity of our social institutions is formed. It is not persuasive if one believes, as does Sidney Hook, that the "welfare state" offers hope for the reform of decaying social institutions and has shown ". . . that democratic political processes could affect the operation of the economic system, abolish some of its worst evils and open a perspective for profound change in the power relations of different classes."[19] Those who agree with Hook have been trapped by the "false consciousness" which is sustained by the illusion of progress and measures progress quantitatively. Although they may believe that Vietnam was a tragic mistake and that we must avoid further military entanglements in the Third World, if they fail to oppose the growing world hegemony of the American Empire in all its forms, they cannot hope to achieve social reconstruction, the rehabilitation of the cities, the salvaging of the physical environment and the eradication of racism at home. All of these social "ills" are a consequence of the inverted priorities forced upon us by the managers of the Permanent War Economy in their quest for an American Empire, and they cannot be cured without the breakup of that Empire.

If "the production of ideas, of conceptions, of consciousness" is, as Marxism postulates, based on "the material intercourse of men," then our consciousness must reflect the crisis of the existing class structure, both at home and abroad. If our politics, law, morality, religion and metaphysics are repressive, this is an indication that the class structure is repressive. If, in our semantic confusion, we describe our society as "free" or "democratic," we have not yet extricated ourselves from the false consciousness imposed on us by those who control the American Empire. Our failure to recognize the direct link between the domestic and the foreign repression of the American Empire constitutes the most terrible fact of our time, that we have become our own oppressors, that, as Herbert Marcuse has said, "the majority of the people is the majority of their masters. . . ."[20]

A full understanding of the historical process which has led us to become, in a real sense, our own oppressors, rests on a comprehension of how social control is exercized in society. Although social control is a function of the relative powerlessness of the individual in a society dominated by powerful and interlocking institutions, there is also the factor of internalization, by which the individual incorporates the repressive demands of these institutions and carries them out unbidden. Social theorists such as C. Wright Mills have asserted that the American Empire is controlled and directed by a "power elite" composed of the corporate, military and political leaders of the Empire.[21] Although the power wielded by these few hundred men is, indeed, massive, it should be kept in mind that we do not feel the daily lash of this power because we have adopted its assumptions and almost automatically and uncritically carry out its demands.

It has been almost two decades since Mills dissected the "power elite." Since that time, its membership has changed considerably through death, retirement and defeat. But the places in the elite, and the power conferred by membership in the elite, have not changed significantly. It is important to avoid considering the men who manage the American Empire as conscious members of a "conspiracy," whose motives and goals are directed at personal profit and power. Desire for such profit and power may motivate men to climb the ladder to the "power elite," but it is the position itself which confers these rewards, and the structure of the American Empire which establishes the positions. Rather than a conscious conspiracy, what we actually have is a "community of interest" in which those who fill the positions of power and those who work for them, directly and indirectly, are in basic agreement. Our social institutions are repressive to the extent that most of us have internalized this structure and have become part of the "community of interest."

The United States is not the only repressive society in the world, of course, and the growth of Imperial America did not bring racism and chauvinism in its wake. But liberation from the grip of repressive institutions is dependent on the breakup of that empire. The full magnitude of the extent to which the "American way of life" is based on the enforced subservience and poverty of the Third World is embedded in the statistics cited by Lyndon Johnson in a 1964 commencement speech: "It has been estimated that if everyone in the world were to rise to the standard of living of the United States we would then have to extract about 20 billion tons of iron, 300 million tons of copper, 300 million tons of lead, and 200 million tons of zinc. These totals are well over 100 times the world's present annual rate of production."

Since it is inconceivable, barring a stunning technological breakthrough, that production of these crucial raw materials could expand a hundredfold within many years, the inescapable conclusion is that as long as Americans treasure and are willing to fight any threat to their "standard of living," American institutions will operate to preserve this system. As long as six per cent of the world's people insist on producing and consuming half of the world's goods, American affluence and Third World poverty will be inextricably linked.

Karl Mannheim has written that "Political discussion is, from the very first, more than theoretical argumentation; it is the tearing off of disguises. . . ."[22] Those who control the American Empire have for decades disguised themselves behind the masks of patriotism and public service. The militarization of American Society, our growth into a Garrison State, has been disguised behind the mask of "anti-communism." The growing concentration of corporate power into the hands of an interlocking oligopoly has been disguised behind the mask of "people's capitalism." If our political discourse is to be more than "theoretical argumentation," its primary function must be to tear off the disguises, semantic and ideological, behind which the power of the Empire is concealed. We have, in the last decade, grown increasingly conscious of the full dimensions of the American Empire and the links it has forged between repressive institutions and imperialism. Losing a war abroad to the forces of revolutionary nationalism has sobered many of us, and has rudely focused our attention on the domestic consequences of imperialism. Watching and experiencing, if only vicariously, the struggle of our oppressed minorities here at home has added to this consciousness. Feeling the repressive weight of our institutions, as they are torn by the conflicting demands of tradition and the accelerating changes in values and technology, has revealed to some of us the necessity of revolution. But our growing consciousness, our awareness of the bond between our ideas and our "material intercourse," does us little good until it is transformed into a commitment to the ultimate goals of the revolutionary struggle.

The consciousness which liberates men and women from repression and frees them to become the advocates of the oppressed has always been a reality in our history, even when submerged by the waves of "false consciousness." People such as Denmark Vesey, "Mother" Jones, Big Bill Haywood, Eugene Debs and A. J. Muste, ignored or dismissed in the textbooks written for "future managers of the Empire," have kept alive the revolutionary consciousness which no repressive force can extinguish. The more clearly we see and feel, as they did, the repressive nature of the American Empire, the more conscious we will become of the necessity to bring it to an end.

Notes

[1] Marx and Engels, *The German Ideology* (New York, International Publishers), p. 13.

[2] Quoted in Paul Baran and Paul Sweezy, *Monopoly Capital* (New York, Monthly Review Press, 1968), pp. 181-182.

[3] William A. Williams, *The Tragedy of American Diplomacy* (New York, Dell), p. 43.

[4] Quoted in Williams, *op. cit.*, p. 17.

[5] *Ibid.*, p. 56.

[6] *Ibid.*, p. 52.

[7] Quoted in Eric Mann and Dan Gilbarg, *We Won't Be Used to Put Down the Vietnamese Revolution* (Boston, SDS, 1969), p. 24.

[8] *The New York Times* (January 20, 1944), p. 8.

[9] *Business Week* (December 9, 1967), p. 118.

[10] Mira Wilkins, "The Businessman Abroad," *The Annals of the American Academy* (November, 1966), p. 85.

[11] *The New York Times* (February 16, 1968), p. 2.

[12] Bob Goodman, "Textbooks are Bullshit," *Liberation* (January, 1969), p. 29.

[13] Patricia Cayo Sexton, *Education and Income: Inequalities of Opportunities in Our Public Schools* (New York, Viking, 1969), p. ix.

[14] Quotes and statistics from *The New York Times* (April 19, 1969), p. 29.

[15] Hans Gerth and C. Wright Mills, eds., *From Max Weber: Essays in Sociology* (New York, Oxford University Press, 1946), p. 78.

[16] *Ibid.*

[17] *The New York Times* (November 2, 1966), p. 16.

[18] *The Atlantic* (May, 1969), p. 11.

[19] *The New York Times* Book Review (April 20, 1969), p. 8.

[20] H. Marcuse, *An Essay on Liberation* (Boston, Beacon Press, 1969), p. 64.

[21] C. Wright Mills, *The Power Elite* (New York Oxford University Press, 1956).

[22] Karl Mannheim, *Ideology and Utopia* (New York, Harcourt, Brace and World, 1936), p. 39.

20

American Imperialism and the Peace Movement

One of the weaknesses of the American peace movement as presently constituted is that it lacks a clearly defined theory of imperialism. Various elements within the movement as a whole do hold definite views on this question, but there is neither general agreement as to their relevance nor much inclination to test conflicting interpretations against the available evidence. Precisely because the war in Vietnam is so manifestly unjust and inhuman, the protest against that war has stemmed in large part from a sense of outrage which requires no theoretical analysis or justification. What we are all beginning to discover, however, is that protest is one thing and political action another. If the peace movement is to break out of its current isolation and begin to build a political base in this country, it must learn to relate its opposition to the war in Vietnam to a continuing struggle against the policies which have produced that war and which must inevitably produce new

311

Vietnams in the future. For this task of long-range political education protest is not enough. What is needed among other things is an analysis both of the origins of the current conflict, and of the nature of American foreign policy in general. What is needed, in brief, is a theory of American imperialism.

By the term "American imperialism" I mean that system of political, economic and military domination by means of which the United States today controls the greater part of what is sometimes known as the Free World. For almost twenty years the United States has sought directly or indirectly to manipulate the internal political life of the entire non-socialist world in order to simultaneously bar the way to indigenous social revolution and maximize opportunities for American capital investment and American access to strategic raw materials. This system of global domination has taken different forms in different areas; only as a last resort has it led to outright military intervention. Military bases and military training programs, large scale capital investment, economic and military aid, CIA-sponsored coups, covert support for European colonial regimes: these are the "neo-colonial" techniques through which the United States normally pursues its objectives. The ramifications of this global strategy are too broad to be explained in terms of such subjective attitudes as anti-Communist hysteria or racism or a lust for power on the part of individuals in high places. American imperialism is in fact characterized by such attitudes; but its causes, its underlying goals, must ultimately be sought in the fundamental economic and political structure of American society itself.

Proceeding from this assumption, the logical starting point for any discussion of American foreign policy is the classical Marxist interpretation of imperialism, as formulated by Lenin in 1916. Simply stated, the Leninist thesis asserts that imperialism arises out of the growing inability of monopoly capitalism to invest surplus capital at home, and the consequent necessity of subjugating foreign nations in order to create a new, more profitable sphere for capital investment abroad. The relevance of this interpretation to contemporary American imperialism has been repeatedly demonstrated and requires no elaborate discussion here. As of 1963 American investments abroad were in excess of $40 billion, a sum which represented an increase of nearly six-fold since 1946. With close to $10 billion of that total invested in Latin America alone, it is not difficult to understand why the United States should want to overthrow the Cuban regime or to topple bourgeois nationalist governments in Guatemala, Brazil or the

Dominican Republic. Valuable in themselves, these foreign holdings are of particular importance for the economy as a whole due to a range of special factors: the high rate of profit which they help to sustain; their concentration in the hands of the largest and most influential corporations; the access to strategic raw materials which they provide. That American capitalism has a real economic stake in preventing the spread of socialism in the Third World is an elementary fact which no serious analysis of American imperialism can afford to disregard.

Nonetheless, as a comprehensive theory of American imperialism, the Leninist thesis is open to criticism on several grounds:

(1) Despite its growing importance during recent years, foreign investment still accounts for less than five per cent of total American capital investment. For example, whereas the direct capital outflow from the United States in 1963 was just short of $2 billion, domestic investment in new plant and equipment (excluding farm and residential construction) reached almost $40 billion. One may well argue that this five per cent of the total, magnified by the special factors noted above, does provide the economy with a crucial extra margin which represents the difference between stagnation and growth. All the same, it remains true that foreign investment does not play the same role for contemporary American capitalism as it did for, let us say, classical British capitalism—upon which Lenin's theory of imperialism was based.

(2) More important, although the scope of American investment abroad varies sharply from one region to another, American foreign policy is everywhere characterized by the same rigid anti-Communism and fear of change. Almost sixty per cent of American foreign holdings are concentrated in Western Europe and Canada, two areas in which relatively little direct American intervention is now required in order to preserve the status quo. On the other hand, only seven per cent of American foreign holdings are to be found in Asia (including the Middle East), a fact which does not prevent the United States from pursuing an extremely rigid and ambitious course in this area. American investments in Latin America are more than twice as great as those in all of Asia and Africa put together; but the control of Vietnam is nonetheless deemed as vital as the control of Venezuela. In short, there is a certain disproportion between the actual pattern of American foreign investment and the global scale and uniform character of American foreign policy.

(3) Finally, the Leninist thesis does not adequately account for the belligerence of American policies *vis-à-vis* the socialist world. The United States has long since abandoned the hope of restoring capitalism in the Soviet Union or China; but it continues to encircle these countries with a ring of military bases and to threaten them with its gigantic nuclear arsenal. The American military presence in Western Europe and Southeast Asia clearly derives at least as much from a desire to isolate and encircle the Soviet Union and China as it does from the need to check social revolution in these areas. It is true that one reason for American belligerence is a desire to prevent Soviet or Chinese support for revolution in the Third World; but here again, there is a disproportion between the kind of support which the Soviet Union or China is actually prepared to give (as witness the current struggle in Vietnam) and the massive character of the American military threat.

On balance, then, it seems to me that the Leninist thesis provides a necessary but not a sufficient explanation for the basic policies of American imperialism. American foreign policy is indeed designed to protect American investments abroad; the point is that it *over-protects* them, that it operates on a scale and in a way which is all out of proportion to the magnitude of the interests at stake. American imperialism cannot be understood without reference to the Leninist thesis; but that thesis alone will not suffice to account for the global scale of American policies.

A second theory which is sometimes advanced, often in conjunction with the first, is that American imperialism seeks to check the spread of socialism not only because its foreign holdings are endangered, but also because a capitalist America could not long survive in a socialist world. The emphasis here is less upon the direct economic effects of revolution abroad as it is upon the political and ideological repercussions of such a trend within the United States itself. From this standpoint, every social revolution, no matter what the immediate interests at stake, poses a long term threat because it represents a further step in the direction of a socialist world. Indeed, if the United States (or even the United States and Western Europe) were to find itself isolated in this way, it is hard to see how profound political and ultimately economic changes could be avoided. That American policy makers are conscious of this possibility is perfectly evident; their constant harping on the theme of Munich has no other significance.

The chief difficulty with this theory is that it assumes that the triumph of socialism throughout the entire Third World is in fact so imminent that only the most desperate measures can turn the tide. There is, quite frankly, little evidence to support such a hypothesis. Since 1945 the dominant force in the Third World has been nationalism rather than socialism; although the Nassers and Sukharnos cannot resolve the fundamental problems which confront their emerging nations, it seems likely that a considerable period of time must elapse before genuine social revolutions can take place in such countries. Of course one of the reasons why social revolution in the Third World has not proceeded at a more rapid pace is precisely the role of American imperialism, without whose intervention more than one bastion of the Free World would by now have fallen. On the other hand, it must also be remembered that American imperialism often tends to strengthen the very forces which it seeks to oppose. In Vietnam and elsewhere the effect of American intervention has been to invest socialist movements with a broad national appeal, thus recreating those conditions which proved so conducive to the growth of socialism during the Second World War. Given the continuing viability of the nationalist alternative throughout much of the Third World, it is far from clear why American policy makers should be so obsessed with the threat of socialist encirclement as to embark upon a course of global repression whose political disadvantages may well offset whatever temporary military gains are achieved.

Yet another approach to the problem is the one adopted by, among others, the late Paul Baran in *The Political Economy of Growth*. Basing himself upon the Leninist thesis, Baran nonetheless admits that the economic importance of American foreign investment is of "incidental significance" in comparison to the economic importance of the means used to protect foreign investments, namely military spending and related expenditures. Arguing that "the means of imperialist policy overshadow almost entirely its original ends," Baran compares the relationship between the two to "an errant stone setting into motion a mighty rock." His point is that in order to assess properly the economic significance of imperialism, one must consider the impact not only of foreign investment, but also of the entire military establishment, which exists only in order to safeguard the former.

That military spending and its by-products are of decisive significance for the functioning of modern American capitalism is a fact which no one can seriously question. Baran's estimate is that such expenditures directly or indirectly account for almost twenty per cent of the annual Gross National Product, and the figure is undoubtedly not too high. It was defense spending and defense spending alone which enabled the American economy to pull out of the depression at the end of the 1930's, and which averted another depression at the end of the 1940's. For the last fifteen years through hot wars and cold the economy has received its annual $50 billion shot in the arm; and of late, it has even proved necessary to increase the dosage by another $10 billion. But while Baran's conclusions are unassailable, his logic is not; for if foreign investment, on his own finding, is merely an "errant stone," why is an enormous military establishment required to protect it? In *The Political Economy of Growth,* Baran provides no clear answer to this question, but the whole effect of his analysis is to demonstrate that American imperialism cannot be understood except in relation to its domestic repercussions. If we are to transcend the limitations of the Leninist thesis, it is from this standpoint that we must now proceed.

Whatever the need to protect foreign investments by military means, there is certainly an intimate connection between American foreign policy and military spending. It was the American commitment to the "defense" of Western Europe which provided the original rationale for the creation of a vast nuclear arsenal; and it was the American commitment to the "defense" of Southeast Asia which led to the massive build-up of our conventional military forces as well. At the same time as it has served to justify military spending, moreover, American imperialism has also had important political repercussions on the domestic scene. The link between the Korean War and the rise of McCarthyism is well known; but it is sometimes forgotten that despite the demise of McCarthy the continuation of the Cold War has made it possible to transform McCarthyism into a permanent feature of the American political landscape. The elimination of the Communist Party as an active factor in American politics, the emasculation of the liberal and socialist left, the domestication of the trade union movement, all this and more can be traced in large part to the combined economic and political impact of American imperialism upon American society. In brief, there can be no doubt that imperialism has played an absolutely central role in assuring the survival and continued growth of capitalism in the United States.

To state the position in this form, it seems to me, is inevitably to raise the question: to what extent are military spending and domestic reaction not only the consequence but also the cause of imperialism abroad? The mere existence of the military establishment and the political attitudes associated with it tends to militate against the adoption of a foreign policy which might result in a lessening of international tensions and hence a reduction in military spending. As everyone knows, those who have the greatest vested interest in the military establishment are also ardent advocates of a hard line in foreign affairs. What ought to be remembered, however, is that the demands of the war hawks in the Pentagon are hardly more extreme than the actual policies followed during the last twenty years. After all, John F. Kennedy, the architect of the so-called *détente* with the Soviet Union, took office on a pledge to increase military spending and promptly discovered a Berlin crisis which justified that increase. And Lyndon Johnson, everybody's peace candidate in 1964, finds it so essential to defend freedom in Vietnam that he must ask Congress for an additional $13 billion in military appropriations. Is it not possible that the determination with which Kennedy and Johnson confront the foe in Berlin and Vietnam is related to the immense economic and political advantages to be gained from such a course?

In approaching the problem from this angle I do not mean to ascribe any deep Machiavellian cunning to the policy makers in Washington. To the contrary, there is every reason to believe that these men do in fact see themselves faced with a world-wide Communist conspiracy which must be resisted at every turn if the American way of life is to be preserved. The source of this perception is to be found in the actual spread of socialism since 1917; and the source of their opposition to that trend is to be found in the very real economic interests which social revolution abroad endangers. But while Washington seeks to defend real interests, it seeks to do so on the basis of a mythological view of the world, a view which derives from a total inability to understand the spread of socialism except in terms of foreign aggression, mysterious subversion and Great Power intervention. Precisely because Washington itself pursues its goals by no other means, it believes its own propaganda which attributes the same techniques to the other side. Precisely because the United States is an imperialist nation, it finds no difficulty in accepting the myth of Soviet and Chinese imperialism. Were this mythological perception of no value to the system or even a positive hindrance, it would have long since been corrected. What perpetuates and gives substance to the myth is the massive military spending and atmosphere of political reaction which it engenders. The ultimate proof of the existence of the Communist conspiracy is that it is so profitable to combat. Just as the mythology of anti-Communism serves to justify military spending and domestic reaction, so military spending and domestic reaction serve to reinforce and preserve the mythology of anti-Communism and the foreign policies which derive from it.

It is, in the final analysis, this continuing interaction between imperialism abroad and its repercussions at home which give rise to that element of over-protection in American foreign policy noted earlier. Because it is now virtually an economic and political necessity to perceive the world through the categories of the myth, American imperialism has become increasingly incapable of distinguishing between real and unreal threats. Despite all the evidence to the contrary, it continues to behave as if by isolating and encircling the Soviet Union and China, it could halt the course of revolution in the Third World. Despite all the evidence to the contrary, it continues to act as if the socialist world were a monolithic bloc and the triumph of socialism in Vietnam a victory for Chinese imperialism. Despite all the evidence to the contrary, it continues to believe that if it does not intervene everywhere in the world, socialism must be everywhere victorious tomorrow. The final irony, of course, is that by pursuing such policies the United States ends by transforming its phantasies into realities. By treating the Cuban regime as a Soviet outpost in the Western Hemisphere, it compels the Soviet Union to place missiles in Cuba. The mythology of anti-Communism not only justifies military spending and domestic reaction; it also provides the necessary confirmation for its own distorted perceptions. In this sense one might almost argue that the real goal of American imperialism today is not so much to preserve capitalist holdings abroad as it is to preserve and give substance to the myth upon which capitalism at home now rests.

In no case has this mythological function of American imperialism been of more decisive significance than in Vietnam. The main reason why the war has aroused so much opposition within the ranks of the Cold War Establishment itself is that it is justified by neither economic nor strategic considerations commensurate with the grave risks involved. Not only are American investments in Vietnam of negligible significance, but American holdings in the entire Far East (as of 1963) totalled only $1.5 billion, of which the greater part was invested in Japan and the Philippines, two countries which are not even part of the Asian mainland. Even if the economic stake in the rest of the Far East were greater than it is, moreover, there is little reason to believe that the triumph of socialism in South Vietnam would endanger it to any significant degree. Ironically enough, some radical critics of the war have been compelled to accept the Administration's own rationale, the "domino theory," because they are rightly unwilling to attribute American policies to Johnson's personal caprice. All the same, the evidence that the United States is fighting in Vietnam in order to defend its interests in Southeast Asia is no stronger when presented by the left than by the right. The victory of the Viet-Minh in 1954 had no major international repercussions; and there is no country in Southeast Asia today, with the possible exception of Laos, where revolutionary forces are strong enough to derive a real impetus from an NLF victory in South Vietnam. As Johnson's liberal critics have not failed to point out, the actual effect of the war has been rather to undermine American influence in the area, most notably in Cambodia. Of course one might still insist that even if an NLF victory did not immediately alter the balance of forces in Southeast Asia, the knowledge that the United States could be forced to withdraw would provide a source of tremendous encouragement to other revolutionary movements throughout the world. It is likely that the Administration believes this; but what it ignores is that the desperate conditions which produce revolutions do not permit revolutionaries to pause and consider whether or not they will offend the United States. The lesson of Vietnam—if it is intended as a lesson—is no lesson at all.

In order to understand American policy in Vietnam, it seems to me, one must have reference to the self-justifying logic of anti-Communism and military spending described above. Not only does the war provide a suitable occasion for an increase in military appropriations and a series of repressive measures—such as the attempt to register the Du Bois Clubs—directed against the left; it also serves to bolster that anti-Communist mythology without which even the normal rate of military spending could not be sustained. Both Kennedy and Johnson (prior to 1965) could easily have withdrawn from Vietnam without the slightest damage to American prestige or their own political standing. They had only to blame the whole thing on the perfidy of the South Vietnamese ruling class, whose belief in its own capacity to retain power had declined in direct proportion to the increase in its deposits in Swiss banks. They chose to remain because to have withdrawn would have been to give the lie to the whole myth of "aggression from the North" which they had so assiduously propagated. They chose to remain because to have withdrawn would have been an admission that there was no real reason for being there in the first place. They chose to remain because to have withdrawn would have dealt a serious blow to that whole doctrine of global resistance to Communist aggression which American capitalism no longer knows how to dispense with. Unwilling to expose the American people to such a rude awakening, and fortified by the economic and political advantages to be derived from such a course, first Kennedy and then Johnson determined to stay in Vietnam; and in order to stay, in the face of a rapidly deteriorating military situation, they were compelled to become ever more deeply involved.

The point at which American policy passed entirely into a phantasy world of its own creation was in February of 1965, when Johnson embarked upon the bombing of North Vietnam. It is quite possible that Johnson believed that by bombing the North he could compel Ho Chi Minh to call off the war in the South. Such a notion, although totally mistaken, would be consistent with Washington's conception of what revolution is all about. But even this theory does not suffice to explain why Johnson continues the bombings long after their military and political futility has become entirely obvious. In the final analysis, Johnson is bombing North Vietnam because he wants to prove to himself, to his critics and to the American people that the United States is in fact confronted with a clear case of Communist aggression in the South. By devastating the North, Johnson declares: here is the proof of your complicity, for why else would we attack you? There is a strict historical parallel between this exercise in mad logic and Hitler's Final Solution to the Jewish question. The basic function of the extermination camps was not so much to eliminate actual enemies—political prisoners were not usually sent to Auschwitz—as it was to give substance to mythical ones. Every Jew who perished in the gas chambers became by his very death a confessed enemy of the German race: for why else was he killed? This is the logic not of Descartes but of Kafka, and Vietnam today is America's Penal Colony. The people of Vietnam, North and South, must be punished for their aggression, for without the punishment there would be no aggression and without the aggression no possible justification for that gigantic military-industrial complex which stands at the very core of American economic and political life.

This parallel between the American treatment of Vietnam and the Nazi treatment of the Jews is not accidental; it stems from a fundamental resemblance between twentieth century German and American imperialism. For German capitalism even more than for

American capitalism, capital investment abroad was always of secondary importance in comparison to the role of military spending at home. The early twentieth century German equivalent to the American nuclear arsenal was a vast and costly fleet which never served any military purpose whatsoever. Having embarked upon a program of military spending of this kind, Germany found itself compelled to pursue a foreign policy commensurate with its military preparations; the effect of this system was to imbue German imperialism with an aggressive character all out of proportion to either the foreign interests at stake or the actual magnitude of German resources. The mad dreams of conquest entertained by Hitler during the Second World War were hardly more grandiose than the German war aims formulated during the course of the First World War and embodied in the treaty of Brest-Litovsk. If Johnson behaves like Hitler in Vietnam, it is not because Johnson is a fascist or America a fascist country, but rather because American imperialism like German imperialism has been driven to act out its phantasies in order to preserve them. To the extent that American foreign policy goes beyond the task of safeguarding American holdings abroad, to that extent does it threaten to recapitulate the truly insane and disastrous history of Germany in the twentieth century.

What follows from the above is that the monstrous irrationality which characterizes American policy in Vietnam also causes American imperialism to pose a very real threat to world survival itself. British and French imperialism, for all of its barbarous atrocities, was at least compelled to preserve the peoples which it sought to exploit; and when it could no longer maintain its domination through military means, it found ways of accommodating itself to the changing situation. American imperialism, insofar as it derives from the implacable need to justify its own myths, can make no such accommodation. Mythical interests, unlike real ones, cannot be compromised or negotiated; they must stand or fall as an integral whole. Already during the Cuban missile crisis Kennedy proved that the United States government was perfectly capable of threatening nuclear war in order to preserve its own mythological universe intact. In Vietnam today only the incredible forebearance of the Soviet Union and China has prevented another major confrontation with the United States. Almost fifty years ago Lenin noted that imperialism, from the political standpoint, was more than a striving after foreign conquest, that it was "in general, a striving towards violence and reaction." It is this amorphous "striving towards violence and reaction" which has come to constitute the most dangerous feature of American imperialism today. Unless a way is found to wake the United States from that phantasy world in which it now acts, there is good reason to believe that the ultimate nightmare of nuclear war may also be played out on the stage of the real world.

There are two distinct and partially contradictory implications which can be derived from this analysis. On the one hand, it suggests that American imperialism is so integrally bound up with the American capitalist system that it will prove difficult to modify the former to any significant degree without also transforming the latter. Such a conclusion is implicit in any theory based upon the Leninist thesis; it relates to the traditional Marxist argument that the effects of capitalism cannot ultimately be remedied without changing the system itself. On the other hand, the above analysis also suggests—and this in contradistinction to the Leninist thesis—that there is no inherent economic *necessity* for certain key aspects of American imperialism. Military spending belongs in the public rather than the private domain; it can be acted upon in a way that foreign investment cannot. Although the military establishment now forms an integral part of the American capitalist system, it is possible, at least in theory, to envisage a capitalist economy organized along different lines and geared to a different type of government spending. Were the United States to abandon large scale military spending and the mythological perceptions which both reflect and justify it, then American imperialism would no longer pose the same kind of threat to world survival as it does today. Of course it may well be that no government will prove capable of abolishing the military-industrial complex unless it is also capable of abolishing the capitalist system itself. To argue along these lines, however, means to argue that American imperialism must continue to play out its phantasies until the triumph of socialism in the United States. Since there is no way to test this hypothesis in practice at the present time, I prefer to assume that it may be possible to gain a partial victory over imperialism, a victory which will provide both the necessary time and the necessary political climate for the task of eliminating the roots of imperialism altogether.

It is at this point that the peace movement comes in. Peace has always been an issue for the left; but it is an issue which is of special relevance to the conditions created by the existence of the modern American military-industrial complex. That dependence upon a mythological world view which makes American im- perialism so dangerous also renders it extremely vulnerable to attack. In the case of Vietnam the gap between myth and reality has become so great as to arouse serious disquiet in the most unexpected places. Moreover, given the self-justifying character of American foreign policy, any critique of its effects tends to lead into a critique of its causes. Merely by calling into question the need for American involvement in Vietnam, the peace movement acts to undermine that military establishment which is in large part responsible for the war in the first place. Merely by calling into question the reality of an "aggression from the North," the peace movement acts to discredit that doctrine of global resistance to Communist aggression in whose name the war is being fought. It is for this reason that the relatively ineffective and isolated protest against the war in Vietnam has aroused such a hysterical reaction in certain quarters. The peace movement is not yet at the point where it can have any appreciable effect upon the outcome of the war itself; but by virtue of its very existence, it has already succeeded in posing a real challenge to the ideological framework which the war is designed to sustain.

If the peace movement is to achieve any lasting gains in the struggle against imperialism, however, it must learn to translate its implicit condemnation of American foreign policy into explicit terms. It is not enough to repudiate the anti-Communist crusade in Vietnam; one must also develop a frank and comprehensive critique of the entire doctrine of global resistance to Communist aggression. It is already clear to everyone except SANE and its allies that one cannot protest the war in Vietnam in the name of a more sophisticated version of anti-Communism without thereby lending credence to the very myths which have produced that war. What is not generally understood is that Vietnam is not a special case, that the lies which are used to justify American policy today have also served to justify the policies of the last twenty years. What this means in practice is that the peace movement must make a concerted effort to demonstrate to the American people and to its own members that there is not and never was any such thing as Soviet or Chinese imperialism. It means that the peace movement must not only call for an American withdrawal from Vietnam but must also press for a complete abandonment of those global commitments which make a new Vietnam inevitable. It means, in brief, that the peace movement must launch a concerted assault upon the basic doctrines of anti-Communism as applied both at home and abroad. By refusing to meet this issue head-on some elements in the movement may assure themselves of a certain respectability, but they will have done little to counteract the policies which must eventually produce not only future Vietnams but also a world conflagration.

If such a critique of the anti-Communist mythology is to gain wide acceptance, it must be accompanied by the progressive dismantling of the economic and political foundation of the myth, the military-industrial complex. It is at this point that the real difficulties begin; for military spending and the military establishment are so closely bound up with the whole fabric of American society that many persons, even within the peace movement, have ceased to regard their abolition as a realistic goal. The workers whose jobs depend upon defense contracts, the professors whose salaries are paid by corporate grants to institutions of higher learning, the scientists whose pure research is financed by General Dynamics, all of these potential allies of the peace movement are also accomplices in the bombing of Vietnam. It is precisely this sense of involuntary complicity which underlies much of the protest against the war; but the guilt which feeds the protest also defines the limits of that protest. The reluctance of some elements in the peace movement to repudiate openly the doctrine of anti-Communism stems directly from their involvement in a system whose monstrous consequences they are—to their credit—unwilling to accept. It must also be remembered that protest is not the only way of expiating guilt, and that the same atrocities which outrage some are a source of satisfaction to others. The inability of the peace movement to expand its current base within the academic and professional middle class strongly suggests that the guilt of suburbia will not suffice to build a mass opposition to the war. If the peace movement is to transcend its present limitations, it must begin to ask itself how one creates an opposition to a system which knows how to make accomplices out of its critics.

There are no easy answers to such questions; but one point is already clear. For millions of Americans military spending means nothing but higher taxes, inflation, impoverished social services and the blood tax of the draft. Even those who may directly or indirectly benefit from military spending in one way are almost sure to be victimized in another. It is to the victims of the military establishment—not only the urban poor but also blue and white collar workers—that the peace movement must learn to address itself if it is to build a real political base in this country. The chief obstacle to such an approach, of course, is that those who benefit least from military spending are also those who are for good reason least optimistic about the possibility of effecting any significant change in American foreign policy. Unable to exercise even the slightest control over the basic conditions which determine their lives, the victims of the war see little chance of ending the war. As many in the peace movement have already discovered, there is little point in telling people about the connection between military spending and poverty unless one is also prepared to help give them some concrete experience of acting to eliminate both the one and the other.

In the final analysis, then, the struggle for peace and against imperialism cannot succeed if it continues to be waged on a single-issue basis. Precisely because American imperialism is so deeply rooted in the whole military-industrial complex, it must be fought on the level of domestic as well as international policy. In order to draw the connection between military intervention abroad and the inability of the government to meet basic human needs at home, we must learn how to organize the victims of the war around a program which provides meaningful solutions to those needs. In order to put an end to military spending we must learn how to build a movement capable of achieving the political power to make such changes. That many in the peace movement are already aware of this necessity is apparent in the growing trend towards political action, community organization and a multi-issue approach. The whole point of the above analysis has been to show that there is nothing arbitrary or wilful about this trend, that it flows from the very logic of the movement itself. Only by transcending its own immediate objectives can the peace movement hope to achieve those objectives. This is the task—and also the opportunity—which confronts us today.

21

RONALD ARONSON

Socialism: the Sustaining Menace

Robert Wolfe raises a key issue for peace activists, for radical intellectuals working towards an illuminating account of contemporary society, and, indeed, for liberals who simply oppose United States involvement in Vietnam: does the spread of socialism really endanger American capitalism? Wolfe's answer is that, in Vietnam at least, this threat is more myth than reality. But, he argues, this myth of the Red Menace is the sole *raison d'être* for the military-industrial complex whose rulers hold positions of key economic and political power. To permit a Communist victory in Vietnam would deny the very basis of this power: that a mortal threat confronts us. In order to justify its own existence, the Cold War apparatus must oppose Communism wherever it appears, no matter how slight may be the American economic stake. In reaching this conclusion Wolfe rejects those explanations which turn on either the threat of socialism to

327

American capitalism's actual foreign economic stake, or the eventual consequences of socialist encirclement of a capitalist America. The issue is perplexing because every explanation, taken by itself, seems compelling. Wolfe is right: a military-industrial class, whose lifeblood is Cold War mobilization, *needs* the Communist threat. Their prosperity and power, as well as that of their brethren throughout the oligarchy, seem to require the wartime economy. But American capitalism *does* have a vital economic stake in foreign areas, and it *does* fear the example, the precedent of successful socialist revolutions. Moreover, the Soviet Union, as a working proof of socialism's viability, *is* a threat to a depression-prone, poverty-ridden, war-generating capitalist society.

Wolfe has illuminated a single and historically very recent phase of the political economy's foreign policy needs. But in arriving there he has cast away other vital dimensions of the historical development of American foreign involvement. Thus I think his discussion is a partial, a distorted view of the Behemoth that confronts us.

What shall we do in our search for a complete explanation of the connection between American foreign policy and the spread of socialism and socialist movements? If none of the explanations is complete, shall we lump them all together? I think this would be incorrect. We certainly need a full-scale description of this Behemoth, its major needs, difficulties and tendencies. But we can see precisely how far situations like Vietnam are connected to the basic workings of the system only if we clearly grasp those basic workings.

In these pages I will try to sketch some of the lines of a fuller description of American capitalism's relationship to socialism abroad. I will try to indicate the place of those key elements, like foreign investment, which I believe Wolfe's discussion wrongly minimized. And I will sketch what I feel to be the prospects ahead for American foreign involvement. My goal is obviously not a full analysis, but a point of view on the whole. Much work has to be done, and there are many materials available to us: Marx, the theories of imperialism, Mills, Marcuse, Baran and Sweezy. Our goal, eventually, should be a theoretical model of contemporary American society which explains its basic workings, needs, contradictions and lines of development. Here I can only argue for a specific perspective for that eventual work, and present a few insights.

My major point is that the contest with socialism has become *the* decisive fact of the American political economy, the framework within which it operates. American capitalism's needs, problems and tendencies are developed and expressed in a Cold War context which affects, influences and even determines them. Communism, as the Enemy, has become a constituent of American society which the society needs in order to keep functioning, and yet which threatens it. Such general phrases encompass the concrete and possibly conflicting dimensions of the American stake *vis-à-vis* socialism; protection of the foreign economic empire; response to the threatening example and alternative of socialism; the economic and political basis for Cold War mobilization; the attempt to keep the American people's support for capitalism; and the Cold War consciousness required for the waste consumption which helps to support the economy. Let us examine each of these areas.

II

Imperialism proper refers to the direct economic stake of the developed capitalist nations in foreign lands. As distinguished from Wolfe's all-embracing use of the term to include the Cold War apparatus, it originally meant the conquest of the markets, areas of investment and raw materials necessary to capitalism's continued growth. While other devices and tendencies have since been introduced to buoy up the economy, such as armaments spending, non-competitive pricing and massive waste consumption, the role of foreign investment has certainly not diminished in importance. Here I directly disagree with Wolfe.

If anything, the relationship of the metropolitan economy to its colonial satellites has grown more interdependent, sophisticated and complex, as Baran and Sweezy point out.[1] American capitalism must be described as an international system, and the protection of its foreign interests is a keystone of American political and military involvement overseas. The full description of American foreign policy must begin with America's economic empire.

As regards Vietnam, Wolfe rejects this position. As he indicates, the issue in Vietnam is not America's slight current stake there. But what then? Can we say that world-wide interests of American capitalism are at stake in Vietnam? Wolfe's answer is that foreign investment is only five per cent of total American capital investment. Centered as it is in Europe and Latin America, Wolfe argues, this relatively small percentage of total investment could hardly justify the rigidity and militancy shown *everywhere* by the American government, especially in Vietnam. I think Wolfe's position here is based on a misreading of the data and a misunderstanding of the truly global character of American capitalism's stake.

First, the most telling figures indicate not the amount of American capital invested, but the percentage of total profits *drawn from* overseas—about 11 per cent. Distinguishing developed from underdeveloped countries, the breakdown is even more striking. While less than two per cent of total American capital invested, domestic and foreign, is located in underdeveloped areas, such areas pay to the United States—after re-investment of part of the earnings—a sum equal to about eight per cent of the total domestic after-tax corporate profits. This makes up nearly one dollar in every six paid in dividends. The profit rate in underdeveloped countries is a staggering 15 per cent, compared with a rate of eight per cent in developed countries. Furthermore, this exploitation of underdeveloped countries is focused in a very specific and strategic area—raw materials. Most of this enormously profitable investment is in extractive industries, chiefly petroleum and mining, which would be difficult if not impossible to replace were these countries liberated from American exploitation.[2]

Now most of the capital invested abroad is centered in the giant corporations—45 corporations control half of American overseas investments. Just as in domestic politics, the vital needs of the handful of giant corporations are likely to become the "national interest," rather than those of the sum total of domestic businesses of all sizes. We are dealing here with the fact of power concentration: American foreign holdings are perceived as vital to the large corporations in the center of policy-making. This has been the case from the beginning of American economic expansion overseas. Corporate America has vigorously asserted control over its economic domain, ordering the military to intervene whenever and wherever its interests were affected. As today, countries were occupied, governments were overthrown, favorable local cliques were promoted. (In the 90 years from 1851 to 1940, over 120 instances of overseas intervention are reported by the State Department. See *Studies on the Left*, Vol. III, No. 2, "The Use of United States Armed Forces Overseas, 1851-1945.") Thus long before socialism threatened the empire, a military apparatus had been developed to assure the control of that empire by elements favorable to the needs of American corporations.

Today it is socialism that threatens this long-established domain of American capitalism. At stake in this struggle, according to Baran and Sweezy, is the international monopoly character of the major corporations. They require, more than ever, to dispose without hindrance over an enormous variety of foreign resources in order to secure their most profitable utilization. Here the threat of socialism is obvious: a successful revolution establishes a precedent for local control over local resources. The danger posed by Cuba lies in its effect on the rest of the American empire.

Wolfe rejects this notion of the *example* of Vietnam, Cuba, etc. But his disregard for the incentive and precedent offered by successful socialist revolution is hardly shared in Washington. There the fear of being proved a paper tiger seems real, and the desire to provide a terrifying example of the fate of "the new Chinese tactic" of wars of national liberation seems equally real. I would suspect that the Vietnam outcome is equally important, especially in terms of morale and confidence, to the guerrilla movements in the hills of Central and South America.

My point is that American response is not and should not be expected to be in direct proportion to the immediate stake involved in Cuba, say, or Vietnam. The long-range purpose of terror in any system of subjugation is the same: to keep the entire population in line. Terror works by example. On this level the American destruction of Vietnamese villages is intended at least as much for the peasants of Central and South America as it is for the Vietnamese villagers who support the National Liberation Front. High policy statements from Washington make it clear that American actions in Vietnam must be taken as an example of what will happen to all who rebel.

Imperialist economic interest thus remains a basic strand of American foreign policy. As we have seen, this economic stake, and the military involvement stemming from it, is prior to and was originally independent of the Cold War. Whether or not Communism exists, American capitalism has always sought to protect its vital foreign interests.

At this point, with the foreign stake of key American corporate interests clearly before us, we may still dispute the role of Vietnam. Wolfe argues that American policy is marked by a rigidity everywhere, and not merely in the American economic empire proper. In a "conservative" estimate Baran and Sweezy list 14 countries plus Latin America as belonging to the American empire.[3] Cuba may be considered vital because of its proximity both to the United States and to Latin America. But, the argument goes, why Vietnam, where the role of American investment is comparatively slight?

I think two interconnected historical developments account for this world-wide inflexibility and militancy in protecting what seems to be a less-than-world-wide empire. The first turns on the nature of American economic involvement overseas, and the second turns on the polarizing effects of the Cold War context. First, in pursuing its interests overseas, American capitalism has not required direct colonial rule of its economic empire. A wide and sophisticated variety of devices, including proprietorship through foreign-based subsidiary corporations, diplomatic pressures, CIA and USIA activities, military aid to the cooperating ruling class, and, when necessary, direct military intervention, have created the proper climate for investment. With few exceptions, American capitalism has always sought conditions favorable for American investment rather than direct colonial rule. And today the historical situation makes a widespread renewal of direct colonial control unthinkable.

Thus the subtle and indirect character of many of its forms of control make American capitalism's empire an invisible one. Without overt American political control, actual control over a country is always a matter of degree, subject to shifting local political situations and the success of various manipulative tactics. This character of the American overseas stake means that all "Free World" nations belong in some degree to the American empire. This very lack of boundaries extends rather than diminishes the defense perimeter of American capitalism. If almost every country is a partial member, all must be "protected." Brazil's status, for example, is quantitatively, not qualitatively, different from Vietnam's in spite of the more extensive American investments there. Where American control is indirect it is also more fragile. The example of the successful defection of a country with slight American investments threatens those areas under more direct control. The invisible nature of the empire, therefore, makes it necessary to provide a firm, unmistakable example of American intentions towards all who rebel, regardless of the size of the American stake.

The notion of the "Free World" makes clear this all-embracing commitment to defend American capitalism everywhere. But it does this with reference to the second element determining the world-wide character of American involvement, the Cold War. The role of the Cold War in American society will be discussed further below. We may say here, however, that the specific threats to the American network of control and influence have become Communist-oriented national liberation movements. The American empire is at stake against its alternative, Communism. The recent Cold War polarization of political forces throughout the world has wedded the defense of the American empire to the struggle against socialism. This polarization leaves only two sharply different alternatives for colonial peoples: continued domination and stagnation under capitalism, or economic development under some form of socialism. All forces struggling to throw off foreign economic domination must increasingly look towards a national liberation movement whose goal is socialism; Cold War polarization permits no more moderate solution. In this context, a victory for one is a defeat for the other: a successful Communist-oriented revolution in areas *not* under American hegemony and economic control still spreads the example of socialism. Regardless of direct economic stake, then, the defense perimeter of the American empire has extended to the entire non-socialist world.

III

Since the Cold War began, foreign intervention on behalf of the economic interests outlined above has been consistently justified by the "danger of Communism." But Cold War mobilization was not originally rooted in those specific interests: it represents a new and different stage in the development of American foreign involvement. The military-industrial elements most directly served by Cold War mobilization are not those most interested in foreign economic exploitation; the Cold War itself occupies a place in the development of American capitalism initially quite distinct from that of American imperialism.

Certainly the Truman Doctrine and the Marshall Plan encompassed areas in which American investments are today enormous, and the Soviet occupation of Eastern Europe withdrew other areas from investment. But this division of Europe had been accepted by the major powers long before the Cold War began. The Truman Doctrine and the Marshall Plan were simply attempts to secure those capitalist spheres of influence, already conceded by Stalin, from indigenous Communist movements. Seen as American capitalism's response to the post-war threat of Communism, these policies hardly required American mobilization against the Soviet Union.

But if Cold War mobilization was not an attempt to regain lost areas and protect threatened ones, it clearly served other more visible needs. The old Marxian notion that foreign wars are projections outward of internal contradictions and class conflicts may illuminate these needs. This notion appears obscure to us because class conflict seems to have vanished from the United States, and because the contradictions of the economic system seem to be so neatly contained. But that of course is just the point: the Cold War mobilization has been so successful as to disguise its function. To recall the Great Depression puts the matter in a clearer light. In 1939, immediately before mobilization began for World War II, one-sixth of the labor force was unemployed, nearly 30 per cent of industrial capacity unused. The Great Depression had not yet stimulated a social revolution in the United States, but the economy had found no solution to its malfunctioning. American capitalism continued to limp along. Demands for social reform continued to come from a growing, militant working-class movement. On the other hand, the Soviet Union demonstrated that a rational economy was possible under socialism.

Only the war ended the stagnation of the economy, returning it to full employment and productivity. Without war, American capitalism was a system unable to overcome its own structural malfunctioning, which generated a potentially large internal opposition, and which had before it the working example of a rational alternative. After the war the unresolved structural threat of returning to stagnation and mass unemployment, plus the visible extension of the alternative, socialism, to vast new areas, provided the basis for transferring the threat from within to without. If it had not united against this external threat, the system's own internal dynamic, contained during the war, might well have resumed after the post-war boom cycle subsided.

The system, then, *was* threatened. Was it threatened by the Soviet Union? Although it posed no military threat, the Soviet Union certainly embodied the alternative to a structurally faulty capitalism. Capitalism's own malfunctioning was the real threat, and socialism the visible embodiment of that threat. The institutional response was obvious: unite all forces against that external embodiment.

The Cold War, then, was quite an understandable course, given the developed interests in wartime mobilization, the threat of the Great Depression, and the presence of socialism. Mobilizing against the Soviet Union helped to contain the threats to the system. The economic fruits are obvious: assured demand at assured profits for the specific interests in armaments research and production, and a powerful stimulant to demand and production throughout the economy. The political consequences of the situation are also obvious. Owing to the "threat of Communism" a far-reaching "national interest" is proclaimed which absorbs class differences and overt political struggles. The remaining internal opposition is identified with the external Enemy. The existence of Communism abroad permitted both the suppression of the system's malfunctioning and the suppression of the alternatives implied by that malfunctioning. The system was rescued from the potential threat of socialism at home. Capitalism's Enemy became its deliverer.

We can now see Wolfe's point more clearly: the Vietnamese involvement is to be explained by referring to the domestic stake in continued Cold War mobilization, to military-industrial interests which have their own need to "overprotect" their brothers' foreign empire. But even aside from the question of the American overseas economic stake, I disagree with Wolfe here. He emphasizes a specific class, with specific interests in mobilization which are not necessarily shared by the remainder of the oligarchy. Thus he can conceive of an American capitalism purged of its Cold War apparatus. I think he arrives at such utopian hopes by failing to examine the stake in the Cold War of the entire oligarchy. I have argued above that the political economy as a whole has come to need Communism as the Enemy, for without mobilizing against that Enemy, the system's own threatening dynamic would be resumed. Real needs, and not mythical ones, are at stake, although, as Wolfe points out, those needs can only be served by erecting the colossal myth of the Communist military threat. Certainly specific military-industrial interests have come to depend most immediately on mobilization; they direct it and live entirely by it. But in spite of their more militant ideology and their more distorted perception of reality, they serve the interests of the oligarchy in general. That, after all, is the reason for their position and power. Their immediate interests may well diverge from those of other sectors of the oligarchy, but this does not cancel American capitalism's basic stake in the Cold War.

IV

I have said that by casting the threat outward and mobilizing against the Soviet Union, American capitalism has managed to preserve itself intact, to contain its own internal dynamic of boom and depression. Thus the system's irrationality leads it to a bizarre solution: *American capitalism now requires the existence of Communism.* But on the other hand, as I have tried to show, foreign economic interests are vital to the stability of American capitalism, and they must therefore be protected. There are here two major strands of American foreign involvement, stemming originally from the needs of different periods in the development of American capitalism, and most directly benefiting different corporate sectors.

If imperialist and Cold War interests nevertheless emphasized different dimensions, the recent challenge to capitalism from pro-Communist movements in the colonial world has made possible their amalgamation. The chief threats to American imperialism were once posed by other imperialist powers, such as Japan, or by nationalist leaders, such as Mossadegh or Nasser. Today the chief threats are Communist-oriented national liberation movements. The original Enemy of the military-industrial complex was Soviet Communism: it is now guerrilla nationalism-Communism. The Communism which threatens vital imperialist interests also justifies the new "counter-insurgency" direction of Cold War mobilization. In Santo Domingo, Vietnam, Cuba and the Congo, the vital needs of both interests coalesce. The direct military threat of the Soviet Union was a myth: the threat to American business in Vietnam is actual.

This suggests that American capitalism, far from being stabilized and consolidated, has yet to face its sharpest threats. While the pseudo-threat of the Red Army was compatible with nuclear sabre-rattling and big-power diplomacy, the actual threat to America's foreign empire is not easily defeated. Diplomatic chess games and the threat of annihilation cannot stop the revolution in Vietnam, just as it could not stop the revolution in Cuba. In each case American intervention only intensifies the movements. Bombing the North and genocide in the South, incredible political maneuvering among the local military cliques, and plans for "social revolution" drawn up by the United States State Department—these are frantic castings about for an answer. But no answer has yet been found. Because it is uncontrollable, this threat to American capitalism is all the greater.

Contrast the uncontrollable situation in Vietnam with the litany of State Department liberals: the long-range interests of American security and economic stability can best be served by promoting rapid economic development, parliamentary democracy and the growth of a middle class. Popular revolutions must be accepted when they are inevitable, treated gently and even subsidized, in order to counteract their most radical tendencies. Partial nationalization must be permitted, as in Mexico. In the light of the current Latin American counter-revolution, of Cuba, the Congo, Vietnam and the Dominican Republic, it is grimly ironic to rehearse these prescriptions. For the opposite is actual American policy everywhere. James O'Connor has listed the new forms of United States imperialism in Latin America in *Studies on the Left,* Vol. IV, No. 4. Although as O'Connor points out, "the counter-revolution has grasped the initiative and intends to retain it at nearly any cost," this policy hardly serves the long-range economic interests of American capitalism. For that, intense economic development and a loosening of class structure would be necessary: but the Alliance for Reaction can hardly be expected to benefit the Latin American peasant. The short-term prospect may be more profits and more repression, but the long-term prospect under such conditions can only be ever more furious, ever more violent revolution.

Certainly this deviation of the immediately secure but ultimately threatening real policy from the liberal ideal is rooted in the balance of actual forces at play. I would add one further element to those which restrict American options and make a more "enlightened" policy inconceivable: the Cold War itself.

Obviously if anyone is to formulate and carry out a policy whose long-range goal is to protect American interests, it cannot be the corporations themselves. Their response when confronted by any threat is to call for government military intervention to protect their immediate interests. A more intelligent and foresighted course must come from elsewhere. This is what happened in the New Deal: the government assumed the role of protecting those long-range interests which the majority of capitalists were incapable of protecting, and often understanding, because of their own fixation on their immediate interests.

A more sophisticated colonial policy must thus come from elsewhere than the colonialists themselves. But can a government whose entire orientation is to sustain and promote the Cold War abandon its Cold War responses and categories upon approaching the colonial world? In fact it cannot: the Cold War apparatus, whose insight into the colonial peoples cannot reach beyond defining them as *personnel* and their homes as *structures,* plus the immediate needs of business interests, make a rigid posture all but inevitable. Here I think is the place of Wolfe's major point—that the military-industrial apparatus does seek a policy which justifies itself, for its existence and pressure limit the options actually available to the government. Of course this is only possible insofar as the government itself and all the interests it represents remain committed to the Cold War and perceive reality according to its categories. And now that the Cold War against socialism has become amalgamated with the defense of the empire, now that Communism does directly threaten vital national interests, no voice of sanity—representing capitalism's own long-range interests—will be heard. There is no sphere in ruling circles from which it can come. Having created the Cold War to sustain itself, American capitalism must move within the narrowing space of its own political and conceptual trap—eliminating the slight chance for a more foresighted policy. Repressive and manipulative techniques carry a clear message to the colonial peoples: meaningful change can come only through revolution. And given the Cold War polarization of political forces, that revolution has no choice but to align with the Communist camp. American capitalism leaves no alternatives.

While temporary stability may be won (see the O'Connor article mentioned earlier), the long-range prospects have barely begun to show themselves. American landings, CIA-installed governments, support for the most reactionary and despised elements: the American response re-creates those conditions of foreign occupation under which the wartime resistance movements flourished. American capitalism is creating the need abroad for violent and bloody revolution. Through the New Deal reforms and the Cold War it has contained the dynamic which would generate its own gravediggers at home. But its gravediggers are being created by its own operation—in the colonial world. Having shifted its contradictions overseas through imperialism and the Cold War, it has also shifted the class struggle there. Its various props and devices have only succeeded in postponing that struggle.

V

I have argued so far that American capitalism's dynamic and problems have been decisively shifted overseas through the struggle against socialism. This suggests that basic domestic problems are at an end, that the American people have become tied to the system, and that their support in this struggle may be taken for granted. But the struggle is, at least in part, *for* the support of the American people. At a time of post-war prosperity and comparative Soviet poverty and tyranny it was relatively easy to create popular support for mobilization—without the actual sacrifices of war—against the apparent foreign designs of the Red Army. But it will be far more difficult to sustain popular support for the actual sacrifices involved in counter-revolutionary wars against whole peoples, especially as socialism, exemplified by the Soviet Union, grows more attractive and less frightening.

There is already difficulty in sustaining public support for the war in Vietnam. Although capitalism's stake is not obvious, it is clear that American soldiers are dying to sustain a right-wing military clique. Only the right wing at home considers this war anything but a regrettable burden whose purpose is unclear. Thus, to disguise the real imperial interest at stake and to promote popular support for the war, an external enemy must be located which seeks, in line with Cold War rhetoric, to "conquer" South Vietnam. To prevent erosion of popular support, the would-be foreign conqueror of the South Vietnamese people must be attacked: first North Vietnam, and then perhaps China. Here I think Wolfe's discussion is most insightful, pointing as it does to the domestic need, as well as the more questionable military need, to attack North Vietnam. The split developing in Washington around the war indicates that the government has failed to deceive at least some of the liberals that its stated goals are its real goals. As the war draws on without any improvement in the American position the problem of support will probably grow acute.

We are talking here about the problem involved in sustaining the identification of interest of rulers and ruled in fighting colonial wars. In fact this identification came about only through wartime mobilization and has been consolidated only through the Cold War. It presents difficulties on a completely different level: the competition between the United States and the Soviet Union.

I have suggested that the Soviet Union was and is an actual threat to American capitalism because it pointed to a rational, working alternative to the chaos and inequity of the American economic system. The consequence of this is relevant at this point: by making the Soviet Union into the Enemy, thereby creating the basis for suspending any possible class struggle at home, American capitalism took on the burden of its challenge. It must outperform socialism.

The Cold War message to the American working class is twofold: you are threatened by an evil and ruthless tyranny which seeks to conquer you and destroy everything you value. Not only is it a menace, but socialism, embodied in the Soviet Union, offers a form of life far inferior to that of American capitalism. This is central to its very nature as a menace. In mobilizing against socialism, then, American capitalism takes on two burdens: to defend itself against the real and supposed threats; and to convince its people that it is the superior society. As the rulers of East Germany and South Korea know, a freer and more prosperous alternative is a vital danger.

This is the point: the Soviet Union, as the Enemy, *must not* become the superior society. Having organized itself against Communism, having made the invidious comparison with Communism central to its public support, American capitalism is endangered if Communism does prove to offer a superior way of life. A system not organized against an Enemy may be able to withstand unfavorable comparison. But the *raison d'être* of American capitalism in the Cold War is its superiority to Communism: to fall behind is to endanger the domestic consensus based on the menace and inferiority of the Enemy.

But in thus projecting its problems onto the international scene, American capitalism has in one important sense placed them beyond its control. For the Soviet Union is itself developing. American militancy can force continued mobilization of the Soviet Union and thus hinder the full productivity of a more rational economy, but it can not basically control Soviet development. Soviet growth demands American growth. Its successes demand American successes. Its progress towards elimination of poverty demands an American attack on poverty. From this point of view the competition with the Soviet Union can be seen to be one spur behind many domestic reforms.

But peaceful competition favors the most rationally organized system—the Soviet Union. By staking its domestic support on its alleged superiority over the Soviet Union, American capitalism has placed its future on a very precarious footing. If and when the Soviet Union does produce more, demand fewer hours of work, offer a freer and better life, as Isaac Deutscher has pointed out in *The Great Contest,* the alternatives available to the American oligarchy may be only two—the rational one of drastic changes at home, or the irrational one of nuclear war.

In connection with this Cold War competition, the American government's need to convince the public that its foreign wars are intended to defend freedom against Communism will restrict its ability to suppress dissent against those wars. Cold War justification of counter-revolutionary wars will necessarily limit the fascistic tendencies of American politics. "Freedom" must be sold to the American people as the reason for their sacrifices. Otherwise the very propaganda basis for what is at heart an economic struggle will be cut from under it. Thus there are very real difficulties involved in maintaining support for a long series of counter-revolutionary wars. Opposition will probably have to be tolerated, but counter-revolutionary wars are long wars. The base of public support will likely dwindle unless the wars are continually expanded. In this respect as well, then, the long-range alternatives facing American policy-makers are narrow and unencouraging.

If its intense struggle with socialism reveals American capitalism's problems in keeping the support of the American people, this competition also serves American capitalism well in relation to the demands it must make on that public! The economic system has come to require that the American people consume enormous quantities of goods far beyond their actual needs for physical and psychological well-being. A key new dimension has been added to the economy since the onset of the Cold War: the need to produce and consume waste. To this end, individuals' vital needs do not suffice, they must be induced to *believe* they need things which stunt rather than promote their development, which provide socially acceptable forms of consolation rather than well-being, which violate all rational standards of use, durability and production. These things must be the very goods that the system turns out in great quantities, and at sufficiently high profits. We enter here a basic problem in the critique of American society, one at the heart of many liberal-radical disputes (see the Gans-Weinstein-Lynd exchange, *Studies on the Left*, Vol. VI, No. 1): who is to say what individuals *really* need?

The key, I think, is that life-patterns and life-commitments develop in relation to the actually available alternatives. Where no alternatives are available, individuals may freely choose a life of senseless labor and spiralling waste consumption. As Herbert Marcuse has pointed out, where meaningful alternatives are rigorously excluded, the subjective feeling of freedom may well coincide with actual enslavement. The basic question to ask in determining whether free choice has any content is, what are the alternatives?

This helps to illuminate the relationship between the Cold War and waste consumption as a needed prop of contemporary American capitalism. My point is that a one-dimensional consciousness, in Herbert Marcuse's term, is necessary to waste consumption, a consciousness which has no alternative before it but continued expansion of the same style of life. And the Cold War, in terms of its effect on consciousness, is precisely mobilization against any alternative. In however distorted a form it may take in the Soviet Union, socialism *is* the alternative form of society, and the Cold War has made it into the Enemy. To foreclose the alternative form of society, as the Cold War has done, is to foreclose meaningful alternatives for consciousness. Social change is excluded, and a society is created whose goal is larger and larger quantities of itself. Individuals succumb to it not because they want to, not because they approve, but because they have no alternative towards which to orient themselves. Thus they direct themselves, however cynically, at the accepted goals of American society—to buy beyond their needs—to the great benefit of American capitalism.

If a class struggle existed *within* American society rather than having been projected out onto the international scene, it would pose the goal of socialism, of another, a humane way of life. This massive waste production would then be impossible. Choices and possible commitments would exist which are now unavailable. Other standards for evaluation would exist than the self-validating ones of American capitalism itself. The unsatisfying and irrational nature of the American style of life is intelligible only if measured in terms of something else. But the Cold War eliminates the internal opposition which would make this possible, and taboos the alternative. Thus the struggle against socialism is basic to the ever-expanding waste production of American capitalism.

VI

What emerges from this discussion is the tremendous dependence of American capitalism on the struggle against socialism. On the one hand the system *needs* this struggle, has organized itself around it and won stability through it. On the other hand the struggle is beyond control. American capitalism seems unable to prevent itself from generating the conditions for revolution throughout its empire. And, having pitted itself against the Soviet Union, it faces possible Soviet developments in productivity and the reduction of the working day which it may be incapable of equalling. The most vital wars, counter-revolutionary ones, do not lend themselves to the ready use of Cold War rhetoric to maintain popular support; yet the professed commitment to freedom required for public support makes it difficult to suppress the opposition to those wars at home.

Being dependent on and yet threatened by socialism, American capitalism is far from being the firmly entrenched, stable Behemoth we are accustomed to see it as. It is already in trouble, and the trouble will grow. What matters is the long-range perspective, not the immediate containment of its malfunctioning, of colonial revolution, of the prospects for an internal opposition movement. The system is not stable, but fragile, for it depends on a dynamic beyond its control.

Thus, while I agree with Robert Wolfe that the key thrust of political organizing should be to combat anti-Communism, I think that to do so is to attack more than the prop holding up a specific sector of the ruling class. It is to do no less than attack the whole. If successful, the attack on anti-Communism will become a revolution. The present conditions for such success are slight, but in the long range, I believe we have every reason to hope.

Notes

[1] See Paul A. Baran and Paul M. Sweezy, *Monopoly Capital, An Essay on the American Economic and Social Order* (New York and London, Monthly Review Press, 1966) Ch. 7.

[2] The source of this information, the U.S. Department of Commerce's monthly *Survey of Current Business* (see the issues of August 1964 and September 1965) was suggested by a communication from John Maher—who disagrees with the conclusions drawn from the figures.

[3] *Ibid.*, pp. 183-4.

22

STOKELY CARMICHAEL

Black Power and the Third World

The following is the text of a speech made by Stokely Carmichael at the OLAS (Organization of Latin-American Solidarity) conference held in Havana in the period July 31st-August 10th, 1967.

We greet you as comrades because it becomes increasingly clear to us each day that we share with you a common struggle. We have a common enemy. Our enemy is white Western imperialist society. (Note that we use the term white Western *society* as opposed to white Western *civilization.* The West has never been civilized. It has no right to speak of itself as a civilization.) Our struggle is to overthrow this system which feeds itself and expands itself through the economic and cultural exploitation of non-white, non-Western peoples—the THIRD WORLD.

We share with you also a common vision of the establishment of humanistic societies in the place of those now existing. We seek

345

with you to change the power base of the world, where mankind will share resources of their nations, instead of having to give them up to foreign plunderers, where civilizations can retain their cultural sovereignty instead of being forced to submit to foreign rulers who impose their own corrupt cultures on those civilizations they would dominate.

Anglo society has been nearly successful in keeping all of us—the oppressed of the Third World—separated and fragmented. They do this for their survival, because if we felt our unity we would know our strength. Especially here on this continent, where the Anglo is in the minority, he has for hundreds of years succeeded in keeping all of us who are oppressed from realizing our common plight. But the call of Che Guevara for a continental struggle against a common enemy would seem to ameliorate this fragmentation among those who would resist Western imperialism.

We speak with you, comrades, because we wish to make clear that we understand that our destinies are intertwined. Our world can only be the Third World; our only struggle, for the Third World; our only vision, of the Third World.

Until recently, most African-Americans thought that the best way to alleviate their oppression was through attempts at integration into the society. If we could enjoy public accommodations in the United States (motels, hotels, restaurants, etc.) our condition would be alleviated, many of us believed. This attitude was characteristic of the "Civil Rights movement" and clearly points up the bourgeois character of that "movement." Only the *bourgeoisie* are in a position to be concerned about public accommodations.

The African-American masses, on the other hand, do not have any jobs, any housing worthy of the name "decent," nor the money to enjoy restaurants, hotels, motels, etc. The "Civil Rights movement" did not actively involve the masses, because it did not speak to the needs of the masses. Nonetheless, the "Civil Rights movement" was a beginning, and because its aims met resistance throughout the United States, depths of racism heretofore unrecognized were laid bare. It had been thought that the aims of the "Civil Rights movement" would be easily realizable, because the United States Constitution supported them. But thousands of African-Americans were jailed, intimidated, beaten, and some murdered, for agitating for those rights guaranteed by the Constitution, but only available to whites.

Eventually, the United States Congress passed a Civil Rights Bill and a Voting Rights Bill, assuring us of those rights for which we had been agitating. By this time, however, more and more of us were realizing that our problems would not be solved by the enacting of these laws. In fact, these laws did not begin to speak to our problems. Our problems were an inherent part of the capitalist system and therefore could not be alleviated within that system. The African-American masses had been outside the "Civil Rights movement." For four years they watched to see if any significant changes would come from the non-violent demonstrations. It became clear to us that nothing would change and in the summer of 1964, only a couple of weeks after the Civil Rights Bill was passed, the first of what are now over one hundred rebellions occurred. The following year, the same year that the Voting Rights Bill was enacted, one of the largest rebellions occurred in Watts.

These rebellions were violent uprisings in which African-Americans exchanged gunfire with policemen and army troops, burned down stores and took from the stores those commodities that are rightfully ours—food and clothing—and which we never had. These rebellions are increasing in intensity and frequency each year until now practically every major city has seen us rise to say, "We will seize the day or be killed in the attempt."

The "Civil Rights movement" could never attempt and hold the young bloods who clearly understood the savagery of white United States and who are ready to meet this savagery with armed resistance. It is the young bloods who contain especially the hatred Che Guevara speaks of when he says, "Hatred is an element of the struggle . . . relentless hatred of the enemy that impels us over and beyond the natural limitations of man and transforms us into an effective, violent, selected and cold killing machine."

The Black Power movement has been the catalyst for the bringing together of these young bloods: the real revolutionary proletariat, ready to fight by any means necessary for the liberation of our people. In exposing the extent of racism and exploitation which permeates all institutions in the United States, the Black Power movement has unique appeal to young black students on campuses across the country. These students have been deluded by the fiction that exists in white North America that if the black man would educate himself and behave himself he would be acceptable enough to leave the ranks of the oppressed and join white society.

This year, when provoked by savage white policemen, students on many campuses fought back, whereas before they had accepted these incidents without rebellion. As students are a part of these rebellions they begin to acquire a resistance consciousness. They begin to realize that white North America might let a very few of them escape one by one into the mainstream of her society, but as soon as blacks move in concert around their blackness, she will reply with a fury which reveals her true racist nature.

We are moving to control our African-American communities as you are moving to wrest control of your countries—of the entire Latin continent—from the hands of foreign imperialist powers. Therefore there is only one course open to us.

We must change North America so that the economy and politics of the country will be in the hands of the people. Our particular concern is our people—African-Americans. But it is clear that a community based on the community ownership of all resources could not exist within the present capitalist framework. For the total transformation to take place, whites must see the struggle that we're engaged in as being their own struggle. At the present time, they do not. Even though the white worker is exploited, he sees his own best interest lying with the power structure. Because of the racist nature of this country, we cannot work in white communities, but have asked those whites who work with us to go into their own communities to begin propagandizing and organizing. When the white workers realize their true condition, then there will exist the possibilities for alliances between ourselves and them. However, we cannot wait for this to happen, or despair if it does not happen.

The struggle we are engaged in is international. We well know that what happens in Vietnam affects our struggle here and what we do affects the struggle of the Vietnamese people. This is even more apparent when we look at ourselves not as African-Americans of the United States, but as African-Americans of the Americas.

At the present moment, the power structure has sown the seeds of hate and discord between African-Americans and Spanish-speaking people in the large cities where they live. In the State of California, Mexican-Americans and Spanish-speaking people comprise almost 50 per cent of the population, yet the two view each other with suspicion, and sometimes outright hostility. We recognize this as the old trick of "divide and conquer" and we are working to see that it does not succeed this time.

Last week Puerto Ricans and blacks took to the streets together in New York City to fight against the police, which demonstrates success in this area. Our destiny cannot be separated from the destiny of the Spanish-speaking people in the United States and of the Americas. Our victory will not be achieved unless they celebrate their liberation side by side with us. For it is not their struggle, but our struggle.

We have already pledged ourselves to do what we are asked to aid the struggle for the independence of Puerto Rico, to free it from domination by United States business and military interests. And we look upon Cuba as a shining example of hope in our hemisphere. We do not view our struggle as being contained within the boundaries of the United States as they are defined by present-day maps. Instead, we look to the day when a true United States of America will extend from Tierra del Fuego to Alaska, when those formerly oppressed will stand together, a liberated people.

Our people are a colony within the United States; you are colonies outside the United States. It is more than a figure of speech to say that the black communities in America are the victims of white imperialism and colonial exploitation. This is in practical economic and political terms true.

There are over thirty million of us in the United States. For the most part we live in sharply defined areas; in the rural black belt areas and shanty-towns of the South, and more and more in the slums of the northern and western industrial cities. It is estimated that in another five to ten years, two-thirds of our thirty million will be in the ghettos—in the heart of the cities. Joining us are the hundreds of thousands of Puerto Ricans, Mexican-American and American-Indian populations. The American city is, in essence, populated by people of the Third World, while the white middle class flee the cities to the suburbs.

In these cities we do not control our resources. We do not control the land, the houses or the stores. These are owned by whites who live outside the community. These are very real colonies, as their capital and cheap labor are exploited by those who live outside the cities. White power makes the laws and enforces those laws with guns and night-sticks in the hands of white racist policemen and black mercenaries. The capitalist system gave birth to these black enclaves and formally articulated the terms of their colonial and dependent status, as was done, for example, by the *apartheid* Government of Azania (South Africa), which the United States keeps alive by its support.

The struggle for Black Power in this country is the struggle to free these colonies from external domination. But we do not seek to create communities where, in place of white rulers, black rulers control the lives of black masses and where black money goes into a few black pockets: we want to see it go into the communal pocket. The society we seek to build among black people is not an oppressive capitalist society, for capitalism by its very nature cannot create structures free from exploitation. We are fighting for the redistribution of wealth and for the end of private property inside the United States.

The question that may be asked is, how does the struggle to free these internal colonies relate to your struggle to destroy imperialism? We realistically survey our numbers and know that is is not possible for black people to take over the entire country militarily and hold large areas of land. In a highly industrialized nation the struggle is different. The heart of production and the heart of commercial trade is in the cities. We are in the cities. With our rebellions we have become a disruptive force in the flow of services, goods and capital.

Since 1966, the cry of the rebellions has been "Black Power." In this cry, there was an ideology implied which the masses understood instinctively. It is because we are powerless that we are oppressed, and it is only with power that we can make the decisions governing our lives and our communities. Those who have power have everything; those who are without power have nothing. Without power we have to beg for what is rightfully ours. With power we will take our birthright, because it was with power that our birthright was taken from us.

Black Power is more than a slogan; it is a way of looking at our problems and the beginning of a solution to them. It attacks racism and exploitation, the horns of the bull that seeks to gore us.

The United States is a racist country. From its very beginning it has built itself upon the subjugation of colored people. The Europeans who settled the United States systematically stole the land and destroyed the native population, the Indians, forcing them eventually on to reservations where they live today, a mere 0.3 per cent of the total population. And at the same time the United States was waging genocide against the Indians, it was raping the African Continent of its natives and bringing them to the Americas to work as slaves.

To enslave another human being, one needs a justification; and the United States has always found this justification in proclaiming the superiority of whites and the inferiority of non-whites. We are called "niggers"; Spanish-speaking people are called "spics"; the Chinese "chinks"; the Vietnamese "gooks." By dehumanizing us and all others of color, it therefore becomes just, in the mind of the white man, that we should be enslaved, exploited and oppressed. However, it becomes even easier to keep a man a slave when he himself can be convinced that he is inferior. How much easier it is to keep a man in chains by making him believe in his own inferiority! As long as he does, he will keep himself in chains. As long as a slave allows himself to be defined as a slave by the master, he will be a slave, even if the master dies.

This technique has been successfully practised not only against us, but wherever people have been enslaved, oppressed and exploited. We can see it happening today in the schools of large United States cities, where Puerto Rican and Mexican children are not allowed to speak Spanish and are taught nothing of their country and their history. It is apparent in many African countries, where one is not considered educated unless one has studied in France and speaks French.

Black Power attacks this brain-washing by saying, WE WILL DEFINE OURSELVES. We will no longer accept the white man's definition of ourselves as ugly, ignorant and uncultured. We will recognize our own beauty and our own culture and will no longer be ashamed of ourselves, for a people ashamed of themselves cannot be free. Because our color has been used as a weapon to oppress us, we must use our color as a weapon of liberation. This is the same as other people using their nationality as a weapon for their liberation.

This coming together around our race was an inevitable part of our struggle. We recognize, however, that this is not the totality, only the necessary beginning. Black Power recognizes that while we are made to feel inferior, this is only so that we may be more easily exploited. Even if we destroy racism, we would not necessarily destroy exploitation. Thus, we must constantly launch a two-pronged attack; we must constantly keep our eyes on both of the bull's horns.

Color and culture were and are key in our oppression. Therefore our analysis of history and our economic analysis are rooted in these concepts. Our historical analysis, for example, views the United States as being conceived in racism. Although the first settlers themselves were escaping from oppression, and although their armed uprising against their mother country was around the aggravations of colonialism—"taxation without representation," etc.—the white European settlers could not extend their lofty theories of democracy to the Indian, whom they systematically exterminated as they expanded into the interior of the country. Indeed, in that same town where the settlers set up their model of government based on the theory of representative democracy—in that same town the first slaves were brought from Africa.

In our economic analysis our interpretation of Marx comes not only from his writings, but from how we see capitalism's relationships to people of color.

The Labor movement of the United States, while in the beginning containing some great leaders in the struggle against the absolute control of the economy by the industrial lords, essentially fought only for more money. Those few who had the vision of extending the fight for workers' control of production, never succeeded in transmitting their entire vision to the rank and file. This Labor movement found itself asking the industrial lords not to give up their control but merely to pass out a few more of the fruits of this control. Unlike us, they do not raise questions of redistributing the wealth inside the United States.

Thereby did the United States anticipate the prophecy of Marx and avoid the inevitable class struggle within the country by expanding into the Third World and exploiting the resources and slave labor of people of color. United States capitalists never cut down on their domestic profits to share with the workers. Instead they expanded internationally and threw the bones of their profits to the American working class.

The American working class enjoys the fruits of the labors of the Third World workers. The proletariat has become the Third World; the *bourgeoisie* is white Western society.

The true potential revolutionaries in this country are the black youths of the ghettos; those who have developed insurgence in the cities are African-American and Latin communities, where past rebellions have taught important lessons in dealing with the Government's armed reaction to our uprisings.

These rebellions should not be taken lightly. In the past three years, there have been over one hundred uprisings in the internal colonies of the United States. These are no doubt reported to you as "minor disturbances initiated by a few malcontents." These are major rebellions with large numbers of participants who are developing a consciousness of resistance.

It is with increasing concern that we see the United States will by any means necessary attempt to prevent the liberation struggles sweeping across the Third World. But in particular we know that the United States fears most the liberation struggle on this continent. In order to secure itself geographically, the United States must have Latin America—economically, politically and culturally. It will not do for the Anglos to be isolated on a continent of hostiles.

"Black Power" not only addresses itself to exploitation, but to the problem of cultural integrity.

Wherever imperialism has gone, she has imposed her culture by force on other peoples, forcing them to adopt her language and way of life. When African slaves were brought to this country, the Anglo saw that if he took away the language of the African, he broke one of the bonds which kept them united and struggling. Africans were forbidden to speak to each other in their own language. If they were found doing so, they were savagely beaten into silence.

Western society has always understood the importance of language to a people's cultural consciousness and integrity. When it moves into the Third World, it has moved to impose its own language. In Puerto Rico, where Yankee cultural imposition is at its height, English is taught in all high schools for three years, while Spanish is taught for two years.

Anglo society learned other valuable lessons from the enslavement of Africans in this country. If you separate a man's family, as was done to the slaves, you again weaken his resistance. But carry the separation further. Take a few of the weaker slaves and treat them as house pets—the lighter skinned slave (the offspring of the master's rape of the African woman) was preferred. Give him the crumbs from the master's table and cast-off clothing and soon he will fear to lose these small comforts. Then use his fears by getting him to report on the activities of the bad slaves, report the impending revolts and uprisings. Distrust and dissent is created among the Africans, and thus they will fight among themselves instead of uniting to fight their oppressors.

Today's descendants of African slaves brought to America have been separated from their cultural and national roots. Black children are not taught of the glory of African civilization in the history of mankind; they are instead taught about Africa, the dark continent inhabited by man-eating savages. They are not taught of the thousands of black martyrs who died resisting the white slave masters. They are not taught of the numerous uprisings and revolts where hundreds of brave Africans refused to submit to slavery. Instead, their history books read of "happy slaves singing in their fields . . . content with their new lives." Those "few" slaves who did resist are called "troublemakers," "malcontents," "crazy."

Black children in North America grow up aspiring only to enter white society—not only because white society eats better, is housed and clothed better and can make a better living, but also because they have been bombarded by the white-controlled communications media and educated by black teachers with white minds (our petty Yankees) that white IS better, white is beautiful. Anglo features, manner of speech and aspirations are to be acquired if one is to be successful, even *within* the black community.

The white man hardly needs to police his colonies within this country, for he has plundered the cultures and enslaved the minds of the people of color until their resistance is paralyzed by self-hate. An important fight in the Third World, therefore, is the fight for cultural integrity. Wherever Western society has gone, as Frantz Fanon tells us, she has imposed through force her culture. Through force and bribery (the giving of a few crumbs to a few petty Yankees) the people of a conquered country begin to believe the Western culture is better than their own. The young people begin to put aside the richness of their native culture to take on the tinsel of Western culture. They become ashamed of their roots and inevitably can only be trapped in a life of self-hate and private pursuit for self-gain.

Thus does the West entrap whole peoples with little resistance. One of our major battles is to root out corrupt Western values, and our resistance cannot prevail unless our cultural integrity is restored and maintained. It is from our people's history, therefore, that we know our struggles and your struggles are the same. We have difficulty getting the information we need on what is happening in your countries. In so many ways we are illiterate of your heroes, your battles and your victories. We are working now to increase the consciousness of the African-American, so it will extend internationally. The United States fears this more than anything else, not only because such a consciousness would destroy within black communities the minority complex so carefully cultivated by the Anglos, but because it knows that if the black man realizes that the counter-insurgency efforts of this country are directed against his brother, he will not go, he cannot go. Then it will become crystal clear to the world that the imperialist wars are racist wars.

During the past year we have instituted a black resistance to the draft movement, not only because we are against black men fighting their brothers in Vietnam, but also because we are certain that the next Vietnam will be on this continent. Perhaps Bolivia, where there are now "special forces advisers"; perhaps Guatemala, Brazil, Peru or the Dominican Republic.

The African-American has tried for the past four hundred years to exist peacefully inside the country. It has been to no avail. Our history demonstrates that the reward for trying to coexist peacefully has been the physical and psychological murder of our peoples. We have been lynched, our houses have been bombed and our churches burned. We are now being shot down in the streets like dogs by white racist policemen and we can no longer accept this oppression without retribution. We must join those who are for armed struggle around the world.

We understand that as we expand our resistance and internationalize the consciousness of our people, as our martyred brother Malcolm X taught us, retaliation from the Government will come to us as it did to him. As the resistance struggle escalates, we are well aware of the reality of Che Guevara's words that the "struggle will not be a mere street fight . . . but will be long and harsh." In the end our common brotherhood sustains us all, as we struggle for our liberation by any means necessary.

But Black Power means that we see ourselves as part of the Third World; that we see our struggle as closely related to liberation struggles around the world. We must hook up with these struggles. We must, for example, ask ourselves: when black people in Africa begin to storm Johannesburg, when Latin Americans revolt, what will be the role of the United States and that of African-Americans?

It seems inevitable that this nation will move to protect its financial interests in South Africa and Latin America, which means protecting white rule in these countries. Black people in the United States, then, have the responsibility to oppose—at least, to neutralize—that effort by the United States. This is but one example of many such situations that have already arisen around the world—with more to come.

There is only one place for black Americans in these struggles, and that is on the side of the Third World. Frantz Fanon, in *The Wretched of the Earth,* puts forth clearly the reasons for this and the relationship of the concept of a new force in the world:

> Let us decide not to imitate Europe; let us try to create the whole man, whom Europe has been incapable of bringing to triumphant birth.
>
> Two centuries ago, a former European colony decided to catch up with Europe. It succeeded so well that the United States of America became a monster, in which the taints, the sickness and the inhumanity of Europe has grown to appalling dimensions. . . .
> The Third World today faces Europe like a colossal mass who aim should be to try to resolve the problems to which Europe has not been able to find the answers. . . .

It is a question of the Third World starting a new history of man, a history that will have regard to the sometimes prodigious theses which Europe has put forward, but that will also not forget Europe's crimes, of which the most horrible was committed in the heart of man, and consisted of the pathological tearing apart of his functions and the crumbling away of his unity.

No, there is no question of a return to nature. It is simply a very concrete question of not dragging men toward mutilation, of not imposing upon the brain rhythms—which very quickly obliterate it and wreck it. The pretext of catching up must not be used to push man around, to tear him away from himself or from his privacy, to break and kill him.

No, we do not want to catch up with anyone. What we want to do is go forward all the time, night and day, in the company of man, in the company of all men.

23

ERNESTO CHE GUEVARA

Create Two, Three, Many Vietnams

> Now is the time of the furnaces, and
> only light should be seen.
>
> *José Martí*

Twenty-one years have already elapsed since the end of the last world conflagration; numerous publications in every possible language celebrate this event, symbolized by the defeat of Japan. There is a climate of apparent optimism in many areas of the different camps into which the world is divided.

Twenty-one years without a world war, in these times of maximum confrontations, of violent clashes and sudden changes, appears to be a very high figure. However, without analyzing the practical results of this peace (poverty, degradation, increasing exploitation of enormous sectors of humanity) for which all of us have stated that we are willing to fight, we would do well to inquire if this peace is real.

It is not the purpose of these notes to detail the different conflicts of a local character that have been occurring since the surrender of Japan, neither do we intend to recount the numerous and increasing instances of civilian strife which have taken place during these years of apparent peace. It will be enough just to name, as an example against undue optimism, the wars of Korea and Viet Nam.

In the first of these, after years of savage warfare, the Northern part of the country was submerged in the most terrible devastation known in the annals of modern warfare: riddled with bombs; without factories, schools or hospitals; with absolutely no shelter for housing ten million inhabitants.

Under the discredited flag of the United Nations, dozens of countries under the military leadership of the United States participated in this war with the massive intervention of U.S. soldiers and the use, as cannon fodder, of the drafted South Korean population. On the other side, the army and the people of Korea and the volunteers from the People's Republic of China were furnished with supplies and technical aid by the Soviet military apparatus. The U.S. tested all sorts of weapons of destruction, excluding the thermonuclear type, but including, on a limited scale, bacteriological and chemical warfare.

In Viet Nam, the patriotic forces of that country have carried on an almost uninterrupted war against three imperialist powers: Japan, whose might suffered an almost vertical collapse after the bombs of Hiroshima and Nagasaki; France, that recovered from that defeated country its Indo-China colonies and ignored the promises it had made in harder times; and the United States, in this last phase of the struggle.

There have been limited confrontations in every continent although in Our America, for a long time, there were only incipient liberation struggles and military coups d'état until the Cuban Revolution sounded the alert, signaling the importance of this region. This action attracted the wrath of the imperialists and Cuba was finally obliged to defend its coasts, first in Playa Girón, and again during the October [Missile] Crisis.

This last incident could have unleashed a war of incalculable proportions if a US-Soviet clash had occurred over the Cuban question.

But, evidently, the focal point of all contradictions is at present the territory of the peninsula of Indo-China and the adjacent areas. Laos and Viet Nam are torn by civil wars which have ceased being such by the entry into the conflict of U.S. imperialism with all its might, thus transforming the whole zone into a dangerous powder keg ready at any moment to explode.

In Viet Nam the confrontation has assumed extremely acute characteristics. It is not our intention, either, to chronicle this war. We shall simply remember and point out some milestones.

In 1954, after the annihilating defeat of Dien Bien Phu, an agreement was signed at Geneva dividing the country into two separate zones; elections were to be held within a term of 18 months to determine who should govern Viet Nam and how the country should be reunified. The U.S. did not sign this document and started maneuvering to substitute the emperor, Bao Dai, who was a French puppet, for a man more amenable to its purposes. This happened to be Ngo Dien Diem, whose tragic end—that of an orange squeezed dry by imperialism—is well known by all.

During the months following the agreement, optimism reigned supreme in the camp of the popular forces. The last redoubts of the anti-French resistance were dismantled in the South of the country and they awaited the fulfillment of the Geneva Agreements. But the patriots soon realized there would be no elections—unless the United States felt itself capable of imposing its will in the polls, which was practically impossible even resorting to all its fraudulent methods. Once again fighting broke out in the South and gradually acquired full intensity. At present the U.S. invading army has increased to nearly half a million troops, while the puppet forces decrease in number and, above all, have totally lost their combativeness.

Almost two years ago the United States started systematically bombing the Democratic Republic of Viet Nam, in yet another attempt to overcome the resistance of the South and impose, from a position of strength, a meeting at the conference table. At first, the bombardments were more or less isolated occurrences and were represented as reprisals for alleged provocations from the North. Later on, as they increased in intensity and regularity, they became one gigantic attack carried out by the air force of the United States, day after day, for the purpose of destroying all vestiges of civilization in the Northern zones of the country. This is an episode of the infamously notorious "escalation."

The material aspirations of the Yankee world have been fulfilled to a great extent, despite the unflinching defense of the Vietnamese anti-aircraft artillery, of the numerous planes shot down (over 1,700) and of the socialist countries' aid in war supplies.

This is the sad reality: Viet Nam—a nation representing the aspirations, the hopes of a whole world of forgotten peoples—is tragically alone. This nation must endure the furious attacks of U.S. technology, with practically no possibility of reprisals in the South and only some of defense in the North—but always alone.

The solidarity of all progressive forces of the world with the people of Viet Nam today is similar to the bitter irony of the plebeians urging on the gladiators in the Roman arena. It is not a matter of wishing success to the victim of aggression, but of sharing his fate; one must accompany him to his death or to victory.

When we analyze the lonely situation of the Vietnamese people, we are overcome by anguish at this illogical fix in which humanity finds itself.

U.S. imperialism is guilty of aggression—its crimes are enormous and cover the whole world. We already know all that, gentlemen! But this guilt also applies to those who, when the time came for a definition, hesitated to make Viet Nam an inviolable part of the socialist world; running, of course, the risks of a war on a global scale—but also forcing a decision upon imperialism. The guilt also applies to those who maintain a war of abuse and maneuvering— started quite some time ago by the representatives of the two greatest powers of the socialist camp.

We must ask ourselves, seeking an honest answer: is Viet Nam isolated, or is it not? Is it not maintaining a dangerous equilibrium between the two quarrelling powers?

And what great people these are! What stoicism and courage! And what a lesson for the world is contained in this struggle! Not for a long time shall we be able to know if President Johnson ever seriously thought of bringing about some of the reforms needed by his people—to iron out the barbed class contradictions that grow each day with explosive power. The truth is that the improvements announced under the pompous title of the "Great Society" have been poured down the drain of Viet Nam.

The largest of all imperialist powers feels in its own guts the bleeding inflicted by a poor and underdeveloped country; its fabulous economy feels the strain of the war effort. Murder is ceasing to be the most convenient business for its monopolies. Defensive weapons, and never in adequate number, is all these extraordinary Vietnamese soldiers have—besides love for their homeland, their society, and unsurpassed courage. But imperialism is bogging down in Viet Nam, is unable to find a way out and desperately seeks one that will overcome with dignity this dangerous situation in which it now finds itself. Furthermore, the Four Points put forward by the North and the Five Points of the South now corner imperialism, making the confrontation even more decisive.

Everything indicates that peace, this unstable peace which bears the name for the sole reason that no world-wide conflagration has taken place, is again in danger of being destroyed by some irrevocable and unacceptable step taken by the United States.

What role shall we, the exploited people of the world, play? The peoples of the three continents focus their attention on Viet Nam and learn their lesson. Since imperialists blackmail humanity by threatening it with war, the wise reaction is not to fear war. The general tactics of the people should be to launch a constant and a firm attack on all fronts where the confrontation is taking place.

In those places where the meager peace we have has been violated, what is our duty? To liberate ourselves at any price.

The world panorama is of great complexity. The struggle for liberation has not yet been undertaken by some countries of ancient Europe, sufficiently developed to realize the contradictions of capitalism, but weak to such a degree that they are unable either to follow imperialism or to start on their own road. Their contradictions will reach an explosive stage during the forthcoming years—but their problems and, consequently, their solutions are different from those of our dependent and economically underdeveloped countries.

The fundamental field of imperialist exploitation comprises the three underdeveloped continents: America, Asia, and Africa. Every country has also its own characteristics, but each continent, as a whole, also presents a certain unity. Our America is integrated by a group of more or less homogeneous countries and in most parts of its territory U.S. monopoly capital maintains an absolute supremacy. Puppet government or, in the best of cases, weak and fearful local rulers, are incapable of contradicting orders from their Yankee master. The United States has nearly reached the climax of its political and economic domination; it could hardly advance much; any change in the situation could bring about a setback. Its policy is to maintain that which has already been conquered. The line of action, at the present time, is limited to the brutal use of force with the purpose of thwarting the liberation movements, no matter of what type they might happen to be.

The slogan "we will not allow another Cuba" hides the possibility of perpetrating aggressions without fear of reprisal, such as the one carried out against the Dominican Republic, or before that, the massacre in Panama—and the clear warning stating that Yankee troops are ready to intervene anywhere in America where the established order may be altered, thus endangering their interests. This policy enjoys an almost absolute impunity: the OAS is a suitable mask, in spite of its unpopularity; the inefficiency of the UN is ridiculous as well as tragic; the armies of all American countries are ready to intervene in order to smash their peoples. The International of Crime and Treason has in fact been organized. On the other hand, the national bourgeoisies have lost all their capacity to oppose imperialism—if they ever had it—and they have become the last card in the pack. There are no other alternatives; either a socialist revolution or a make-believe revolution.

Asia is a continent with different characteristics. The struggle for liberation waged against a series of European colonial powers resulted in the establishment of more or less progressive governments, whose ulterior evolution has brought about, in some cases, the reaffirming of the primary objectives of national liberation and in others, a setback towards the adoption of proimperialist positions.

From the economic point of view, the United States had very little to lose and much to gain in Asia. These changes benefited their interests; the struggle for the overthrow of other neocolonial powers and the penetration of new spheres of action in the economic field is carried out sometimes directly, occasionally through Japan.

But there are special political conditions, in Asia, particularly in Indo-China, which create certain characteristics of capital importance and play a decisive role in the entire U.S. military strategy.

The imperialists encircle China through South Korea, Japan, Taiwan, South Viet Nam, and Thailand, at least.

This dual situation, a strategic interest as important as the military encirclement of the People's Republic of China and the penetration of these great markets—which they do not dominate yet—turns Asia into one of the most explosive points of the world today, in spite of its apparent stability outside of the Vietnamese war zone.

The Middle East, though geographically a part of this continent, has its own contradictions and is actively in ferment; it is impossible to foretell how far the cold war between Israel, backed by the imperialists, and the progressive countries of that zone will go. This is just another of the volcanoes threatening eruption in the world today.

Africa offers an almost virgin territory to the neocolonial invasion. There have been changes which, to some extent, forced neocolonial powers to give up their former absolute prerogatives. But when these changes are carried out without interruption, colonialism continues in the form of neocolonialism with similar effects as far as the economic situation is concerned.

The United States had no colonies in this region but is now struggling to penetrate its partners' fiefs. It can be said that following the strategic plans of U.S. imperialism, Africa constitutes its long-range reservoir; its present investments, though, are only important in the Union of South Africa and its penetration is beginning to be felt in the Congo, Nigeria and other countries where a sharp rivalry with other imperialist powers is beginning to take place (non-violent up to the present time).

So far, it does not have great interests to defend there except its assumed right to intervene in every spot of the world where its monopolies detect the possibility of huge profits or the existence of large reserves of raw materials.

All this past history justifies our concern over the possibilities of liberating the peoples within a moderate or a short period of time.

If we stop to analyze Africa we observe that in the Portuguese colonies of Guinea, Mozambique, and Angola the struggle is waged with relative intensity, with particular success in the first and with variable success in the other two. We still witness in the Congo the dispute between Lumumba's successors and the old accomplices of Tshombe, a dispute which at the present time seems to favor the latter, those who "pacified" a large area of the country for their own benefit—though the war is still latent.

In Rhodesia we have a different problem: British imperialism used every means within its reach to place power in the hands of the white minority, now in control. The conflict, from the British point of view, is absolutely unofficial; this Western power, with its habitual diplomatic cleverness—also called hypocrisy in plain language—presents a facade of displeasure before the measures adopted by the government of Ian Smith. Its crafty attitude is supported and followed by some Commonwealth countries, but is attacked by a large group of countries belonging to Black Africa, even by some that are still docile economic vassals of British imperialism.

Should the efforts of Rhodesia's black patriots to organize armed rebellion crystallize and should this movement be effectively supported by neighboring African nations, the situation in that country could become extremely explosive. But for the moment all these problems are being discussed in such innocuous organizations as the UN, the Commonwealth and the OAU.

Nevertheless, the social and political evolution of Africa does not lead us to expect a continental revolution. The liberation struggle against the Portuguese should end victoriously, but Portugal means nothing in the imperialist field. The confrontations of revolutionary importance are those which place at bay all the imperialist apparatus, though this does not mean that we should stop fighting for the liberation of the three Portuguese colonies and for the deepening of their revolutions.

When the black masses of South Africa or Rhodesia start their authentic revolutionary struggle, a new era will dawn in Africa. Or when the impoverished masses of a nation rise up to rescue their right to a decent life from the hands of the ruling oligarchies.

Up to now, army putsches have followed one another; a group of officers succeeds one another or replaces rulers who no longer serve their caste interests and those of the powers who covertly manage them—but there are no great popular upheavals. In the Congo these characteristics appeared briefly, generated by the memory of Lumumba, but they have been losing strength in the last few months.

In Asia, as we have seen, the situation is explosive. The points of friction are not only Viet Nam and Laos, where actual fighting is going on, but also Cambodia, where a direct U.S. aggression may start at any time, Thailand, Malaya, and, of course, Indonesia, where we cannot assume that the last word has been said, despite the annihilation of the Communist Party of that country carried out by the reactionaries when they took power. And also, naturally, there is the Middle East.

In Latin America armed struggle is underway in Guatemala, Colombia, Venezuela, and Bolivia and the first uprisings are appearing in Brazil. Other foci of resistance appear and are later extinguished. But almost every country of this continent is ripe for a type of struggle that, in order to achieve victory, cannot be content with anything less than establishing a government of a socialist nature.

On this continent, for all practical purposes, only one tongue is spoken (with the exception of Brazil, with whose people those who speak Spanish can easily make themselves understood, owing to the great similarity of both languages). There is also a great similarity among the classes of the different countries, and an identification exists among them, as an "international American" type, much more complete than that of other continents. Language, customs, religion, a common foreign master, unite them. The degree and forms of exploitation are similar for both the exploiters and the exploited in many of the countries of Our America. And rebellion is ripening swiftly.

We may ask ourselves: how will this rebellion come to fruition? What type will it be? We have maintained for quite some time now that, owing to the similarity of national characteristics, the struggle in Our America will achieve, in due course, continental proportions. It will be the scene of many great battles fought for the liberation of humanity.

Within the overall struggle on a continental scale, the battles which are now taking place are only episodes—but they have already furnished their martyrs, who will figure in the history of Our America as having given their necessary quota of blood in this last stage of the fight for the total freedom of Man. These names will include Major Turcios Lima, the priest Camilo Torres, Major Fabricio Ojeda, Majors Lobatón and Luis de la Puente Uceda, all outstanding figures in the revolutionary movements of Guatemala, Colombia, Venezuela, and Peru.

But the active mobilization of the people creates new leaders; César Montes and Yon Sosa raise the flag of battle in Guatemala; Fabio Vázquez and Marulanda in Colombia; Douglas Bravo in the western half of the country and Américo Martín in El Bachiller direct their respective fronts in Venezuela. New uprisings will take place in these and other countries of Our America, as has already happened in Bolivia; they will continue to grow in the midst of all the hardships inherent in this dangerous profession of the modern revolutionary. Many will perish, victims of their errors; others will fall in the hard battle ahead; new fighters and new leaders will appear in the heat of the revolutionary struggle. The people will produce their fighters and leaders in the selective process of the war itself—and Yankee agents of repression will increase. Today there are military "advisers" in all the countries where armed struggle exists, and the Peruvian army, trained and advised by the Yankees, apparently carried out a successful action against the revolutionaries in that country. But if the foci of war grow with sufficient political and military wisdom, they will become practically invincible, obliging the Yankees to send reinforcements. In Peru itself many new figures, practically unknown, are now tenaciously and firmly reorganizing the guerrilla movement. Little by little, the obsolete weapons which are sufficient for the repression of small armed bands will be exchanged for modern armaments and the U.S. military "advisers" will be substituted by U.S. soldiers until, at a given moment, they will be forced to send increasingly greater numbers of regular troops to ensure the relative stability of a government whose national puppet army is disintegrating before the attacks of the guerrillas. It is the road of Viet Nam; it is the road that should be followed by the peoples of the world; it is the road that will be followed in Our America, with the special characteristic that the armed groups may create something like Coordinating Councils to frustrate the repressive efforts of Yankee imperialism and contribute to the revolutionary cause.

America, a forgotten continent in the world's more recent liberation struggles, which is now beginning to make itself heard through the Tricontinental in the voice of the vanguard of its peoples, the Cuban Revolution, has before it a task of much greater relevance: to create a Second or a Third Viet Nam, or the Second and Third Viet Nam of the world.

We must bear in mind that imperialism is a world system, the last stage of capitalism—and it must be defeated in a great world confrontation. The strategic end of this struggle must be the destruction of imperialism. Our part, the responsibility of the exploited and underdeveloped of the world, is to eliminate the foundations of imperialism: our oppressed nations, from which they extract capital, raw materials, cheap technicians and common labor, and to which they export new capital—instrument of domination—arms and every kind of article, submerging us in absolute dependence.

The fundamental element of this strategic end is, then, the real liberation of all peoples, a liberation that will be brought about in most cases through armed struggle and will, in Our America, almost certainly have the characteristic of becoming a Socialist Revolution.

In envisaging the destruction of imperialism, it is necessary to identify its head, which is no other than the United States of America.

We must carry out a general task which has as its tactical purpose drawing the enemy out of his natural environment, forcing him to fight in places where his living habits clash with the existing reality. We must not underrate our adversary; the U.S. soldier has technical capacity and is backed by weapons and resources of such magnitude as to render him formidable. He lacks the essential ideological motivation which his bitterest enemies of today—the Vietnamese soldiers—have in the highest degree. We will only be able to triumph over such an army by undermining its morale—and that is accomplished by causing it repeated defeats and repeated punishment.

But this brief scheme for victory implies immense sacrifice by the people, sacrifice that should be demanded beginning today, in plain words, and which perhaps may be less painful than what they would have to endure if we constantly avoided battle in an attempt to have others pull our chestnuts out of the fire.

It is probable, of course, that the last country to liberate itself will accomplish this without armed struggle and that people may be spared the sufferings of a long and cruel war against the imperialists. But perhaps it will be impossible to avoid this struggle or its effects in a global conflagration and the last country's suffering may be the same, or even greater. We cannot foresee the future, but we should never give in to the defeatist temptation of being leaders of a nation that yearns for freedom but abhors the struggle it entails and awaits its freedom as a crumb of victory.

It is absolutely just to avoid all useless sacrifice. For that reason, it is necessary to study carefully the real possibilities that dependent America may have of liberating itself through peaceful means. For us, the answer to this question is quite clear: the present moment may or may not be the proper one for starting the struggle, but we cannot harbor any illusion, and we have no right to do so, that freedom can be obtained without fighting. And the battles will not be mere street fights with stones against teargas bombs, nor pacific general strikes; neither will they be those of a furious people destroying in two or three days the repressive superstructure of the ruling oligarchies. The struggle will be long, harsh, and its battle fronts will be the guerrilla's refuge, the cities, the homes of the fighters—where the repressive forces will go seeking easy victims among their families—among the massacred rural population, in the villages or cities destroyed by the bombardments of the enemy.

They themselves impel us to this struggle; there is no alternative other than to prepare it and decide to undertake it.

The beginnings will not be easy; they will be extremely difficult. All of the oligarchies' powers of repression, all of their capacity for brutality and demagoguery will be placed at the service of their cause. Our mission, in the first hour, will be to survive; later, we will follow the perennial example of the guerrilla, carrying out armed propaganda (in the Vietnamese sense, that is, the propaganda of bullets, of battles won or lost—but fought—against the enemy). The great lesson of the invincibility of the guerrillas will take root in the dispossessed masses. The galvanizing of the national spirit, preparation for harder tasks, for resisting even more violent repressions. Hatred as an element of struggle; relentless hatred of the enemy that impels us over and beyond the natural limitations of man and transforms us into effective, violent selective and cold killing machines. Our soldiers must be thus; a people without hatred cannot vanquish a brutal enemy. We must carry the war as far as the enemy carries it—to his home, to his centers of entertainment—in a total war. It is necessary to prevent him from having a moment of peace, a quiet moment outside his barracks or even inside; we must attack him wherever he may be, make him feel like a cornered beast wherever he may move. Then his morale will begin to fall. He will become still more savage, but we shall see the signs of decadence begin to appear.

And let us develop a true proletarian internationalism, with international proletarian armies; let the flag under which we fight be the sacred cause of redeeming humanity, so that to die under the flag of Viet Nam, of Venezuela, of Guatemala, of Laos, of Guinea, of Colombia, of Bolivia, of Brazil—to name only a few scenes of today's armed struggle—would be equally glorious and desirable for an American, an Asian, an African, or even a European.

Each drop of blood spilled in a country under whose flag one has been born is an experience for those who survive to apply later in the liberation struggle of their own countries. And each nation liberated is a step toward victory in the battle for the liberation of one's own country.

The time has come to settle our discrepancies and place everything we have at the service of the struggle.

We all know that great controversies agitate the world now fighting for freedom; no one can hide it. We also know that these controversies have reached such intensity and such bitterness that the possibility of dialogue and reconciliation seems extremely difficult, if not impossible. It is useless to search for means and ways to propitiate a dialogue which the hostile parties avoid. But the enemy is there; it strikes every day, and threatens us with new blows and these blows will unite us, today, tomorrow, or the day after. Whoever understands this first, and prepares for this necessary union will earn the people's gratitude.

Because of the virulence and the intransigence with which each cause is defended, we, the dispossessed, cannot take sides with one or the other form of manifestation of these discrepancies, even if we at times coincide with the contentions of one party or the other, or in greater measure with those of one part than with those of the other. In time of war, the expression of current differences constitutes a weakness; but as things stand at this moment, it is an illusion to hope to settle these differences by means of words. Time will erase them or give them their true explanation.

In our struggling world, all discrepancies regarding tactics and methods of action for the attainment of limited objectives should be analyzed with the respect that the opinions of others deserve. Regarding our great strategic objective, the total destruction of imperialism via armed struggle, we should be uncompromising.

Our aspirations to victory may be summed up thus: total destruction of imperialism by eliminating its firmest bulwark: imperialist domination by the United States of America. To carry out, as a tactical method, the gradual liberation of the peoples, one by one or in groups forcing the enemy into a difficult fight far from its own territory; liquidation of all of its sustaining bases, that is, its dependent territories.

This means a long war. And, we repeat once more, a cruel war. Let no one fool himself at the outstart and let no one hesitate to begin in fear of the consequences it may bring to his peoples. It is almost our sole hope for victory. We cannot elude the call of this hour. Viet Nam is pointing it out with its endless lesson of heroism, its tragic and everyday lesson of struggle and death for the attainment of final victory.

There, the imperialist soldiers encounter the discomforts of those who, accustomed to the vaunted U.S. standard of living, must face a hostile land, the insecurity of those who are unable to move without being aware of walking on enemy territory, death to those who advance beyond their fortified encampments, the permanent hostility of an entire population. All this provokes internal repercussions in the United States and propitiates the resurgence of a factor which was attenuated in the full vigor of imperialism: class struggle even within its own territory.

What a luminous, near future would be visible to us if two, three or many Viet Nams flourished throughout the world with their share of death and their immense tragedies, their everyday heroism and their repeated blows against imperialism obliging it to disperse its forces under the attack and the increasing hatred of all the people of the earth!

And if we were all capable of uniting to make our blows more solid and more infallible so that the effectiveness of every kind of support given to the struggling peoples were increased—how great and how near that future would be!

If we, those of us who, on a small point of the world map, fulfill our duty and place at the disposal of this struggle whatever little we are able to give: our lives, our sacrifice, must some day breathe our last breath in any land, not our own yet already ours, sprinkled with our blood, let it be known that we have measured the scope of our actions and that we consider ourselves no more than elements in the great army of the proletariat, but that we are proud to have learned from the Cuban Revolution, and from its maximum leader, the great lesson emanating from Cuba's attitude in this part of the world: "What do the dangers or the sacrifices of a man or a nation matter, when the destiny of humanity is at stake?"

Our every action is a battle cry against imperialism, and a call for the peoples' unity against the great enemy of mankind: the United States of America. Wherever death may surprise us, it will be welcome, provided that this, our battle cry, reach some receptive ear, that another hand be extended to take up our weapons and that other men come forward to intone our funeral dirge with the staccato of machine guns and new cries of battle and victory.

24

LIN PIAO

Defeat U.S. Imperialism by People's War

The Chinese revolution is a continuation of the great October Revolution. The road of the October Revolution is the common road for all people's revolutions. The Chinese revolution and the October Revolution have in common the following basic characteristics: (1) Both were led by the working class with a Marxist-Leninist party as its nucleus. (2) Both were based on the worker-peasant alliance. (3) In both cases state power was seized through violent revolution and the dictatorship of the proletariat was established. (4) In both cases the socialist system was built after victory in the revolution. (5) Both were component parts of the proletarian world revolution.

Naturally, the Chinese revolution had its own peculiar characteristics. The October Revolution took place in imperialist Russia, but the Chinese revolution broke out in a semi-colonial and semi-feudal country. The former was a proletarian socialist revolution, while the latter developed into a socialist revolution after the complete victory of the new-democratic revolution. The October Revolution began with armed uprisings in the cities and then spread to the countryside, while the Chinese revolution won nation-wide victory through the encirclement of the cities from the rural areas and the final capture of the cities.

Comrade Mao Tse-tung's great merit lies in the fact that he has succeeded in integrating the universal truth of Marxism-Leninism with the concrete practice of the Chinese revolution and has enriched and developed Marxism-Leninism by his masterly generalization and summation of the experience gained during the Chinese people's protracted revolutionary struggle.

Comrade Mao Tse-tung's theory of people's war has been proved by the long practice of the Chinese revolution to be in accord with the objective laws of such wars and to be invincible. It has not only been valid for China, it is a great contribution to the revolutionary struggles of the oppressed nations and peoples throughout the world.

The people's war led by the Chinese Communist Party, comprising the War of Resistance and the Revolutionary Civil Wars, lasted for twenty-two years. It constitutes the most drawn-out and most complex people's war led by the proletariat in modern history, and it has been the richest in experience.

In the last analysis, the Marxist-Leninist theory of proletarian revolution is the theory of the seizure of state power by revolutionary violence, the theory of countering war against the people by people's war. As Marx so aptly put it, "Force is the midwife of every old society pregnant with a new one."[1]

It was on the basis of the lessons derived from the people's wars in China that Comrade Mao Tse-tung, using the simplest and the most vivid language, advanced the famous thesis that "political power grows out of the barrel of a gun."[2]

He clearly pointed out:

> The seizure of power by armed force, the settlement of the issue by war, is the central task and the highest form of revolution. This Marxist-Leninist principle of revolution holds good universally, for China and for all other countries.[3]

War is the product of imperialism and the system of exploitation of man by man. Lenin said that "war is always and everywhere begun by the exploiters themselves, by the ruling and oppressing classes."[4] So long as imperialism and the system of exploitation of man by man exist, the imperialists and reactionaries will invariably rely on armed force to maintain their reactionary rule and impose war on the oppressed nations and peoples. This is an objective law independent of man's will.

In the world today, all the imperialists headed by the United States and their lackeys, without exception, are strengthening their state machinery, and especially their armed forces. U.S. imperialism, in particular, is carrying out armed aggression and suppression everywhere.

What should the oppressed nations and the oppressed people do in the face of wars of aggression and armed suppression by the imperialists and their lackeys? Should they submit and remain slaves in perpetuity? Or should they rise in resistance and fight for their liberation?

Comrade Mao Tse-tung answered this question in vivid terms. He said that after long investigation and study the Chinese people discovered that all the imperialists and their lackeys "have swords in their hands and are out to kill. The people have come to understand this and so act after the same fashion."[5] This is called doing unto them what they do unto us.

In the last analysis, whether one dares to wage a tit-for-tat struggle against armed aggression and suppression by the imperialists and their lackeys, whether one dares to fight a people's war against them, means whether one dares to embark on revolution. This is the most effective touchstone for distinguishing genuine from fake revolutionaries and Marxist-Leninists.

In view of the fact that some people were afflicted with the fear of the imperialists and reactionaries, Comrade Mao Tse-tung put forward his famous thesis that "the imperialists and all reactionaries are paper tigers." He said,

> All reactionaries are paper tigers. In appearance, the reactionaries are terrifying, but in reality they are not so powerful. From a long-term point of view, it is not the reactionaries but the people who are really powerful.[6]

The history of people's war in China and other countries provides conclusive evidence that the growth of the people's revolutionary forces from weak and small beginnings into strong and large forces is a universal law of development of class struggle, a universal law of development of people's war. A people's war inevitably meets with many difficulties, with ups and downs and setbacks in the course of its development, but no force can alter its general trend towards inevitable triumph.

Comrade Mao Tse-tung points out that we must despise the enemy strategically and take full account of him tactically.

To despise the enemy strategically is an elementary requirement for a revolutionary. Without the courage to despise the enemy and without daring to win, it will be simply impossible to make revolution and wage a people's war, let alone to achieve victory.

It is also very important for revolutionaries to take full account of the enemy tactically. It is likewise impossible to win victory in a people's war without taking full account of the enemy tactically, and without examining the concrete conditions, without being prudent and giving great attention to the study of the art of struggle, and without adopting appropriate forms of struggle in the concrete practice of the revolution in each country and with regard to each concrete problem of struggle.

Dialectical and historical materialism teaches us that what is important primarily is not that which at the given moment seems to be durable and yet is already beginning to die away, but that which is arising and developing, even though at the given moment it may not appear to be durable, for only that which is arising and developing is invincible.

Why can the apparently weak new-born forces always triumph over the decadent forces which appear so powerful? The reason is that truth is on their side and that the masses are on their side, while the reactionary classes are always divorced from the masses and set themselves against the masses.

This has been borne out by the victory of the Chinese revolution, by the history of all revolutions, the whole history of class struggle and the entire history of mankind.

The imperialists are extremely afraid of Comrade Mao Tse-tung's thesis that "imperialism and all reactionaries are paper tigers", and the revisionists are extremely hostile to it. They all oppose and attack this thesis and the philistines follow suit by ridiculing it. But all this cannot in the least diminish its importance. The light of truth cannot be dimmed by anybody.

Comrade Mao Tse-tung's theory of people's war solves not only the problem of daring to fight a people's war, but also that of how to wage it.

Comrade Mao Tse-tung is a great statesman and military scientist, proficient at directing war in accordance with its laws. By the line and policies, the strategy and tactics he formulated for the people's war, he led the Chinese people in steering the ship of the people's war past all hidden reefs to the shores of victory in most complicated and difficult conditions.

It must be emphasized that Comrade Mao Tse-tung's theory of the establishment of rural revolutionary base areas and the encirclement of the cities from the countryside is of outstanding and universal practical importance for the present revolutionary struggles of all the oppressed nations and peoples, and particularly for the revolutionary struggles of the oppressed nations and peoples in Asia, Africa, and Latin America against imperialism and its lackeys.

Many countries and peoples in Asia, Africa, and Latin America are now being subjected to aggression and enslavement on a serious scale by the imperialists headed by the United States and their lackeys. The basic political and economic conditions in many of these countries have many similarities to those that prevailed in old China. As in China, the peasant question is extremely important in these regions. The peasants constitute the main force of the national-democratic revolution against the imperialists and their lackeys. In committing aggression against these countries, the imperialists usually begin by seizing the big cities and the main lines of communication, but they are unable to bring the vast countryside completely under their control. The countryside, and the countryside alone, can provide the broad areas in which the revolutionaries can maneuver freely. The countryside, and the countryside alone, can provide the revolutionary bases from which the revolutionaries can go forward to final victory. Precisely for this reason, Comrade Mao Tse-tung's theory of establishing revolutionary base areas in the rural districts and encircling the cities from the countryside is attracting more and more attention among the people in these regions.

Taking the entire globe, if North America and Western Europe can be called "the cities of the world," then Asia, Africa, and Latin America constitute "the rural areas of the world." Since World War II, the proletarian revolutionary movement has for various reasons been temporarily held back in the North American and West European capitalist countries, while the people's revolutionary movement in Asia, Africa, and Latin America has been growing vigorously. In a sense, the contemporary world revolution also presents a picture of the encirclement of cities by the rural areas. In the final analysis, the whole cause of world revolution hinges on the revolutionary struggles of the Asian, African, and Latin American peoples who make up the overwhelming majority of the world's population. The socialist countries should regard it as their internationalist duty to support the people's revolutionary struggles in Asia, Africa, and Latin America.

The October Revolution opened up a new era in the revolution of the oppressed nations. The victory of the October Revolution built a bridge between the socialist revolution of the proletariat of the West and the national-democratic revolution of the colonial and semi-colonial countries of the East. The Chinese revolution has successfully solved the problem of how to link up the national-democratic with the socialist revolution in the colonial and semi-colonial countries.

Comrade Mao Tse-tung has pointed out that, in the epoch since the October Revolution, anti-imperialist revolution in any colonial or semi-colonial country is no longer part of the old bourgeois, or capitalist world revolution, but is part of the new world revolution, the proletarian-socialist world revolution.

Comrade Mao Tse-tung has formulated a complete theory of the new-democratic revolution. He indicated that this revolution, which is different from all others, can only be, nay must be, a revolution against imperialism, feudalism and bureaucrat-capitalism waged by the broad masses of the people under the leadership of the proletariat.

This means that the revolution can only be, nay must be, led by the proletariat and the genuinely revolutionary party armed with Marxism-Leninism, and by no other class or party.

This means that the revolution embraces in its ranks not only the workers, peasants and the urban petty bourgeoisie, but also the national bourgeoisie and other patriotic and anti-imperialist democrats.

This means, finally, that the revolution is directed against imperialism, feudalism and bureaucrat-capitalism.

The new-democratic revolution leads to socialism, and not to capitalism.

Comrade Mao Tse-tung's theory of the new-democratic revolution is the Marxist-Leninist theory of revolution by stages as well as the Marxist-Leninist theory of uninterrupted revolution.

Comrade Mao Tse-tung made a correct distinction between the two revolutionary stages, i.e., the national-democratic and the socialist revolutions; at the same time he correctly and closely linked the two. The national-democratic revolution is the necessary preparation for the socialist revolution, and the socialist revolution is the inevitable sequel to the national-democratic revolution. There is no Great Wall between the two revolutionary stages. But the socialist revolution is only possible after the completion of the national-democratic revolution. The more thorough the national-democratic revolution, the better the conditions for the socialist revolution.

The experience of the Chinese revolution shows that the tasks of the national-democratic revolution can be fulfilled only through long and tortuous struggles. In this stage of revolution, imperialism and its lackeys are the principal enemy. In the struggle against imperialism and its lackeys, it is necessary to rally all anti-imperialist patriotic forces, including the national bourgeoisie and all patriotic personages. All those patriotic personages from among the bourgeoisie and other exploiting classes who join the anti-imperialist struggle play a progressive historical role; they are not tolerated by imperialism but welcomed by the proletariat.

It is very harmful to confuse the two stages, that is, the national-democratic and the socialist revolutions. Comrade Mao Tse-tung criticized the wrong idea of "accomplishing both at one stroke," and pointed out that this utopian idea could only weaken the struggle against imperialism and its lackeys, the most urgent task at that time. The Kuomintang reactionaries and the Trotskyites they hired during the War of Resistance deliberately confused these two stages of the Chinese revolution, proclaiming the "theory of a single revolution" and preaching so-called "socialism" without any Communist Party. With this preposterous theory they attempted to swallow up the Communist Party, wipe out any revolution and prevent the advance of the national-democratic revolution, and they used it as a pretext for their non-resistance and capitulation to imperialism. This reactionary theory was buried long ago by the history of the Chinese revolution.

The Khrushchev revisionists are now actively preaching that socialism can be built without the proletariat and without a genuinely revolutionary party armed with the advanced proletarian ideology, and they have cast the fundamental tenets of Marxism-Leninism to the four winds. The revisionists' purpose is solely to divert the oppressed nations from their struggle against imperialism and sabotage their national-democratic revolution, all in the service of imperialism.

The Chinese revolution provides a successful lesson for making a thoroughgoing national-democratic revolution under the leadership of the proletariat; it likewise provides a successful lesson for the timely transition from the national-democratic revolution to the socialist revolution under the leadership of the proletariat.

Mao Tse-tung's thought has been the guide to the victory of the Chinese revolution. It has integrated the universal truth of Marxism-Leninism with the concrete practice of the Chinese revolution and creatively developed Marxism-Leninism, thus adding new weapons to the arsenal of Marxism-Leninism.

Ours is the epoch in which world capitalism and imperialism are heading for their doom and socialism and communism are marching to victory. Comrade Mao Tse-tung's theory of people's war is not only a product of the Chinese revolution, but has also the characteristics of our epoch. The new experience gained in the people's revolutionary struggles in various countries since World War II has provided continuous evidence that Mao Tse-tung's thought is a common asset of the revolutionary people of the whole world. This is the great international significance of the thought of Mao Tse-tung.

Since World War II, U.S. imperialism has stepped into the shoes of German, Japanese, and Italian fascism and has been trying to build a great American empire by dominating and enslaving the whole world. It is actively fostering Japanese and West German militarism as its chief accomplices in unleashing a world war. Like a vicious wolf, it is bullying and enslaving various peoples, plundering their wealth, encroaching upon their countries' sovereignty and interfering in their internal affairs. It is the most rabid aggressor in human history and the most ferocious common enemy of the people of the world. Every people or country in the world that wants revolution, independence and peace cannot but direct the spearhead of its struggle against U.S. imperialism.

Just as the Japanese imperialists' policy of subjugating China made it possible for the Chinese people to form the broadest possible united front against them, so the U.S. imperialists' policy of seeking world domination makes it possible for the people throughout the world to unite all the forces that can be united and form the broadest possible united front for a converging attack on U.S. imperialism.

At present, the main battlefield of the fierce struggle between the people of the world on the one side and U.S. imperialism and its lackeys on the other is the vast area of Asia, Africa, and Latin America. In the world as a whole, this is the area where the people suffer worst from imperialist oppression and where imperialist rule is most vulnerable. Since World War II, revolutionary storms have been rising in this area, and today they have become the most important force directly pounding U.S. imperialism. The contradiction between the revolutionary peoples of Asia, Africa, and Latin America and the imperialists headed by the United States is the principal contradiction in the contemporary world. The development of this contradiction is promoting the struggle of the people of the whole world against U.S. imperialism and its lackeys.

Since World War II, people's war has increasingly demonstrated its power in Asia, Africa, and Latin America. The peoples of

China, Korea, Vietnam, Laos, Cuba, Indonesia, Algeria and other countries have waged people's wars against the imperialists and their lackeys and won great victories. The classes leading these people's wars may vary, and so may the breadth and depth of mass mobilization and the extent of victory, but the victories in these people's wars have very much weakened and pinned down the forces of imperialism, upset the U.S. imperialist plan to launch a world war, and become mighty factors defending world peace.

Today, the conditions are more favorable than ever before for the waging of people's wars by the revolutionary peoples of Asia, Africa, and Latin America against U.S. imperialism and its lackeys.

Since World War II and the succeeding years of revolutionary upsurge, there has been a great rise in the level of political consciousness and the degree of organization of the people in all countries, and the resources available to them for mutual support and aid have greatly increased. The whole capitalist-imperialist system has become drastically weaker and is in the process of increasing convulsion and disintegration. After World War I, the imperialists lacked the power to destroy the new-born socialist Soviet state, but they were still able to suppress the people's revolutionary movements in some countries in the parts of the world under their own rule and so maintain a short period of comparative stability. Since World War II, however, not only have they been unable to stop a number of countries from taking the socialist road, but they are no longer capable of holding back the surging tide of the people's revolutionary movements in the areas under their own rule.

U.S. imperialism is stronger, but also more vulnerable, than any imperialism of the past. It sets itself against the people of the whole world, including the people of the United States. Its human, military, material and financial resources are far from sufficient for the realization of its ambition of dominating the whole world. U.S. imperialism has further weakened itself by occupying so many places in the world, overreaching itself, stretching its fingers out wide and dispersing its strength, with its rear so far away and its supply lines so long. As Comrade Mao Tse-tung has said, "Wherever it commits aggression, it puts a new noose around its neck. It is besieged ring upon ring by the people of the whole world."[7]

When committing aggression in a foreign country, U.S. imperialism can only employ part of its forces, which are sent to fight an unjust war far from their native land and therefore have a low morale, and so U.S. imperialism is beset with great difficulties. The people subjected to its aggression are having a trial of strength with U.S. imperialism neither in Washington nor New York, neither in Honolulu nor Florida, but are fighting for independence and freedom on their own soil. Once they are mobilized on a broad scale, they will have inexhaustible strength. Thus superiority will belong not to the United States but to the people subjected to its aggression. The latter, though apparently weak and small, are really more powerful than U.S. imperialism.

The struggles waged by the different peoples against U.S. imperialism reinforce each other and merge into a torrential world-wide tide of opposition to U.S. imperialism. The more successful the development of people's war in a given region, the larger the number of U.S. imperialist forces that can be pinned down and depleted there. When the U.S. aggressors are hard pressed in one place, they have no alternative but to loosen their grip on others. Therefore, the conditions become more favorable for the people elsewhere to wage struggles against U.S. imperialism and its lackeys.

Everything is divisible. And so is this colossus of U.S. imperialism. It can be split up and defeated. The peoples of Asia, Africa, Latin America and other regions can destroy it piece by piece, some striking at its head and others at its feet. That is why the greatest fear of U. S. imperialism is that people's wars will be launched in different parts of the world, and particularly in Asia, Africa and Latin America, and why it regards people's war as a mortal danger.

U. S. imperialism relies solely on its nuclear weapons to intimidate people. But these weapons cannot save U.S. imperialism from its doom. Nuclear weapons cannot be used lightly. U.S. imperialism has been condemned by the people of the whole world for its towering crime of dropping two atom bombs on Japan. If it uses nuclear weapons again, it will become isolated in the extreme. Moreover, the U.S. monopoly of nuclear weapons has long been broken; U.S. imperialism has these weapons, but others have them too. If it threatens other countries with nuclear weapons, U.S. imperialism will expose its own country to the same threat. For this reason, it will meet with strong opposition not only from the people elsewhere but also inevitably from the people in its own country. Even if U.S. imperialism brazenly uses nuclear weapons, it cannot conquer the people, who are indomitable.

However highly developed modern weapons and technical equipment may be and however complicated the methods of modern warfare, in the final analysis the outcome of a war will be decided by the sustained fighting of the ground forces, by the fighting at close quarters on battlefields, by the political consciousness of the men, by their courage and spirit of sacrifice. Here the weak points of U.S. imperialism will be completely laid bare, while the superiority of the revolutionary people will be brought into full play. The reactionary troops of U.S. imperialism cannot possibly be endowed with the courage and the spirit of sacrifice possessed by the revolutionary people. The spiritual atom bomb which the revolutionary people possess is a far more powerful and useful weapon than the physical atom bomb.

Vietnam is the most convincing current example of a victim of aggression defeating U.S. imperialism by a people's war. The United States has made South Vietnam a testing ground for the suppression of people's war. It has carried on this experiment for many years, and everybody can now see that the U.S. aggressors are unable to find a way of coping with people's war. On the other hand, the Vietnamese people have brought the power of people's war into full play in their struggle against the U.S. aggressors. The U.S. aggressors are in danger of being swamped in the people's war in Vietnam. They are deeply worried that their defeat in Vietnam will lead to a chain reaction. They are expanding the war in an attempt to save themselves from defeat. But the more they expand the war, the greater will be the chain reaction. The more they escalate the war, the heavier will be their fall and the more disastrous their defeat. The people in other parts of the world will see still more clearly that U.S. imperialism can be defeated, and that what the Vietnamese people can do, they can do too.

History has proved and will go on proving that people's war is the most effective weapon against U.S. imperialism and its lackeys. All revolutionary people will learn to wage people's war against U.S. imperialism and its lackeys. They will take up arms, learn to fight battles and become skilled in waging people's war, though they have not done so before. U.S. imperialism, like a mad bull dashing from place to place, will finally be burned to ashes in the blazing fires of the people's wars it has provoked by its own actions.

Notes

[1] Karl Marx, *Capital,* Vol. I, Eng. ed. (Moscow, Foreign Languages Publishing House, 1954), p. 751.

[2] Mao Tse-tung, "Problems of War and Strategy", *Selected Works,* Vol. II, Eng. ed. (Peking, FLP, 1965), p. 224.

[3] *Ibid.,* p. 219

[4] V. I. Lenin, "The Revolutionary Army and the Revolutionary Government", *Col-*

lected Works, Vol. VIII, Eng. ed. (Moscow, Foreign Languages Publishing House, 1962), p. 565.

[5] Mao Tse-tung, "The Situation and Our Policy After the Victory in the War of Resistance Against Japan", *Selected Works,* Eng. ed., FLP, Peking, 1961, Vol. IV, pp. 14-15.

[6] Mao Tse-tung, "Talk with the American Correspondent Anna Louise Strong", *Selected Works,* Vol. IV, Eng. ed. (Peking, FLP, 1961), p. 100.

[7] Mao Tse-tung, Statement Supporting the People of the Congo (Leopoldville) Against U.S. Aggression, November 28, 1964.

A BIBLIOGRAPHICAL GUIDE TO U.S. IMPERIALISM

The following bibliography contains first a section representing the most revealing, influential, and theoretically significant works for understanding contemporary imperialism in general; and second, a section of critical works on U.S. imperialism in particular. In the interest of brevity, we have omitted independent essays and articles, except those in anthologies, thus limiting our selection to the most important books on the subject. As for those major works which have not been cited, most are written in foreign languages beyond the competence of the average reader.

I. General Works

Baran, Paul, *The Political Economy of Growth*, New York, Monthly Review Press, 1957.

Brown, Michael Barratt, *After Imperialism*, rev. ed., London, Merlin, 1970.

Bukharin, N. I., *Imperialism and World Economy*, London, Martin Lawrence, 1930.

Dutt, Palme, *World Politics 1918-1936*, New York, International Publishers, 1936.

——, *The Crisis of Britain and the British Empire*, New York, International Publishers, 1953.

Fanon, Frantz, *The Wretched of the Earth*, New York, Grove, 1963.

——, *Studies in a Dying Colonialism*, New York, Monthly Review Press, 1965.

Fieldhouse, D. K., ed., *The Theory of Capitalist Imperialism*, New York, Barnes & Noble, 1967.

Fleming, D. F., *The Cold War and its Origins*, 2 vols, New York, Doubleday, 1961.

Grant, Madison, *The Passing of the Great Race*, New York, Scribner, 1916.

Halevy, E., *Imperialism and the Rise of Labour*, 2nd rev. ed., London, Benn, 1951.

Hobson, J. A., *Imperialism: A Study*, London, Allen and Unwin, 1954.

Jalée, Pierre, *The Pillage of the Third World*, New York, Monthly Review Press, 1968.

Kemp, Tom, *Theories of Imperialism*, London, Dennis Dobson, 1967.

Lenin, V. I., *Imperialism: The Highest Stage of Capitalism*, New York, International Publishers, 1939.

Luxemburg, Rosa, *The Accumulation of Capital,* New York, Monthly Review Press, 1964.

Mackinder, Halford Jr., *Democratic Ideals and Reality,* New York, Norton, 1962.

Moon, P. T., *Imperialism and World Politics,* New York, Macmillan, 1947.

Nkrumah, Kwame, *Neo-Colonialism: The Last Stage of Imperialism,* New York, International Publishers, 1965.

Schumpeter, Joseph A., *The Sociology of Imperialisms,* New York, Meridian, 1955.

Semmel, Bernard, *Imperialism and Social Reform,* New York, Anchor, 1968.

Spengler, Oswald, *The Hour of Decision,* New York, Knopf, 1934.

Stoddard, Lothrop, *The Rising Tide of Color Against White World-Supremacy,* New York, Scribner, 1916.

Strachey, John, *The End of Empire,* New York, Random House, 1960.

Varga, E. and Mendelsohn, L., *New Data on Lenin's Imperialism,* New York, International Publishers, 1940.

Winslow, E. M., *The Pattern of Imperialism: A Study in the Theories of Power,* New York: Columbia University Press, 1948.

Woolf, Leonard, *Economic Imperialism,* London, Howard Fertig, 1920.

II. Case Studies of U.S. Imperialism

Agruilar, Alonso, *Pan-Americanism from Monroe to the Present: A View from the other Side,* New York, Monthly Review Press, 1969.

Alperovitz, Gar, *Atomic Diplomacy,* New York, Simon & Schuster, 1965.

Arevalo, Juan J., *The Shark and the Sardines,* New York, Lyle Stuart, 1961.

Bosch, Juan, *Pentagonism: A Substitute for Imperialism,* New York, Grove Press, 1968.

Carmichael, Stokely and Charles V. Hamilton, *Black Power,* New York, Vintage, 1967.

Castro, Fidel, *Fidel Castro Speaks,* New York, Grove Press, 1970.

Chomsky, Noam, *American Power and the New Mandarins,* New York, Vintage, 1969.

Cleaver, Eldridge, *Post-Prison Writings,* New York, Grove Press, 1970.

Lockwood, Lee, *Conversation with Eldridge Cleaver in Algiers,* New York, Dell, 1970.

Cook, Fred J., *The Warfare State,* Collier, 1964.

Crabb, Cecil V. Jr., *American Foreign Policy in the Nuclear Age,* 2nd ed., New York, Harper & Row, 1965.

Dozer, Donald M., *Are We Good Neighbors?: Three Decades of Inter-American Relations, 1930-1960,* Gainesville, University of Florida, 1959.

Ferrero, Gugliemo, *Ancient Rome and Modern America,* New York, Putnam's Sons, 1914.

Frank, André Gunder, *Capitalism and Underdevelopment in Latin America,* New York, Monthly Review Press, 1967.

_____, *Latin America: Underdevelopment or Revolution,* New York, Monthly Review Press, 1969.

Galeano, Eduardo, *Guatemala: Occupied Country,* New York, Monthly Review Press, 1969.

Gerassi, John, *The Great Fear in Latin America,* rev. ed., New York, Collier, 1965.

Gettleman, Marvin, *Vietnam,* New York, Fawcett, 1965.

Horowitz, David, *The Free World Colossus,* New York, Hill and Wang, 1965.

_____, ed., *Containment and Revolution,* Boston, Beacon Press, 1967.

_____, *Empire and Revolution,* New York, Random House, 1969.

Horowitz, Irving L., *The War Game: Studies of the New Civilian Militarists,* New York, Ballantine, 1963.

Jordan, Winthrop, *White over Black,* Chapel Hill, University of North Carolina Press, 1968.

Kaplan, Lawrence S., *Recent American Foreign Policy: Conflicting Interpretations,* Homewood, Ill., Dorsey, 1968.

LaFeber, Walter, *The New Empire: An Interpretation of American Expansion 1860-1898,* Ithaca, Cornell University, 1967.

Lewis, Gordon K., *Puerto Rico: Freedom and Power in the Caribbean,* New York, Monthly Review Press, 1963.

Magdoff, Harry, *The Age of Imperialism: The Economics of U.S. Foreign Policy,* New York, Monthly Review Press, 1969.

Malone, Dumas and Basil Rauch, *America and World Leadership,* New York, Appleton-Century-Crofts, 1965.

May, Stacey and Galo Plaza, *The United Fruit Company in Latin America,* Washington, D.C., National Planning Association, 1958.

Morray, J. P., *The Second Revolution in Cuba,* New York, Monthly Review Press, 1962.

Nearing, Scott and Joseph Freeman, *Dollar Diplomacy,* New York, Monthly Review Press, 1969.

Nirumand, Bahman, *Iran: The New Imperialism in Action,* New York, Monthly Review Press, 1969.

O'Connor, Harvey, *The Empire of Oil,* New York, Monthly Review Press, 1955.

———, *World Crisis in Oil,* New York, Monthly Review Press, 1962.

Oglesby, Carl and Richard Shaull, *Containment and Change,* New York, Macmillan, 1967.

Perlo, Victor, *American Imperialism,* New York, International Publishers, 1951.

Russell, Bertrand, *War Crimes in Vietnam,* New York, Monthly Review Press, 1967.

Scheer, Robert, *How the United States Got Involved in Vietnam,* Santa Barbara, Center for the Study of Democratic Institutions, 1965.

Spykman, Nicholas John *America's Strategy in World Politics,* New York, Harcourt & Brace, 1942.

Tully, Andrew, *The CIA, The Inside Story,* New York, Morrow, 1962.

Van Alstyne, Richard W., *The Rising American Empire,* Chicago, Quadrangle, 1965.

Williams, William A., *The Tragedy of American Diplomacy,* rev. ed., New York, Delta, 1962.

———, *The United States, Cuba, and Castro,* New York, Monthly Review Press, 1962.

Wise, David and Thomas B. Ross, *The Invisible Government,* New York, Random House, 1964.

INDEX

East India Company, 26, 27, 152, 199
ECLA. *See* United Nations Economic Commission for Latin America
Economic surplus, 45-59, 62-65
Economic Weekly, 247
Eisenhower, Dwight D., 14, 18, 86, 299
Electric Bond and Share Company, 60, 211
Empresa Eléctrica, 250
Engels, Friedrich, *The German Ideology,* 91, 184, 269, 296
Ethiopia, financial domination of, 41
Europe
  division of, 333
  foreign competition and, 279-287
  United States investments in, 57, 283-285
European Common Market, 39, 40, 56, 95, 208
European Economic Community. *See* European Common Market
Export-Import Bank, 17, 58, 252

Fanon, Frantz, *The Wretched of the Earth,* 354, 355
FAO. *See* United Nations Food and Agricultural Organization
Farm surpluses, xii-xiii
Federal Communications Commission, 111
Federal University of Rio de Janeiro, 210
Fieldhouse, D., 29
Ford Foundation, 143
Ford Motor Company, 80
Foreign aid
  United States, 175-176, 299
  See also Alliance for Progress; Good Neighbor Policy
Foreign Assistance Act of 1961, 82
Foreign capital, political independence and, 50-52
Foreign competition, and United States, 268-270, 279-287
Foreign exchange assets, control over, 41-42
Foreign investments, 15-16, 209-213
Foreign policy, 59-62, 297-299
Fourth International, 276
France, in Vietnam, 358
Frank, André Gunder, 13, 165, 168-169, 212, 237-248
Frantz, Jacob, 239
Free trade, 14-15
Frelinghuysen, Frederick, 121-122
Frondizi, Arturo, xiv

Galbraith, John K., 266
Galeano, Eduardo, 205-223
Gallagher, J., 34, 36
Garfield, James, 121-122
General Electric Corporation, 35, 78, 108
German Colonial Congress, 36-37
German economy, 34
German Ideology, The (Marx and Engels), 91, 184, 269, 296
Ghana, intervention in, 92
Gillman, Joseph, 30, 46, 50
Good Neighbor Policy, 18, 170
Gordon, Lincoln, xiv
Goulart, João, xiv, 29, 241-242
Great Britain
  colonization of India, 199
  foreign investments of, 26-27
  foreign policy of, 59, 61
  imperialism, xv, 41-42
  nineteenth century exports, 55
  Sterling Area countries, 51, 56
  See British Empire
Great Contest, The (Deutscher), 340
Great Depression, the, 334
Guatemala
  counter-revolution in, 16, 18, 59-60, 364, 365
  United States foreign aid to, 249-255
Guevara, Ernesto Ché, 16, 346, 347, 355, 357-370
Guinea, 363
Gulf Oil Company, 211

Hammarskjold, Dag, xii
Hanna Mining Company, 211
Hanson, Simon
  Inter-American Economic Affairs, 245
  Latin American Letter, 245
Harding, Timothy F., 13-22
Harrison, Benjamin, 123
Harrison Company, 252
Hay, John, 297
Haywood, Bill, 308
Hilferding, Rudolf, 69
Hobson, John A.
  criticism of theories of, 33-38 *passim*
  on economic imperialism, 1-2, 13, 44
  Imperialism, 30-31
Honduras, Alliance for Progress aid to, 17-18
Hook, Sidney, 305
Hoskyns, Catherine, *The Congo Since Independence,* 9

ACKNOWLEDGEMENTS

"Peace Through Resistance to American Imperialism," by Bertrand Russell, originally appeared in *War Crimes in Vietnam,* published by George Allen & Unwin Ltd., London. It is reprinted here by permission of George Allen Unwin Ltd.

"Contemporary Forms of Imperialism," by Conor Cruise O'Brien, originally appeared in *Studies on the Left,* Volume 5, Number 4, Fall 1965. It is reprinted here by permission of the author.

"The New Imperialism In Latin America," by Timothy F. Harding, originally appeared as a comment on Conor Cruise O'Brien's "Contemporary Forms of Imperialism" in *Studies on the Left,* Volume 5, Number 4, Fall 1965. It is reprinted here by permission of the author.

"The Meaning of Economic Imperialism," by James O'Connor, originally appeared in pamphlet form, published by the Radical Education Project, Box 625, Ann Arbor, Michigan. It is reprinted here by permission of the author.

"Notes on the Theory of Imperialism," by Paul Baran and Paul M. Sweezy, originally appeared in *Problems of Economic Dynamics and Planning: Essays in Honour of Michal Kalecki,* Polish Scientific Publishers, Warsaw, Poland, 1964. It was published in this country in *Monthly Review,* Volume 17, Number 10, March, 1966, and is reprinted here by permission of Monthly Review Press.

"The Third Stage of Imperialism," by L. Marcus, originally appeared as a pamphlet published by the National Council of Labor Committees, New York, 1967. It is reprinted here by permission of the author.

"Notes on the Multinational Corporation," by Harry Magdoff and Paul M. Sweezy, originally appeared in *Monthly Review,* Volume XXI, Numbers 5 and 6, October and November, 1969. It is reprinted here by permission of Monthly Review Press.

"The Vicious Circle of American Imperialism," by William Appleman Williams, originally appeared in *New Politics,* Volume

IV, Number 4, New York, 1965. It is reprinted here by permission of the author and the publisher.

"Militarism and Imperialism," by Harry Magdoff, originally appeared in *Monthly Review,* Volume XXI, Number 9, February, 1970. It is reprinted here by permission of Monthly Review Press.

"Scarce Resources: The Dynamic of American Imperialism," by Heather Dean, originally appeared in pamphlet form, published by the Radical Education Project, Box 561-A, Detroit, Michigan. It is reprinted here by permission of the Radical Education Project.

"Dependency and Imperialism: The Roots of Latin American Underdevelopment," by Sue Bodenheimer, published for the first time in this volume. It is reprinted here by permission of the author.

"On Underdevelopment," by Fidel Castro, is taken from the official transcript of a speech made at the University of Havana, Havana, Cuba, on March 13, 1968.

"Colonialism, Hunger, and Progress," by Josué de Castro, originally appeared in *World Marxist Review,* Volume IV, Number 10, October, 1961. It is reprinted here by permission of *World Marxist Review.*

"Latin America and the Theory of Imperialism," by Eduardo Galeano, originally appeared in *Monthly Review,* Volume 21, Number 11, April, 1970. It is reprinted here by permission of Monthly Review Press.

"The Structure of Dependence," by Theotonio Dos Santos, is taken from the transcript of a paper presented at the annual meeting of the American Economics Association in 1969, and is published here by permission of the author.

"On the Mechanisms of Imperialism: The Case of Brazil," by Andre Gunder Frank, originally appeared in *Monthly Review,* Volume 16, Number 5, September, 1964, and is reprinted here by permission of Monthly Review Press.

"Foreign Aid: The Case of Guatemala," by David Tobis, originally appeared in *Monthly Review,* Volume 19, Number 8, January,

1968, and is reprinted by permission of Monthly Review Press.

"Where Is America Going?" by Ernest Mandel, originally appeared in *New Left Review,* Number 54, March-April, 1969, and is reprinted here by permission of *New Left Review.*

"Who Will Bring the Mother Down?" by Martin Nicolaus, originally appeared in *Leviathan,* Vol. I, No. 5, September, 1969, and is reprinted here by permission of Leviathan Publications.

"On Repressive Institutions and the American Empire," by Peter Irons, originally appeared in *The New Left: A Collection of Essays,* Porter Sargent Publisher, Boston, 1969. It is reprinted here by permission of the author, with author's alterations.

"American Imperialism and the Peace Movement," by Robert Wolfe, originally appeared in *Studies on the Left,* Vol. VI, No. 3, May-June, 1966, and is reprinted here by permission of the author.

"Socialism: The Sustaining Menace," by Ronald Aronson, originally appeared in *Studies on the Left,* Vol. VI, No. 3, May-June, 1966, and is reprinted here by permission of the author.

"Black Power and the Third World," by Stokely Carmichael, is taken from a speech made at the OLAS conference in Havana, Cuba, 1967, and appeared in *The New Revolutionaries: A Handbook of the International Radical Left,* Tariq Ali, ed., published by William Morrow and Co., New York, 1969, copyright © 1969 by Peter Owen Ltd. It is reprinted here by permission of William Morrow and Company, Inc., and Peter Owen Ltd.

"Create Two, Three, Many Vietnams," by Ernesto Che Guevara, originally appeared as "Message to the Tricontinental," a transcript of a speech given in Havana, Cuba, April 16, 1967, and published by the Executive Secretariat of the Organization of the Solidarity of the Peoples of Africa, Asia, and Latin America.

"Defeat U. S. Imperialism by People's War," by Lin Piao, is taken from *Long Live the Victory of People's War,* a speech given in commemoration of the 20th anniversary of victory in the Chinese People's War of Resistance Against Japan, and published September 3, 1965, by Foreign Languages Press, Peking, China.